Politics, People & Potpourri

BY THE SAME AUTHOR

Mulroney: The Making of the Prime Minister
Free Trade: Risks and Rewards (Ed)
From Bourassa to Bourassa: Wilderness to Restoration
Leo: A Life (with Leo Kolber)

L. Ian MacDonald

Politics, People & Potpourri

For Rod,
All good wishes,
L. IM.
December, 2009

Published for *The Gazette*
by
McGill-Queen's University Press
Montreal & Kingston · London · Ithaca

© McGill-Queen's University Press 2009
ISBN 978-0-7735-3685-2

Legal deposit fourth quarter 2009
Bibliothèque nationale du Québec

Printed in Canada on acid-free paper that is 100% ancient forest free (100%) post-consumer recycled), processed chlorine free

McGill-Queen's University Press acknowledges the support of the Canada Council for the Arts for our publishing program. We also acknowledge the financial support of the Government of Canada through the Book Publishing Industry Development Program (BPIDP) for our publishing activities.

LIBRARY AND ARCHIVES CANADA
CATALOGUING IN PUBLICATION

MacDonald, L. Ian
Politics, people, & potpourri / L. Ian MacDonald.

A selection of columns previously published in the Montreal Gazette.
ISBN 978-0-7735-3685-2

1. Canada – Politics and government – 1993–.
2. Politicians – Canada.   I. Title.

FC176.M35 2009   971.07   C2009-904861-2

Set in 11/14 Sabon with Gill Sans
Book design & typesetting by
Garet Markvoort, zijn digital

For Grace and Zara,
the ladies in my life

CONTENTS

Author's Note   ix

PART ONE: POLITICS

1 The Liberal Leadership Wars   3
2 Uniting the Right   14
3 The Sponsorship Scandal   24
4 Elections 2004, 2006, 2008   46
5 America—from Bill Clinton to Barack Obama   74
6 Issues and Attitudes   101

PART TWO: PEOPLE

7 Brian Mulroney   125
8 Jean Charest   139
9 Paul Martin   153
10 Stephen Harper   162
11 Stéphane Dion   174
12 Michael Ignatieff   182
13 Profiles   197
14 Tributes   225

PART THREE: POTPOURRI

15 Montreal Landmarks   253
16 Cities   273
17 Living   284
18 Cottage Life   305
19 Gracie   319

AUTHOR'S NOTE

Most of the columns and articles in this collection appeared in *The Gazette*, beginning in 1997, when publisher Michael Goldbloom and editor Alan Allnutt were kind enough to ask me back to the paper, where I had been the national affairs columnist before going off to work for the prime minister, Brian Mulroney, as his chief speechwriter from 1985 to 1989. Subsequently, I went to Washington to serve as head of the public affairs division at the Canadian Embassy, and later worked there as a communications consultant before returning to Montreal to host a radio morning show in 1996. One day, when Michael and Alan were appearing on the show to promote a new design for *The Gazette*, they spontaneously invited me back to resume writing at the paper, which had always been, and remains, my professional home. At first, they asked me to write a weekly city, business, and lifestyle column, and some of those pieces, as well as profiles and tributes, appear in this book. But I'm primarily a political writer, and when they asked me to write once and then twice a week on the op-ed page, that was also a homecoming. Later, another editor, Peter Stockland, moved me to the op-ed three days a week, a practice continued by his successor, Andrew Phillips. Twelve years on, Alan has returned to the newsroom as editor as well as publisher, and *The Gazette* has been very supportive in publishing this book in conjunction with McGill-Queen's University Press.

When I first asked Pat Duggan of *The Gazette* library if she could send me the archive of columns as an e-mail, she burst out laughing. "It will take many e-mails," she said. "It's over 800,000 words, and that's just up to the end of 2005." Another 550,000 words brought *The Gazette* word count to 1.35 million words up to the spring of 2009. Then 150,000 words from my weekly column in the *National Post* brought the count to 1.5 million words. Yikes. Several longer political articles from *Policy Options*, the magazine of which I'm also editor, rounded out the archive.

When I decided it would be fun to put out a collection of columns and other pieces, getting it into shape – cutting, tossing, choosing, and cutting again – proved to be much more work than I ever imagined. It will be for the readers to decide how well it stands up. And that's a basic test. A political columnist interprets events as they occur, but our role is also to get things right looking down the road. A sense of history helps, which is different than simply looking in the rear-view mirror.

The pieces selected went into nineteen different chapter boxes on politics, personalities, and lifestyles. The title, *Politics, People & Potpourri*, was an easy alliterative choice. It is what it is, a collection. All of us who work writing the first draft of history are indebted to our role models. In my case, it was sports columnists, beginning with the great hockey writer Red Fisher and *Gazette* columnist Dink Carroll, who got me reading the paper as a boy. Later, as a high school senior at Loyola in Montreal, I organized a senior class trip to Ottawa in 1965. Waiting to go into question period, we ran into a Loyola graduate, Robert Lewis, who was a young parliamentary correspondent and would later become editor of *Maclean's*. The House of Commons was consumed by the battles between Lester Pearson and John Diefenbaker, and it was a very exciting place to be. Looking down at Bob in the Press Gallery from the visitors' gallery above, I thought, "that's what I want to do." I've never lost that sense of excitement, and I'm very aware of having a privileged seat as a witness to history. But I've been equally privileged to have worked at the centre of government, as chief speechwriter to a prime minister, and later as minister of public affairs at our embassy in Washington. There was never a day, when I went to work at the Langevin Block in Ottawa, or our magnificent chancery in Washington, when I wasn't thrilled by the view of Parliament Hill or the U.S. Capitol. It was an honour to work in both. When I resumed writing for myself rather than other people, I realized that my work as a columnist would be informed by my experience in government in Ottawa and Washington.

The Americans have always understood this value-added difference and have long been more accepting of writers moving from government back to journalism. Presidential speechwriters, from William Safire to Michael

Gerson, are deemed to have something important to say because of the privileged place they have worked – the White House. In Canada, we are much harder on journalists working in government, who are seen to have sold out, or become damaged goods, when they are actually in a much better position to share insights and perceptions of public policy, as well as politics, from having worked on the inside, especially a central agency such as the Prime Minister's Office. I have Michael and Alan to thank for inviting me home, which prompted some internal grumbling at the time. Then again, working for Brian Mulroney, I developed a thick skin.

The columns and articles in this collection cover a political period in Canada and the United States, from the end of one century through the first decade of the next. In Canada, Jean Chrétien was prime minister and, in a very Canadian coup, was deposed by Paul Martin, who was eventually defeated by Stephen Harper, who nearly brought down his own newly elected government in the parliamentary crisis of 2008. The failed Three Stooges coalition led to a palace revolt in the Liberal Party and the installation of Michael Ignatieff as its new leader. Being descended of Russian nobility, I noted that he knew how to organize a palace coup without having his fingerprints on the gun, a very admirable trait in a public intellectual, proving that he's tough enough, as well as smart enough, to be in the game at this level. The stage has now been set for the next election.

In the United States, the period covered by these selected columns begins with the impeachment of Bill Clinton in 1998 and ends with the inauguration and first 100 days in office of Barack Obama. Along the way, there was the controversial presidency of George W. Bush and the presidential election of 2008, a campaign for the ages, especially in the epic Democratic primary race that saw Obama defeat Hillary Clinton for the party's nomination. Obama was an electrifying candidate of hope and change, with a compelling personal narrative. It was clear from his sensational debut, at the Democratic convention in Boston in 2004, that he was presidential material. The Clintons thought it was her turn, but it turned out to be his time. It was a season in which the candidate of change was always going to beat the candidate of continuity, whether it was Clinton in the primaries or John McCain in the general election.

The final part of this book is a section on lifestyles, from vacations in Maine, to summers at our cottage at Lac St. Pierre-de-Wakefield in the Gatineau Hills of Quebec, to my daughter Grace at various stages of her childhood. When she reached a certain age, about ten, out of respect for her privacy, I essentially stopped writing about her, except as an occasional narrator of the story. But many readers have stopped me in the years since to ask, "How's Gracie doing? How old is she now? Where's she going to school?" The answer is that she's now nineteen, living in Washington again and going to college at the American University there.

In the chapter on living, there were two pieces that triggered huge reader response, the first on selling my Miata, and the second on a personal journey through the public and private health-care system when I had eye surgery in 2005. This long form piece, on Dr. John Chen and his great team at the McGill University Health Centre, provoked hundreds of e-mails. Finally, there are some comparative notes on cities – beginning with Montreal landmarks. It was Mark Twain who famously said, "Throw a rock in Montreal and break a church window." Two of those churches are St. Patrick's, Montreal's Irish basilica, and St. Monica's, where I grew up. Other landmarks include Place Ville Marie, Windsor Station, and the Royal Montreal Curling Club, oldest in North America, where I found a trophy with my father's name on it.

So that's it, *Politics, People & Potpourri*. One thing for sure, I'm not going to wait twelve years to publish the next collection of columns. Quite enough work has gone into this one.

There are the usual people to be thanked, in my professional and private lives.

First and foremost, Philip Cercone, the executive director of McGill-Queen's University Press, publisher of my last three books. Philip has taken McGill-Queen's from the Gutenberg Galaxy to the age of the Internet, selling and making books available online and making a profit doing so. In an era when book publishers are challenged by secular change, as well as a cyclical downturn, Philip has responded to the challenges and opportunities of new platforms. More than half of his list is exported – he was a free trader long before it became generally accepted in Canadian cultural industries that we live in a globalized economy. Publishing a book of newspaper columns is not within the normal scope of his mandate as an academic publisher, but he has been kind enough to see this one as a body of work about events shaping people, and people shaping events.

Philip and his team at McGill-Queen's are, as always, a joy to work with, none more so than Joan McGilvray, coordinating editor of all my books with the Press. Judith Turnbull has been the copy editor on the last two, responsible for many good catches. I hasten to add that any errors, of fact or fancy, are entirely my own. Thanks also to Anna Lensky, rights and projects manager, and Jeff Dalziel, director of marketing, for their initiatives and ideas on this book. Special thanks for design and proofreading to Garet Markvoort.

At *The Gazette*, I want to thank Alan and Michael most of all. At a recent lunch, for which he characteristically picked up the tab, Alan reminded me of the origins of this journey. "What was the name of that editor again?" Allnutt. As my editor and publisher, he has always done what good editors and publishers do – stood behind me and skated any complainers into the boards. He was immediately enthusiastic about this project, and delighted to put *The Gazette*'s brand behind it, not to mention its award-winning marketing vice president, Bernard Asselin. Michael has since moved on, first to the *Toronto Star* as publisher, then to McGill University as a vice-principal, now to Bishop's University as principal. They are lucky to have him. Larry Smith, during his sojourn as *Gazette* publisher, was unfailingly supportive.

Then, Peter Stockland and Andrew Phillips, who were equally supportive of my column during their tenures as editor of the paper. And Brian Kappler, editor of the editorial page, has been unstinting in his support. Wayne Lowrie, editor of the op-ed, has been my peerless and imperturbable editor for a decade. And in *The Gazette* library, special thanks, as always, to Pat Duggan and Michael Porritt. "Don't forget to send us a copy," she said. I won't. I won't forget her help, either. Other colleagues in the newsroom who have handled the column over the years include Dave Bist; thanks to them all for taking my late-night calls with late changes or corrections.

At the *National Post,* thanks to editor Doug Kelly, with special thanks to Jonathan Kay, managing editor of the Comment section, and Marni Soupcoff, who usually does the copy edit on my weekly column.

Special thanks to our proprietors, Leonard and David Asper, respectively CEO of Canwest Global Communications and chairman of the *Post*. They are the best kind of owners to work for – the kind who never tell you what to write. The same can be said of Conrad Black, former proprietor of *The Gazette* and visionary founder of the *Post*. He raised industry standards, brought needed competition to the marketplace, paid top dollar, and never interfered with his writers. It simply wouldn't occur to him to do so. Conrad is one of the people profiled in this book, and he certainly deserves to be in a much better place than where he is now, as he has himself put it, as a guest of the United States government. Free Conrad Black! Now there's a Facebook page I'll sign up for.

At the Institute for Research on Public Policy, publisher of *Policy Options*, I'm very much indebted to two presidents, Hugh Segal, who brought me in as editor of the magazine in 2002, and Mel Cappe, his successor, who has been no less staunch in his support of our efforts to make the magazine a must-read among Canada's political class and public policy community. There isn't another think-tank magazine like it anywhere, and I'm very proud of it. Though the circulation is only 3,000, it is all the right people, and we are approaching one million article downloads a year online. But it's still nice to actually hold the magazine in your hands, and it's a joy to produce it. But it wouldn't come out ten times a year without an amazing stable of writers and our great team. That begins and ends with our production co-ordinator, Chantal Letourneau, associate editor Sarah Fortin, copy editor Francesca Worrall, webmaster Jeremy Leonard, communications director Kate Shingler, vice-president of research France St. Hilaire, and vice-president of operations Suzanne Ostiguy-McIntyre, affectionately known around the office as "the minister of finance." And thanks to our designer, Jenny Schumacher of Schumacher Design, for the covers of this book.

On a personal note, there are special friends to be thanked, beginning with Brian Mulroney, Canada's eighteenth prime minister. I have always said it's an honour to serve any prime minister, and I was honoured to serve mine. He afforded me the unique opportunity of not only seeing history in the making but playing a small part in writing it. His marginal notations on his speech drafts, all in a filing cabinet in my basement, are proof that he worked as hard on his speeches as I did. And they were the great issues of the day – Free Trade, Meech Lake, Acid Rain, and the fight against apartheid, among others.

Other friends who have been encouraging in this project include Bill Fox, my best friend of all the years. Anthony Wilson-Smith, former editor of *Maclean's,* is always good at keeping in touch from his current listening post as a senior vice-president of Canada Post. And Bernie St. Laurent, my colleague and confidant at CBC Radio, has also offered his unfailing encouragement.

Finally, a special word of thanks to two of "the girls" – Rinku Mondal and Rocio Lozano, whose friendship on a personal level means more to me than I can say.

The last page written in this book is the first one – the dedication to my daughters, Grace and Zara. Gracie has been the great joy of my life for the last nineteen years, and she figures in these pages, from the child she was to the young woman she has become. Zara, newly arrived, will bring joy to the rest of my life, and will certainly keep her father young.

L. Ian MacDonald
Montreal and Lac St. Pierre-de-Wakefield, July 2009

PART ONE

Politics

1

THE LIBERAL LEADERSHIP WARS

THE WAR OF THE ROSES

The struggle for the Liberal leadership, now fully joined, is unprecedented in the history of the party and, for that matter, of the country. Never in Canadian history has a sitting prime minister, much less one running thirty points ahead in the polls, been threatened with eviction by his own party.

Yet that is the perilous predicament in which Jean Chrétien finds himself as he nears the mid-point of his third consecutive majority mandate and at a time when the country is prosperous and remarkably at peace with itself.

Chrétien must be wondering how it came to this, how he came to be engaged in desperate battles on three fronts – with the media, who have declared war on him; with the civil service, where he foolishly fingered "a couple of bureaucrats" for the sponsorship scandal; and within the Liberal Party itself on the question of leadership and succession.

And while the Chrétien government regroups in the capital, with plans for a fall throne speech, Paul Martin is barnstorming the country, while his supporters organize for next February's scheduled Liberal leadership review.

The PM's loyalists can't control the public service or the media, but they can try to recapture the agenda by putting together a throne speech over the summer. And they can send out signals to the Martin camp that they would be interested in a truce.

As the price of peace, Chrétien would have to agree to a definite time for his departure, say after the 40th anniversary of his first election to Parliament in April, but before his 10th anniversary as prime minister in November 2003, so that the party could have a leadership convention before next summer. Or, once Chrétien sees the writing on the wall, he could simply announce his resignation before Christmas and ask for a convention in the spring.

This is the only way left for Chrétien to avoid a leadership review he appears almost certain to lose.

It was a significantly bad omen for Chrétien when the Liberal Party's national executive refused to take the hint and cancel the leadership review. It is increasingly apparent that the Martin forces control both the executive and the process.

Then, head counts of the national caucus resulted in almost half going public with their preference for a change of leadership.

Touring the country, Martin drew 2,000 people to an event in Vancouver, and about the same number to a $30-a-plate pancake breakfast at the Calgary Stampede. Those are very unusual turnouts in high summer. Something is going on out there, something like the Liberal Party making up its mind on the leadership.

Something else: as the Martin forces organize, they're not running into the Chrétien people on the ground. That's as revealing as the dog that didn't bark. As of now, Chrétien doesn't have the numbers, and isn't doing much to get them. In which case, it's done, and so is he.

July 2002

LOSING THE CAUCUS

A leader's hold on his party is measured, first and last, by his relations with the parliamentary caucus. "You can't lead without the caucus," Brian Mulroney used to say.

John Diefenbaker lost his caucus, and the Conservative leadership, in 1967. Joe Clark lost his caucus, and the Tory leadership, in 1983. Stockwell Day lost his caucus, and the Canadian Alliance leadership, in 2001. Each, at the time, was leader of the opposition.

Jean Chrétien is in the process of losing his caucus, and the Liberal leadership, in 2002. But he, uniquely among federal leaders who have faced caucus revolts, is prime minister.

A prime minister's leadership of caucus is greatly enhanced by the perks and pleasures of power. A prime minister can invite MPs for cocktails and conversation at 24 Sussex. The most obscure backbencher can count on invitations to state occasions such as Royal Visits by the Queen. An MP can propose his riding executives for the thousands of appointments in the pleasure of the prime minister.

The prime minister names the chairmen of parliamentary committees and all the parliamentary secretaries to cabinet ministers. Most of all, the PM can dangle the prospect of promotion to cabinet, the one phone call MPs are always hoping to receive.

With all of that, Chrétien is losing the Liberal caucus. It is rather late in the day for him to be inviting backbenchers around for drinks. Given the circumstances of the Liberal leadership review, his motives would be highly suspect.

For fifteen years, Pierre Trudeau held the Liberal caucus members together because they admired him as the smartest guy in the room. But he also consulted them on major issues such as patriation of the constitution and would never have gone ahead without their support, particularly the Quebec MPs.

Mulroney kept the Conservative caucus together for a decade because of its affection for him, and because he never stopped working the room. Selected MPs were invited for breakfast at 24 Sussex every week before the national caucus. Backbenchers were forever receiving handwritten notes of appreciation for a speech they'd made in an empty House of Commons, but which Mulroney would catch on the parliamentary channel.

As a result, the Tory caucus followed him down many politically hazardous paths, from Meech Lake to free trade and the GST.

Chrétien is not particularly held in either admiration or affection by the current Liberal MPs. But for nearly a decade, they've had to respect his success at the polls – his record of three consecutive majority governments. Even now, Chrétien could threaten the Liberal caucus with the dread prospect of an election that he would win, yet again.

It is mainly his electoral success, and the discipline of power, that has kept his caucus together, until this remarkable summer of Liberal discontent.

August 2002

THE SHIFTING SAND

Thomas D'Arcy McGee, the most eloquent father of Confederation, once observed that the politician who "seeks after popularity, builds upon a shifting sand."

Jean Chrétien's entire leadership of Canada has been built upon his popularity, but now in the summer of 2002, the sand has shifted beneath him.

For nine years, he has hoarded his popularity, without giving Canadians an indelible impression of what he stands for, and so now they have concluded that he stands only for power.

Because of the leadership spat, Chrétien's numbers have gone splat.

The timing couldn't be worse for Chrétien, as he prepares for the Liberal summer caucus in Chicoutimi. Dozens of caucus members are already openly supporting a leadership review; dozens more, nominally loyal to the leader, have added the caveat that their riding associations want a change.

The overwhelming desire for change in the country only validates that. There go the people, we must follow them.

It's ironic that Chrétien confronts his new-found unpopularity with the argument that he was elected by the people and, for the sake of democracy, intends to serve his full term.

He's quite right about that. The insurrection in Liberal ranks amounts to a very Canadian kind of coup. A sitting prime minister, not halfway through his majority mandate, is in the process of being thrown out of office not by the voters but by card-carrying members of his own party.

There's nothing in Canadian constitutional convention about leadership review. It's the caucus, not the Liberal rank and file, that has the constitutional heft. The leader of the party in the Commons that enjoys the confidence of the voters, enjoys the confidence of the House – so long as he enjoys the confidence of his own caucus.

That's what makes the Chicoutimi caucus such a dangerous moment for Chrétien.

If a majority of caucus endorses his leadership, he can soldier on and face the leadership review. If a majority is emboldened to call for his retirement, then it's over. Just like that.

As for the leadership review, it is a modern political invention, concocted by the Tories as a means of dumping John Diefenbaker. But leadership reviews have since taken on a life of their own, as purported tests of accountability with party rank and file, even if a lot of the ranks have recently joined the file for the sole purpose of ditching the incumbent.

In the real world, if Chrétien can't win this vote, then he can't let it come to a vote. Chrétien is finally the victim of the politics of popularity, which he has practised so successfully for so long. When his popularity evaporated, so did the rationale for his leadership. Truly, he built upon a shifting sand.

August 2002

∞

THE LONG GOODBYE

If Jean Chrétien were really concerned about the "unique integrity" of his office, he wouldn't hang on to power for another year and a half.

In the interest of the Liberal Party, and the country, he would leave office much sooner, in early 2003 rather than 2004, assuring a timely transfer of power to his successor.

But of course, it's not about the party or the country. It's about him. It's about him remaining in office for the 40th anniversary of his first election to Parliament in April of next year. It's about him marking a decade as prime minister in November 2003. It's about him being in office on his 70th birthday in January 2004.

It's not business; it's personal.

It's not at all clear that Chrétien can maintain the timeline for his departure with the Liberal Party. It is quite clear that the government cannot function effectively for such a long period with a lame-duck prime minister.

Not to put too fine a point on it, Chrétien is dictating the terms and timing of his departure to a caucus in full revolt and a party on the verge of dumping him in a leadership review.

A sitting prime minister, with all the discipline of power and all the appointments at his pleasure, was able to muster only half his caucus to sign a loyalty pledge, an ill-considered gesture conceived as a show of strength that only served to demonstrate his weakness.

However the Liberals resolve the issue internally, the PM's long goodbye has profound implications for the conduct of public policy. For another eighteen months, he will be making appointments to the judiciary, managing the trade-based economy, overseeing federal-provincial relations and conducting foreign policy.

Moreover, in hanging around for so long, Chrétien is running a very big risk that the media will refocus on the ethics and patronage files, which could get extremely messy for him in his legacy phase.

Finally, he is bucking the Canadian convention of the elegant exit, staged over three to four months by his predecessors Lester Pearson, Pierre

Trudeau and Brian Mulroney. Chrétien's exit timetable is unprecedented, and might well prove to be untenable.

Behold, as Trudeau once wrote, "the rouged face of power."

August 2002

THE TWILIGHT ZONE

Ottawa has become a twilight zone, the time of day *"entre chien et loup"* when it is impossible to distinguish one from the other. In the fading light, the most dangerous time of day on the road, it's hard to tell if that's Jean Chrétien or Paul Martin up ahead.

One is still prime minister but no longer leader of the Liberal Party except in name. And the other is Liberal leader in all but name but not yet prime minister.

And when Martin is acclaimed leader, the twilight zone will become even murkier. Instead of leaving within ten to fourteen days after a change of leadership, the traditional Canadian timeline for a transition, Chrétien still insists on sticking around until next February.

Normally, the governor-general invites the leader of the party that enjoys the confidence of the House to form a government. And since Chrétien will no longer be leading that party, how can he cling to office for a further three months? It's simple – when the House and Senate rise for the Remembrance Day break at the end of the first week of November, they will not sit again until the passage of power is finally complete.

That will spare both Chrétien and Martin the cringing embarrassment of both sitting in the House, one as PM and the other as leader, while the opposition parties have a field day asking which one of these guys is actually running the country.

For the moment, it would appear they both are.

Since clinching the Liberal leadership, Martin has toured towns ravaged by forest fires in British Columbia and inspected the damage caused by the hurricane in Nova Scotia and Prince Edward Island. He was acting in the role of a prime minister, surveying the scenes of natural disasters and bringing words of comfort to the victims.

He has invited the provincial premiers to a tailgate party at the Grey Cup in Regina, the very weekend of his formal accession to the leadership in Toronto. He just wants to sit around with the boys and talk a little football and transfer payments.

The finance minister, John Manley, has curtailed the normal consultations leading to a February budget because, as he has acknowledged, he cannot bring in a budget in February. Like everyone else in Ottawa, he is "waiting for Paul." The best Manley can do is provide a budget update in November, again before the House rises, never to return on the watch of this government.

In a perverse way, it's a measure of the confidence markets have in both Martin and Manley, as well as the solid fundamentals of the Canadian economy, that there hasn't been negative fallout in financial and currency markets. The markets detest uncertainty, but they are also "waiting for Paul."

The weirdness of this Ottawa twilight is compounded by the sputtering merger talks between the Canadian Alliance and the Progressive Conservatives. They've agreed to call themselves the Conservative Party, to consolidate their debts and to grandfather all sitting MPs at the next election.

They just haven't been able to agree on how to elect a leader, by one person, one vote as the Alliance has insisted or by a delegated convention at the riding level, as the Tories would prefer.

If it had been left to the negotiators, they would probably have a deal by now. On both sides, they know where the cutting edge of the deal is: Right down the middle in a place called the Canadian compromise.

But the two leaders, Stephen Harper and Peter MacKay, have to control skittishness within their caucus ranks, and rein in their own egos.

They look and sound like two principals in a labour negotiation, constantly threatening to walk, just before they make a deal.

October 2003

THE CHRÉTIEN YEARS—A MIXED LEGACY

The Chrétien years can be summarized in the title of a spaghetti western: *The Good, the Bad, and the Ugly.*

The good part includes the major achievements of balancing Canada's books after three decades of deficits, and the Clarity Act that sets the rules of the road for Quebec's independence.

The bad part includes the breakdown of accountability in government and a succession of unseemly scandals, and a transactional leadership style that has left the country adrift.

The ugly part is the last fifteen months since Chrétien announced his retirement, and the worst of it is yet to come if the prime minister insists on clinging to office until February.

First, the good part. Paul Martin gets most of the credit for balancing the budget and creating the fiscal dividend. But there's no way he could have done either without the unstinting support of the PM. Until the end of his years in office, when he became preoccupied with legacy baubles, Chrétien was very good at skating Liberal spenders into the boards.

When the budget was finally balanced in 1997, Canada's federal debt was approaching $600 billion. As Chrétien prepares to leave office, it has been paid down to about $510 billion. Debt, as a percentage of national output, has fallen from 70 per cent a decade ago to below 50 per cent today, and Canada has gone from worst to first among G7 countries. It's an impressive achievement, and Chrétien deserves his share of the credit.

He deserves all the credit for the Clarity Act, just as he deserves much of the blame for the near-death experience of the 1995 referendum. Chrétien's policy of don't-worry-be-happy, followed by panic mode, could well have cost Canadians their country. The Clarity Act, which he proposed against the advice of many Quebec federalists, has actually been well accepted by most Quebecers, precisely because it requires a clear question and a clear majority.

Those are two big things for which Chrétien will be well remembered, among others. His recent campaign finance reform is another. The severe limits on corporate donations in general elections and their elimination in leadership campaigns is welcome in terms of the transparency of government.

But in far too many instances, Chrétien has governed simply by being there. And he has always hoarded his political capital, rather than spending it. This has worked well enough for him in three elections, but it's not going to wear well in the history books.

And he has been inadequate on the vision thing. In a decade in office, he has failed to propose what the French call a *projet de société*. By comparison with the Pearson, Trudeau and Mulroney years, Chrétien's achievements shrink. There was no equivalent to the Canada-Quebec Pension Plan or medicare on social policy, nothing like the Charter of Rights redefining the social contract between citizens and the state, nothing at all like the Canada-U.S. Free Trade Agreement that re-engineered the Canadian economy, creating four out of every five new jobs in Canada in the last decade.

In management terms, the two most important files on a prime minister's desk are Canada-U.S. relations and the federal relationship with the provinces. Here, Chrétien's record is mixed. He got along famously with Bill Clinton for seven years, but is hardly on speaking terms with George W. Bush.

This is not entirely Chrétien's doing – Bush's determination for war in Iraq, with or without UN sanction, with or without proof of Iraqi weapons of mass destruction, created painful divisions in the NATO alliance and across the Atlantic community. But neither can Canada conduct its most important strategic and commercial relationship when the prime minister is unwelcome at the White House.

As for federal-provincial relations, Chrétien's achievements include the Social Union Agreement. On the downside, can anyone remember the last time there was an open first ministers' conference?

And in terms of moral leadership, Chrétien has been a failure. Accountability is the central attribute in the corporate governance of government. From the time of the Airbus hoax, to his highly unethical interventions in the Shawinigan loan files, Chrétien has allowed the standards of government to deteriorate to the point where the integrity of the public service itself has been called into question. When senior bureaucrats book Caribbean cruises, something is very rotten at the centre.

For a long time, Chrétien was very good at reading the mood of the country. After the tumult of the Trudeau era and the wrenching turmoil of the Mulroney years, Chrétien's minimalist style suited the national mood.

But he has badly miscalculated the mood for change that took hold after he announced his intention to retire, but to remain in office for a further eighteen months.

The Liberal Party is getting a new leader. And the country is waiting for a new government. Not in three months, but in two weeks. If you think it has been ugly between the Paul Martin forces and the Chrétien camp, stay tuned. You ain't seen nothing yet.

November 2003

WHAT KIND OF PRIME MINISTER

Part of Paul Martin's problem in his acceptance speech at the Liberal convention was that he was following his own opening act. Bono rocked the joint with his speech on AIDS and debt relief in Africa.

Then, expectations of Martin's speech were so high that he could never possibly meet them. That being said, Martin missed a unique opportunity to introduce himself to the country and propose a vision for Canada. Instead he settled for what amounted to a budget speech with a few rhetorical ruffles and flourishes.

Uniquely in modern Canadian history, the Liberal convention was a coronation rather than a contest, creating an opening for a U.S.-style acceptance address.

After fifteen years in public life, including nearly nine years as an outstanding finance minister, Canadians know a lot about Martin's record, without knowing much about how he sees the country and where he wants to take it.

They know he's superbly prepared to be prime minister. They have little idea what kind of prime minister he will be.

They know he has won the struggle for the crown, but don't yet know how it fits on his head.

They know of his sense of public service, but little of his sense of country.

Not that Martin and his speechwriters didn't give it a try.

"Have you ever, on a cloudless night, looked down from a passing aircraft flying over Canada?" he asked. "Endless, glowing strings of cities, towns and homesteads. Stretching on and on, one province to the next. With only the stars in the distance."

Wait, there's more.

"Have you ever done so by daylight, when the stunning features of our country's face stare back at you? In all their exquisite variety, magnitude, ruggedness and beauty?"

So, it's a big country, by night and by day.

"It's a palette of enormous colour and range."

Uh-hunh.

"But more than that, it's a profile of character, our character, seen from above. A vision of possibility that knows no bounds – except for the far-off curve of the horizon. Rough hewn in places, beckoning in others, bountiful in land and sea and the riches they give."

Here comes the clincher.

"And like all of you, I just love it."

Enough, already.

Martin's strategic positioning was that he represented a change of government, not just a change of leadership; a change in the way government does business rather than business as usual.

Martin proposed a "politics of achievement," and in case anyone missed the point, repeated it twice within the next minute. Why? Because it fits with how Canadians perceive Martin, as someone who gets things done for the country.

But then Martin's speech became what is known in the speechwriting trade as a Christmas tree, full of trinkets, with something under it for everyone.

Fed-prov relations? He wants to end the "uniquely Canadian combination of regional discord and intergovernmental bickering."

Canada-U.S. relations? "We need a proud partnership based on mutual respect with our closest friends and neighbours. Two nations with many shared values but acting independently." So, close but sovereign.

Canada's role in the world? "Our foreign policy must always express the concerns and Canadians about the poor and underprivileged of the world." That's why Bono was there, "because he cares, because we care." There's never a re-write around when you need one.

Universal health care? He's for it. His dad would have been proud. Cities? He promised "a New Deal." Parliament? It must become meaningful again.

Transparency and accountability in government? Martin pledged "a government that treats taxpayers' money like it is your money, because it is."

This was actually the best line in the speech, and on Jean Chrétien's side of the Air Canada Centre, they were sitting on their hands, looking quite annoyed.

As the Chrétien and Martin entourages sat on different sides of the Air Canada Centre, their mutual loathing was all too apparent.

This was Martin's first problem as Liberal leader, healing the wounds left by the ouster of a sitting prime minister.

November 2003

2

UNITING THE RIGHT

MERGER TALKS

The merger talks between the Progressive Conservatives and the Canadian Alliance have a real chance of succeeding because there are serious people at the table.

Never mind the bitching by Tory backbenchers who read about it in the papers, after Alliance Leader Stephen Harper had briefed his caucus, proving once again there is no such thing as caucus secrecy.

Until then, the negotiators had managed to keep a tight lid on the merger talks for weeks, with a very small loop including the two leaders, Harper and Peter MacKay, as well as a few influential advisers and party elders.

The names of the negotiators alone, and the good working relationship they've developed, are sufficient grounds to take the talks, and the prospects of success, quite seriously.

For the Tories, there's the former deputy prime minister, Don Mazankowski. There's the former four-term premier of Ontario, Bill Davis, the man who made Brampton famous. And there's the party's house leader, Loyola Hearn, representing the parliamentary caucus.

From the Alliance, there's Senator Gerry St. Germain, a former president of the Conservative Party. There's Ray Speaker, a former Reform MP from Alberta, who has known Maz forever. And there's Scott Reid, a thoughtful MP from the Ottawa area not inclined to pound the table about social conservatism.

If you want to know where the middle of the road is, it's where you'll find Mazankowski and Davis. More than pragmatists, they're both accomplished dealmakers. If there's a good deal to be got for MacKay and the Tory party, they'll get it.

Mazankowski and Davis are also very close to the former Conservative prime minister, Brian Mulroney. They would not even be at the table if he wasn't supportive of the idea. Equally, there's no chance that they will do a deal Mulroney doesn't privately recommend to MacKay.

At this point, it's the Alliance that has developed a more detailed agenda in the form of fourteen points, not Woodrow Wilson's, but Stephen Harper's.

One thing the Alliance negotiators have already agreed to is that they would call themselves the Conservative Party of Canada. And why not? That's where all the brand equity is. Nor do the Tories have any problem with the Alliance proposal that all sitting MPs for both parties would be automatically nominated by the new one. It makes perfect sense – protect each caucus and bring them both on board.

But Harper has one demand that's a deal-breaker. He's wants a one-member, one-vote system at a founding leadership convention. Forget it, Stephen. The Tories will never agree to it, for two very good reasons.

First, there is no excitement and suspense in holding a leadership vote on the Internet. It's lousy television and the only reason for holding a leadership convention is to get three days of hoopla on prime time TV. That means some kind of "delegated" convention, where there would be as many members as Harper wanted, but only so many delegates per riding, pledged to one candidate for the first ballot, but free to move after that. There's no point doing this if everyone doesn't have some fun.

Second, the Alliance has about 200,000 members, compared with fewer than 50,000 Tories. Even with the membership numbers driven up by a leadership campaign, there's no way the Conservatives can pull even with the Alliance in a few short months.

"We would get swamped," says one top Tory strategist from Toronto. "It would be a crowning of Stephen Harper. No way we'll go for that."

There are other problems in selling a deal to both sides. For example, the Tory leader has a problem with David Orchard, the anti-free trader who threw his support to MacKay at last spring's leadership convention on the written promise of no merger with the Alliance.

Even with the difficulties, the stars might finally be aligned for a merger on the right. For one thing, the leaders who carried the baggage of bitterness between them have all left the stage. As far as that goes, even Mulroney thinks it's time to turn the page.

Then, another election cycle is fast approaching with the imminent change of the Liberal leadership; as of today, Paul Martin is Liberal leader in all but name. Do the Alliance and Tories really want to hand the Liberals a fourth consecutive majority just by splitting the opposition vote?

Then, the Alliance runs behind the Conservatives in every region of the country except the West. In the 210 seats east of the Lakehead, they are polling in single digits, and east of Ontario, they don't even have a pulse. For their part, while the Tories are competitive in the Atlantic, they are only a distant second in Ontario.

These talks might yet fail. But it's Friday night, and the dance has begun.

August 2003

IT'S A DEAL

It wasn't a dread of the next prime minister that drove the Alliance and Progressive Conservative leaders to unite the right so much as a fear of the outgoing prime minister's campaign-finance reform, which virtually eliminates corporate donations to political parties and leadership candidates.

The immediate timeline concentrating the minds of the two opposition leaders wasn't really an April election being called by Paul Martin. It was the looming implementation of Jean Chrétien's election and leadership expense reform legislation, limiting corporate donations to $1,000 at the riding level in general elections, and outlawing them outright in leadership campaigns.

This means the Canadian Alliance and PCs have less than three months to raise corporate donations for a combined campaign war chest, even as the Liberals harvest millions of dollars at a final round of fall fundraisers, some of them starring Martin after the Liberal leadership coronation.

It also means any and all prospective candidates to lead the new Conservative Party have until year's end to raise the millions of corporate dollars that have always been the financial mainstays of leadership campaigns in mainstream Canadian political parties.

So while Alliance leader Stephen Harper and Tory leader Peter MacKay will always have a claim on posterity for making this deal, Chrétien has also played an important role as an unacknowledged instigator of the pact to unite Canada's conservative forces. Campaign finance reform, already an important aspect of Chrétien's legacy agenda, might yet prove to be part of his revenge on Martin for overthrowing him as Liberal leader.

For as long as Chrétien might have run for a fourth term as prime minister against a fragmented and feeble opposition, election-expense reform was never on his radar screen.

Even as Chrétien's bagmen cynically exploited the ticking clock by going to the corporate trough one last time, the Liberals could not have foreseen the message corporate Canada was also sending to the Alliance and the Tories.

Quite simply, they were told: Don't come here again looking for money for two opposition parties, when the country wants only one. And by the way, as of January, we are actually out of this business, so you have only until then to get it together.

In the talks that began in secret over the summer, this imposed a deadline between Labour Day and Thanksgiving, depending on when the process went public. But the emissaries of both sides – notably Don Mazankowski and Bill Davis for the Tories, and Ray Speaker and Gerry St. Germain for the Alliance – were not only accomplished deal-makers, but respected figures in the two parties. Moreover, two elder statesmen, Brian Mulroney for the Tories and Preston Manning for the Alliance, were not only prepared to turn the page on the past, but strongly supportive of the merger process.

At the negotiating table, there was a sense Harper's fourteen-point plan represented a shopping list, while MacKay's blank page represented flexibility. If Harper knew what he wanted, MacKay also knew he had problems with the Red Tory wing of his caucus, including former leader Joe Clark and his sole Quebec MP, André Bachand.

For as long as MacKay allowed his caucus to delay an agreement, the Tories were sorely divided; once he decided to stop counting and start leading, they began to fall into line. Clark might remain outside the consensus, but that would leave him on the margins of his own party, with the David Orchard hostile-takeover crowd.

There will be interesting moments ahead in the selling of this deal, to say nothing of the three-month leadership campaign beyond the mid-December date for ratification by the membership of both parties.

But in doing the merger, the Tories and Alliance have not only acknowledged a divided right only elects the Liberals in perpetuity, but also that they hear Canadians saying whoever forms the government, this country needs a competitive democracy again.

In that sense, all Canadians are winners.

October 2003

THE MAGNA MAGNATE

It's one thing to be a political junkie, and hang with former prime ministers, premiers and even American presidents. It's quite another to decide, with no political experience of any kind at any level, that you'd like to be prime minister yourself.

But such is the case with Belinda Stronach, the Magna magnate, who is "seriously considering" a run for the Conservative leadership, and is expected to announce in her home town of Aurora, Ontario, that she's in.

She's never run for public office, never belonged to a political party, never made a major speech on public policy.

Which, as it happens, is an asset as well as a liability. She's not a professional politician. Precisely.

But as the president and CEO of Magna International, the auto parts and entertainment empire built by her father, Frank Stronach, she can hire the best campaign consultants and advisers in the business. Indeed, she already has the Conservative Party's top campaign strategist, John Laschinger, on the payroll.

This, in and of itself, lends credibility to the Stronach campaign. In Laschinger's last outing, the Toronto mayoralty race, he took David Miller from seven per cent in the polls last spring to 44 per cent and victory in the November election. But Miller had at least the experience of being a Toronto city councillor.

Stronach has no experience, meaning one of two things. Either her campaign will crater, or she'll demonstrate a capacity for growth and benefit from low expectations.

What's her position on same-sex unions, softwood lumber, mad cow, defence spending, Canada-U.S. relations, the war on terror, federal-provincial relations, Senate reform? If she doesn't have answers in a book of Q&As, her opening press conference could turn into a drive-by shooting.

French? Nope. But she's working on it, spending an hour a day with a tutor, and apparently is committed to becoming bilingual.

Money? Next question. There are no legal limits as to how much of your own money you're allowed to spend in a leadership race. But she would do well to ditch the corporate jet and fly commercial, indeed to fly economy, for the duration of the campaign. Then the story line changes from privilege to one of meeting Canadians as they fly about the country on their business.

Endorsements? Not a problem. She has a former prime minister, Brian Mulroney, and two former Ontario premiers, Bill Davis and Mike Harris, on the Magna payroll. Since none of them has succeeded in talking her out the race, all of them will be supportive of her making it. Davis and Harris are prepared to go public, while Mulroney, as a former PM, should stay on the sidelines.

The ease with which an untested and unknown political candidate is picking up support is both impressive and troubling. It is reminiscent of Kim Campbell's run for the Tory leadership in 1993, which was more preemptive than substantive. Would-be contenders with far more impressive resumés than her own, including Michael Wilson and Perrin Beatty, decided to sit it out rather challenge her. But at least Campbell had sat in the federal cabinet for four years.

As to whether she's in this just for the leadership campaign, or whether she's committed to a career in politics, she might take that off the table in her Aurora announcement by declaring she intends to run to be an MP there no matter the outcome of the Conservative convention.

Her bio is an interesting one. As the daughter of a penniless immigrant who built what is now a $15-billion business, she can say she wants to give something to a country that's been very good to her and her family.

At a minimum, she'll bring some sizzle and excitement to what otherwise looks like a very boring race. We're always saying it's difficult to attract good people into politics. On that basis, she can hardly be criticized for wanting to get in the game. But this is the bigs. She better know her stuff.

January 2004

THE RIGHT MAN WINS—HARPER

The right person won. It's a general rule of leadership conventions the winner is the best-qualified candidate, with the best organization, and enough support in every region of the country to win the day. On Saturday, that person was Stephen Harper, winning the leadership of the Conservative Party with 56 per cent on the first ballot, to 35 per cent for Belinda Stronach, and 9 per cent for Tony Clement.

The margin of Harper's victory in the Conservative leadership vote left no room for bitterness, no room for doubt and every opportunity for Harper to unite the new party around his leadership, and offer the country a competitive alternative to the Liberals.

This was the challenge of Harper's acceptance address, and he passed with flying colours. It was a very smart speech, strongly delivered – gracious to his opponents and generous to moderate Conservatives.

And with all most television networks carrying his speech, just before *Hockey Night in Canada*, Harper strategically planted the new Conservative banner on the middle ground, where elections are won in this country.

Right-wingers looking for red meat from Harper got their share in his nomination speech the previous evening, when gun and pervert registries, along with other family values, were on the agenda. That was Harper, speaking to the party.

In his acceptance address the next day, he was speaking to a wider audience – the country. He pointedly began by referring to Conservatives as the party of John A. Macdonald and Brian Mulroney. Indeed, Harper later placed a call to Mulroney, who happened to be out for dinner on his 65th birthday.

He congratulated Stronach for bringing "unprecedented" interest to a race that would otherwise have been mired in boredom. "Dare I say," he added, "and I'll concede this, she generated significantly more glamour than I was able to do." Equally, he congratulated Clement for the ideas he brought to the race, and later said both his opponents would have a prominent place on the front bench, that is to the cabinet, in any eventual Conservative government.

To moderate Conservatives, he said: "We need the Red Tory vision of important national institutions and sustainable social programs because Conservatives will never leave the most vulnerable behind."

On the imperative of inclusiveness, he said: "My Conservative Party will not be built by listing the types of people we don't want in our party."

On Canadian diversity, Harper said: "The Conservative Party believes that Canada's multicultural society is a valued reality and accepts the need to foster understanding and equality while promoting common values across Canada."

On Quebec, he said a lot of the right things in perfectly acceptable French, which is already better than most people thought.

Say hello to Stephen Harper, centrist.

Stronach was also a big winner. Beginning as a rank novice and complete outsider, she proved capable of growth over two months, held her campaign together through the convention, and later served notice in a pumped-up speech to supporters that she's in the game for keeps. She even put down a little marker of her own, about the necessity of the Conservatives being "a party of the mainstream."

The new Conservative brand emerged the biggest winner of all. The former Progressive Conservatives wanted the merger for the critical mass of the Canadian Alliance, which acquired the brand equity of the Conservatives, the party to which Canadians always turn when they're preparing to throw out the Liberals.

With five networks carrying the candidates' speeches, the country saw a much more competitive and interesting show than the one staged by the Liberals at the coronation of Paul Martin. They also saw three young candidates – Harper, Clement and Stronach – representing a new generation of Canadian leadership.

The leadership vote, held across the country, could have presented major problems for the Conservatives had the process failed or dragged on into the evening. The major networks had already put the Tories on notice that they were going off the air at 6 o'clock no matter what. If the vote ran any later, as the CBC's Peter Mansbridge quipped, "it'll be a crawl" across the bottom of the screen during Hockey Night.

When a party's not in power, the only thing the voters have to judge its competence to govern is the competence of the organization. And on Saturday, the Conservatives looked very competent. They got on the stage and off the air in plenty of time. They appeared united behind the new leader.

And now their guns are pointed squarely at the Liberals rather than each other. Canadian democracy is competitive again.

March 2004

MARCHING TO THE CENTRE

In organizational terms, the Canadian Alliance completed its takeover of the Progressive Conservative Party at their convention in Montreal. In policy terms, the PCs completed their merger with the Alliance.

Both sides got what they wanted on the floor of the convention. Stephen Harper got complete control of the party apparatus to go along with a clear 84 per cent endorsement of his leadership – a free pass through the next election. The former PCs got what they wanted, and Harper got what he needed, in that the Conservative Party moved closer to the centre on a volatile mix of social-policy issues.

Moderate, or sensible right of centre, resolutions prevailed at the policy plenary, attended by nearly 3,000 Tories bleary-eyed from a night on the town that knows how to party. Harper showed impressive floor management skills, and the rank and file demonstrated remarkable discipline, gaining a qualified yes to the question of whether they appeared competent enough to govern.

They also appeared moderate enough to govern, on most of the contentious issues on the floor, none more so than abortion.

Harper supported a resolution that a Conservative government would not introduce abortion legislation, and when it passed, another resolution to ban late term abortions became moot. The first resolution passed by a surprisingly close margin of only 55 to 45 per cent, but Harper will take it. Abortion is off the table, and Harper has an opportunity to close a significant gender gap. Instead of dodging questions on abortion, he can point to the number of articulate women winning leading roles in his caucus, the ones arranged closely around him on the podium.

Then, same-sex marriage. The party adopted a hard-line resolution affirming traditional marriage by a 75 to 25 per cent margin. Yet the entire party understands that Harper also supports a more generous position, affirming full equality rights under the Charter of Rights for same-sex civil unions, while maintaining the traditional definition of marriage.

Two basic tenets of the old Reform movement, recall and referendums, were given an unceremonious burial. The first, the notion of recalling MPs who displease their constituents, was always a nutty idea, quite apart from being unconstitutional. The second, the Reform referendum of the month club, was another stupid idea whose time never came.

The Quebec delegates, mostly remnants of the former PCs, got what they demanded from Harper's office to organize a provincial wing. They also got what they wanted in one resolution recognizing the fiscal imbalance between Ottawa and the provinces, and another supporting official bilingualism.

The only policy skirmish won by the Alliance faction was a resolution not to have a youth wing in the Conservative Party, and it barely carried. The Tories may want to reconsider this. Without the youth, there's no beer at conventions, and no one to plaster the hall with posters.

The one the PC wing of the party needed to win, and the one Harper passed the word it must win, was the defeat of a resolution tying riding representation to the number of members, rather than all ridings being equally represented.

This was snuck by the rooster in a workshop early on Friday morning. The proposer, Ontario MP Scott Reid, was one of three persons at the table for the Alliance during the merger talks. He knew perfectly well this was a deal breaker, and that Peter MacKay, as the co-founder of the Conservative Party, could never let it pass.

MacKay said he felt betrayed, and made it abundantly clear that all ridings are created equal, or else. With all hell breaking loose on Friday afternoon, Harper put it out that Reid's resolution should die on the floor of the Saturday plenary, which it did, by a 2-1 margin. A win-win for both Harper's leadership, and MacKay's stand for a bedrock principle.

But not before Harper's entire day had been thrown off message, and his team's floor management skills called into question.

The strain showed backstage after a sound check Friday afternoon, where Harper kicked over a chair, yelled at his staff and for good measure, booted the chair again. All this in full view of several CPAC television technicians, who passed it along to the anchor booth. Well, Harper was having a bad day.

But he recovered with a strong opening keynote, taking down Paul Martin for "promises made, promises broken," and staking his own positions on same-sex marriage and abortion, as well re-opening the missile defence debate, saying a Conservative government would bring Canada back to the table with the United States.

His closing speech was the opening salvo of the next campaign, when he flayed the Liberals as "corrupt, incompetent and visionless," and warned they had no monopoly on Canadian values, affirming the Conservatives proposed a "moderate, mainstream program which reflects Canadian values proudly and faithfully."

Because he has moved his party to the centre, and the leader and party appeared competent in doing so, Canadians may now be more disposed to listen.

March 2005

3

THE SPONSORSHIP SCANDAL

A PERFECT STORM

The perfect storm that threatens to engulf the Martin government began with the news of a fire suspected as arson at the Auberge Grand-Mère, scene of the crime in more ways than one.

The highly suspicious nature of the fire rewound the videotape on the story to the beginning in 1996, when Jean Chrétien, as prime minister, personally lobbied the president of the Business Development Bank for a loan to a constituent, Yvon Duhaime, for the Auberge Grand-Mère, of which Chrétien was once part-owner, adjoining a golf course he was trying to sell.

Chrétien pressed BDC president François Beaudoin on three different occasions, including one conversation at 24 Sussex. You could call this a conflict of interest, or an abuse of power, or both, because the president of the BDC is appointed by the prime minister and serves at his pleasure. The bank eventually succumbed to the pressure, approving a $615,000 loan in 1997, which Beaudoin later recommended recalling in 1999 after the hotel went into default.

Instead, Beaudoin was systematically stripped of his authority as CEO and terminated with severance and a pension, which the bank later cancelled. By this time, Chrétien's former operations director, Jean Carle, was executive vice-president and a longtime Chrétien supporter, lawyer Michel Vennat, formerly non-executive chairman of the BDC, had replaced Beaudoin as president and CEO.

Their role in attempting to ruin Beaudoin is the second element of the perfect storm, "an incalculable injustice," as Superior Court Justice André Denis recently wrote in a scathing judgment. No one in Montreal legal circles can ever recall such a devastating judgment. The bank was advised "to raise the white flag" rather than appeal. Its conduct was "abusive." Carle's testimony was blasted as having "no credibility," while Vennat's was dismissed for inconsistencies.

The bank and Chrétien's operatives were blasted for the "ferocity and maliciousness" with which they pursued Beaudoin, seeking to "break and ruin his career." It was clear that Beaudoin had been looking after the bank's interests, while they were looking after Chrétien's.

The third part of the perfect storm blew up with the release of the auditor-general's long-awaited report on the sponsorship scam. Among all the shocking headlines in war type, one stood out in the *Toronto Star*, the house organ of the Liberal Party: "Your money, their friends."

In a story of unparalleled cynicism and corruption, $100 million of public money went missing at the hands of the Chrétien government in collusion with three Montreal advertising agencies. Millions was laundered through five crown corporations – the BDC, the Old Port of Montreal, Via Rail, Canada Post and the RCMP. The ad agencies – Groupaction, Lafleur Communication, and Groupe Everest – skimmed the misappropriated funds with commissions and finder's fees, and all were generous donors to the Liberals. Of the many shadowy figures in this affair there is one, Jean Lafleur, with links to Alfonso Gagliano, the disgraced former public-works minister. It is hardly conceivable that Chrétien's then chief of staff, Jean Pelletier, was unaware of these scandalous events.

But Paul Martin said he was unaware, because as finance minister and chief financial officer of the government at the time, he was out of the room when it all happened. And that was the fourth component of the perfect storm. Even if true, hardly anyone believed it. Martin made things even worse for the Liberals and himself when he blamed the whole sorry scandal on a few rogue civil servants. This was incredibly stupid, not only a complete abdication of leadership, but also an invitation to the bureaucracy to take down the government.

The perfect storm reached its peak when Martin, in a hastily called news conference, admitted political oversight and warned Chrétien-appointed henchmen at crown corporations that "they will answer for their actions."

He did not name names. He did not have to. André Ouellet, the chairman of Canada Post. Pelletier, now head of Via Rail. Vennat of the BDC. "Anybody who knew anything about that, and did nothing, should resign immediately," Martin said.

Inside the Liberal Party, it was a declaration of war. Though he must know the consequences, Martin appeared to find his footing. He was staking the high ground for himself, and Chrétien be damned. "Let me assure you that those who are responsible," he said, "regardless of who they are, where they work or may have worked in the past, will face the full consequences of their actions." Make no mistake, it is war.

Centrifugal forces have now been unleashed inside the Liberal Party. It is far from clear that Martin can ride out the perfect storm through to the safe shore of a new electoral mandate.

February 2004

A CULTURE OF ENTITLEMENT

A lot of the paper trail in the sponsorship scandal leads directly to Jean Chrétien's office. But some of the witnesses at the Gomery Commission put the story in his living room.

Jean Carle, for one, was like a son to Chrétien. Jacques Corriveau, for another, was a top Quebec organizer in his two leadership campaigns and all his subsequent elections. "A good friend," the former prime minister acknowledged in his testimony before the commission in Ottawa. Close to Chrétien, close to his family. Chrétien's son Michel worked for Corriveau's company, Pluri Design, and reportedly once lived at his house.

As Chrétien's diaries indicate, Corriveau was an occasional guest at 24 Sussex and the Prime Minister's Office on Parliament Hill. Records from Elections Canada indicate that during the Chrétien years, Corriveau, his wife and his two companies contributed $60,000 to the Liberal Party and to Chrétien himself. Corriveau had every reason to be generous to Chrétien, because the Liberal Party and the Chrétien government were exceedingly generous to him.

Corriveau designed the maple leaf logo for the $60,000 in neckties given away on foreign trips, for which he was paid by Jean Lafleur, the man at the very centre of the scandal. Most of "the gadgets," as the ties, corkscrews and Jean Chrétien signature golf balls are known, were supplied by Lafleur's son, Eric.

This is the first time Corriveau has been directly linked with Lafleur, and it raises the question of whether or not he received any other small jobs from Lafleur Communications, which for years was the main supplier of communications products and services for Via Rail.

Corriveau was also in the printing business. In all three of Chrétien's national campaigns, he got the printing work for all the Liberal signs in Quebec. But in the 1997 campaign, he never got paid. He complained directly to Public Works Minister Alfonso Gagliano and Chrétien's chief of staff, Jean Pelletier, and was given millions of dollars of sponsorship subcontracts.

So a supplier to the Liberals was paid not by the party, but by the government.

It's odd in another way. In the weeks before the 1997 election, Chrétien gave half a dozen small dinners at Sussex to raise $1.5 million for the campaign in Quebec. But the printer, usually one of the first to get paid, never got paid. So where was the extra money spent? That's a very good question.

After a decade in office, with all the fundraising tools available to a party in government, the federal Liberals in Quebec were not only broke, but several million dollars in debt. If legitimate suppliers weren't getting paid, who was?

Then there's Carle, the surrogate son and former director of operations in Chrétien's office, who was parachuted into the Business Development Bank as senior vice-president of public affairs, even though he had no background in public relations.

One of his main roles there was to keep an eye out for Chrétien on the Shawinigan loan file, but he also got tangled up with Lafleur in the sponsorship files.

In front of Gomery, Carle reluctantly agreed with the judge's assertion a sponsorship deal involving the bank was akin to "money-laundering" in drug deals.

But that's the problem with the culture of entitlement that flourished in Ottawa during the Chrétien years. Chrétien treated the bank, a crown corporation whose CEO and board were named by him, as if it were his bank, strong-arming its president, François Beaudoin, not to foreclose the Shawinigan hotel loan, having him fired when he refused to comply, and then turning all the powers of the state, including the police, on him in one of the most disgusting abuses of power ever seen in Canada.

Chrétien's associates broke all the rules of transparency and process, not in the name of saving Canada from the separatists, but in their own partisan interests.

Typically, Lafleur had the effrontery to write to Pelletier in 1998 complaining that his sponsorship contracts fell off to $2.5 million from $8.5 million the previous year.

This wasn't about Canada. This was about greed. They thought of it as their money, not yours.

January 2005

∞

SMALL TOWN CHEAP

In public life, there's only one thing more dangerous than attacking a man's wife, and that's attacking his daughter.

What was Jean Chrétien thinking, then, when he brought Judge John Gomery's daughter into his theatrical stunt about signature golf balls before the sponsorship inquiry?

Here's one from George Bush, and another from Bill Clinton, with the seal of the president of the United States. Pretty funny. Why, here's another one from Ogilvy Renault, the Montreal law firm where Brian Mulroney and Gomery commission counsel Bernard Roy are partners, and where Sally Gomery is in their Ottawa office.

Mulroney and Roy were fair game for Chrétien, they're both public figures. But the judge's daughter is not. Her only crime is to have passed the bar exam and be hired by the one of the biggest law firms in Canada.

But you can always count on Chrétien, ever the schoolyard bully, to overplay his hand. His shot against the judge's daughter was not only cheap, and small town cheap doesn't begin to describe it, it was stupid. He gave Gomery a sword.

Besides, there's a difference between Chrétien's signature golf balls and the one he was holding from Ogilvy Renault. Chrétien's balls were paid for with public funds for distribution at golf tournaments to raise money for Chrétien's political campaigns. It's illegal to divert public funds for partisan gain.

The Ogilvy Renault balls were paid for by the private sector for distribution at private events. Nobody broke the law. That's the difference.

Chrétien's appearance before the commission was undeniably good theatre, but it wasn't very enlightening.

Much was left unanswered, and much was left unasked.

What was the ongoing nature of the relationship, for example, between Chrétien and Jean Carle, after he left the Prime Minister's Office as director of operations and was parachuted into the Business Development Bank of Canada as senior vice-president of public affairs? Did Carle and Chrétien stay in touch about the Shawinigan loan file and the firing of BDC president François Beaudoin, who wanted to foreclose the loan? Chrétien followed the loan file closely. Was he also aware that BDC chairperson Michel Vennat, a close supporter, cancelled Beaudoin's severance and that the bank authorized a legal witch-hunt against him.

These are not sponsorship issues, they are about the larger abuses of power under Chrétien's rule. But so far as that goes, would Chrétien have agreed that it was "money laundering" for Carle to agree to the BDC taking a $125,000 television sponsorship off the hands of Public Works, which didn't want it on their books?

What about Chrétien's relationship with Jacques Corriveau, his long-time top Quebec organizer and close family friend? In addition to printing all Quebec signage during the Chrétien years, he also did conventions for the Quebec wing of the Liberal Party. When he wasn't paid for his work in the 1997 campaign, he complained to Alfonso Gagliano and Chrétien's chief of staff, Jean Pelletier, and was paid millions of dollars in sponsorship contracts.

And what about going back to the beginning of this mess in 1996, when Chrétien's own deputy minister, clerk of the Privy Council Jocelyne Bourgon, warned him in writing to set up a proper process before distributing any sponsorship money?

He signed off on the first $17 million anyway. Bourgon's memo was very direct and blunt. Perhaps Chrétien never read it.

No, Chrétien has left a lot of questions unanswered. As for Paul Martin, he stuck to his story that he was out of the room when it all happened.

But the fact is that as finance minister, and by his own testimony, he signed on off a $50-million contingency reserve in the PMO that was start-up money for the sponsorship program. This could only have occurred at Chrétien's request. Martin's fingerprints aren't on the smoking gun, he just provided the money to buy it.

As deputy president of the Treasury Board, Martin hardly ever attended this cabinet committee, and then only to settle a dispute. As a senior Quebec minister, he was never aware of administrative problems in the sponsorship program. No one ever told him anything.

Then he was never in Montreal, never attended Liberal cocktails and dinners, where all these high rollers were usually in attendance, trolling for even more government contracts.

Montreal is a small town. Advertising and public relations is a small milieu, where each firm envies the success of the next. Long before the story broke, there was talk on the political street about irregularities in the sponsorship program.

When the commission moves its hearings to Montreal, that's when the whole story will come out. It's going to go kaboom.

February 2005

ALL IN THE FAMILY

As long as the Gomery commission was sitting in Ottawa, the script was about the bureaucracy and how it got its arm twisted by the Chrétien government. Now that the inquiry has moved to Montreal, the story shifts to the heads of the advertising agencies and their network of greed.

Consider Jean Lafleur of Lafleur Communications, the man at the very centre of the scandal. He had his whole family on the federal payroll. Between 1995 and 2000, Lafleur paid himself, his wife, his son and his daughter more than $12 million out of $66 million of billings to the federal government and crown corporations.

Lafleur himself was the big breadwinner, making nearly $2 million a year during the period, while his wife, Dyan, made $400,000 a year, his son, Eric, $200,000 a year, and his daughter, Julie, earned a paltry $115,000 a year.

How did he land all this work?

"We demonstrated an extraordinary level of know-how," Lafleur told Gomery.

Or more to the point, as he acknowledged in a burst of candour: "We had our network of contacts across Quebec."

It was a precisely that, a network of high rollers. There was the Cigar Club. They met for dinner in the best restaurants in the Ottawa area, in private salons of the Rideau Club and Cafe Henry Burger across the river in Hull. Good food, the best wines, and fine Cuban cigars.

André Ouellet, chairman of Canada Post, was a member. During his tenure, he gave Lafleur contracts for the rollout of thirty commemorative stamps, including the Series of the Century hockey stamps launched in NHL arenas across Canada.

Alfonso Gagliano was also a member. As minister of Public Works, he was the boss of sponsorship paymaster Chuck Guité.

There was Martin Cauchon, justice minister and minister responsible for Quebec's economic development, who was Lafleur's salmon fishing guest in the Gaspé.

That's a pretty high level network of contacts, social contacts who were also business contacts.

In the Gomery Commission's press room in the conference centre of Complexe Guy-Favreau, there were eighteen separate binders of documents relating to Lafleur Communication Marketing. There's one on the Montreal Expos and federal signage at the Olympic Stadium. There's one on the Grand Prix of Canada. There's one on the Maurice Richard television series.

And there's a big, fat file on *Via* Magazine, published by Lafleur when he was the main supplier of communications products and services to Via Rail, the Montreal-based crown corporation. The magazine was printed by Satellite Publishing, a wholly owned subsidiary of Lafleur Communications, which billed Lafleur back more than $40,000 per month for Via Rail's advertising and editorial copy in its own magazine.

But Via Rail was not the only government advertiser in the magazine. Here's a Lafleur invoice to Chuck Guité at Public Works for $185,000 in 1998 for five months of tourism "publi-reportage" in the magazine. Here's another in 1998 for $188,000 for four months of tourism advertising. Here's another 1998 invoice for $248,000 for four months of tourism advertising and promotional articles, reduced from a draft invoice dated the same day for $353,000. Lafleur finally gave them the government rate.

Again in March 1999, two invoices dated the same day, billing Public Works $236,000 and $252,000 for advertising between August 1998 and March 1999. Both invoices were addressed to Guité, and both were marked paid.

There's more – an internal 1998 Via Rail request for an "advance – Via's participation re *Via* Magazine" in 1999, in the amount of $287,000. Then there was another contract with Public Works, our old friend Chuck again, for $336,000 for "Logos Canada Via."

But the best story of all is about the salmon-fishing museum at Grande Cascapedia. In 1998, Lafleur billed $150,000 for a sponsorship, taking a 15 per cent commission of $22,500. He also charged $48,500 in creative and site management fees. Then he charged another $4,400 for his time.

Then there's the $3.8 million for the purchase of flags. Guité wanted flags. "I'm a businessman," Lafleur shrugged. "The client asked me to buy flags." For which, of course, he took a commission, not the usual 15 per cent, but a smaller one. How patriotic of him.

There's enough fascinating paper trails in those eighteen binders to keep him on the stand for a month. Not that he's going to say very much. "I have no precise memory for the moment," he said.

But one thing is certain – he never forgot to send his bill.

February 2005

∞

A NETWORK OF GREED

It's a small world when lawyer Doug Mitchell, who brilliantly represented François Beaudoin against the Business Development Bank, turns up at the Gomery commission on behalf of the Liberal Party, whose operatives tried to ruin his client's life.

As president of the federally owned BDC, Beaudoin was encouraged by Jean Chrétien's chief of staff, Jean Pelletier, to hire Jean Carle as senior vice-president of public affairs.

Carle, formerly Chrétien's director of operations and surrogate son to him, kept an eye on the Shawinigan loan file, and when Beaudoin refused to extend it, participated in the witch hunt against him. Not only was Beaudoin fired and his compensation package withdrawn, the bank organized RCMP raids at his home, cottage and golf club.

Mitchell courageously took Beaudoin's case for his small firm when none of the big firms in town would go near it. It was considered bad for trade to take on a client who was not only suing the feds, but essentially going after the prime minister himself. This is not a good way to get federal mandates.

Yet there was Mitchell at the inquiry, rushing in on behalf of the Liberal Party to explain that Chrétien's close friend and Quebec organizer Jacques Corriveau had, indeed, been paid $207,000 for his printing services to the 1997 campaign, though not until 1998 and 1999.

This was long after Corriveau complained, as he should have, he wasn't paid for legitimate services rendered. But it was also after he billed Eric Lafleur's firm a $60,000 annual retainer for nothing more than making himself available, and then billed another $115,000 for design services on some of Eric's sponsorship gadgets. After all, Corriveau came highly recommended, by Eric's dad, Jean Lafleur.

The fact he was on a $60,000 annual retainer to a company whose principal business was billing Public Works Canada for sponsorship trinkets is an important piece of information. The auditor-general didn't have it because she was looking into the government's books, and Corriveau didn't show up there.

The only reason we know now is Gomery's forensic accountants turned the advertising firms' books inside out.

And the hits just keep on coming. The other day, out tumbled the story of the L'Encyclopedie du Canada, a $1.2-million project turned down by Heritage Canada, but picked up as a Millennium Fund project over Public Works. Guess who charged a 12 per-cent commission of $144,000 for getting the money from the government to the publisher? Why, none other than that enterprising entrepreneur Jean Lafleur. He then charged another $136,000 for distributing the books.

Wait, it gets better. Hundreds of left-over copies were dumped in a landfill. The auditor-general didn't have that, either.

And there is much more to come. The auditor-general's report, devastating as it was, examined the sponsorship scandal primarily as a bureaucratic nightmare, an Ottawa story. Gomery followed that trail, too, in the Ottawa phase of his hearings.

But what's unravelling in Montreal is an astonishing network of greed. He knows where to look – for the boxes and season tickets at hockey games charged back to the government; for salmon-fishing trips with federal cabinet ministers from Quebec, for very expensive bottles of wine.

This is the kind of stuff that makes people very angry, because they understand it. Why should anyone have season tickets in the reds for the Canadiens, and charge them back to the government as an expense?

As for Doug Mitchell, he might want to make sure his client pays his bills. The Liberal Party is habitually broke, and notoriously slow to pay its bills. Ask Jacques Corriveau.

March 2005

EVERY TREE IN THE FOREST WILL FALL

In every political scandal, there's a guy who refuses to take the fall. In Watergate, it was James McCord, who famously wrote that "every tree in the forest will fall."

In the sponsorship scandal, it is Jean Brault, the former head of Groupaction, whose explosive testimony has blown the doors off the Gomery commission.

Brault had a lot to say, and in five riveting days of testimony, he said it all. He remembered everything and told everything. More than a co-operative witness, he was a compelling one.

Not only did he tell everything, he kept everything. The paper trail he gave the commission – five years of phone records, diaries, invoices and cancelled cheques – corroborates his amazingly detailed recollections of what took place, and where, of who got paid how much, and when.

But there was more to Brault than his testimony and his records. There was also his impressively calm demeanour. He was the best witness since John Dean, and for the same reason. Having decided to tell all, he appeared completely serene.

Most scandals are about money, greed, kickbacks or corruption. Adscam is about all of those things, and in Brault's case, all of them at once.

With the lifting of the publication ban, Canadians now understand why Ottawa is reeling from Brault's testimony.

He hired a Liberal fundraiser, Alain Renaud, and paid him $1.1 million over five years to open doors for Groupaction in Ottawa. From $14,000 in government contracts in fiscal 1996, Brault's business book with the feds grew to $47 million in 2001.

His advertising clients included the federal gun registry, and facing competition for renewal of the lucrative contract, he met with Joe Morselli, Alfonso Gagliano's organizer and bagman.

"He said, '$100,000 cash, your problem is solved.'" Brault paid in two cash installments and the competition was never held.

Morselli, whose car was blown up outside his house one night in 1989, turns up later in a restaurant scene right out of *Goodfellas*.

Brault brought $5,000 cash in an envelope to a meeting with Morselli at Chez Frank restaurant, left it on the table, excused himself to go to the washroom, and when he returned, the envelope was gone.

On another occasion, Brault delivered $25,000 cash to Morselli at a Christmas fundraiser hosted by Gagliano in 2001.

"I was told the party counted a lot on me and my financial aid," Brault said. And how.

In addition to $280,000 of illegal cash contributions, and $166,000 of legal donations to the Liberals, Brault also illegally donated $220,000 of value in kind – carrying Liberal organizers on his payroll when they worked for the party.

Who asked for the cash donations? Usually Jacques Corriveau, Jean Chrétien's top organizer and close friend, who also received millions of dollars of sponsorship sub-contracts that never showed on the government's books. Or Benoît Corbeil, president of the Liberal Party's Quebec wing. Or Alain Renaud, Liberal bagman and Groupaction rainmaker.

It was Corriveau, Brault said, who asked him to hire John Welsh at $80,000 a year while he worked for the party. Welsh is now chief of staff to Heritage Minister Liza Frulla. At least two other party workers carried on Brault's payroll have worked for Quebec ministers in the current Martin government.

Fortunately for the Liberals, Brault spread his largesse around, donating $100,000 to the Parti Québécois over two years in the 1990s in the hope of landing a lucrative $4.5 million contract with the Société des alcools du Québec. Since corporate donations have been illegal under Quebec law since 1977, Brault donated the maximum $3,000 through employees and illegally reimbursed them. In the 1998 campaign, at the request of Chuck Guité, he gave $50,000 to Groupe Everest to be donated to Jean Charest's first campaign as Quebec Liberal leader. It's not clear what happened to the money then.

Brault's testimony alone is enough to topple the government. He has clearly linked the sponsorship program and advertising contracts to the Liberal Party by way of illegal cash contributions, tollgating, skimming and kickbacks, not to mention paying the salaries of party organizers. And that's just the illegal stuff.

But there is more, much more, to come, some of it apparently just as shocking. Justice John Gomery himself warned yesterday that we are entering "an explosive phase" of the inquiry.

Every tree in the forest will fall.

April 2005

CUTTING UP THE CASH

Some political organizers call it walking around money. Others call it black money. Either way, it's cash money. And as Yogi Berra once observed, you get cash and it's as good as money.

Even better, for the federal Liberals in Quebec during the 1997 campaign. There was up to $300,000 in cash, which was never reported to Elections Canada and for which no receipts were ever issued, in violation of the law.

Who asked for the money? Michel Béliveau, then director-general of the Liberal Party's Quebec wing and former riding organizer for Jean Chrétien going back to the 1960s. Who delivered it? Jacques Corriveau, senior Quebec organizer of Chrétien's leadership campaigns in 1984 and 1990, and supplier of all Liberal signs and brochures for the three elections of the Chrétien era.

In 1997, just before the writ was dropped, Corriveau brought between $75,000 and $100,000 cash in an envelope to Liberal Party headquarters in Montreal. The cash, Béliveau told the Gomery commission, was "in $100 bills or $20 bills, 100s, or 20s, or both."

It must, as Justice John Gomery drily observed, have been quite a big envelope.

Where did the money come from? Béliveau never asked his colleague, whom he had known since at least the 1984 leadership campaign. And Corriveau never told him. Nor did they ever inform Chrétien. Nor would they have, since the first rule of politics is to protect the king, sometimes from knowledge of inappropriate activities on his behalf.

And Chrétien, had he known, would surely have disapproved. In fairness to him, while he worked hard to raise millions for the Liberal Party, he always played within the rules.

Where did the money go? To Benoît Corbeil, then Béliveau's deputy and later his successor, to help the Liberals organize "orphan ridings" held by the Bloc Québécois.

There was another $200,000 in cash for Marc-Yvan Côté, the former Bourassa cabinet minister and the Quebec Liberal Party's top organizer for eastern Quebec, who ran that part of the province for the federal Liberals in 1997.

How did Corriveau get his hands on up to $100,000 cash in 100s and 20s? You can't go to the bank and withdraw $100,000 cash. The banks won't give you that much cash. What they'll do is ask you to step into the manager's office, while they call the cops.

And even if Corriveau could get that much cash, how would he have that much cash on hand? Though he benefited from nearly $8 million in sponsorship money, this was early 1997, before the sponsorship money started to flow. Corriveau was the owner of a small printing company, Pluri Design, and no small business keeps that much cash on hand. It had to come from somewhere. So did the $200,000 cash for Côté.

What happened to the cash? Béliveau never asked Corbeil, because he had confidence in him.

The cash became walking around money for organizers. Béliveau admitted it was "an irregularity." But though he broke the law, he is beyond the law, since infractions of the Elections Act must be acted upon within eighteen months.

In addition to the $300,000 in illegal cash, the Liberals dedicated another $1.5 million to something called Fonds 1, raised legally and specifically for the campaign in Quebec.

Chrétien himself pitched in by hosting half-a-dozen small fundraising dinners at 24 Sussex, raising the $1.5 million for Quebec.

It wasn't complicated. The Liberals, starting with the prime minister, wanted to improve their score in Quebec over the 1993 campaign, when the Bloc won 54 seats and *les rouges* won only 19 ridings.

The extra effort paid off. The Bloc was reduced to 44 seats, while the Liberals won 26. Those seven seats were the Liberals' margin of majority in the election. The Chrétien Liberals won 155 seats in 1997, four more than a bare majority of 151 in what was then a 301-seat House.

History might have taken another turn altogether if Jean Charest, then leading the Progressive Conservatives, hadn't been caught in a squeeze between the Liberals and the Bloc in the closing days of the campaign.

Charest was on a roll out of the leaders' debates and his voting intention soared well into the high 30s, which might have delivered as many as 40 seats to him off the island of Montreal. It was then that Chrétien gave a television interview saying that a 50-per-cent-plus-one Yes vote was "not enough" to achieve Quebec's sovereignty in a referendum. The campaign then polarized around two choices, federalism or sovereignty, and most voters who had migrated to Charest went home to the Liberals and the Bloc.

In the end, Charest won just five seats, with 20 per cent of the vote, in Quebec. Had he held on to some of his earlier gains at mid-campaign, Charest would have reduced Chrétien to minority status in the House. In that context, Charest would never have left Ottawa in 1998 to become leader of the Quebec Liberals. And today he might be prime minister of Canada rather than premier of Quebec.

Reading about Corriveau delivering the cash to Béliveau, Charest must wonder how his life might have turned out differently.

May 2005

FOLLOW THE MONEY

Benoît Corbeil was saying he couldn't remember precisely when he picked up the two payments totaling $50,000 in cash from Jean Brault, the Groupaction guy. He could only say it was at the beginning of the November 2000 election campaign, when he was director-general of the Liberal Party of Canada's Quebec wing.

Was it at the end of September, the beginning of October, mid-October? "Right at the beginning," was all he could say.

"But the date is important," insisted Doug Mitchell, the party's lawyer.

"He doesn't remember," said Justice John Gomery. "That's the advantage of a cheque, and the disadvantage of cash, *n'est-ce pas?*"

N'est-ce pas!

This was illegal cash for the 2000 election, not to be confused with the illegal cash for the 1997 election.

In Corbeil's mind, there was no confusion at all. He was very clear that of the $75,000 to $100,000 cash delivered to Michel Béliveau by Jacques Corriveau in April 1997, he got only $9,000 of it, $5,000 for Denis Coderre's campaign in Bourassa, and another $4,000 for Yvon Charbonneau in Anjou.

What happened to the rest of it, either $66,000 or $91,000? Mitchell, on a mission to destroy the witness, did a pretty good job of insinuating it went into Corbeil's pocket around the same time, in April 1997, that he bought a cottage on Lac Nominingue in the Laurentians.

Either Corbeil got it, or Béliveau kept it, and disbursed it himself. But Béliveau himself wasn't around that much longer, as by Corbeil's account he bailed out, "not three days but three weeks" before the election, to save Jean Chrétien's seat in Shawinigan.

Béliveau, Corbeil's predecessor as director-general at party headquarters in Montreal, had been Chrétien's organizer in St. Maurice going back to the 1960s. And in the spring of 1997, Chrétien was in a tough fight against Yves Duhaime, a former Péquiste cabinet minister running for the Bloc. In the end, Chrétien's organization pulled it out for the prime minister, delivering 22,215 votes to 20,656 for Duhaime.

That was a lot closer than it should have been, but not as close as it was when Béliveau first got there. Did some of that walking-around money for organizers end up in the PM's riding? Well, there was one unpaid bill in St. Maurice for which Béliveau picked up another $8,000 in cash from Corriveau. This is not to be confused with the other $8,000 in cash from Corriveau to settle the campaign debts of Hélène Scherrer, the defeated candidate in Louis-Hébert, who is today principal secretary to Prime Minister Paul Martin.

As for Corbeil, he's quite clear on how he cut up the $50,000 cash. About $15,000 went down river to Quebec City, while the rest went to eight political attaches on unpaid leave from their jobs. Three of them immediately served Corbeil with a subpoena threatening a libel suit unless he retracted.

Two of them work for Jean Lapierre, Martin's Quebec lieutenant. Oh, by the way, Corbeil said he got a phone call from Alfonso Gagliano, demanding to know why he'd hired Guy Bertrand as his lawyer, and promising everyone would call him a liar if he named names. In some jurisdictions, a judge might call this witness tampering.

Did I mention the $120,000 in cash for Marc-Yvan Côté to distribute around his 21 ridings in eastern Quebec? The former health minister in Robert Bourassa's government was long the Quebec Liberal Party's senior organizer for that part of the province, and hired out to the feds in 1997.

In one of Côté's very competitive ridings, Bellechasse-Etchemins-Montmagny-L'Islet, Liberal Normand Gilbert defeated the Bloc's François Langlois by only 80 votes. In another, in the Gaspé, Liberal incumbent Patrick Gagnon lost to the Bloc's Yvan Bernier by less than 200 votes.

You get the idea. A very good case can be made that if the Liberals didn't steal the 1997 election, they bought it with illegal cash.

Yet a party literally rolling in cash was perpetually broke. In 2000, the Quebec wing's line of credit was expanded from $60,000 to $2.1 million and again to $3 million.

"And you're telling me your line of credit was maxed out?" Mitchell asked Corbeil.

"To be clear," Gomery interjected, "the party's line of credit."

"You can include mine, too," Corbeil replied.

This is why Corriveau's legitimate bill for $234,000 as the party's printer for the 1997 campaign wasn't settled until 1998 and 1999. It would explain why BCP, the party's advertising agency, was paid $200,000 for the 2000 campaign only in 2002.

Usually the guy who does the signs, and the guys who do the commercials, are among the first suppliers to get paid. In this party, they were the last. Everyone else, it seems, was smart enough to demand cash.

May 2005

∞

JUST A GUY NAMED JOE

John Gomery walked into the Van Houtte coffee shop down the mall from his hearings at Complexe Guy-Favreau, grabbed a tray and ordered lunch.

"Do you have a soup?" he asked.

"Cream of broccoli," replied the woman behind the counter. "For here or to go?"

He also ordered a wrap and a coffee, and paid at the cash. No one took any notice of him as he sat at a floor-to-ceiling window table, in full view of passers-by. He was just a man on his lunch, reading his *Gazette*.

Half an hour later, he was again sitting under the television lights in his hearing room, listening to Joe Morselli, who earlier had also been thinking about lunch when he asked for an early adjournment.

One thing the judge had in common with the witness, each paid for his own lunch. Morselli said he always picked up the tab, especially at Chez Frank, "to make sure I was indebted to no one." But if Jean Brault invited him to Club St. Denis, that was different. "He was the member, he paid."

Joe's rules.

He paid. You ate. Maybe you talked. Maybe not. "We talked about everything, including the weather," he said about one of his lunches with Brault.

Morselli paid for a lot of lunches during Alfonso Gagliano's reign as minister of Public Works, political minister for Quebec, and chief organizer of the Liberal Party in Quebec. Gagliano was Morselli's friend through all the years since they first organized St. Leonard for the provincial Liberals in 1976, and later when they were commissioners together on the Jérôme–Le Royer school board in the 1980s. But it was while Gagliano held this power, from 1997 to 2002, that Morselli himself became a man of influence.

If Jacques Corriveau was unhappy that two of his favourite musical ensembles hadn't received a sponsorship, why Joe would just call up Pierre Brodeur on Gagliano's staff, and put in a good word. If Alain Renaud wanted him to meet his former employer, Jean Brault, Joe was happy to do so. It might help him move some tickets for a $500-a-head cocktail planned for the fall of 2001.

"So you're telling us," Gomery interjected, "that you accepted an invitation in April to meet Mr. Brault, whom you didn't know, at the request of someone who no longer worked for him, with the objective of selling tickets for an event in October."

Sure. Who wouldn't want to meet Joe? "Because," as he said of another meeting, "I paid for the lunch, and because I was interesting."

If Brault wanted his advertising agency to win new clients in the ethnic and anglophone communities, Morselli was happy to introduce him to Beryl Wajsman, whom Joe had brought into Liberal Party headquarters as an organizer. Was there any cash in an envelope at their first meeting at Chez Frank? "I didn't see an envelope, Mr. Commissioner," Morselli said.

But he did remember being angry at Daniel Dezainde, "this so-called director-general" of the party, for firing Wajsman. Morselli added: "If I'd had a stick, I would have hit him. Did I say it's war between us? Probably. It was the only time I lost my cool."

He lost it again when Gomery wouldn't allow him to speak to Brault's character. "My God!" Morselli exploded, protesting that Brault had been permitted to say things about him.

If Benoît Corbeil, the former director-general of the Liberal Party, needed money for his municipal election campaign under Pierre Bourque's Vision Montreal banner in 2001, Morselli was happy to solicit a donation from Brault. He went to Groupaction's office on Sherbrooke Street, and picked up an envelope with $5,000 in cash. But it never got to Corbeil. Morselli put it in his pocket in payment for the value in kind he had supplied at his Buffet Trio restaurant and catering business.

Once when Morselli was leaving Liberal headquarters for a lunch with Brault in 2001, Corbeil said, "tell him to send me some paper ... paper for the office."

"Paper, what paper?" Gomery asked.

"Paper. Paper for the printer, paper for the photocopier. Paper."

How much paper?

"Boxes of paper. Otherwise, I imagine it wasn't worth the trouble."

Which only deepens the mystery of how a party in government was perpetually in debt and had trouble even paying the rent. The Liberals didn't even pay for their own paper.

At least Joe paid for his own lunch.

May 2005

∞

LE BAL DES AVOCATS

The Gomery commission has been *le bal des avocats*, the lawyers' ball, with dozens of parties seeking standing or representation before the inquiry into the sponsorship scandal and government advertising.

This week, in the last public phase of the inquiry, Justice John Gomery has been hearing closing arguments from lawyers on behalf of their clients; there isn't a courtroom lawyer in town who wouldn't kill for such an opportunity. But in pleading before so many colleagues, they've also been arguing before a jury of their peers.

Because the hearings have been televised, many of the lawyers have acquired a measure of celebrity. Two of the commission's counsel, Guy Cournoyer and Marie Cossette, have become media stars. It was Cournoyer's deposition of Michel Béliveau that resulted in the inquiry's most devastating revelation: That up to $300,000 in illegal cash tainted, and may have bought, the 1997 election for the Liberals in Quebec.

Cossette could charm the birds down from the trees, which made her very dangerous. Packing up her bankers' boxes late one afternoon after totally destroying one witness, she gave a colleague a jubilant high-five. Their boss, commission counsel Bernard Roy, had a way of laying out timelines that left the credibility of forgetful witnesses, notably Jean Lafleur and Jacques Corriveau, in tatters.

And then there was Doug Mitchell, representing the Liberals, the same crowd that tried to ruin the life of a previous client, former Business Development Bank president François Beaudoin in the case that made Mitchell's name. Considering the hand he was dealt, Mitchell made the most of it. While acknowledging some illegal money got to the party, he maintained most of it didn't. That would be because it was in cash, Doug, and was never intended to get there. His client also tried to turn him into a spin doctor, a hazardous line for any lawyer to cross.

Sitting beside Mitchell these many months has been the Conservative Party's lawyer, Arthur Hamilton, who was hampered by his client's lack of full standing before the commission. Finally given a full opportunity at the podium, Hamilton laid out a compelling, though partisan, check list on the origins of the scandal.

But in every roomful of lawyers, there is one who stands out from the rest, and in this room it has been Guy Pratte, representing Jean Chrétien's former chief of staff, Jean Pelletier, surgical in cross examination, and simply brilliant in his closing. All the francophone lawyers at the inquiry have a remarkable facility in both languages, but Pratte effortlessly switches back and forth from French to English in mid-sentence.

Yesterday, he argued Chuck Guité's testimony "does not hold water, *ne tiens pas la route*."

Later, Gomery interrupted to tell him what he meant to say.

"Nudge, nudge, wink, wink," said the judge.

"What did I say?" Pratte asked.

"Nod, nod, wink, wink."

"My French is getting in the way of my English."

Not really. He made a powerful case for Pelletier's public service. And there is no doubt his PMO was one of the best run in the last thirty years – in the top tier with Jim Coutts and Derek Burney under Pierre Trudeau and Brian Mulroney. Which isn't to explain what Pelletier was doing in meetings with Guité at the PMO, but that's for Gomery to figure out.

"He has earned the right," Pratte said of his client, "to walk with his head up in Quebec City, where he was mayor for twelve years."

Then this: "Guilt by association is not a concept to which our laws subscribe."

And: "Just because people were on the scene at the time does not mean they should become victims of a drive-by shooting."

Finally, and most compellingly: "If in this country we persist in bringing down people who serve the public interest … then we are in big trouble."

It was not only brilliant, it was riveting. Pratte defined a delicate balance that Gomery must strike between determining the truth and protecting reputations that, once destroyed, can never be remade.

June 2005

∞

A STOLEN MAJORITY

At the heart of Justice John Gomery's damning narrative is the compelling story of how the Liberals tried to steal the 1997 federal election with illegal cash in Quebec.

The Liberals were returned to office on May 2, 1997, with 155 seats in a 301-seat House of Commons, a bare majority of four. But in Quebec, they improved their score over the 1993 election from 19 to 26 out of the province's 75 seats.

Those seven seats were Jean Chrétien's margin of majority. And it was in those "orphan ridings," among others, that hundreds of thousands of dollars of cash was illegally distributed to local campaigns.

At the very centre of the story are Chrétien's two closest campaign operatives in Quebec, Jacques Corriveau and Michel Béliveau.

Corriveau was the Quebec organizer of Chrétien's two leadership campaigns in 1984 and 1990. He was vice-president of the Quebec wing of the Liberal Party as well as national francophone vice-president in the 1980s.

His firm, Pluri Design, was the supplier of outdoor signs, advertising and handouts in Quebec during the election campaigns of the Chrétien years. He was close enough to Chrétien to be invited to sleep over at 24 Sussex.

Béliveau was a Chrétien organizer in the St. Maurice riding going back to the 1965 election, and was chief organizer of the 1984, 1993 and 2000 campaigns in Shawinigan. In 1997, he was director-general of the Quebec wing of the party in Montreal.

And here is where Gomery picks up the story, at Béliveau's office, to which Corriveau brought as much as $100,000 in cash stuffed in a rather large envelope.

Gomery recounts Béliveau's testimony "he received directly from the hands of Mr. Corriveau, at the party's headquarters, a thick envelope in which there was $75,000 to $100,000 in bills of $20 and $100, although he did not count them." The money was for orphan ridings in western Quebec.

It was part of a plan to raise "a total of $250,000 to $300,000, of which $175,000 to $200,000 was needed in the eastern ridings and $75,000 to $100,000 in the western part of the province." Every nickel of it was illegal.

In the event, Béliveau disbursed $120,000 in two cash payments for the twenty-one ridings of eastern Quebec. The first payment of $60,000 was made at the opening of Chrétien's Quebec campaign in Shawinigan. The entire amount was handed over to Marc-Yvan Côté, a legendary Liberal organizer for eastern Quebec.

He also testified to a further cash payment "amounting to $7,000 or $8,000 which was paid to a volunteer in Quebec City to reimburse him for out-of-pocket expenses incurred in the riding of St. Maurice."

That would be Jean Chrétien's riding of St. Maurice, to which Béliveau retreated in mid-campaign, because the prime minister was in an extremely competitive race with Yves Duhaime, a former Parti Québécois cabinet minister running for the Bloc Québécois.

By pulling out all the stops, Chrétien won by 22,215 votes to Duhaime's 20,656, a margin of only 1,557 votes.

Among the ridings secured with illegal cash was the prime minister's own.

Gomery writes Béliveau recalled "another delivery of cash in the sum of $8,000, which was received at a later date, and paid to a businessman in Quebec City who had provided services during the 1997 campaign in the riding of Louis-Hébert." The defeated Liberal candidate was Hélène Scherrer, who is today principal secretary to Prime Minister Paul Martin.

At the conclusion of his testimony, Béliveau broke down and wept in shame. He had testified, Gomery writes, that Corriveau "was the person to whom, he, as executive director" of the party, "could turn for money, that Mr. Corriveau did not disappoint him when he was asked for financial assistance, and that the money received in cash came from unrecorded and improper sources."

And where did Corriveau get the money? Gomery concludes some of it came from the $7 million of sponsorship sub-contracts Corriveau received as a third-party supplier to the advertising agencies, which is how Chrétien's top political organizer in Quebec never appeared on the government's books, and never attracted any attention.

The Liberal's Party preoccupation with improving its score in Quebec was understandable. Indeed, the need to do better is even recorded in the minutes of a 1996 cabinet retreat, an unusual subject of government business.

Chrétien even hosted half a dozen private dinners at 24 Sussex in the spring of 1997, which quite legally raised and reported another $1.5 million dedicated to the Quebec campaign.

Jean Charest, then Conservative leader, always believed the Liberals tried to buy or steal the 1997 election. The testimony before Gomery, and his report, proves it.

November 2005

4

ELECTIONS 2004, 2006, 2008

2004: A MINORITY HOUSE

It's 1957 all over again. Or 1962. Or 1963. Or 1965. Or 1972. Or 1979. Six elections in the last half-century have resulted in minority governments. The polls are telling us we might be headed there again.

Paul Martin must hope it's like 1963, the election that returned the Liberals to office under Lester B. Pearson. In successive minority governments, in only five years in office, Pearson left the most impressive legislative legacy in modern times.

Despite petty scandals completely forgotten today, despite being tormented every step of the way by John Diefenbaker, Pearson's record of achievement included the Auto Pact, forerunner of free trade, and the entitlements of medicare, the Canada-Quebec Pension Plan, the Canada Assistance Plan and the Guaranteed Income Supplement. Not to mention the Canadian flag, adopted after a tumultuous debate also forgotten today, and the spirit of co-operative federalism still regarded as the gold standard of federal-provincial relations.

In both 1963 and 1965, Pearson came up a few seats short of a majority, and was left in a workable minority situation in which the NDP held the balance of power. The support of the NDP came at a cost, but it happened to fit with Pearson's domestic agenda of social innovation. Although some argue Pearson's social programs sowed the seeds for decades of deficits to come, he managed to govern with the last balanced budgets Ottawa would see for the next thirty years.

Just as the NDP's founding leader, Tommy Douglas, exacted a price for his support of the Pearson Liberals, so would Jack Layton have his terms for supporting the Martin Liberals.

He's already made them clear. Electoral reform, for openers, which would fit Martin's fascination with redressing "the democratic deficit." If the provinces can take a leadership role in discussing a mixed proportional system, as Quebec is doing, then it's time Ottawa joined the debate. It's not complicated – in our first past the post system, the NDP is under-represented in Parliament. A Liberal minority would allow the NDP to leverage its demands for parliamentary reform.

On health care and other social-policy issues, the NDP's position is clear from Layton's talking points out of the budget. The government is paying down the mortgage on the house at a time when the roof needs fixing and your mother needs an operation. The surplus would be reallocated for social programs in the first budget of a minority Martin government, which might be the best argument for not electing one.

Stephen Harper hopes it's 1957 again, with an election returning a minority Conservative government on its way to electing a big Conservative majority in the one after that. Such was the case with Diefenbaker in 1957, when he brought twenty-two years of successive Liberal rule to an end. The next year, Quebec jumped on the bandwagon and Dief was returned with the landslide of 208 seats.

This was also the hope of Joe Clark in 1979, when the Conservatives ended another sixteen years of consecutive Liberal rule. Their expectation was that, just as in 1957–58, they would defeat the Liberals in two stages, with Quebec coming aboard after the departure of its favourite son, Pierre Trudeau. Instead, Clark mistakenly chose to govern as if he already had a majority, though he was half a dozen seats short. Which proved to be exactly the margin of his defeat, 139-133, when his government famously fell over John Crosbie's "no pain, no gain" budget. The rest being history, Trudeau came out of his brief retirement and won his third majority mandate in 1980.

Like Dief in 1957, like Clark in 1979, Harper is challenged to win this election without winning seats in Quebec. What makes Harper's job easier than his predecessors is the presence of the Bloc Québécois. The Bloc and Quebec now stand between Martin and his hopes for a majority. Less than four months ago, when he took office, Martin's campaign strategy was to win 20 more seats in Quebec to make up for anticipated losses in Ontario. But the Liberal brand was already getting sideswiped by the unpopularity of Jean Charest's government in Quebec. And in the political firestorm unleashed by the sponsorship scandal, the Bloc has taken a big lead in the polls.

And while Martin's Ontario advisers are itching to call an election while they have a 20-point lead on the Tories there, his Quebec advisers want to see further improvement and a clear trend away from the Bloc.

As one of them puts it: "I'm in favour of calling an election – when we can win."

March 2004

BRAND EQUITY

An election campaign is a lot like the fast-food business. It's built on brand equity and the menu. And it depends entirely on execution. The party leader is the franchisee, the guy behind the counter asking if you'd like fries.

The Liberals are the McDonald's of Canadian politics, the most accepted trademark in the business. The Conservatives are like Burger King, the clear alternative when people get tired of McDonald's and want a change. The NDP are like Harvey's – Canadian, eh?

The Bloc? They're a regional brand, available only in Quebec, with poutine stands across the province. They're giving the other guys so much trouble that they're putting poutine on the menu, too.

They all make hamburgers, with fries. You look at the menu board, just as you choose among the party platforms. Apart from the menu (the things you pay for) there are the promotions (the stuff you get for free).

But if you don't execute in this business, if the food is cold, if the supply chain breaks down, if the washrooms are dirty, then the whole thing fails. Customers drift away to competitors. The brand takes a hit. This is the equivalent of the leaders' tours.

In this campaign, the Liberal brand is flailing, the Conservative brand is growing, the NDP brand is a competitive third, and the Bloc brand is cleaning up at poutine stands all over Quebec.

The Grits aren't even running on the Liberal name. They're running as Team Martin. This is like McDonald's running as George Cohon. It is the salesman as the brand.

The Liberals rebranded as Team Martin because they sensed the hit from the auditor-general's report on the sponsorship scandal, and anticipated collateral damage because of unpopular Liberal governments in Quebec, British Columbia and Ontario.

The Liberals knew about the sideswipe effect of the Ontario budget, since Martin's campaign director, David Herle and his colleagues at Earnscliffe Communications, advised Dalton McGuinty on the budget brought down only days before the May 23 federal election call. The political class is still stunned that Martin's own advisers sent him into a perfect storm.

The Martinites treated the sponsorship scandal as if it were Mad Cow, and decided to kill off their supply chain, and with it the golden arches. Instead of Mad Cow, they offered Mad as Hell. They took Jean Chrétien's scandal and made it their own.

Meanwhile, the Conservatives were also rebranding, but in a manner guaranteed to grow, rather than shrink, their market share. The western Canadian Alliance brand, which stopped at the Lakehead, merged with the weak eastern Progressive Conservative brand. The Alliance bought out the PCs, not for the number of stores, but for the brand equity of the Conservative trademark, to which Canadians turn whenever they get tired of the Liberals. You can look this up under Robert Borden in 1911, R.B. Bennett in 1930, John Diefenbaker in 1957, Joe Clark in 1979 and, because Clark blew it, Brian Mulroney in 1984.

They turn to the Conservatives only when they feel the Liberals, the comfort brand, have been too long in office, too arrogant and too susceptible to scandal. Only when they feel comfortable with the menu offered by the Tories, and the guy asking if you'd like fries.

Once the Conservatives were a national brand again, they were able to grow their market share. Once they chose Stephen Harper as their leader, they could offer fries in two languages. The fact they were a national brand meant they could offer a menu of change, provided they could execute.

In this campaign, at least until their mishap clumsily connecting Martin to child porn, they looked quite competent. For an opposition party, Canadians can judge their competence to govern only on the competence of their campaign. It starts with the strategy in the war room, and ends on the leader's tour. This is what is known as fast-food management.

It is the Liberals, the party of power, whose tour has broken down. When they pulled Martin out of the G8 summit a day early to resume the campaign in Montreal, only to cancel because there were no hotel rooms due to the Grand Prix, that was a telling moment. Millions of Canadians actually know the F1 race is held in Montreal in the second week of June.

Martin desperately needs to put the Liberal brand back in the window. He needs to say: "We are the party of Lester B. Pearson and the Canadian flag. We are the party of Pierre Trudeau and the Charter of Rights. We are the party of Jean Chrétien and the Clarity Act. Together, in a decade of achievement, Mr. Chrétien and I put this country in the black."

The Liberals are the party of the Big Mac and golden arches. Martin has ignored that brand equity at his own peril. When the entire campaign is put on the shoulders of the leader, and the leader stumbles, what does the party have to fall back on?

Nothing.

June 2004

∞

A LIBERAL MINORITY

If you'd asked Canadians to pick their preferred result in this 2004 election, they would have said a Liberal minority propped up by the NDP, with the Conservatives keeping a watchful eye on both of them, and the Bloc Québécois denied the balance of power.

Pending recounts, the Liberals have 135 seats, the NDP 19 – together one seat short of a majority, while the Tories won 99 seats and the Bloc 54.

As they say in golf, you couldn't walk it out there any better.

The voters have punished the Liberals without defeating them. They've told the Conservatives, not yet, not until we're comfortable with you as a moderate alternative to the Liberals. And with the Bloc, Quebecers have sent a strong deputation to defend their interests in Ottawa, without creating a backlash in the rest of the country.

Make no mistake, if the separatists had held the balance of power in a weak minority Parliament, there would have been a firestorm of anger in English-speaking Canada, much of it directed at Paul Martin and the Liberals for their stupidity in calling an unnecessary election.

The country dodged this doomsday scenario thanks to a late Liberal surge in Ontario, where they won 77 seats to the Conservatives' 22. Undetected by polls published as late as the weekend, undecideds were deciding Liberal, and NDPers, terrified at the prospect of a Conservative government, switched to the Liberals.

Instead of winning Ontario by five points, 40-35, as projected in the polls, the Liberals surged to a 44-32 margin, sweeping the Toronto and southern Ontario ridings that had been in jeopardy throughout the campaign. Had the Conservatives won another 25 Ontario seats, as pollsters predicted before the weekend, they would have formed a minority government.

Typically, in the suburban 905 belt around Toronto, Conservative star candidate Belinda Stronach, was leading by nearly thirty points two weeks into the campaign, but hung on to win by only a few hundred votes.

But the Conservatives have only themselves to blame. The constant friendly fire on social issues, together with the disgusting Liberal attack ads, finally took a fatal toll on Stephen Harper's campaign.

Unless Harper gains control of his caucus, and reserves a special place in hell for bozos like Cheryl Gallant and Randy White, Canadians will never trust him with government. The Conservatives were at 37 per cent, heading to majority territory, when Gallant made her comment comparing abortion to the beheading of American Nicholas Berg. It stopped the momentum and started the Conservative slide. At his first meeting of the Conservative caucus, Harper should make it abundantly clear that the reason they are in the room is because of some of the people in the room.

Harper himself made two critical errors, first following the leaders' debates by talking of a Conservative majority government – the last thing voters wanted to hear about. And then, over the final weekend, by returning to the old Reform theme of "the West wants in," a strange way of trying to close the deal in Ontario. It just drove voters to the Liberals, whose best-case scenario was then 125 seats.

Moreover, while Martin pushed himself to the limit, including a frantic dash across the country on Sunday, Harper's final week on tour was almost a leisurely walk in the park. At the beginning of the last week, he took an entire day off. At mid-week, he was in northern Ontario when he should have been in southern Ontario, bussing down the 401 and the Queen Elizabeth Way. At the weekend, he was in Alberta, which was a lock. Amateur hour.

All the conditions for the throwing the bums out, from the sponsorship scandal to the Ontario budget, were there. Sixty per cent of the voters wanted a change of government, but only 30 per cent voted for the Conservatives. They should ask themselves some hard questions about their failure to provide the comfort level voters were looking for. The Conservatives blew it.

While the NDP doesn't quite have the balance of power, it is close enough that Jack Layton can write up his shopping list, from health care to the environment. Liberal-NDP minorities tend to be expensive, but they can also be productive, as during the two minorities of the Pearson years, which produced the social programs that endure to this day.

This promises to be that kind of minority Parliament, one that will last at least two years, if not three. Certainly, Gilles Duceppe will not be in any hurry to force a federal election before the next Quebec election in 2007.

With 54 members, he has 54 offices in Ottawa, and 54 riding offices in Quebec, all fully staffed, as branch offices for the Parti Québécois. Duceppe's job is to stay in Ottawa and help elect the PQ. And his activities will be fully financed by the new federal finance reform, which gives each party $1.75 per voter per year. The Bloc got 1.6 million votes. Do the math. Ottawa is now financing the sovereignty movement.

As for Paul Martin, he gets to keep his job, after the near-death experience of the campaign. Whether he proves a caretaker prime minister or something more remains to be seen. He has escaped the fate of John Turner, a prime minister who inherited office only to lose it. Yet Martin has also paid a big price. He has been exposed as just another politician who will say, and do, anything to win.

June 2004

DODGING A BULLET

The still photographers behind the curtains in the House of Commons knew what they wanted – Peter MacKay and Belinda Stronach in the same shot. In question period the picture was perfectly framed – MacKay on his feet, turned away from her toward the speaker, while she sat in her new place on the Liberal side of the floor.

His body language was as eloquent as her tight-lipped expression – it was a difficult moment for them both. On any other day, it would have been the defining moment. But with the government's fate hanging in the balance of a non-confidence vote, it was only a teaser.

The outcome of the vote was actually determined earlier in the week when Stronach crossed the floor for a cabinet seat. Had she remained with the Conservatives, they would have won the vote, and the Liberals would have lost it, 153-151. In the actual vote, they tied 152-152, with the speaker breaking the deadlock in favour of the government. House of Commons rules, in this instance, are the same as in baseball – a tie goes to the runner.

And so the Conservatives have to consider what to do next. Do they stand down, as promised earlier this week, and allow the government to survive through the summer until at least the fall? Or do they return to the charge again at the next opposition day on May 31?

Having lost his best opportunity to topple the government, by failing to keep his own ranks together, Stephen Harper is the biggest loser. He is not without responsibility in Stronach's decision to bolt. Not only did he freeze her out, he went out of his way to offend her.

At a Conservative candidates' college the Harper team showed one of her photo ops as an example of how not to stage one.

As if they all had degrees in event management.

Two weeks ago, she was summoned to Stornoway to be dressed down for a newspaper interview in which she warned against a spring election. Harper told her she would never be leader of the Conservative Party.

MacKay has felt equally frozen out by Harper and his office. Though a co-founder and deputy leader of the party, his loyalty has been questioned at every turn by the insensitive clods around Harper.

Instead of reining in Harper's anger, they've fanned the white-hot indignation that has burned a hole through the television screen, turning voters off in droves.

Letting his anger get the better of him again, he dismissed Stronach as someone not known for her ability to discuss complex issues. Well, that's one way to address the gender gap. Stronach might be a crass opportunist, but at least she knows how to stay on her message track.

Conservative strategists were resigned to losing the vote, and the sensible ones among them were privately relieved. Increasingly, they had a sense of foreboding about going into an election with the Liberals bouncing back to lead most polls, notably in Ontario.

What happened to the Conservative lead, which was as much as nine points, 36 to 27 per cent? That's easy – the Gomery effect got them to 36 per cent, and they did nothing to stay there. The Liberals reinforced voters' doubts about Harper, with help from Harper himself.

A summer of corn roasts and strawberry socials, with his family in tow, might soften Harper's hard edges. If he has a feminine side, he badly needs to get in touch with it. And he should reflect on the lessons of the last few weeks, in which his office and his campaign team have been outmanoeuvred by the Liberals at every turn.

One of the tests of leadership is knowing when to change the entourage. Sometimes it involves a realization that the people who brought you here can't take you there.

All the players in the events of this week have lost something. Martin once again appears as a man who would do and say anything to remain in office. He invited a stranger into his home and gave her a cabinet job. Stronach won a seat at the cabinet table, but paid a Faustian price.

May 2005

∞

ALICE IN WONDERLAND

You know the story of *Alice in Wonderland*. She falls down the rabbit hole and ends up at a tea party, where everyone says what they mean, except when they don't, then everything is the opposite of what they say.

Here's Alice, with the Hatter, the March Hare and the Dormouse sitting at a table under a tree. When Alice wants to guess some riddles, the March Hare warns: "You should say what you mean."

"I do," Alice hastily replied, "at least, I mean what I say – that's the same thing, you know."

"Not the same thing a bit," said the Hatter. "You might just as well say that 'I see what I eat' is the same as 'I eat what I see.'"

"You might just as well say," added the March Hare, "that 'I like what I get' is the same as 'I get what I like.'"

"You might just as well say," added the Dormouse, who seemed to be talking in his sleep, "that 'I breathe when I sleep' is the same as 'I sleep when I breathe.'"

Alice, that's you, the voter, a bit mystified and slightly appalled by a world turned upside-down. The Hatter, the March Hare and the Dormouse are perfectly represented by Gurmant Grewal, Tim Murphy and Ujjal Dosanjh.

It's just the kind of crazy conversation they had on tape, about Grewal and his wife, Nina, also a Conservative MP, crossing the floor, or staying out of the House, to assure the survival of the Liberal government in the May 19 confidence vote on the budget.

In this world, saying what you mean isn't the same as meaning what you say, as the Hatter, the March Hare and the Dormouse make perfectly clear.

Of course, the March Hare could also be played by Belinda Stronach, liking what she gets, and getting what she likes. I digress.

Then it turns out there were gaps on the tapes, up to 14 minutes, the kind of gap that made Rosemary Woods famous at Watergate, which was not a fairy tale but a morality play. But while the tapes were in an altered state, nothing changed the fact of Tim Murphy, the prime minister's chief of staff, saying Paul Martin was aware of the meeting, and was prepared to meet Grewal. Why, the Liberal Party is a welcoming one, "a welcome mat that has a lot of nice, comfy fur on it."

Of course, "you didn't approach, we didn't approach." Or as Lewis Carroll wrote of the tea party: "And here the conversation dropped, and the party sat silent for a minute."

If comfort was what Grewal was seeking, Murphy could arrange a quick ruling from the ethics commissioner, that everything was in order in terms of one public official soliciting or receiving benefits, while others offered them, in return for a vote, in violation of the Criminal Code.

"That would be really nice," Murphy told Grewal, "if we could get the ethics commissioner to give an interim report or something to take the cloud off."

Murphy must have this ethics commissioner, an independent officer of Parliament, mixed up with the former ethics counsellor, an employee of the Prime Minister's Office.

The ethics commissioner, Bernard Shapiro, immediately let it be known he didn't appreciate having his name bandied about in such fashion, suggesting he was a PMO lackey. Shapiro also agreed to investigate Grewal and Dosanjh's role in the sordid affair, though he's not able to investigate Murphy as a member of Martin's staff.

Murphy suggested co-opting, if not corrupting, a neutral official to a partisan purpose. But Shapiro is unable to investigate Murphy because he's not an MP. Well, commissioner, pull up a chair at the tea party.

There's a place now, with Grewal having flown the coop. He was last seen at Vancouver airport, apparently trying to persuade passengers on an Air Canada flight to take a package on a flight he was not taking, in violation of security regulations.

The one thing he is taking is stress leave. He won't attend the House. He won't sit in the Conservative caucus. This is a bargain struck with Stephen Harper, to keep Grewal at a distance while keeping his vote, provided he doesn't sell it.

Elsewhere in Wonderland, MP Pat O'Brien, an opponent of same-sex marriage, bolted the Liberal caucus because the government is fast-tracking the same-sex bill to clear the House before summer. It seems O'Brien and 11 other Liberal dissenters had their own tea party in the East Block, and considered ways to bring down their own government.

Meanwhile, over in the Senate, Conservative Senator Anne Cools said she had been hit by other senators. And this just in – Belinda Stronach gave $100,000 to defray the campaign debt of a leadership opponent, Tony Clement, back in her Conservative days. And Bloc leader Gilles Duceppe will run for the leadership of the Parti Québécois, unless he doesn't.

That's quite the party, Alice.

June 2005

∽

HOGWARTS, END OF TERM

It was a scene straight out of Harry Potter – Hogwarts, end of term. Before being called to order, members of rival houses mixed and mingled on the floor of the great vaulted chamber, shaking hands and saying farewell. Before announcing who had the most points for the school cup, the headmaster had a brief announcement.

MPs were invited to a reception, said Speaker Peter Milliken, "to permit members to exchange Christmas greetings." This was met with much laughter, in view of what was to happen next. The speaker then read the motion: "That this House has lost confidence in the government."

A simple declarative statement, without rhetoric or recriminations. A moment of truth. The speaker then called the vote, and the roll call of MPs standing in their places was interrupted by applause for some of them who waved goodbye to their colleagues. For a revered few, including the NDP's Ed Broadbent, there was a standing ovation from all sides of the House.

The clerk read the result: Yeas, 171, Nays, 133. "I declare the motion carried," said the speaker. And with that, the government was defeated, and the 38th Parliament of Canada was over.

Class dismissed. No caps were thrown in the air, and there were no whoops. And no one lingered in the chamber. They all hurried to house meetings down the hall. The Liberals and Conservatives met across the hall from one another. As the doors to both caucus meetings were left open, the cheers and applause from one eerily resonated across the corridor to the other.

In the Liberal caucus, the leader stood alone on stage, with the Canadian flag as his backdrop. The voters, said Paul Martin, "will judge the alliance among the neo-Conservatives, the separatist Bloc and the NDP." It was a message he repeated later at Rideau Hall, after obtaining a writ for the January 23 election. He referred again in both languages, to "the Conservatives and the separatist Bloc, with the NDP." Not the sovereignist Bloc, the separatist Bloc, even in French. On the first day of the campaign, the Liberals were already down to where they were on the last week of the previous campaign: a vote for the Bloc is a vote for separation.

It is a bid to play the unity card in the rest of the country. Get ready for it: The election of the Conservatives without representation from Quebec would create a winning condition in the next referendum. And it is an attempt to polarize the vote between federalists and separatists, by telling potential supporters of the NDP and Conservatives in Quebec that they have no alternative but to vote for the Liberals, the party whose sponsorship scandal has driven support for the Bloc Québécois to historic levels.

There's a logical disconnect to that, but fear is a higher motivator than logic. And fear is the Liberals' ultimate weapon in this campaign. Fear of Stephen Harper eating your children. Fear of a hidden Conservative agenda. And fear of another referendum.

It's interesting, as Harper pointed out at his news conference in front of the Commons, that Martin would rather campaign against Boisclair than work with Jean Charest, "the most federalist Quebec premier in my lifetime."

Fully two years before Charest's Quebec Liberals must face the voters, the federal Liberals have essentially written him off. And it creates an opportunity for Harper to strike his own alliance with Charest, a former federal Conservative leader with whom he has a natural affinity on issues such as the vertical fiscal imbalance between Ottawa and the provinces.

It was also interesting that Harper was changing the conversation. It's no longer enough, he said, "to tell the public just what you're against, we have to offer a positive vision of the country."

While the Liberals promoted the culture of entitlement, Harper said: "We have to turn the page and make a change."

That's a powerful message. Harper has eight weeks to persuade Canadians to overcome their doubts about the messenger.

November 2005

∞

2006—THE WINDS OF CHANGE

There is a place in Oshawa called the Polish Hall, which is an obligatory campaign stop on the political pilgrimage to power. When Stephen Harper went there on the final Friday before the January 23 election, the hall was filled to overflowing with 2,500 people, easily the biggest meeting of his campaign.

This was in Ed Broadbent's Oshawa. More to the point, it was in Buzz Hargrove's Oshawa, home of General Motors and spiritual centre of the Canadian Auto Workers, whose leader had urged his members to vote strategically for the Liberals.

Looking out over the surging crowd from the podium, Harper noticed it didn't consist of Tory blue-rinsers or the party rank and file bussed in from other ridings. It consisted mostly of suburban families, parents who had brought their kids along to see the history of it – the making of a prime minister. People like Harper, dads who drove their sons to hockey practice and their daughters to ballet on Saturday mornings. People who, as he said in a campaign refrain borrowed from Bill Clinton, "work hard, pay their taxes and play by the rules."

"This," Harper thought, as he later told Senator Marjory LeBreton, "is a middle class revolt."

These were the voters who had bought into his promises on daycare, the GST, and the health-care guarantee. On these issues, Harper and the Conservatives successfully aligned themselves with consumers, while the Liberals and the NDP were captives of the service providers.

On daycare, Harper promised parents $100 a month for every child under the age of six. Paul Martin and Jack Layton wanted to create more publicly-funded spaces, more jobs for daycare workers.

On the GST, Harper promised to reduce the consumption tax, from 7 per cent to 6 per cent to 5 per cent over five years. For someone buying a $30,000 car, that would mean a saving of $600. Harper was appealing to consumers doing their Christmas shopping. Martin's appeal was to economists, supporting the GST as an efficient tax.

On health care, Harper was endorsing Liberal Senator Michael Kirby's 2002 proposal for allowing patients to go outside the system, and even the country, for publicly-funded treatment if elective surgeries were not available within acceptable waiting times. Martin initially said he supported the Canada Health Act, and the recommendations of Roy Romanow, whose royal commission wanted to force semi-private and private health-care providers out of business and back into the public sector, a system that is broken, as anyone who has been to an emergency room can attest. One-hundred thousand Canadians are waiting for elective eye surgery.

Harper won all three issues before the holiday break, aligning himself with the middle class voters who turned up in Oshawa. Martin was not only aligned with the service providers, he had no space between himself and Jack Layton, from whom he needed qualitative and quantitative distance in order to close his proposed deal with strategic voters. Layton's positions on daycare and health care at least resonated with his base. Martin lost out on conviction, and was left with an appeal to pragmatism – the Conservative hordes are at the gates, hold your nose and vote Liberal to stop them.

Paul Martin's Liberals, as they styled themselves to the detriment of the renowned Liberal brand, also made several strategic errors at the outset of the campaign. First, they thought they could roll the tape from the 2004 election, when their vicious attack ads on Harper were performance-validated by a series of damaging bimbo and bozo eruptions by Conservative candidates.

Then Martin tried to transform the election in Quebec into a referendum, as a choice between federalists and "separatists," between federalism and "separatism," terms most francophone Quebeccrs haven't used for two decades, preferring instead the softer formulation of "sovereignty" as the choice of "sovereignists." Martin's message track was incoherent from the beginning.

Third, in his famous bear hug with Hargrove, Martin played the strategic voting card at the end of the first week of the campaign, rather than at the end of the last week as he had in 2004. Finally, the Liberals underestimated their opponent, always a fatal miscalculation in politics. The Liberals assumed Harper had learned nothing from his mistakes in 2004. They equally assumed he would fold in the stretch of the unusually long eight-week campaign in 2006. Instead, they were confronted with the re-make of Harper, who had learned the remorseless rules of campaign discipline – stay on message, meet the retail demands of kissing babies, and, above all, as his handlers told him every night as he tucked in – keep smiling.

In the first half of the campaign, Harper and the Conservative high command also discovered a secret weapon – Laureen Teskey Harper, an independent, attractive and articulate woman who narrowed her husband's gender gap, and reminded suburban voters that the Harpers were just like them – parents of young kids.

It wasn't just the turtlenecks, open collar shirts and re-styled hair that invited women to take another look at Harper. It was also the increasing presence of his wife in the news coverage.

By the time the campaign resumed in early January, she was clearly her husband's greatest asset. By the time it ended, she was a central figure in the campaign, as vivacious as he is reserved. If she saw something in him, some women thought, then he must have something going for him.

The daily announcements highlighted the first phase of the Harper campaign before the holidays, a time when it seemed the Conservatives were on the field alone, not scoring touchdowns, but moving the ball downfield. The Liberals, meanwhile, ran nothing but threes and out, punting on every possession of the ball, while the Tories had them back on their heels on defence.

Not only was Harper inoculating himself against the inevitable Liberal attempts to demonize him, he was demonstrating newly developed skills as a field general. With every passing day in the first half of the campaign, he appeared increasingly confident and serene – quiet, calm and measured in his daily sessions with the media. In an important leadership moment, in a scrum just before the holidays, Harper brushed off Martin's aggrieved demand for an apology for suggesting the Liberals preferred the separatists to be in power in Quebec. "I don't go around asking for apologies," Harper said. "I can take a punch." And in his stump speeches, his newfound confidence translated into a politician who had found his voice, and his cadence, in both languages.

At the start of the campaign's second half on January 2, Harper presented a top-five check list for a Conservative government: the Accountability Act, daycare cheques, the GST cut, the health-care guarantee and a crackdown on crime. At this event, he confidently ditched his podium, walking around the stage like Phil Donahue, with a hand-held mike. The same day that Harper was announcing his priorities for government, Martin went to a bagel shop in Ottawa.

The Harper campaign presented a portrait of competence, and of a leader moving his party to the centre, where elections are won and lost in this country. But Harper also caught some major breaks over the holidays, supposedly the period of the Christmas truce. The juvenile and insulting Rob Klanders Web site reinforced the impression of the Liberal "beer and popcorn" campaign, the frat boys. The Boxing Day drive-by shooting in downtown Toronto dramatized the issue of murderous gang warfare in the heart of the country's largest city. Most Canadians didn't see it as sociological issue of communities failing young blacks. They saw it instead as a question of restoring law and order in the peaceable kingdom, which played to Conservative strength.

Then on December 28, the RCMP announced a criminal probe into the income trust leak, and the resulting war-type headlines not only reinforced the impression of Liberal entitlements, they validated a Conservative attack ad in which customers in a coffee shop sat slack-jawed while Paul Martin, on television behind the counter, insisted "the Liberal Party is not corrupt." It was the tipping point. The Liberals, who had been leading by 10 points in the final CPAC tracking poll before Christmas, went into free fall.

On the afternoon of the French debate on January 10, the Liberals delivered a flight of twelve attack ads to television outlets across the country. Within hours, they were forced to pull one, the one about Harper proposing to station "soldiers in the streets of our cities." In the ensuing furor, Martin told both CTV and CBC that he had approved the ads, then said that he hadn't. Liberal candidates across the country angrily distanced themselves from the ad, which insulted veterans and Canadians in uniform.

But the biggest story of the campaign wasn't on television, it was the Conservative momentum surge in Quebec. Barely nudging 10 per cent in the polls there before the holidays, Harper grew to 20 per cent by the January debates, and 25 per cent by election day. On who would be the best prime minister, a leading indicator of voting intention in Quebec, Harper rose to 31 per cent in the final CPAC poll on January 22, while Martin plummeted to 13 per cent, dead last as a sitting prime minister in his own province. Pollsters say there comes a point where the numbers are talking to you, and by the last week of the campaign, Harper's numbers were talking. They were talking because 25 per cent was an efficient number, concentrated in the 418 area in Quebec City and the South Shore. The question was, could the chronically weak Conservative ground game deliver those numbers with help from Jean Charest's Big Red Machine? Or was the Conservative tide rising high enough that it would deliver itself?

There was another question – how real was the Conservative momentum on the ground in Quebec? And the answer, in the final week of the campaign, was very real indeed. No one in his right mind would have suggested, at the beginning of the campaign, or even a week before the end, that Stephen Harper would spend three days in the final week of the campaign barnstorming in Quebec.

But there he was on the morning of January 17, crossing the St. Lawrence by ferry from Quebec City to Lévis. Harper had awakened that morning to the very good news of an endorsement by André Pratte in *La Presse*. In *Le Soleil*, the dominant paper in Quebec City and eastern Quebec, there was a front page story of a CROP poll that indicated Josée Verner in Quebec City and Maxime Bernier in the Beauce were both leading their Bloc opponents by margins of at least 2-1 and heading to certain victory. The long awaited *percée bleu* was at hand, the only question was how many more seats Harper would win. But there was no other way to read those numbers as anything less than 10 seats.

"Then, I'll be dancing," Harper said privately on the Thursday before the vote.

At the Conservative Party convention in Montreal in March 2005, Harper moved the party to the centre when he took hot-button issues like abortion off the table, and killed stupid Reform era ideas like recall referendums for MPs. As Brian Mulroney told him: "It's very simple, Stephen, you just have to figure out how to move your furniture from Stornoway to 24 Sussex."

In the previous four campaigns going back to 1993, the Liberals and the Bloc had been the joint beneficiaries of a polarized vote, in which the Conservatives were marginalized. The truth is the Liberals and Bloc had a symbiotic relationship. They needed each other, and they knew it. That was the implicit bargain between them.

But in 2006, the Liberals were burdened by a legacy of scandal and Quebecers were determined to punish them. As for the Bloc, it turned out to be a two-trick pony, scandal and sovereignty being the only things on offer from Duceppe. In this campaign, the remainder of his platform was exposed as meaningless, since he could never implement it. Harper offered something more, as he put it, "pride and power." It was an extremely resonant message.

Voters who had been held captive by the Liberals and Bloc for more than a decade were told by Harper in December that the election wasn't about a choice of country, but about a choice of policies. And the policies he rolled out before the holidays had strong appeal to Quebecers, especially on daycare and the GST.

But it was Harper's December 19 speech on "open federalism" that caught the interest of frustrated federalists and soft nationalists – the voters of the former Mulroney coalition. In what is destined to become known as the Quebec City speech, Harper acknowledged the existence of the vertical fiscal imbalance between Ottawa and the provinces, under which Ottawa sits on a ton of surplus cash while the provinces are going back into deficits providing federally mandated programs such as health care. He also pledged that Quebec could be represented at international forums such as UNESCO in areas of its constitutional jurisdiction, such as culture and education, according to the Mulroney-Johnson formula, which enabled the creation of la Francophonie in 1985.

Harper also promised to respect the division of powers in the British North America Act, vowing not to invoke the federal spending power in areas of exclusive provincial jurisdiction without the approval of a majority of provinces. This is a classic Conservative constitutional perspective, in a line of Conservative prime ministers from Macdonald to Mulroney. Ottawa does what Ottawa does in section 91 – peace, order and good government. The provinces do what the provinces do in section 92 – health, education and cities. The asymmetrical nature of the federation is apparent in sections 93 and 133, allowing for confessional schools in Quebec at the time of Confederation and the recognition of French and English as languages of the courts and legislature of Quebec. Without the division of powers, without the asymmetric features of the Constitution, Sir John A. Macdonald wouldn't have been the father of our country. While the Liberals are the Charter party, the Conservatives are the BNA party.

Harper also made an important emotional connection with Quebec and Quebec City. Speaking in French, the boy from Toronto who became the man from Calgary, said: "Quebec is the heart of Canada." Just as significant as Harper's speech, as he said privately at the time, was Martin's immediate response, completely repudiating his own support of the identical position articulated in a speech in Laval in May 2004. "Canada speaks with one voice," Martin replied, "not two and not ten." That's the Trudeauesque view of the world, and it has no constituency in Quebec.

Quebecers were immediately onto Martin. He wasn't speaking to them. He was talking over their heads, to Ontario. It was the precise moment Quebecers finally gave up on a prime minister who had once held so much promise for renewing the federation.

The policy rollouts gave Quebec voters something to think about. The Quebec City speech gave them a respectable place to go.

And here was Harper, in the dead of a Canadian winter, forcing a Conservative spring. The ferry crossing provided what would become the photo of the campaign. The Tories didn't have a photo op for the day until an advance man named Jean-Maurice Duplessis thought of the ferry, only the previous day. The forecast was for a cold, clear winter day. They took the 8:30 morning crossing, just as the sun was coming up over the gabled rooftops of the Château Frontenac. The ship's captain agreed to stop the ferry at mid-crossing and steer horizontally to the Quebec City skyline. Harper posed with his area candidates for a thumbs-up shot.

Then, almost as an afterthought, he and Laureen posed against the signature skyline of Quebec City. They looked like any other young couple that goes to Quebec for a romantic weekend at the Château. In *Le Soleil* and *Le Devoir* the next day, the photo played over seven columns across the top of the front page. The headline in *Le Soleil* was about Bloc support bleeding to the Conservatives.

But even as Harper was peaking in Quebec, his momentum was about to be stopped dead in Ontario. In the very last question of a scrum following the morning speech in Lévis, Harper was asked the dreaded question of whether Canadians should be worried about a Conservative majority. No reason to be concerned, he replied. There were the courts and the Senate, as well as the public service, dominated by Liberal appointees, to keep him in check. It was his only serious blunder of the campaign, and with it, any prospect of a majority disappeared.

"Get him out of there," yelled a voice in the Conservative war room, watching the event on the all-news channels. With the characteristic stubbornness of the old Stephen Harper, the new one refused to say he hadn't meant to question the independence of the judiciary. It took him three days to clear up the confusion, and that allowed the Liberals to open the closet and let out all the demons, including abortion.

By the final Thursday night, the Liberals outdid themselves in a new attack ad accusing Harper of refusing to affirm a woman's right to choose. The Conservative numbers, which had been holding steady in Ontario, dropped three points in the closing three days. "Our numbers melted with women between 18 and 44," said Philippe Gervais, the Conservative deputy campaign manager. "We've got to find a better way of closing the deal next time," said campaign manager Doug Finley, as he left the Conservative war room two days after the vote. His final seat projection on the day before the election was in the range of 122 to 152 Conservative members. It was to come in at the lower end of the range.

In Calgary on election night, Harper's team prepared three versions of a victory speech. A slender minority, a comfortable minority and an outright majority. They never prepared a concession speech. They knew they didn't need it. And Stephen Joseph Harper is the 22nd Prime Minister of Canada.

Policy Options, March 2006

2008—A MISSED RENDEZVOUS WITH A MAJORITY

Chatting with a visitor to his Langevin Block office in mid-August 2008, Stephen Harper reflected on the daunting math of a majority, and acknowledged it was an unlikely outcome of an election.

He ran through the scenarios of what he called "four competitive parties in the House," and concluded that a majority probably wasn't in the cards, let alone the numbers.

The math of a majority was simple – 155 seats out of 308 in the House of Commons. Getting there was another matter, as the prime minister explained. First, he said, the Bloc Québécois would normally win 40 to 45 seats out of 75 in Quebec. Then, the NDP would be good for about 30 to

35. Throw in a couple of independents and in no time at all, you're down to 230 competitive seats available to the Conservatives and the Liberals, the two major national parties.

One of them, in order to form a majority government, would have to win 67 per cent, or two-thirds, of all the seats available to the two main parties. An odds-against proposition.

Why then, just three weeks later, did he call an election? Because, in that same moment of summer, he saw an opportunity for a majority in the fall. He saw it in his poll numbers in Ontario and Quebec, as well as British Columbia, the three biggest battlegrounds on the electoral map, with 106, 75 and 36 seats respectively, 217 seats in all.

Over the summer recess, Ontario looked exceptionally promising for the Conservatives, especially in the 905 belt around Toronto and the 519 region of southern Ontario. In Quebec, the Conservatives were running even with the Bloc in the polls, with the prospect of an historic breakthrough in the 50 battleground ridings outside Montreal. And in B.C., Stéphane Dion's Green Shift was political poison from the moment on July 1 that a provincial carbon tax was introduced by the Liberal government of Gordon Campbell.

Even as Harper spoke about the difficult math of a majority, the stars were aligning for him. And even in the worst-case scenario of an early election call, Harper would likely be returned with another minority, probably a more comfortable one than that of the government he had been leading for the previous two and a half years.

After thirty months in office, the Harper minority had equaled the two Pearson governments' tenures in office, from 1963 to 1965 and from 1965 to 1968, as the longest-serving minority governments in modern times. And the House, the PM concluded, was becoming a dysfunctional place, especially in its committees which had become, in his words, "a kangaroo court."

In a highly partisan speech to a packed party rally in St. Agapit, during the Conservatives' national summer caucus in Quebec at the end of July, Harper had already taunted Dion, telling him it was time to "fish or cut bait" on defeating the government. And Dion, not having a political bone in his body, rather than saying he would decide when to defeat the government, said he hadn't made up his mind. Rather than cutting bait, he went for it.

And then in Cupids, Newfoundland, on August 14, Harper lit the election fuse in response to a reporter's question. "Quite frankly," he said, "at some point I'm going to have to make a judgment in the next little while as to whether this Parliament can function effectively."

Oh, really? And what about Bill C-16, the fixed election law, which established October 19, 2009, as the date of the next election? Was Harper about to break his own law, one of his pet projects, to force an unnecessary $300-million election on the country?

Not on a careful reading of it. Months earlier, Marjory LeBreton, the Government Leader in the Senate and a member of the inner cabinet Priorities and Planning Committee, had handed a visitor to her office a copy of Bill C-16, with one paragraph highlighted in yellow: "Nothing in this section affects the powers of the Governor-General, including the power to dissolve Parliament at the Governor-General's discretion." Quote, unquote.

In other words, Harper had an escape clause written into his own fixed election law. Anytime he thought it was a nice day for an election, all he had to do was cross the street from 24 Sussex to Rideau Hall for coffee or tea with Her Excellency.

As the month of August came to a close, the Conservatives put up a flight of TV ads featuring Harper in a blue sweater, talking about family, veterans and the splendour of Canada's North, with a tagline wrapped in the Canadian flag. The thirty-second spots were very reminiscent of the famous "Morning in America" theme of Ronald Reagan in 1984. In the pre-writ period, the cash-rich Conservatives were the only party on the air, especially in Ontario, and the ads drove their numbers near majority territory before the election call.

In Quebec, the Conservatives also ran a series of effective spots shot by their francophone ad guru, Robert Beaudoin. In one, Harper was sitting around a table at Harrington Lake with his Quebec cabinet colleagues, talking about how they had delivered the goods for Quebec. In another, several Quebecers struck a similar theme, politely pointing out that in Ottawa one party adopted the Québécois nation resolution, resolved the fiscal imbalance and increased family allowances for child care, and that *"ce n'est pas le Bloc."* And these messages also moved the numbers in Quebec.

From the morning the election writ dropped on September 7, Harper proposed a ballot question on the economy, what he called proven leadership for uncertain times. He had no idea that by mid-campaign his preferred ballot question would be redrafted as "Who do trust with your money?" Or what's left of it.

For in the second week of the campaign, the stock market crashed in New York in the fallout from the subprime mortgage disaster, and a liquidity crisis swept over the investment banks, brokerages and even the insurance companies of Wall Street. In the space of a few days, the venerable investment banking firm Lehman Brothers went belly up. Merrill Lynch, famously bullish on America, sold itself to Bank of America in the middle of the night. Goldman Sachs and Morgan Stanley, the last two investment banking giants standing on Wall Street, announced they were reorganizing as retail bank holding companies, to receive better protection from the federal government and the Federal Reserve. The U.S. government threw Freddie Mac and Fannie Mae – which together hold $6 trillion in mortgages, half of all the mortgages in America – into trusteeship. Washington bought an $85-billion interest in AIG, the giant insurer, and announced a $700-billion bailout for the failing financial services sector, even as Washington Mutual and Wachovia cratered. In the space of two weeks, in the middle of the American presidential and Canadian elections, Washington nationalized Wall Street. And for every day the Dow lost $1 trillion of market capitalization, the TSX usually lost $100 billion. Canadian voters dared not open their monthly investment, mutual fund and retirement statements for September. But that was the good news. The bad news was that the October statements would be even worse. And all this turmoil in global markets happened because, as it turned out, there was no such thing as a free house.

Stephen Harper wanted an election on the economy. Well, he got one, as well as a reminder of the ancient proverb: beware of what you wish for.

As it turned out, the inherent Conservative advantage on the economy had already been priced into Harper's stock. But when uncertainty turned to fear, and then fear into panic, Harper's stock was discounted, and the advantage of incumbency became a posture of doing nothing when the sky was falling. The fundamentals of the Canadian economy were strong, Harper insisted, sounding for all the world like John McCain after the stock market crashed in New York. Harper was right as far as that went – Canada's fundamentals were much stronger than those of the U.S. Our banking system has a stronger regulatory framework; down payments must be made on mortgages, which are guaranteed by the government; and the Canadian fiscal framework is a paradigm of sound management compared to that of the U.S.

But it was Harper and the Conservatives who asked for additional time on the global financial crisis in the leaders' debates on October 1 and 2, and it was Harper who failed to show up with a plan to deal with it. Stéphane Dion had a five-point plan to have a plan, to have meetings about having meetings within thirty days of forming a government. While it was obviously written by his advisers on the back of an envelope, at least Dion showed up with something to say. And relative to expectations, he also won just by turning up for the debates. It was Harper who took the hit in the French debate where he was cool to the point of being disengaged, the iceman; and in the English debate when he said Canadians weren't in danger of losing their homes. Once again, his empathy deficit was showing.

Even worse, he was a man without a plan. He finally showed up with one, the morning after the election at his news conference in Calgary, where he outlined a clear, crisp six-point plan to deal with the global financial crisis, including an early recall of Parliament with a fiscal update, calling for a First Ministers' Meeting on the economy, putting the crisis on the agenda of a pending Canada-European summit and "taking whatever appropriate steps are necessary to ensure that Canada's financial system is not put at a competitive disadvantage."

In other words, to the question of what he would do to protect Canada's economy in these extraordinary circumstances, Harper's answer on the morrow of the election was, "Whatever it takes." If he had shown up at the debates with that plan, and proposed it forcefully in front of opponents who had nothing sensible to say, he might still have gained a majority. Instead, he sat unresponsively through Jack Layton's taunt asking him where his plan was, "under your sweater?" Ouch.

And then Harper made matters worse for himself four days later in Toronto, when he committed a potentially fatal unforced error at a news conference following a major economic address and platform release that were to have been the highlights of the Conservatives' closing push in the final week of the campaign. Quite inexplicably, Harper stepped on his own message when he said the unprecedented turmoil in markets represented "a buying opportunity." And then, in a television interview with CBC anchor Peter Mansbridge, quite unprompted, he said it again. It was an astonishing lapse of judgment by Harper. A prime minister never comments on the stock market any more than on currency exchange rates. And here was Harper, a sitting prime minister, effectively urging people to go into the stock market before it had made a bottom after a crash that obliterated the portfolios of countless Canadians. For Harper and the Conservatives, with exactly a week to the election, this was the low moment of the campaign, a campaign that had been taking incremental hits in English Canada for two weeks and big hits on values and identity that were to crush Harper's hopes for a breakthrough in Quebec, for which he had no one to blame but himself.

The Conservative campaign peaked in Quebec on September 19, a glorious late-summer day that saw Harper appearing at a campaign rally for Michael Fortier in Fortier's chosen riding of Vaudreuil-Soulanges, off the western tip of the island of Montreal.

In order for Fortier to win this seat, a Conservative tide would have to rise in area 450, the suburban ring around Montreal.

And that day, it was rising. A Leger Marketing poll for the Quebecor newspapers and the TVA network showed the Conservatives moving into a 34-32 province-wide lead over the Bloc, with the Liberals trailing at 20 per cent and the NDP at only 9 per cent. Pollster Jean-Marc Léger told TVA's Jean Lapierre privately that those numbers broke out to between 25 and 30 seats in Quebec for the Conservatives, who had become the competitive federalist alternative to the Bloc everywhere but on the island of Montreal, and even there, Léger reported, the Conservatives were growing.

But at the very moment the Conservatives were flying high in Quebec, a series of incredibly stupid mistakes were about to bring them crashing back to earth.

On the Sunday morning, two days after the Leger poll appeared, the Conservatives unveiled a mobile billboard asserting that Quebecers had wasted $350 million voting for Bloc candidates since 1990. In an arrogant, in-their-face gesture, the Conservatives staged the event in front of Bloc headquarters in Duceppe's own riding in east end Montreal. And the messenger for this lesson in democracy was none other than Michael Fortier – from the unelected Senate. The blowback, from the print media to talk shows, was immediate and furious. Not only was the messenger wrong, the message was badly distorted. Rather than suggesting the Bloc *"a eu son temps,"* had had its day in Ottawa, the Conservatives were saying that the Bloc was "useless" and that voting for it had been a waste of money.

The next day, September 22, Harper released his proposed revisions to the Young Offenders Act, which would see repeat offenders for the worst crimes, such as murder and rape, locked up with adults from as young as the age of 14, and 16 in Quebec (the provinces are in charge of the administration of justice). It was evident from the questions at Harper's daily news conference that the youth crime story was going to play out very differently in Quebec than in the rest of Canada. English-language media asked easy questions about urban crime that played into voters' fears in the suburbs of English-speaking Canada. But the French-language media went immediately to the advisability of locking up young teenagers with adults. Duceppe pounced, accusing Harper of feeding "fresh meat" to pedophiles in what he called "universities of crime."

The following day, Harper suffered a major self-inflicted wound when, in response to a question about the Conservative cuts to cultural programs, which had been denounced from the stage of Radio-Canada's television awards show *Les Jumeaux*, he replied that average Canadians had different concerns from those attending "rich galas" subsidized by the very government being denounced. Noted for his message discipline, Harper went way off message, and he clearly knew it the moment the words left his lips, since he declined to repeat them in French. It didn't matter – within an hour, his comments led all the French-language newscasts anyway, with the added insinuation that he had insulted Quebecers by not having the courtesy to repeat them in French – and this about a leader from Calgary who had made it a policy of always reading his prepared statements in French first, even at the White House.

Thus, a perfect storm for Harper, and an incredible gift for Duceppe. This was a ballot question that Duceppe could not lose, and that Harper had no hope of winning, in spite of all that he had delivered for Quebec. As a weary member of the Conservative war room put it when the campaign was over: "How did you like our brilliant plan to put 14-year-old artists in prison?" Quebec's share of the reprofiled arts funding was a measly $15 million, which in terms of what the cuts cost Harper in Quebec alone worked out to $1 million a seat. There went Harper's rendezvous with a majority.

And Quebec, which was supposed to be the road to a Conservative majority, instead became the roadblock to one.

It all could have been avoided, if only Harper had had better advice, and better friends, in Quebec. If only, as Lysiane Gagnon of *La Presse* noted, he hadn't severed his contacts with Mulroney over the Schreiber affair, then he wouldn't have cut himself off from his single best source of advice on Quebec. Moreover, as the campaign wore on, Jean Charest increasingly became a thorn in Harper's side, one day denouncing the cultural cuts and the next showing up with a thirteen-point shopping list of things Quebec wanted from Ottawa. Looking ahead to his own election, Charest was buttressing his position as the principal defender of Quebec's interests. But where he had virtually endorsed Harper after the Prime Minister's "open federalism" speech of the previous campaign, Charest's silence in 2008 was deafening.

"The special relationship between them is over," a close associate of Charest acknowledged before the campaign, and all efforts to recreate it were doomed to failure by the obstinacy of the two principals – Harper in his lingering anger over Charest allocating all $700 million of Ottawa's fiscal imbalance money to a tax cut in the dying days of the 2007 election, and Charest over Harper attending an event with Mario Dumont in late 2007 while the premier was in the midst of turning around public opinion in Quebec. In the summer and even the fall of 2007, Dumont might have been seen by the Conservatives as the coming man in Quebec, but by the autumn of 2008, he was running a bad third everywhere in Quebec, even in his own stronghold of the Quebec City region.

Yet the Conservatives, inexplicably, brought in ADQ organizers to run their Quebec campaign. It was the ADQ staff in the Conservative war room, hard right-wingers, who signed off on the Conservative youth offenders plan. And in Harper's own close circle, his press secretary and Quebec adviser, Dimitri Soudas, had close ties to the ADQ, which made him anathema to Charest. As a consequence of all this, the Quebec Liberal Party, the famed Big Red Machine, sat out the campaign except in the 418-area ridings around Quebec City, where it helped the Conservatives as the only federalist alternative to the Bloc.

As a result of this campaign fiasco, the Conservatives dropped 10 points in as many days – the final Leger Marketing poll on October 11 put the Bloc at 37 per cent, the Liberals at 24 per cent and the Conservatives at 23 per cent in Quebec. It was no mystery: the Bloc was up 5 points from the September 19 poll, the Conservatives down 11 and the Liberals had grown 4 points, once again becoming the block-the-Bloc party in the Montreal region as the Conservative vote collapsed.

In the end, the Conservatives won only 13 per cent of the vote in the Montreal region, but managed to hold on to 32 per cent in the rest of the province and retain 10 seats, the same score as in 2006. As before, all but two of them were in the 418 area around Quebec City. So swift and complete had the Conservative collapse been that only five days before the election they were projected to hold on to, at most, only half a dozen seats in Quebec.

But in the final weekend of the campaign, the real Stephen Harper finally showed up to knock down Duceppe's vitriolic accusations that he was "a liar," "a cheater," "arrogant," "retrograde" and, of course, a clone of George W. Bush. From Longueuil on the South Shore of Montreal to St. Tite, the country-and western capital of Quebec north of Shawinigan, and on to Quebec City, Harper barnstormed courageously across Quebec in the closing days of the campaign. He had two message tracks: the economy, where Duceppe had no resonance, and, once again, delivering the goods for Quebec. Harper was finally getting both messages out, without noise from Duceppe, friendly fire from Charest or unforced errors from his own camp.

In those dying days of the campaign, there was a sense that Harper was growing again, perhaps by enough to take out any projected losses, though clearly not enough to regain the lost breakthrough. Encountered in Quebec City after Harper's bus left his last event there on the Sunday before the vote, Maxime Bernier agreed the Conservatives had run a bad campaign in Quebec, but added, "I think we're going to be okay, we're going to win 10 seats."

At that point, two days before the election, the Conservatives would take that as more, much more, than simply saving the furniture; they would read it as having re-gained their beachhead in Quebec.

And by then, just as fortune had turned on Harper after smiling on him early on, it smiled on him in the closing days after turning on him in Quebec in the last days of September and all across Canada after the debates in the first days of October.

In the early hours of the business day in Europe on Thursday, October 9, the middle of the night in eastern Canada, the prestigious World Economic Forum issued a report on financial services that ranked Canada's banking system as the best in the world. Switzerland's was ranked 14th. The U.S. system was ranked 41st. This was not only an important third-party endorsement, it gave Canadians bragging rights in banking and financial services at a moment when Canadian self-esteem could use the boost. By daylight in Canada, this had become one of Harper's aggressive bullet talking points.

The next day, Friday, October 10, Statistics Canada issued its monthly report on the Canadian labour market, and Harper caught a huge break with the news that the Canadian economy had created a record 106,000 new jobs in September, the strongest month on record; and this was in the middle of a global hurricane, validating his message that while Canada was not an island, it was a shelter from the storm. From that moment on, and for the remaining four days of the campaign, Harper pounded the twin bullets of a sound Canadian banking system and strong Canadian job creation.

And then Harper got lucky again. On Thanksgiving Day, with markets closed in Canada, the Dow rallied 936 points in New York. The next day, election day in Canada, the TSX opened up an amazing 1,600 points before settling in at a 900-point gain for the day, just as voters were streaming home to the polls.

Finally, going into Thanksgiving weekend, the Liberals' brief winning streak was broken by their leader's unfortunate interview with CTV's Atlantic affiliate and the network's decision to air the restarts of Dion's apparent misunderstanding of anchor Steve Murphy's question of what he would have done differently from Harper if he had been running the country. It may not have been fair, but it was fair game, at least to the Conservatives, who held their plane on the ground at Winnipeg so reporters could file on Harper's comments on Dion's apparent inability to articulate why he should be prime minister. Dion had been doing very well in the closing week, as long as he remained off television and the Liberals made it about Harper. But then, going into the final weekend, Dion reappeared to remind voters why they didn't want him as prime minister.

At the end of the day, the numbers talked. The Conservatives, with 38 per cent of the vote, won the election by nearly 12 points over the Liberals, and that could well have left them in majority territory, not 12 seats short at 143 MPs. Quebec should have told them why they weren't there. The Liberals, at 26 per cent, recorded their lowest score in history under Dion, down from their previous low of 28 per cent under John Turner in the Mulroney landslide of 1984, though their count of 77 MPs was a better score than the worst-case scenarios discussed during the campaign. The NDP, at 18 per cent and 37 seats, came up short of the 20 per cent and 43 seats standard of Ed Broadbent in 1988. And while the Bloc won 49 seats in Quebec, its 38 per cent share of the vote was down from 42 per cent, and this only after the Conservatives and Harper had blown a golden opportunity for an historic breakthrough.

Harper and the Conservatives will never again face such a weak opponent as Dion, a leader without a constituency in his home province. In this campaign, the Liberals had a message, the Green Shift, that couldn't be sold, and a leader, Dion, who couldn't sell it. In this sense, the election Harper and the Conservatives called was not only a missed opportunity, but one they blew, with only themselves to blame.

Even so, Stephen Joseph Harper is still prime minister of Canada.

Policy Options, November 2008

5

AMERICA—FROM BILL CLINTON TO BARACK OBAMA

THE IMPEACHMENT OF BILL CLINTON

It is not a stain on a cocktail dress that imperils Bill Clinton's presidency and his place in history.

Rather it is a soundbite he gave as a hostage to fortune, when he said: "I did not have sexual relations with that woman, Ms. Lewinsky."

Maybe she didn't inhale.

"That woman," on whom Clinton pinned a scarlet letter, finally talked in front of Ken Starr's grand jury. She evidently has a different take on what constitutes "sexual relations." And she has the dress to prove it. Or rather, the FBI now has it.

The dress in question, which has been tested for DNA, is under closer security than the Shroud of Turin.

But the "sex dress" as the tabloids delight in calling it, is merely a prop in this high drama, which will move from the court house to the White House for Clinton's testimony.

It is the first time in the history of the American republic that a sitting president will appear in a grand-jury investigation of which he is himself the target. Even Richard Nixon, the "unindicted co-conspirator" of Watergate, never appeared before the grand jury, a star-chamber in which witnesses give secret testimony without the presence of their lawyers in front of twenty-four anonymous panelists.

The grand jury subverts the very presumptions of innocence and due process, and it is independent counsel

Starr's biggest weapon as he closes in on Clinton. There is nothing like the grand jury or the special prosecutor in the Canadian legal or political system. If Starr had been investigating the Somalia scandal and cover-up in the Canadian military, the government could never have closed it down.

Clinton's predicament isn't about sex. It's about lies and videotape. Whether, in the political sense, he lied to the American people. Whether, in the legal sense, he encouraged Lewinsky and others, including his private secretary, to lie about it. That would be suborning of witnesses and obstruction of justice, offences that can be written up in the House of Representatives as articles of impeachment.

The fact that these matters arose out of depositions in the Paula Jones case, which was subsequently thrown out by an Arkansas judge, is immaterial. The fact that none of this would have happened had Clinton settled the Jones case, with costs and an apology for apparently hitting on her in a hotel room seven years ago, is equally immaterial.

Clinton was in denial then, and appears to be in denial still. But then, that's the rule of the League of Guys: deny, deny, deny. It's like stopping and asking for directions: men just can't admit they're lost.

The American people and the news media made a deal with Clinton when he ran for president in 1992 – they cut him some slack, as his wife had, and assumed it would end there. But when he got to the White House, he continued to operate under Arkansas Rules, and that's where his troubles began.

Clinton arrived in Washington as the candidate of the people "who play by the rules," but he developed a different set of rules for himself. He had situational ethics, and he kept moving the goalposts.

The campaign-fundraising scandals were a good example. There was nothing illegal about charging contributors $1 million for a sleepover in the Lincoln Bedroom. But it was pretty cheesy.

Money poured into Clinton's 1996 campaign coffers from places such as the Chinese government, a clear case of illegal meddling by a foreign power in a matter of the utmost sovereignty – the election of a president. Imagine the indignation in Canada if a CIA front had made a donation to Jean Chrétien's re-election, and you have a sense of Clinton's problem on campaign finance.

But, finally, it is Clinton's propensity for bimbos, and his perpetual prevarication about them, that threatens to bring him down. If he, in any way, coached Lewinsky on her previous testimony in the Jones suit, that's witness-tampering. Testifying under blanket immunity for herself and her mother, Lewinsky has no motivation to be anything but truthful.

Clinton's recklessness has already left his presidency irreparably weakened, and has weakened the institution of the presidency itself.

All of Clinton's achievements – balancing the federal budget, enacting the North American Free Trade Agreement, his role in the Mideast, Bosnian and Irish peace processes – have demonstrated his considerable skills as a brokerage politician. And the booming American economy – the Dow Jones industrial average has tripled on his watch – has given him a Teflon coating against scandal.

But the Dow was off 300 points the other day, partly on concerns Clinton is too consumed with his legal problems to focus on the restructuring of the Asian economy. The conduct of U.S. foreign policy has come to a virtual standstill, as has Clinton's legislative program in Congress. The American presidency, the single most powerful office in the modern world, has been caught up in Clinton's zipper problem.

Future presidents have been stripped of the confidential relationship with their Secret Service protectors, and the claim of attorney-client privilege with White House lawyers, as both bodyguards and legal counsel have been compelled to testify in the grand jury.

Lewinsky's involvement with Clinton was obviously consensual, and she clearly went after a presidential trophy. But it is inappropriate in the workplace for a supervisor to encourage the advances of a smitten 21-year-old intern. The CEO of a major corporation would be fired by his board, stripped of his golden parachute and escorted off the premises by security for Clinton's kind of behaviour with Lewinsky.

In this whole tawdry affair, there is still no appetite for impeaching Clinton. And there is an emerging "confession consensus," that Clinton should tell all in the grand jury and then go on television and offer a credible explanation to the American people.

Perhaps he can blame it on the culture of the '90s, in which everyone is a victim, beginning with the president of the United States.

July 1998

A PRESIDENT ON TRIAL

In a system predicated upon the separation of powers, the legislative, executive and judicial branches of American government are all tied up in the trial of the president of the United States.

Such an event is not within the memory of anyone alive, not even Strom Thurmond, the 96-year-old president pro tempore of the Senate. The last president to face trial and removal was Andrew Johnson in 1868. And he was accused of fooling around with the cabinet, not fooling around with the help.

Impeached by the House of Representatives for wrongly firing a cabinet secretary, Abraham Lincoln's successor escaped conviction in the Senate by a single vote. No one thinks it will come to that for William Jefferson Clinton, accused of perjury and obstruction of justice in the Monica Lewinsky matter.

Yet it is still breathtaking to behold the chief justice of the United States presiding over a trial of a president, prosecuted by "managers" from the House of Representatives, before a "jury" of 100 senators. The jury isn't supposed to talk, but it isn't sequestered, and so they talk on *Larry King Live*.

You're not going to see William Rehnquist on *Larry King Live* any time soon, but the chief justice is an unpretentious and endearing figure, the sort who takes his law clerks out to lunch. He once wore Hush Puppies to a dinner at the Canadian embassy in honour of photographer Yousef Karsh. On another occasion, when George Bush hosted Brian Mulroney at Camp David, Rehnquist was seen in the souvenir shop of the presidential retreat, lined up with other guests to buy a memento of the visit.

The mementos of the Clinton trial are the tickets printed for the press and public galleries of the Senate, galleries that are usually empty. On the floor of the Senate, where normally there is barely a quorum, every member's desk is occupied.

The accused, Bill Clinton, tries to maintain the appearance of business as usual in the White House at the other end of Pennsylvania Avenue. Among the things he is preparing is the annual State of the Union Address, normally delivered in the House of Representatives, before what is now his audience of accusers and jurors.

All of which is to say that nothing quite like this has ever happened before – the trial of a president, over lying about sex. It's not clear that Clinton merits removal from office. It is clear that he has demeaned it.

Yet at the moment of his historic peril, Clinton is the most popular president since public opinion began to be measured in the era of Franklin Roosevelt. After his impeachment in the House last month, Clinton's approval rating went up four points overnight to an incredible 72 per cent.

This is partly attributable to the American economy being on a seven-year roll. It took the Dow Jones industrial average nearly a century to reach 3,000. In Clinton's six years in office, it has tripled, and is now closing in on 10,000.

But the American people are also making a distinction between private behaviour and public conduct, and sending a message to Washington that they want this matter settled short of removal. So while Clinton's trial will begin, it will probably end short of the two-thirds vote necessary to convict, with a fine and a bill of censure that Clinton himself will have to sign.

But begin it will, because the Senate is now seized of constitutional obligations. At the heart of the American system is the notion that no person is above the law, least of all the president, who is the chief law-enforcement officer of the United States.

He also happens to be commander-in-chief of the armed forces, where officers are now routinely court-martialed for sexual misconduct with subordinates.

Finally, the Lewinsky affair was sex at the office, for which the head of any organization would be fired before sundown. Whatever transpired between Clinton and Lewinsky, it was clearly inappropriate behaviour by the boss with an intern.

However inappropriate, Clinton wouldn't be in this mess if he hadn't lied about it. And unfortunately for him, the constitution makes no distinction as between lying under oath about sex and lying about bombing Baghdad. Richard Nixon, who knew about these things, once said the problem wasn't the event, "it's when you cover up that hurts."

Still, the public's common-sense conclusion to all this is that if Hillary Clinton can live with a philandering husband, they can live with it in their president. Since he first ran for president in 1992, Americans have known that Clinton is, as the saying goes in his native South, a hard dog to keep on the front porch.

Preparing him for a television debate amid the Gennifer Flowers bimbo eruption back then, Hillary Clinton asked a resonating question.

"You've got to be ready for the Question," she said, as reported by *Newsweek* in its remarkable book, *Quest for the Presidency*. "If you can't keep your promise to your wife, how can we trust you to keep your promises to us?"

January 1999

HANGING BY A CHAD

As Pierre Trudeau might have put it, the universe is unravelling as it should.

Canadians can well imagine a situation like the one in the United States, where one candidate for president apparently won the popular vote, but might well lose the election in the electoral college.

It's a fairly common outcome in this country, with our first past the post parliamentary system. It actually happened to Trudeau in 1979, when he won the popular vote by 40 to 36 per cent, but lost the election in the House of Commons to Joe Clark's Tories, who won 136 seats to 114 for the Liberals.

It happened again in the Quebec election of 1998, when Liberal leader Jean Charest won the popular vote 43 to 42 per cent, but decisively lost the National Assembly, 75 seats to 49.

The U.S. system is somewhat equivalent to ours – the candidate with 270 electoral votes wins the presidency. But not since 1888 has one candidate won the popular vote and lost the presidency.

Until this week. Maybe. Depending on the outcome of a recount, and perhaps the absentee ballot, not to mention the possibility of court challenges in the state of Florida, where George W. Bush won by less than 3/1,000ths of one per cent, out of 6 million votes cast, while apparently losing the national popular vote by one-10th of one per cent out of 100 million votes nationwide.

There's something we can lend Americans – a decimal point to report their results. Make that two decimal points, as in 50.56 to 49.44 per cent, the outcome of the 1995 Quebec referendum.

The American networks, which prefer rounding off their decimals, and had been putting Gore ahead 49-48 in the popular vote, would in Canadian terms be reporting it as 48.70 for Al Gore, and 48.60 for Bush.

But they need no decimals for the electoral college, a constitutional assembly with 538 members, one for each of the 435 seats in the House of Representatives, 100 for the Senate, and three for the District of Columbia, the U.S. capital, which is not represented in the Congress that sits in its own city. Except for two states, Maine and Nebraska, the electoral college is first past the post, winner take all in each state.

The first one to get 270 votes wins the White House. As of yesterday, in the stalemated election and stalled count, Gore had 260 votes, and Bush had 246. Florida has 25 votes. This is not rocket science.

To put it in its most personal terms, if Florida Governor Jeb Bush can deliver his state, his brother wins the electoral college by one vote.

To put it in its most poignant terms, if Gore had won his home state of Tennessee, with its 11 electoral votes, that would have put him over the top.

The uncertainty is by no means confined to Florida. If Bush were to win Oregon with its eight votes, and re-counts in Wisconsin (11 votes), and either Iowa (7 votes) or New Mexico (5 votes), he would still win even if Florida went the other way.

It just doesn't get any closer. And if you pitched a movie with this story line, complete with incorrect network predictions, and retracted concession statements, nobody would buy it.

The U.S. networks managed to get it spectacularly wrong twice, first awarding Florida to Gore, based on exit polls when Bush was well ahead in the hard count, then calling the state and the election when the Texas governor's margin was melting away in the middle of the night.

The networks all subscribe to a vote-gathering service called Voters News Service (VNS), and all went with those forecasts without having an override on their election desks. Thus, garbage in, garbage out. Could it happen here? Not likely, since our networks never make calls when computer projections don't match up with historical data.

One thing that certainly couldn't happen here is the kind of mix-up with voting machines in Florida's Palm Beach county, where thousands of people may have voted inadvertently for third-party candidate Pat Buchanan, and thousands more tried to vote twice, with their votes being disallowed.

In Canada and Quebec, we have paper ballots, counted by hand. It's old-fashioned, but technically fool-proof.

Did someone say every vote counts?

November 2000

∞

KERRY AND THE BIG MO

There is a saying in American presidential campaigns only three tickets get punched out of the Iowa caucuses. John Kerry and John Edwards got tickets. Howard Dean got punched.

Dean represented Democratic voters who were angry at George W. Bush, angry at the war in Iraq, angry at Washington. But when Democrats began thinking about who could beat Bush, change American foreign policy, and run Washington, they turned, in Iowa at least, to Kerry, the presidential-looking senator from Massachusetts.

And now it's on to the New Hampshire primary, suddenly a must-win for both Dean and Kerry. Running twenty points ahead there only a few weeks ago, Dean is now locked in a death struggle with Kerry and Edwards, as well as retired general Wesley Clark and Connecticut Senator Joe Lieberman, who both sat out Iowa.

If Dean can't win in the state next door next week, he has no hope of winning in South Carolina the week after. He needs a firewall in New Hampshire, and he needs all those kids in orange toques to build it for him.

His insurgent candidacy has often been compared to George McGovern's in 1972, particularly with a disastrous November outcome in mind. It's actually much more similar to Eugene McCarthy's anti-war candidacy in 1968 – more a movement than a campaign. Just as McCarthy had his children's crusade, Dean has his true believers who have not only canvassed for him, but also built a virtual candidacy on the Internet, where he has raised tens of millions of dollars in individual donations.

After being the un-candidate for all of 2003, Dean suddenly sounded like a conventional candidate after his first reversal of fortune in 2004. He had the money, the organization and the national campaign, he insisted, to stay in the race until the end. Rolling up his trademark shirtsleeves, he tried to rally the troops with riff that was far too hot for television, concluding with a cackle eerily reminiscent of Dr. Strangelove.

This bizarre sound bite played again and again on cable, undoubtedly leaving some New Hampshire voters to wonder if they wanted this guy's finger on the nuclear trigger.

Deemed to be in a tight race with the fast-closing Kerry in Iowa, Dean actually lost by a margin of more than 2 to 1 – 38 per cent to 18 per cent, while Edwards ran a strong second at 32 per cent. This was too close to call?

Dean's numbers have been drifting south ever since he picked up the endorsement of Al Gore and later, Bill Bradley, the two leading Democratic candidates in 2000. If Dean wanted to continue his insurgent campaign, this was the last thing he needed. There was something counter-intuitive about the anti-establishment candidate being endorsed by the establishment.

Dean even took a half-day off from Iowa to attend church with Jimmy Carter down in Georgia. At some level, it seemed Dean wasn't seeking his party's leadership so much as its approval.

Dean also missed a moment last month when, in a major foreign-policy address, he said Americans didn't feel any safer for the capture of Saddam Hussein. In the intellectual sense, he was quite right. But in the emotional sense, Dean had it wrong. It wasn't that Americans felt safer, but that they felt better.

And then he fell victim to a classic case of gotcha journalism. Just 10 days before Iowa, NBC obtained the Dean tapes, a trail that led back to the richly paneled Mount Stephen Club in Montreal, where he had participated during his years as Vermont governor in dozens of tapings of *The Editors*, a bunch of talking heads seen on PBS.

Let's go to the videotape. Back in 2000, thinking out loud about the caucuses, Dean said "they are all dominated by special interests" and that "he can't stand to listen to everyone's opinion for eight hours about how to save the world."

Naturally, his opponents were shocked and appalled at his contempt for the voters of Iowa, indeed, his contempt for democracy itself. By then, the constant pounding of Dean by his opponents, and the relentless scrutiny by the media, created doubts his suitability for the White House.

Those votes had to go somewhere and many of them went to Kerry, who had recently sharpened his message and campaigned on his record as a hero in the Vietnam War. Last weekend, Kerry's campaign reunited him with a retired Los Angeles sheriff whose life he had saved on a naval patrol thirty-five years ago in Vietnam. In Iowa, that story would play as well as *Field of Dreams*.

Like Dean, Kerry also needs a win in New Hampshire, also partly for the reason he comes from a next-door state – southern New Hampshire is really part of the Boston television market.

But unlike Dean, Kerry's got what the first George Bush once claimed coming out of Iowa, before losing to Ronald Reagan in New Hampshire – the Big Mo.

January 2004

NOBODY WAVED HELLO

How much trouble is George W. Bush in? Well, when the president of the United States flew over Ogunquit Beach in Maine the other day, no one waved.

Bush was on his way from a military base near Portsmouth, New Hampshire, to his father's place at Kennebunkport, for the long July 4 weekend.

Hundreds of people looked up at the passing flight of five military helicopters, four of them in protective formation around the fifth, Marine One. The presidential seal was clearly visible, but there wasn't a friendly wave in sight.

The next morning, when he went fishing off Walker's Point with the first president Bush, CNN duly recorded the video, but also reported Dubya's latest job approval numbers, which were somewhere in the high 20s.

In modern times, only Harry Truman, Lyndon Johnson and Richard Nixon have carried comparable disapproval scores into the late stages of their presidencies. All three were hobbled by foreign wars or domestic scandals. The second George Bush is burdened by both.

Bush's problems began when he shifted the focus of the war on terror from the hunt for Osama bin Laden in Afghanistan to his quest to unseat Saddam Hussein in Iraq. The buildup in 2002 and the invasion in 2003 proved to be the easy part.

There were no terrorists in Iraq then, but there are now in the murderous insurgency that has claimed six times as many U.S. lives as were lost in the invasion, to say nothing of tens of thousands of civilian Iraqi casualties.

Quite apart from the trumped-up rationale for the invasion – weapons of mass destruction that proved to be non-existent – the Americans evidently didn't understand the neighbourhood and the inherent tensions between the Kurds in the north, the Sunnis in the middle and the Shiites in the south. Someone should have left a copy of *Paris 1919* on Bush's bedside table. Anyone who has read it has been struck by Margaret MacMillan's account of how Iraq was cobbled together at the Versailles conference, which determined the geopolitical map after the First World War.

Four years after Bush's invasion, the latest and last best hope for achieving security in Iraq is the American troop surge under the ablest U.S. commander, General David Petraeus, who previously enjoyed significant success in winning hearts and minds.

And then there was the Katrina effect in 2005, the surge of summer storms that lashed the Gulf Coast of the U.S., leaving New Orleans in near ruins. The relief and rebuilding effort has been marked by staggering government inefficiency and shocking incompetence by the Bush administration.

Bush might have hoped that a weekend of summit diplomacy at Poppy's place would have provided some respite. The Man from Vlad, President Putin of Russia, flew in for a couple of days of lobster dinners and bass fishing, but the two leaders remained far apart over U.S. plans to deploy a missile defence system in eastern European countries of the former Evil Empire.

And then there's the blowback over Bush's treatment of Lewis (Scooter) Libby, Vice-President Dick Cheney's former chief of staff. Bush commuted the jail sentence Libby got for perjuring himself during an investigation into who blew the cover of CIA analyst Valerie Plame, whose husband had criticized the Iraq war.

While Bush is within his constitutional prerogatives, his commutation of Libby's jail term raises questions of the rule of law. Gerald Ford's pardon of Nixon in 1974 might have been the right thing to do in terms of turning the page on Watergate, but it probably cost him the election in 1976.

It might already be too late for the Republicans in 2008. Fundraising for presidential campaigns is a leading indicator of a party's prospects, and the *New York Times* reports that the Republicans' fundraising was off sharply in the second quarter.

The top Republican fundraiser, former Massachusetts governor Mitt Romney, raised $14 million in the period, down from $20 million in the first quarter. By contrast, Democratic hopeful Barack Obama raised $31 million, $4 million more than Hillary Clinton.

So, Democrats are raising twice as much money as Republicans. That's one sign of trouble. Another is that the president flew over a Maine beach and nobody waved.

July 2007

ALL ROADS LEAD TO NEW HAMPSHIRE

The American morning begins in Maine, but presidential destinies in the United States begin next door in New Hampshire, home of the first-in-the-nation presidential primary.

It's the law. A 1977 state law requires that New Hampshire hold its primary at least a week before any other state runs "a similar" presidential contest.

But Iowa is always a week before, isn't it? That's different. Those are caucuses, counting heads in a room, not to be confused with a primary.

That's their story in New Hampshire, and they're sticking to it. And they're pretty sticky about it. Any number of states have tried to jump ahead of them, and each time New Hampshire moves up its primary. It was in March in 1968, February in 1992, January in 2004. If need be, they will move it right out of election year, into this year.

It's not just politics. It's a booming cottage industry. All roads lead to New Hampshire, for candidates, their media buys and unhappy reporters. And for many would-be presidents, those roads lead to New Hampshire, even before he (or she) forms an exploratory committee.

The other day, big Fred Thompson was in Bedford, for an invitation-only cocktail with Republicans. He wasn't there to promote the new season of *Law and Order*, in which he stars as the district attorney. So, he's an actor. But so was Ronald Reagan, in a role the Republicans have been trying to recreate since he left the presidential stage in 1989.

Besides, long before he was an actor, Thompson was a Washington hand. As minority counsel to the Watergate committee in 1973, he discovered the Nixon tapes in a deposition of White House administrator Alexander Butterfield. Thompson was Howard Baker's man from Tennessee, and it doesn't come more inside-the-Beltway than that. He also served a term in the Senate in the 1990s, campaigning in Tennessee in a pickup truck.

Thompson could be a serious contender because Republicans don't like the look of all the other white guys – and they are all white guys – in the race.

John McCain? The man who humbled Dubya with his straight talk candidacy in New Hampshire in 2000, now looks too old, and too tied to the discredited Iraq adventure of the Bush White House.

Mitt Romney? Too boring. He has a story line, as a successful Republican governor of Massachusetts, the most liberal state in the union, and previously as the CEO who engineered a turnaround of the organizing committee for the Winter Olympic Games of Salt Lake City. The *Boston Globe* recently ran a massive seven-part series on his life. I read the whole thing, and at the end of it still couldn't think of a single reason to vote for him.

Rudy Giuliani? He had two successful terms as mayor of New York, and was the man of the hour on 9/11. But he's on his third wife, and his own kids are barely on speaking terms with him.

These four are the first tier of candidates on the Republican side. The others are simply taking up space and time in TV debates.

Similarly, the Democrats have a crowded field, but a first tier of only three – Barack Obama, Hillary Clinton and John Edwards.

It gave everyone pause when Obama raised $31 million in the second quarter, more than Clinton and Edwards combined, and more than twice as much as Romney and Giuliani, the leading Republican fundraisers.

While Clinton has name recognition, and a guy named Bill going for her, she also has name recognition, and a guy named Bill, going against her. She is simply all too familiar, and remains a polarizing presence.

Obama is an electrifying figure, and while his resumé might still be thin, his story is a compelling one. The first time he went to New Hampshire, where crowds are measured in the dozens, he drew several thousand people. He's new, he's different, and even while many worry for his safety, he represents hope in a time for change.

July 2007

∞

OBAMA—IN A LEAGUE OF HIS OWN

In the front-end-loaded U.S. presidential race, there are only four days between the Iowa caucuses and the New Hampshire primary.

That's very little time for Hillary Clinton to erect a flood wall against the surging Barack Obama, who beat her by nine points in Iowa, where she actually finished third behind John Edwards.

From the beginning, her candidacy has been built on name recognition and inevitability, as well as money and her standing as the candidate of the Democrat establishment.

But there are two kinds of name recognition, the all too familiar personified by Clinton, and the new and different embodied by Obama.

And after Iowa, she isn't inevitable anymore.

Clinton desperately needs to stem the rising Obama tide in New Hampshire. Already, the field has been winnowed down to three viable candidates, and it isn't clear how competitive Edwards will be in New Hampshire, a state with a very strong record of picking the eventual winner of the nomination. It's really just Clinton and Obama.

The strength of Clinton's candidacy is a fully financed national campaign that is supposed to peak on Super Tuesday, when more than twenty states, including New York and California, will vote in primaries. Her problem is getting there in one piece.

Her real problem is that she is trying to sell herself as the candidate of experience, in a season of change.

Iowa and New Hampshire are two of the most unrepresentative states in America – both are 95 per cent white, and predominantly rural and small town. Obama is the first major African American candidate for president. Jesse Jackson was a candidate of grievance. Obama is a messenger of hope.

He has a compelling story line, draws big crowds, and he has the oratorical skills to bring them to their feet.

Voters in New Hampshire, and across the United States, looking in on Obama's triumph in Iowa, saw one of the most eloquent victory speeches ever delivered, one that left even the most hardened television commentators quite breathless. The voice and cadence were uniquely Obama's own, but there were echoes of both Martin Luther King and Jack Kennedy.

There is no doubt that Obama's showing, and his speech, in Iowa will have given him a momentum surge going into New Hampshire on the weekend.

This was in remarkable contrast to Clinton's remarks, a few minutes earlier, as she awkwardly tried to move forward to New Hampshire as the candidate of both experience and change.

She can't win the change argument, she's already lost it.

And even on experience, she comes with a ton of baggage – her husband's as well as her own.

On Iraq, she voted in favour of the war, which Obama has opposed from the beginning. On health care, Americans remember she was in charge of the file, and botched it completely, under her husband's administration. Free trade? She would reopen the NAFTA, one of the principal legacies and bold vision statements of Bill Clinton's presidency. Obama says globalization is here to stay and quotes Bill Clinton in telling U.S. voters they must "have the courage to change."

Change and hope are the two most powerful forces in any election. When the agent of change and the messenger of hope is an articulate and attractive leader like Obama, he enjoys a huge comparative advantage over all his opponents.

Obama is like Tiger Woods. He takes the game to a new level, his own.

January 2008

MOVING THE GOALPOSTS

In the last week, the Clintons have reminded Americans of two of their important character traits as a couple. First, that they will say and do anything to win, and second that the rules of the game apply to other people, but not to them.

First, it was Bill Clinton playing the race card in South Carolina, with reckless disregard for the consequences. Then, it was Hillary's turn, going into Florida in the last two days of a primary that all candidates had agreed not to contest at the request of the Democratic Party. But rules are for other people. The Clintons make their own.

In South Carolina, Bill Clinton said Hillary didn't stand a chance in the primary because Barack Obama had the black vote sewn up. Then the former president tore into reporters for torquing up his comments. Which is also typical of the Clintons – they never take responsibility for anything.

But this time Bill Clinton got caught, not just by the pundits and outraged Democratic officials, but by the voters of South Carolina, who responded to his intemperate and polarizing comments by delivering an unexpected 2-1 landslide to Obama.

Among those who were appalled by Clinton's comments was John Kerry, the party's 2004 nominee, who accused Clinton of abusing the truth and debasing his statesman's currency as a former president. Clinton's playing of the race card was also a tipping point in Ted Kennedy's decision to endorse Obama.

The backlash against the Clintons was evident in the outcome in South Carolina, where Obama's victory far outpaced even his best showing in the polls.

But Bill Clinton still didn't get it. For the second time, he compared the Obama campaign to Jesse Jackson's failed presidential campaigns of the 1980s, which were never about winning the nomination so much as winning seats in the inner councils of the Democratic Party. Jackson's campaigns were entirely based on his black base. Obama's campaign transcends race.

And then in Florida, where all candidates had agreed not to campaign, Hillary Clinton turned up for a fund-raiser, and was in the state again on voting day, where she addressed a campaign rally after the polls closed, thanking Floridians for their support and promising she would do everything in her power to get their delegates seated at the convention.

But that was the entire point of the party asking the candidates not to campaign there – it was punishing the state party for moving up its primary out of the Super Tuesday lineup so the spotlight could be entirely on Florida.

Asked about this on a Sunday morning television appearance, Obama said he would respect his commitment, play by the rules, and stay out of Florida.

Someone should have told him he wasn't in Kansas anymore, though on Tuesday he was, while Clinton was in Florida. And there she was at her Florida campaign rally, claiming a completely empty victory in a beauty contest over Obama, which she won easily by 18 points.

The Clinton campaign was clearly attempting to generate its own momentum forward to Super Tuesday, in the hope of countering Obama's surge out of South Carolina, and the powerful endorsement of Obama by Caroline Kennedy and her uncle Ted.

There are party rules. And then there are Clinton rules. They make them up as they go along, moving the goal posts with them.

February 2008

∞

HILLARY'S DEAD BUT SHE WON'T LIE DOWN

There's an old Newfoundland saying that applies to Hillary Clinton's presidential campaign – she's dead but she won't lie down.

She has an opportunity to make a graceful exit following her blowout win in the West Virginia primary. More likely, she might well soldier on until the primary season comes to an end in early June.

It doesn't matter. It's over. Barack Obama is going to be the Democratic nominee for president of the United States.

Obama now has an insurmountable lead in pledged delegates, popular vote and number of states won. In the last week, he has also overtaken her lead among super delegates, who were her last hope to achieve an unlikely victory on the floor of the Democratic convention.

It takes 2,025 delegates to win the nomination. After last night's votes were counted and delegates distributed on a proportional basis, Obama was within 140 votes of victory, and she was still about 165 votes behind him.

If the Democrats had the Republicans' winner-take-all rules, Clinton pointed out the other day, "I'd already be the nominee."

Yes, and if pigs had wings, then they could fly.

The Clintons are very good at moving the goalposts, and bending logic to suit their case.

And of course, if you counted the null-and-void primaries in Florida and Michigan, where Obama wasn't even on the ballot, then she would actually be ahead in the popular vote.

Furthermore, Clinton argued, the magic number isn't really 2,025, but 2,212, if the Florida and Michigan delegates were seated. But even if that happened, and it won't, her path to the nomination would be incredibly difficult. Neither candidate campaigned in Florida, where she got 50 per cent of the vote to his 33 per cent. Even under that distribution, Obama would receive a third of Florida's 210 disallowed delegates. As for Michigan, there would have to be another vote or a caucus to achieve any fair allocation of its 156 delegates. And in any vote with his name on the ballot,

Obama would sweep Detroit, with its important black population, and the big university towns of Lansing and Ann Arbor, home of Michigan State and Michigan universities.

Even if the goalposts were moved, as Clinton has suggested, the only result would be to push Obama across the goal line.

And then there's the money. There's always the money. The Clinton campaign is worse than broke. It is $25 million in debt. The Clintons themselves have loaned the campaign $11 million, with the remainder owed to consultants and suppliers. At some point, you can't put a Boeing 757 charter in the air unless the airline gets paid. Obama, on the other hand, has $50 million cash on hand, and no debt.

One of the reasons for her to stay in is to raise enough money to pay down her debt. But staying in costs a lot of money every day. At some point, as in any business, the question becomes when do you stop throwing good money after bad?

Then why doesn't she see it? Why doesn't Bill Clinton see it? Well, they are not quitters. Indeed, she has struck a populist note as the tribune of women and blue-collar, white voters. Economists and pundits universally panned her proposal of a federal gas-tax holiday as a dumb idea. But she said she knew truck drivers would appreciate it.

And while her campaign has been fatally flawed, the candidate has proven she is tournament tough, with no quit in her. Furthermore, no one can tell a leadership candidate when to get out of a race. She has to come through all the stages of grief. But at some point she has to recognize that for the good of the Clinton brand, her husband's as well as her own, this needs to be over. Then there's the well-being of the party, in addition to her own.

There's a point where doomed campaigns start quoting Yogi Berra, that "it ain't over 'til it's over." That's usually when it's over.

May 2008

∞

THE WEST WING, LIVE IN REAL TIME

The U.S. presidential campaign has been compared to the final season of *The West Wing*, with Barack Obama cast in the Jimmy Smits role as the charismatic Democrat, and John McCain standing in for Alan Alda as the good and decent Republican.

But Obama's acceptance speech at Mile High Stadium in Denver was rather more like the climactic scene from *The American President*, an earlier film drama from the same creator, Aaron Sorkin.

"If John McCain wants to have a debate about who has the temperament, and judgment, to serve as the next commander-in-chief, that's a debate I'm ready to have," Obama declared to the crowd of 84,000, and millions more watching on television.

And then: "It's not because John McCain doesn't care. It's because John McCain doesn't get it."

In the 1995 film that preceded the celebrated television series, Michael Douglas as President Andrew Shepherd holds an impromptu White House news conference where he takes down his right wing opponent, Senator Bob Rumson, played by Richard Dreyfuss.

"Bob's problem isn't that he doesn't get it," Douglas says. "It's that he can't sell it."

And then, challenging his Republican opponent, he concludes: "If you want to talk about character and American values, fine. Tell me where and when and I'll show up."

That wasn't the only echo of Hollywood in the evening's production. The set, complete with Romanesque pillars, was meant to invoke the monuments of the Mall in Washington, specifically the Lincoln Memorial, where Martin Luther King delivered his famous "I have a dream" speech, forty-five years to the day before Obama's acceptance address. Actually, it looked more like the set of the chariot race in *Ben-Hur*.

And Obama came both to praise McCain and to bury him. To praise him for his service to America, and to bury him for being the heir of George W. Bush.

Obama started out as the candidate of hope and change. In his acceptance speech he sounded more like a street-smart pol from the south side of Chicago.

He served notice that the Republicans had better not try any of their swift boating tactics on him. No one is going to accuse him of being soft on Osama and the gang.

"John McCain likes to say that he would follow bin Laden to the gates of hell," Obama intoned, "but he won't even go to the cave where he lives."

And where would that be? In the hills of Pakistan. So Obama, having denounced Bush's invasion of Iraq, and decried the unilateral Bush Doctrine in foreign affairs, would presumably invade an unstable nuclear power to get Osama. The rhetoric might be compelling, but the logic is deeply flawed.

It wasn't a great speech, and by Obama's elevated standards of rhetoric, it wasn't even a very good one. You can't take the high road, and travel the low one at the same time. And every time Obama aimed for the high road, he drove into a ditch.

Other than an allusion to the anniversary of King's speech, Obama made no reference to the remarkable fact that he is the first black nominee of a major party for president. Nor did he refer to the challenges that still lie before him in that regard. He might propose a post-racial presidency, but he will have to face down the race issue to get there. It is the elephant in the room.

For the rest, to turn around John F. Kennedy's celebrated New Frontier speech, Obama proposed not a set of challenges but a set of promises, not what he intends to ask of the American people, but what he intends to offer them. A drearily familiar Democratic litany of promises, on everything from health care, to trade unionism, to funding for university tuition.

Instead of a clarion call, Obama offered a shopping list, or what is known in the speechwriting trade as a Christmas tree, weighed down with ornaments.

Perhaps it was a smart speech, as many television commentators observed, in that Obama filled in the blanks on what he meant by change, and served notice that he could play a hard court game of basketball. In those terms, Obama did what he had to do, and it might have been quite effective. But there was nothing new or different about it.

If necessity if the mother of invention, then perhaps politics is the mother of necessity. And that's a great pity.

August 2008

ALL ABOUT THE NARRATIVE

Never mind style over substance, the U.S. presidential campaign has become a matter of story over style. It's not even a question of personality trumping policy. It's all about the candidates' personal narratives, their stories.

Thus, when John McCain named Alaska Governor Sarah Palin as his running mate on the Republican ticket, Democratic candidate Barack Obama framed his response in terms of her story.

"She seems like a compelling person," Obama said, "obviously a terrific story, a personal story."

No doubt about it. In this version of *Northern Exposure*, the former beauty queen and journalism graduate marries her high-school sweetheart, has five kids, and as a self-described hockey mom becomes mayor of a small town, takes down the sitting governor from her own party in a primary, and sweeps the state in a general election.

There's more. The oldest of her five children is about to deploy to Iraq on the anniversary of 9/11, and the youngest, a babe in arms, has Down syndrome, which Palin learned when she was four months pregnant, but decided to have the child anyway. Furthermore, her teenage daughter is five months pregnant and has also decided to keep her baby. The right-to-life movement, a core Republican constituency, is cheering on both counts.

The governor is pro-life, pro-gun, and has taken on her own party on corruption and waste, having killed the $200-million "Bridge to Nowhere," that McCain often cites as the worst example of political pork in Washington (Alaska got the infrastructure money anyway, but that's another story, and a much less compelling one).

McCain's stunning choice signals a return to his own narrative as a maverick, and her right wing credentials have clearly mobilized a Republican base suspicious of McCain as too moderate. Nor should a mother of five, who runs a state as her other full time job, be dismissed as a lightweight. Politicians do very well by being underestimated.

Does she know anything about foreign policy? Is she ready for questions about where is Georgia, and who is president of Iran? She'd better be. Is there something else about her that didn't turn up in the vetting, before her one face-to-face meeting with McCain?

But she wasn't picked for her foreign-policy resumé, she was chosen for her narrative, for her story. And her story, as Obama said, is obviously terrific.

It takes one to know one. Obama's narrative, from the time he first appeared as a keynote speaker at the 2004 Democratic convention, has been the most compelling aspect of his public persona.

McCain has a story, too, being widely repeated this week, the story of the downed naval aviator who survived more than five years as a prisoner of war, and went on to devote a lifetime of service to his country, always marching to his own beat rather than the party drum.

Sometimes the story doesn't have to be a personal narrative, it can be about an event, as in Hurricane Gustav blowing into New Orleans on the third anniversary of Hurricane Katrina.

There were obvious comparisons to a defining moment in the Bush presidency, its tipping point. On the core government attribute of competence, the Bush administration failed miserably. The government of the United

States failed to look after its own people, most of whom happened to be black.

This was not going to happen twice on the Republicans' watch, certainly not in the middle of their nominating convention. George W. Bush and Dick Cheney had been scheduled to deliver farewell speeches to the convention, which were cancelled, ostensibly so that the president could personally take charge of the relief effort, which he failed to do during Katrina.

The cancellation was not only appropriate, it was undoubtedly to the immense relief of McCain, who really doesn't need any more reminders that he's seeking the third term of George W. Bush. This was not exactly a "win one for the Gipper" moment, as Ronald Reagan asked the first George Bush to do for him in an emotional farewell address twenty years ago.

But not content to see the back of Bush, McCain also flew into Mississippi on the weekend, as if that would stop the hurricane, and said it was time to put on hats as Americans, not Republicans, in keeping with his convention theme of "country first."

This is the first time in history that a weather event has run a national political convention. But it's about the story, all about the story.

September 2008

∞

A LOCK FOR OBAMA

This was always going to be a change election in the United States.

Whichever candidate for the presidency captured, articulated and personified the mood for change would certainly enjoy a huge comparative advantage over party rivals in the primaries and his opponent in the general election.

And in that sense, as the candidate of hope and change, this has always been Barack Obama's election to lose, and there is no way for him to lose it. And Hillary Clinton, despite the historic nature of her own candidacy, was always the candidate of continuity in the Democratic primaries. In the general election, John McCain's only hope of capturing change was to play his maverick credentials successfully, running against the Washington establishment of his own party, as well as renouncing the legacy of George W. Bush.

As well, in a general election, there is an important test of competence in that a candidate seeking rather than holding such an office can be measured only by the competence of the campaign.

In September and October, Obama passed that test with flying colours, while McCain failed it abysmally. His choice of Sarah Palin as his vice-presidential running mate proved to be a reflection on his own judgment as much as on her qualifications. Whatever lift his campaign got from her selection disappeared in a series of devastating Tina Fey impersonations on *Saturday Night Live*. "I can see Russia from my house." Ouch.

But McCain really lost the election in mid-September when he suspended his campaign because of the meltdown in the stock market and the near collapse of the U.S. financial system. It was the second time in three weeks he pulled that stunt. First, he delayed the opening of the Republican convention because of a hurricane blowing into New Orleans on the third anniversary of the Katrina disaster, a timely reminder of Republican incompetence.

Delaying a convention is one thing, suspending an entire election campaign because of a crisis in financial and equity markets is quite another, and hardly a solution to the problem.

McCain's response to the financial crisis was one of panicking in the face of it, rather than managing through it. He squandered his inherent advantage as the scarred war hero, ready to be commander-in-chief.

Meanwhile, Obama was cerebral and cool, supporting Washington's bailout package, but offering constructive proposals to improve it. And the competence of his campaign is obvious – just as he had a plan for winning the 2,025 delegates he needed for the nomination in the spring, so he has a plan for winning 270 votes in the Electoral College needed to win the White House in the fall. And not just in Democratic blue states, but in battleground states, and swing states, even Republican states such as Virginia, enough to give him a comfortable cushion in the College as well as the popular vote. And, as no one has before him, he has brought campaigning into the Internet era, and created a standing army of five million volunteers.

And then there's the money. In all, his campaign has raised an unprecedented $700 million, more than $150 million in September alone, most of it in small donations online. Last week's $3-million prime time infomercial on three networks hardly put a dent in his finances, and might have helped him close the deal.

But on the fundamentals, the deal has always been there to be closed. A *New York Times* poll had this key finding on the mood of America in the days before Tuesday's election: "Eighty-nine per cent of people view of the economy negatively and 85 per cent think the country is moving in the wrong direction."

Those are more than change numbers. Those are throw-the-bums-out numbers. To the question of whether America is ready for a black president, the answer might be hidden until Tuesday. But to the question of whether Obama is ready to be president, the answer is yes. He has passed every test, and proven he can take a punch, while setting standards for inspirational rhetoric not heard since John F. Kennedy.

In the *Times* poll, Obama leads by ten points, while other polls have the election as close as three points. But Obama is ahead in every nationwide poll, and well ahead in the state polls he needs to cross the 270 finish line.

U.S. presidential races generally tighten up in the closing days, as voters go home to their normal party preference. But sometimes elections break open, in a decisive moment of change, as was the case with Ronald Reagan over Jimmy Carter in 1980.

Whether Obama wins by a narrow margin or a sweep, he is going to win, because in a year of change, he is the candidate of change.

November 2008

ECHOES OF JFK AND FDR

Barack Obama was born in 1961, the year John F. Kennedy delivered the last great inaugural address by a president of the United States. Justly celebrated for its inspirational eloquence, JFK's "Ask Not" inaugural made no mention, however, of the plight of black Americans.

Millions of African Americans could not even vote, but on Tuesday after his swearing-in, a black American son of a Kenyan student will speak to America and the world as the 44th president of the United States. Later that day, with his daughters and wife Michelle, who is herself descended from slaves, Obama will move into the White House, which was largely built by slaves more than two centuries ago.

Such is the trajectory of Obama's narrative, and of his country, which as he has said, "while not perfect, is perfectible."

Other than JFK's glaring omission on civil rights – his epiphany only came later in 1963, the remainder of his inaugural stands the test of time. As author Thurston Clarke concludes in *Ask Not*, his wonderful book on Kennedy's inaugural address: "Many will read these sentences and mourn a time when a speech could move a nation, and launch an era of idealism, optimism and joy."

Kennedy and his chief speechwriter, Ted Sorensen, set a standard of excellence that is unlikely to be surpassed. It was precisely Kennedy's power as a rhetorical leader that enabled him to become a transformational president. As Obama himself has said: "Sorensen and Kennedy together did an extraordinary job."

Admirable as it is, JFK's "Ask Not" speech may not be the right frame of reference. Obama should also be reading up on Franklin Roosevelt's "Fear Itself". FDR's famous first inaugural was delivered at the height of the Great Depression. Jonathan Alter, in his superb book, *The Defining Moment*, captures the sense of the economic emergency, bordering on panic and desperation, that Roosevelt inherited from Herbert Hoover.

Looking ahead to his inaugural, Obama told George Stephanopolous: "I want to try to capture, as best I can, the moment we are in now … here is the moment we are in, here is the crossroads we are at."

Well, the moment we are isn't at all like 1961, and a lot more like 1933.

Then, as now, the issues were liquidity in the economy and solvency in financial institutions. But the overriding issue was confidence, and FDR radiated confidence. "First of all," he began, "let me assert my firm belief that the only thing we have to fear is fear itself." He went on: "This nation is asking for action, and action now." This was a man who pulled himself out of a wheelchair, and gripped the podium to stay on his feet.

There's another standard of excellence, to which Obama has himself referred, that of Abraham Lincoln's second inaugural, "Malice Towards None."

The moment was March 1865, and the U.S. Civil War was coming to its momentous conclusion. And Lincoln himself was looking past it, though he would not live to see it. "With malice towards none, with charity for all, with firmness in the right as God gives us to see the right, let us strive on to finish the work we are in, to bind up the nation's wounds, to care for him who shall have borne the battle and for his widow and orphan, to do all which may achieve and cherish a just and lasting peace among ourselves and with all nations."

Those Illinois lawyers, they sure have a way with words. Lincoln had a way with brevity. His second inaugural comes in around 700 words, four long paragraphs, one single subject. Eloquence is a benchmark of excellence, but economy is equally to be prized.

But it isn't just the words that define a great public occasion, it's also the context. Lincoln was speaking at the culmination of a great domestic conflict that would redefine his nation, ultimately allowing another legislator from Springfield to succeed him nearly a century and a half later.

Roosevelt was speaking at the height of the greatest economic emergency in American history, from which it would emerge only with the Second World War.

Kennedy was speaking at a great turning point of the 20th century, at the height of the Cold War between the NATO alliance and the Soviet Union, in which the only thing more frightening than "fear itself" was the fear of nuclear war.

Obama will be speaking at what may prove to be a defining moment of the 21st century, a moment when the state of the American economy has eclipsed all other issues, including the state of American power in the world.

But there is, among the famous lines of Kennedy's inaugural, a concluding paragraph that isn't often quoted, but equally commends itself to the new president: "Let us go forth to lead the land we love, asking His blessing and His help, but knowing that here on earth, God's work must truly be our own."

January 2009

A DANGEROUS WORLD

Barack Obama can be forgiven for wondering if the world is a more dangerous place than he bargained for when he ran for president of the United States.

A very strong case can be made that at no time since John F. Kennedy became president in 1961, the year of Obama's birth, have the U.S. and its NATO allies, including Canada, faced such daunting challenges to global security and stability.

NATO and Soviet forces, armed with thousands of nuclear weapons, faced each other in a permanent standoff, across Europe and across the seas, where the only deterrent to global annihilation was the doctrine of mutual assured destruction, aptly named MAD.

But at least the Soviets were a known adversary, and a predictable one. And after both sides went to the brink in the Cuban Missile Crisis of 1962, Kennedy negotiated the ban on atmospheric nuclear testing in 1963, the signal achievement of his presidency, unmatched until the Reagan-Gorbachev arms reduction accords of the late 1980s.

The fall of the Berlin Wall in 1989 and the end of the Cold War signalled what the first George Bush called "the new world order." It could also be called the *Pax Americana*, with a lone dominant superpower, and it lasted only a decade, from the fall of the Soviet Union in 1991 to the fall of the Twin Towers in 2001.

This is the situation Obama inherited from the second George Bush, a world where conventional military forces are tormented by terrorists, insurgents and even pirates.

Obama's morning briefing isn't about the challenge posed by a known state actor, the Soviets, but failed states and rogue states, a highly combustible and unpredictable mix.

The failed states include Somalia, home to the pirates terrorizing maritime commerce along the east coast of Africa; Afghanistan, where the U.S., Canada and NATO are bedeviled by an intensifying Taliban insurgency; and in our own hemisphere, Haiti, a tragically broken nation in which Canada has interests as obvious as the concerns of our governor-general for the fate of her mother country.

The rogue states include North Korea, which tested a missile two weeks ago on the very day Obama made a speech in Prague on arms control; and Iran, which has the scientific and financial wherewithal to build nuclear weapons and deliver them as far away as Israel, which already has nuclear weapons.

And then there's Pakistan, a country of 150 million people, wracked by poverty, seething with secular tensions, and a safe haven for the Taliban and Al-Qaeda, using the wild western region of the country as a staging ground for their insurgency across an unpatrollable border into Afghanistan. Pakistan already has nuclear weapons, dozens of them. It might be the most unstable and dangerous country in the world.

How's the briefing so far today, Mr. President?

Obama is probably getting an idea of what Joe Biden, his vice-president, meant during the campaign when he surmised that Obama would be tested in unforeseen ways in the first months of his presidency. Biden was criticized then for shooting from the lip, but his comments have proven prescient.

We've had some idea of Obama's management style in the way the U.S. faced down Somali pirates last weekend, and we are getting an idea of the choices he is making in Afghanistan, both of which could prove to be defining moments of his presidency.

For the Somali pirates, it is all about the money, and the commercial shipping companies have been paying kings' ransoms to liberate their ships, cargo and crew. This is not something out of Robert Louis Stevenson, it's not Peter Pan against Captain Hook, but a reminder that piracy has been going on for as long as ships have been sailing the seven seas.

Rather than arming their crews with weapons, shipping firms have tried to find safety in numbers, travelling in convoys off the horn of Africa, an area so vast that not even the U.S. Navy can patrol it effectively against brigands travelling in speedboats, and armed with AK-47s.

But when pirates took the U.S. captain of the *Maersk Alabama* hostage, they were surrounded off the Somali coast and taken down by U.S. Navy Seal sharpshooters, in an operation quietly authorized by Obama.

This might prove to be a Reaganesque moment. In 1981, Ronald Reagan fired striking U.S. air traffic controllers, and the Soviets later said this was the moment they learned he meant business.

Similarly, the pirates might learn that Obama, without bluster or threats, means to enforce the law of the high seas. The stability and prosperity of the world, very much including Canada, depends on the safety of maritime commerce. Eighty per cent of global trade moves by ship through shipping lanes like the Horn of Africa and Suez, to ports such as Halifax, Vancouver and Montreal, and from there by rail and intermodal transport to North American and other world markets.

Obama has put the pirates on notice: Don't mess with him. He's from the South Side of Chicago.

April 2009

6

ISSUES AND ATTITUDES

LANGUAGE IN WONDERLAND

Let's see if we've got this right. A lower court judge, appointed by the Parti Québécois, rules that there's no evidence the French language is in danger, and therefore no cause for invoking the Supreme Court's ruling for predominance of French on signs, throws out a case against a couple who had a sign with equal-size French and English lettering.

The PQ, which appointed her, says she's not competent to re-interpret the meaning of the 1988 high court ruling. The secessionist government stands behind the Supreme Court.

Failing appeals which could take years, the separatists could always invoke the notwithstanding clause of the Constitution whose legitimacy they do not recognize, ironically a gift of their great adversary, Pierre Trudeau.

The premier, in California, the home state of his American wife, solemnly declares that French will always be in danger. Lucien Bouchard then goes off to visit a Quebec software icon, SoftImage, which operates in Hollywood in English.

The deputy premier, a noted hard-liner on sovereignty, declares for his part that "independence, as we once dreamed of it ... is a concept that is retrograde per se, and the Parti Québécois knows it." Quote, unquote, Bernard Landry.

Meanwhile, a CROP poll reveals that, after thirty years of debate, 30 per cent of respondents believe a sovereign Quebec would still remain a Canadian province. Another 10 per cent don't know. Clearly, the numbers have been distorted by anglophones voting for dual citizenship.

At this point, then, there are as many Quebecers who don't know what sovereignty means as there are people prepared to vote for it.

Well, no wonder we need Jean Chrétien to clear up the confusion by spelling out the rules of the next referendum. Why, it's right around the corner. The polls show support for the 1995 sovereignty-partnership questions as low as 38 per cent, obviously fulfilling Bouchard's most important winning condition – winnability.

Given this clear and present danger to the federation, it's time for federal legislation on a clear question and a clear majority. What's a clear question and a clear majority? That's for the politicians to argue, said the Supreme Court last year, allowing that Quebec couldn't just declare sovereignty, but that Ottawa would have to negotiate with it.

How does one jurisdiction legislate clarity in another, on a question that hasn't been determined or even discussed?

In the real world, a clear question will be whatever the National Assembly says it is. But for the sake of argument and appearances, let's assume that Bouchard would give Chrétien sign off on a question.

Try this: "Do you give the government of Quebec a mandate to declare sovereignty and negotiate an economic partnership with Canada?" That's clear. Soft, but clear.

Now, as to what constitutes a clear majority, there's where the real argument comes in. The Péquistes have always said that 50 per cent plus one is the basic rule of democracy, and in 1995 Preston Manning agreed with them.

Chrétien replies that you don't break up the best country in the world on a 50 plus one. After all, Quebec is not in colonial status. What, then? Two-thirds plus one, the usual threshold for constitutional change.

Of course, by raising the threshold of secession, the feds would be making it easier for strategic voters to vote Yes, since they wouldn't be part of a 50-plus-one scenario.

Is anybody thinking of that in the PM's office, or over at Stéphane Dion's shop?

These are the same people that brought you the very successful Forum of the Federations at Mont Tremblant, where $3.3 million of taxpayers money went to fund a four-day international symposium on comparative government.

It turned out that they hired a hall, and filled it, for the separatists whom they invited to spoil their party. Ottawa's mistake wasn't in inviting the Péquistes, but in assuming they had some class.

Only the appearance of Bill Clinton at the end, saying this here federalism stuff is a great idea, saved the day for Ottawa. Ever since, the president of the Société St. Jean Baptiste has been dashing off letters to English papers, the only ones paying any attention to him. Guy Bouthillier is deeply concerned for Canadian sovereignty, and scandalized that the American president might hold an IOU on our prime minister.

Meanwhile, back in court, it turns out that the name on the offending bilingual sign is the Wallrus. Right out of Alice in Wonderland.

November 1999

TRUDEAU'S AIRPORT

If an airport is to be re-named for Pierre Trudeau, let it be Mirabel, the white elephant he built in the 1970s, rather than Dorval, which he nearly destroyed in the process.

Mirabel was designed as the airport of the supersonic transport, but it became redundant years before it opened in October 1975, when U.S. president Richard Nixon formally cancelled the SST project in 1971, a year after Congress stopped funding it. The only supersonic ever built, the Anglo-French Concorde, was purchased only by British Airways and Air France and never flew to Montreal on a commercial basis.

But the Trudeau government went ahead with Mirabel anyway, pouring billions into building a completely unnecessary airport. Farmers were thrown off their lands in a massive expropriation meant to absorb sonic booms that were never heard. Airlines, in spite of their protests, had to relocate international flights from Dorval to Mirabel.

Many international carriers responded by simply flying right over Montreal and landing in Toronto instead. And Dorval, once Canada's busiest airport, was relegated to domestic and U.S.–gateway status. Connecting passengers had to endure a 50-kilometre bus ride between the two terminals. Like the airlines, many of them preferred to connect through Toronto.

The Quebec government never finished Autoroute 13, the main highway linking the two airports. And a proposed high-speed rail link was never built. Mirabel, the world's largest airport in terms of land assembly, never received more than a few million passengers per year. But Dorval, hobbled by the loss of international traffic, was allowed to decline for decades.

It was only in the late 1990s that Aéroports de Montréal acknowledged the Mirabel fiasco by returning international flights to Dorval. The upgrades of Dorval's infrastructure, decades overdue, are being financed by a $15 departure tax known by the lovely euphemism, airport-improvement fee.

And now, irony of ironies, Dorval, or more properly Montreal International Airport at Dorval, is being re-named for Trudeau, whose government nearly ruined it. Does this mean no more YUL as we know it, and the beginning of PET on luggage tags?

Many things could, and should, be named for Trudeau. Dorval airport isn't one of them. Quite apart from the Mirabel mess, the Trudeau government and then Transport Minister Jean Marchand thoroughly bungled transportation policy in the 1970s.

Trudeau's legacies are in other areas of public policy, notably the constitution and minority language rights. It would be much more appropriate to name a law library or a human-rights centre in his honour.

Jean Chrétien could have done it with the stroke of a pen, as he has done with Dorval. Such is the unique power of the prime minister in our system. He names cabinet ministers, parliamentary secretaries, senators, judges, ambassadors and executives and board members of all crown agencies. He even gets to rename major airports without consulting anyone.

In fairness to Chrétien, he is not the first prime minister to do so. Trudeau himself, shortly before leaving office, re-named Toronto Airport for Lester B. Pearson. Brian Mulroney re-named three airports, Saskatoon for John Diefenbaker, Quebec City for Jean Lesage and Ottawa for the twin fathers of Confederation, Macdonald and Cartier.

Trudeau was clearly one of the most important prime ministers since the Second World War, but naming Dorval Airport in his honour is inappropriate.

It also takes no account of history. Dorval opened in 1941 and was the headquarters for the famed RAF Ferry Command, which flew thousands of aircraft to Britain from Montreal via Gander and Goose Bay: Avro Lancaster bombers, B-25s, Venturas, Mitchells and De Havilland Mosquitos.

Later reorganized as Number 45 Group of the RAF Transport Command, there were more than 1,300 people based there at the height of the war, including at least 600 members of the RCAF. In 1944 alone, more than 3,700 planes were delivered from Montreal to Europe. In all, more than 9,000 planes were delivered to the Allied command during the war.

The victory in the skies of Europe began on a runway at Dorval. It does no honour to those who flew with such distinction to rename their base in memory of one who famously declined to serve.

August 2003

∞

WELCOME TO 24/7 NEWS

The summer campaign of 1984, which ended the last Liberal dynasty, was also the last election before the digital age. Each campaign since has brought with it new communications breakthroughs that have made it, first incrementally and then exponentially, more difficult for leaders and parties to shape and control their message.

In the 1984 campaign, the leaders' tours could still board their planes in Ottawa and fly to Vancouver, holding the travelling media incommunicado for five hours. The parties could either entertain them with dinner and a movie, or force-feed a policy pronouncement followed by an in-flight briefing. There were no calls to the desk for instructions, much less to the other parties for comment.

By the 1988 free trade election, the communications paradigm shift was under way with the arrival of cellular phones. When Bell Labs brought the first bulky ones out in 1985, they predicted a million cell phones would be sold worldwide by 2000. It turns out to be more like a million a day.

Even in 1988, the impact of cell phones on campaign buses was immediate. Only while airborne were journalists still a captive audience. As soon as the wheels hit the ground, they were talking to their desks, to the other parties for spin, even to their colleagues on the other buses to compare notes. Now there are even in-flight phones.

It is also much more difficult to shape a dominant message, with all the communications developments since. First all-news channels. Then the Internet. Now the BlackBerry.

Every campaign since 1988 has presented important new challenges to parties in getting out the message, and trying to stay ahead of the media curve without falling into the trap of the media's gotcha games.

The arrival of CBC Newsworld in 1989 meant that the 1993 campaign would be run for the first time on a 24/7 news cycle – a ferocious beast that never sleeps. The Internet was then only on the horizon; there were only about a million users and 100 Web sites in the entire world.

By the 1997 campaign, the morning leaders' news conferences became a staple of all-news television, serving as a podium for the day's message or damage control from overnight.

The Internet had arrived, but more as a research tool than the strategic weapon it has become. Parties and local candidates developed Web sites, but more as go-to resources for policy positions than platforms for launching attacks. Attacks on opponents were still sent by facsimile, usually negative or comparative bullet points known as attack faxes.

By the 2000 election, there were five all-news networks – RDI and LCN in French, CTV Newsnet in English, and CPAC in both languages, in addition to Newsworld.

Then there's the BlackBerry, which has replaced the old attack fax. Reporters receive suggested questions from war rooms, which write their e-mail bullet points from live news coverage on cable.

By the time Prime Minister Paul Martin left his health-care announcement, reporters covering him had been sent messages suggesting they ask where he'd find the money for it. As he was making the announcement, reporters on Stephen Harper's tour were watching via satellite as their bus rolled into Fredericton, and when they got there, Harper was ready with his reply.

And then there's Internet blogs. Now, anybody can be a pundit.

May 2004

∞

A FATEFUL VOTE AND A HINGE OF HISTORY

Twenty-five years ago, Joe Clark's minority government fell on a vote of non-confidence, an event on which the hinge of Canadian history has turned ever since.

On December 13, 1979, Clark's Conservative minority was defeated 139-133, on an amendment proposed by the NDP's Bob Rae. Everyone in Ottawa knew the government was going to fall that night, everyone except the prime minister, who could have called off the vote, but didn't.

Clark had until mid-afternoon to reschedule the vote on his budget until February 1980, after the Christmas recess. Instead, he dug in his heels, called the vote when he didn't have the numbers, then called an election he was destined to lose. Even faced with certain defeat in the House, Clark could have prorogued the session and brought in a new Speech from the Throne.

One way or another, had Clark dismissed the House until the winter session of 1980, the political history of the last quarter century would have been very different.

Pierre Trudeau had just announced his retirement as Liberal leader. John Turner had already indicated he would not be running to succeed him in a winter or spring convention, leaving Don Macdonald as the leading candidate. For all his qualities, Macdonald would have been a much less formidable opponent for Clark at the next election than Trudeau, especially in Quebec, which on February 18, 1980, delivered 74 of its 75 seats to the Liberals.

Trudeau, as a retired leader, would never have played the role he did as prime minister in the 1980 Quebec referendum. He would never have delivered his famous "Elliott" speech, or his promise to put his Quebec seats on the line for constitutional reform.

There would never have been a patriation of the constitution without Quebec's signature, and there would never have been a Charter of Rights, which since its adoption in 1982 has redefined the Canadian social contract. There would have been no National Energy Program, Trudeau's disastrous blueprint of economic nationalism.

Brian Mulroney would never have become Conservative leader in 1983 and prime minister in 1984. His opportunity arose only because Clark told Conservatives at a Winnipeg convention in January 1983 that 66.9 per cent support was "not good enough," and, astonishingly, called for a leadership convention that Mulroney won.

There would have been no free-trade agreement with the United States, under which Canada's exports to the U.S. increased from $100 billion in 1988 to $350 billion in 2002. For that matter there would have been no Macdonald Commission recommending the "leap of faith" of free trade in 1985 because Macdonald would have been Liberal leader, rather than chairman of an historic royal commission, which a generation later still stands out as the most outstanding one of its kind in the last half-century.

There would have been no goods and services tax, which, unpopular as it might be as a consumer tax, has proved to be a huge driver of exports. As a visible consumption tax, it comes off at the border, unlike the buried 13.5-per-cent manufacturers' sales tax it replaced, and gave Canadian exports a competitive advantage never before enjoyed.

There would have been no Meech Lake Accord and no need for one, since there would have no need to acquire Quebec's signature, as there would have been no Constitution Act of 1982.

Clark could have avoided disaster and didn't. Even before the vote, Mulroney called Clark's chief of staff. "You've got to buy off the Créditistes,"

ISSUES AND ATTITUDES 107

Mulroney implored Bill Neville, who replied the PM wouldn't hear of it. The support of Fabien Roy and his small band could have been bought with research funds for their staff, and perhaps a small budget update on agriculture. If those six votes had gone the other way, the 139-133 outcome would have been exactly reversed.

At his senior staff meeting that morning, Clark was famously told by a young aide named Nancy Jamieson: "Sir, we do not have the votes." His clerk of the Privy Council, Marcel Massé, told a visitor to his office to stick around the Hill, because the government was going to fall.

After Clark lost the vote that night, an eerily euphoric atmosphere reigned at a government Christmas party. Clark and his entourage thought the country, furious at the Liberals for precipitating an unnecessary election, would reward them with a majority.

Instead, Clark's government turned out to be a footnote to history. And December 13, 1979, turned out to be one of the most important dates in modern Canadian history.

December 2004

∞

COMPETING VISIONS OF DAYCARE

In the spring of 1988, child-care interest groups were invited to a meeting in the Prime Minister's Office to discuss the Mulroney government's daycare initiative.

About thirty of them sat around the table of the second-floor boardroom in the Langevin building as Geoff Norquay, the prime minister's adviser on social policy, briefed them on the government's daycare initiative of $6.4 billion over five years.

Of course, it wasn't enough money for them. It's never enough to satisfy the demands of interest groups. They were also annoyed by the plan's flexibility – part of the money would go to parents, and part to provide daycare spaces in the provinces. The stakeholders wanted all the money dedicated to bricks and mortar in public daycare.

"The conversation was completely driven by ideology," recalls Norquay, now a consultant with the Earnscliffe Group in Ottawa. "For them, there was only one way to go – institutionalization. I called it the nationalization of children."

As Mulroney's chief speechwriter, I was sitting in on the meeting because the PMO wanted the daycare advocates' advice for a speech on the initiative. I was quite taken aback by their hostility. "It's up to you guys," I interjected at one point, "but $6.4 billion is a lot of money. You wouldn't want to leave it on the table, would you?"

"What do you mean?" one of them asked.

"It could die on the order paper when the election is called."

Which, sadly, is precisely what happened. Jake Epp's cherished daycare package cleared the House, but died on the order paper in the Senate, where the Liberals were running a filibuster on free trade, the issue that would define the 1988 election.

And national daycare, which would have become entrenched as a Canadian social value, disappeared from the political radar because of the dogmatic stupidity of the social-policy lobby.

Here we are, all these years later, having the same conversation in another election. But this time, there's a choice, a real social-policy choice on daycare between the Conservatives and the Liberals.

The Conservatives, who have been framing the policy discussion so far in the campaign, were first out of the box again with their announcement of $10.9 billion for daycare over six years. They would give the money to parents, $1,200 per year for each child under 6, to help facilitate their choices in child care.

The Liberals were so annoyed that they leaked their daycare policy overnight before its scheduled announcement yesterday. The story was that they would extend the $5 billion in daycare agreements already signed with the provinces for another five years beginning in 2009. There wasn't a nickel of new money in it, but it did add up to $10 billion over ten years. Then on the way to the announcement, Paul Martin found another $1 billion to extend it another year through 2015. So, $11 billion, a bigger number than $10.9 billion, though over 11 years, not six.

The Liberal plan is about transfer payments to provinces to pay for space. Some daycares are private, some public. Quebec's public daycares are unionized, and have a history of strikes, which is somewhat inconvenient for working parents. Nevertheless, with only 20 per cent of the pre-school children in the country, Quebec provides about half the daycare spaces in Canada with its $7-a-day program that actually costs $48 a day.

So there's an interesting choice, and it was an interesting debate that Ken Dryden, the social development minister, was having with the Conservative critic, Rona Ambrose, on CTV's *Canada A.M.* The Conservative proposal, Dryden acknowledged, "makes things a little easier for parents to do what they're already doing." For the rest, he appeared uncharacteristically annoyed with Ambrose, who somehow gots under his skin (perhaps it has something to do with her calling him "an old white guy" in the House of Commons). Dryden isn't used to people standing in his goal crease.

CTV then ran a live interview with a mother sitting in her Ottawa living room while her three pre-schoolers played behind her. She said the Conservative proposal meant $3,600 a year for her family, which sounded pretty good to her, while she didn't think much of what the Liberal guy said.

If the Tories had the sense to put some soccer moms on the air, talking up their daycare policy during breaks in *Oprah* and *Dr. Phil*, then they might begin to close the gender gap that may well decide this election.

December 2005

THE CHARTER, TWENTY-FIVE YEARS ON

On the morning of September 28, 1981, the Supreme Court delivered a Solomon-like verdict in a famous constitutional reference on whether Ottawa could patriate the constitution from Westminster without the consent of the provinces.

By a 7-2 margin, the court ruled that, legally, it could. But by a 6-3 margin, it also ruled constitutional convention required a "consensus of the provinces."

"What does it mean?" I asked Michel Robert, then known as the "silver-tongued advocate" of the Quebec bar, who had argued Ottawa's case before the high court.

"It means that, technically, we won," said Robert, standing at the top of the double staircase inside the Supreme Court building. "But, politically, it remains to be seen."

A quarter century later, at the opening of the McGill Institute for the Study of Canada's *Charter@25* conference, Robert recalled the historic decision resulting in the first ministers' conference of November 1981, which produced the Canadian Charter of Rights and Freedoms, proclaimed by the Queen in April 1982.

"The court was telling the government to go back to the table with the provinces," said Robert, now chief justice of the Quebec Court of Appeal.

"*C'est ça*," agreed Roger Tasse, then deputy minister of justice, who was editor-in-chief of the Charter.

And what was "a consensus of the provinces" required by the court? Well, because it was a Westminster convention, it wasn't written down. It turned out the number of provinces required, as Jean Chrétien later put it, was "more than two, but fewer than ten."

And that, a quarter century later, remains a flashpoint and a sore point, in that Quebec has never signed the 1982 Constitution Act. Well, except at Meech Lake in 1987, but that's another story.

This was evident in the conference's opening session, in which Pamela Wallin moderated an Oprah-style round table of four backroom boys, three who were in the room, and one who wasn't.

Deal or no deal, that was the question. The three who were in on it were Tom Axworthy, then principal secretary to Prime Minister Pierre Trudeau; Eddie Goldenberg, then senior adviser to Justice Minister Chrétien; and Hugh Segal, who ran the file for Ontario Premier Bill Davis. The one who wasn't was Louis Bernard, then secretary to the Quebec cabinet under Premier René Lévesque.

"I am going to ring different bells than the others," Bernard said at the outset. He spoke of the "betrayal" of Quebec, compared the federal Charter unfavourably to the 1975 Quebec Charter, and concluded that twenty-five years later, there was nothing to celebrate.

Still bitter, after all these years.

For those then unborn, or those who have forgotten, the conversation, which Lévesque would have called a dialogue of the deaf, recalled all the passions and divisions of those days.

The backroom boys also answered some important "what ifs." What if Joe Clark's minority government hadn't been defeated in 1979? Then, as Segal has pointed out, Trudeau would have remained in retirement, and there would have been no Charter.

It was left to Axworthy to recall how the deal finally came together: a straight-up swap, Trudeau's Charter in return for the provinces' 7/50 amending formula – requiring consent of Ottawa and seven provinces representing 50 per cent of the population.

But there was also a deal-maker: the notwithstanding clause. Without it, Alberta's Peter Lougheed, Saskatchewan's Allan Blakeney and even Bill Davis would have walked. Davis made this clear to Trudeau on the fateful night of November 4, 1981, remembered in Quebec to this day as the "night of the long knives," when Quebec was excluded, isolated and humiliated.

What has been forgotten over time was that Lévesque had spontaneously agreed at the closed-door conference to Trudeau's offer to put the whole patriation package to the people in a referendum.

None of us who was there will ever forget the gleam in Trudeau's eye or his words as he unexpectedly came to the microphone in the lobby of the National Conference Centre.

"And so you have a new alliance between the prime minister of Canada and the premier of Quebec," he said. "And the cat is among the pigeons."

Was it ever. The Gang of Eight dissenting provinces was instantly blown up, and the next night, nine provinces cut a deal, and one, Quebec, went home empty-handed.

With consequences, for better or worse, that we are still sorting out to this day.

February 2007

∞

PRESIDENTIAL LIBRARIES

If you want to know how differently Canada and the United States treat their former prime ministers and presidents, you need only look at the network of presidential libraries in the U.S. There's nothing comparable in Canada, nothing at all.

Two of the most significant presidential libraries are on the eastern seaboard, within an easy drive of Montreal, the Franklin D. Roosevelt library at Hyde Park on the Hudson River north of New York, and the John F. Kennedy library on Columbia Point in Boston.

The Roosevelt library is the most historically important of the presidential libraries in that FDR lived and worked there from 1933 to 1945, and donated his family estate while still in office. Much of the Second World War was run from there. Not only did Roosevelt sleep there, so did Churchill, typically on his way to or from meetings in Canada, such as the Quebec Summit of August 1943.

The Roosevelt library established the precedent of private philanthropy and public administration for what would become the presidential library system. Presidential libraries are built with private funds, often at universities, and usually administered by federal government agencies such as the National Archives.

The JFK library, on the University of Massachusetts campus, is typical of a presidential project partnering with a university. How it got there, rather than his own Harvard, is a long story, mostly of disagreements about space, which is in short supply in Cambridge. But it turned out for the best. The Kennedy library is almost completely surrounded by water, and the sea was an important part of Kennedy's story, from his summers at Hyannisport, to the sinking of his PT boat, to the naval blockade of the Cuban missile crisis. The exceptional setting affords a spectacular view across the harbour to downtown Boston, the city that gave Kennedy to America and the world. And the design by I.M. Pei – architect of Place Ville Marie – is a stunning achievement.

The Kennedy library is also typical in that it mixes program activities with its archival role and museum visits. It receives more than 2,000 researchers a year, who have complete access to more than eight million pages of Kennedy's papers. The JFK Web site is also a remarkable online resource, with text and audio of all his presidential speeches available at a touch of the keyboard.

It's the museum visits that sustain the library and nourish the Kennedy legacy. While it lacks the unique authenticity of the FDR estate, the JFK exhibits are in rooms off a long corridor in a representation of the West Wing of the White House, and they take you back to the 1960s. To watch a tape of one of his news conferences is to be reminded of his elegance and aplomb in defusing difficult questions with his disarming sense of humour.

Among the video highlights are the first Kennedy-Nixon debate from the 1960 campaign and Kennedy's 1961 inaugural address. The outstanding feature of the debate reel isn't Kennedy's obvious telegenic advantage over Nixon, but the civil nature of their exchanges under the extreme duress of the first-ever televised debate. As for Kennedy's inaugural address, it is a reminder of the power of rhetoric to set an agenda.

And it being the Kennedy library, the rhetorical flourishes define the man and the times. Two presidential addresses, in challenging open-air settings, stand the test of time. The first is on the space program at Rice University in Texas: "We choose to go to the moon."

And the second, before a million people in Berlin in June 1963, in which he invoked the Berlin Wall as a symbol of the many failings of communism with the powerful refrain: "Let them come to Berlin." At the height of the Cold War, he predicted the failure of the Soviet system. This was nearly a quarter century before Ronald Reagan went to Berlin and famously said: "Mr. Gorbachev, tear down this wall."

Taken together, the two speeches are a continuum. Kennedy, like Reagan, chose to confront the Soviets, but also to pursue a peaceful dialogue with them.

Reagan's Berlin speech is one of the two most memorable and most quoted of his presidency, the other being his address on the cliffs of Normandy on the 40th anniversary of D-Day in 1984. Historian Douglas Brinkley has mined this speech for a lovely book, *The Boys of Pointe du Hoc*. It is known as such for one short and powerful paragraph drafted by the speechwriter, Peggy Noonan: "These are the boys of Pointe du Hoc. These are the men who took the cliffs. These are the champions who helped free a continent. These are the heroes who helped end a war."

Brinkley notes that all of Noonan's research and drafts of the speech are available at the Reagan library in California.

Sadly, nothing like that exists in Canada. Where are Pearson's notes for his speech to the Canadian legion on the flag in 1964? Where are Trudeau's notes for his address to the nation on referendum night in 1980? Where are the drafts of Mulroney's joint address to the U.S. Congress on acid rain and free trade?

Actually, I know the answer to the last question. They're sitting in a filing cabinet in a locker in my basement. And that's not where they should be. Not at all.

July 2007

LIVE TAX-FREE OR DIE

Dick Drisko, my neighbour, friend and landlord at the beach in Maine, commutes from his summer place to his part-time job as a member of the state legislature in Concord, New Hampshire.

With 400 members, it boasts, as Dick says, of being the third-largest parliament in the English-speaking world. Only Westminster, with 645 members of Parliament, and the United States Congress, with 435 members of the House of Representatives, has more members.

And on a per-capita basis, representing a population of only 1.2 million people, the New Hampshire legislature is easily the largest in the anglosphere.

"One seat for every 3,000 people," says Drisko, a Republican member of the legislature from the town of Hollis, about 65 kilometres north of Boston.

By comparison, the Ontario legislature at Queen's Park has 106 seats for a population of 11 million, or one seat for every 100,000 residents. And Quebec, with 125 seats for about 7.5 million people, has one seat for every 55,000 residents.

In the beginning, the idea was that every town would have a seat in the legislature, and as the number of incorporated towns grew, so did the state assembly. In a sense, town-hall democracy was born in New Hampshire, every citizen in town with a say, every town in the state with a vote in the legislature.

While the legislative chamber is definitely a crowded place, members' salaries are not an issue. They are paid $100 per session, plus a very modest mileage allowance.

There is no need for a taxpayer watchdog in New Hampshire. It's in the local DNA.

New Hampshire, famously, has no state income tax and no sales tax. None. Zero. Nada. Massachusetts, the free-spending liberal state next door, is in some flinty New Hampshire circles scorned as Taxachusetts.

No one seeking state-wide office in New Hampshire would ever propose a personal income tax or sales tax. At least, no one with any thought of winning.

"You would have to take the pledge," Drisko says.

No new taxes.

When the first George Bush broke a famous 1988 campaign pledge, "Read my lips, no new taxes," the voters of New Hampshire reminded him of it by punishing him in the 1992 presidential primary, flocking to right wing maverick Pat Buchanan. Bush put out a grim two-word statement, "Message understood."

But how, in the absence of personal tax revenues, does the state run its services and maintain its infrastructure?

Well, there's the revenue from the renowned tax-free state liquor stores. There's the state lottery, tickets available at the liquor stores. There's excise tax on tobacco. There are state tolls on the Interstates. There's a business profit tax, an interest and dividend tax, a state education property tax, a timber tax and even a gravel tax.

But no personal taxes, and no sales tax. Yet the New Hampshire House recently passed a budget that saw expenditures increase by 25 per cent. And this in a state whose constitution requires a balanced budget. How can that be?

It is, Dick explains, covered by the previous year's surplus. So, a state with no taxes usually runs a surplus.

"What would you say," I asked him, "if the government proposed a tax cut, and only 27 per cent of the voters were in favour of it, and 71 per cent favoured investments in new services instead?"

"I'd say that was pretty unusual," he allowed.

I explained this was, indeed, the case in Quebec, New Hampshire's next-door neighbour to the north.

Of course, the two government models aren't exactly the same. Quebec, one of the highest-taxed jurisdictions in North America, allocates about 45 per cent of spending to delivery of public health care, which doesn't exist in the U.S. Quebec also subsidizes private secondary education and public universities to a degree unheard of anywhere else in North America.

Thus, if only 27 per cent of Quebecers wanted a tax cut, that could be because 42 per cent of them don't pay any provincial income tax, and would prefer to receive more services they're not paying for anyway.

Dick Drisko shook his head in wonderment. Of course, New Hampshire goes Quebec one better – 100 per cent of the people pay no state tax.

One begins to understand the state's motto: "Live free or die." Not to be confused, of course, with the current Bruce Willis action movie, *Live Free or Die Hard*.

Which would be the fate of anyone proposing state taxes.

July 2007

1774 AND ALL THAT

In the aim of promoting a secular society, the authors of the Bouchard-Taylor report wrote that "the crucifix must be removed" from the wall behind the speaker's chair in the National Assembly.

"We do not believe that the crucifix in the National Assembly has its place in a secular state," wrote historian Gérard Bouchard and philosopher Charles Taylor, the eminent academics who lent their names to the commission on reasonable accommodation.

Their logic, with a view to advancing what they term "open secularism," is impeccable. But it takes no account of, and is completely at variance with, more than two and a quarter centuries of constitutional tradition that is the foundation of Quebec and Canada itself.

This goes back to the Quebec Act of 1774, and is central to the asymmetrical features of Confederation in the British North America Act of 1867.

The Quebec Act explicitly guaranteed the freedom to practise the Catholic faith. It also restored French civil law alongside British common law.

Furthermore, the Quebec Act allowed Catholics to hold public office, and removed a reference to the Protestant denomination in office holders' oath of allegiance to the king of England. It allowed the Catholic church to collect the religious tax known as the tithe, and permitted the Jesuits to return to Quebec.

These enlightened and generous gestures by the British occupiers were extremely well received by the population. And they achieved their immediate political purpose. The territory formerly known as New France or Canada did not, after the Quebec Act, join in the American Revolution. In other words, the Quebec Act changed the course of North American history, and enabled the emergence of Canada nearly a century later, ending any thoughts of an American takeover following the U.S. Civil War.

It was, in effect, the religious freedoms guaranteed to Catholics, along with the restoration of French civil law, that guaranteed the survival of the French language and culture on the northern half of this continent.

And that was reflected in the BNA Act, which in Article 93 guaranteed the place of Catholic and Protestant schools in Quebec. It required nothing less than a bilateral constitutional amendment, negotiated between the Chrétien and Bouchard governments, to move to linguistic rather than denominational school boards in Quebec.

The status of the English-language minority was also protected in Article 133, which guaranteed both French and English as recognized languages of the courts and legislature. Asymmetrical federalism wasn't invented with the Health Accord of 2004, it has been with us since 1867, and is central to the bargain of Confederation.

Jean Charest saw this immediately when he received his copy of the Bouchard-Taylor report, and even as it was released, the government tabled a motion in the legislature affirming "our attachment to our religious and historic heritage represented by the crucifix."

While Charest was pre-empting any blowback from Catholics, still a big majority of the population, he has the history exactly right.

While all churches might be struggling with attendance, while the Catholic church is no longer a dominant force in Quebec society, the fact remains that it was, until the Quiet Revolution was launched by Jean Lesage after 1960. The role of the church was pre-eminent in schools and hospitals, and in every municipality in the province. A village might not have had a town hall, but it had a church steeple. Generations of Quebecers were baptized, married and buried from there.

Anecdotally, here's a story involving the crucifix in the Quebec legislature. In the days when Georges-Émile Lapalme was Liberal leader, the party's finance critic was Maurice Hartt, a Jewish member from Montreal. Once, when he asked a question in the House, the reply of the premier, Maurice Duplessis, was that Lapalme sent a Jew to speak on his behalf.

Hartt pointed to the crucifix and replied: "There is a Jew who has been speaking to you for 2,000 years and you haven't heard him."

May 2008

SECURITY CLEARANCE

If any good is to come of the Julie Couillard affair, perhaps it might result in a thorough review of security clearances and access to classified documents in Canada. We've never really taken either very seriously in this country.

Allow me to illustrate with a personal anecdote.

In late 1985, when I went to work in the Prime Minister's Office, I was given a Top Secret security clearance, meaning as the PM's speechwriter I could see the most sensitive government documents, security reports and intelligence assessments.

But first, I was informed by my contact at the Privy Council Office, I would have to pass a routine security check. No problem, I just had to fill out a form that included two references.

I wrote down, Brian Mulroney, prime minister of Canada and Robert Bourassa, premier of Quebec.

My PCO contact called back. "You can't use these names," he said.

"Why not?"

"They have to be real people, people you know."

"But I do know them."

"They have to be people we can call."

What kind of questions would they be asking people they could call?

"Whether you knew any communists," he replied.

In fact, I did know one communist, Nick Auf der Maur, who had famously been tossed out of the Soviet Union for loudly proposing a toast to a free Czechoslovakia in the presence of President Leonid Brezhnev. Nick had also been locked up during the October Crisis. I wasn't going to use him as a reference. Besides, he would have ruined the careers of any young RCMP officers sent to interview him – they would have been last seen on Crescent Street.

Then, when I began writing speeches, and circulating drafts, I discovered that there was no system for classifying them. So I made one up. If the PM was speaking at the 100th anniversary of Thurso (yes, Guy Lafleur's home town), that would be unclassified. If he was making an address on women's issues, that would be confidential. If he was making a Joint Address to the United States Congress, that was secret.

The hardest part of the job, other than giving the PM what he wanted, was reconciling the competing interests in government. Mulroney's 1988 speech to the U.S. Congress went through nearly forty drafts that were circulated to the PMO, PCO, Foreign Affairs, Defence, Environment Canada and our embassy in Washington. Everyone wanted a piece of it, and everyone thought he was a writer.

Sometimes the system made me crazy. For example, in 1987, Mulroney was speaking to a NATO Assembly meeting in Quebec City, and wanted to send a positive signal to Mikhail Gorbachev on his policies of *glasnost* and *perestroika*. "Mr. Gorbachev is a reformer," the draft read, "and in the Soviet Union there is much in need of reforming."

The foreign affairs branch of PCO sent back the following marginal notation: "It has not yet been conclusively demonstrated that Mr. Gorbachev is a reformer." Institutional caution, not to say stupidity, got the better of them. At PCO's insistence, we took it out. By the time Mulroney got around to saying it, a year later in his Washington speech, it had become a statement of the obvious. And the PCO wondered why we cut them out of the loop.

In the matter of Julie Couillard, while she was dating Maxime Bernier, she received no security clearances. It turns out that, as a biker chick, she was well known to the police. But if no one had asked about her, then there wouldn't have been a background check on her.

And here's the thing – the RCMP don't do security clearances on spouses or companions of cabinet ministers, and haven't since the 1980s. The private lives of ministers are deemed to be their own business. So if Julie Couillard was accompanying Max Bernier, that was enough to get her into a receiving line to meet the president of the United States. Why not? It was enough to get her into Rideau Hall.

What is wrong here, other than Bernier's shocking lack of judgment in the company he kept, is the lack of vetting. Similarly, when he left a briefing book at her place, the system never knew it had gone missing. His carelessness was stupid enough, but the system was equally stupid.

Sex, lies and videotape. Who said Canadians were boring?

June 2008

☯

BEV AND THE SUPREMES

The rapidity with which the Supreme Court heard the Bell buyout case, and the unprecedented speed with which it overturned the Quebec Court of Appeal's ruling that would have derailed the deal, sends an unmistakeable message to the appeal bench to get its act together on commercial law.

The Supremes' unanimous 7-0 decision, with costs thrown in as well, is a stinging rebuke to the Quebec court, which had ruled in a unanimous 5-0 judgment that bondholders, as stakeholders, deserved the same consideration as shareholders in the Ontario Teachers' Pension Fund's $52-billion bid to take BCE Inc. private in the biggest leveraged buyout in world history.

It's not the first time the Supremes have overturned the top Quebec court, but the magnitude of the Bell case, and the consequences of it, dramatize the message from on high. In fact, the Supreme Court has previously reversed seven out of nine commercial rulings from the Quebec court, including five out of five unanimous judgments, in the last five years.

From 0 for 5 to 0 for 6, for a batting average of .000. These are not great numbers in any World Series. But for serious court watchers, the intent of the Supremes, if not the outcome, was evident in the swift manner in which they expedited the Bell case on their calendar, so it could be heard before the deal closed on June 30. The deal would have cratered as a result of the stunning Quebec Court of Appeal ruling, which essentially aimed to rewrite Canadian business law in a way that would have made it legally impossible to sell a publicly listed company without placating other stakeholders as well as maximizing value for shareholders – the first tenet of corporate governance.

Following the Quebec court decision, the Supremes granted leave to appeal a week later, called for written factums by June 6 and oral arguments on June 17. This extended timeline was set out in the high court's initial response on May 26.

Then consider what happened in the High Court. The court heard arguments on Tuesday. It decided the case on Wednesday. It put out a notice of its decision on Thursday. It released the judgment, while reserving its reasons, in a single paragraph at the close of markets on Friday.

A unanimous judgment of the Quebec court was unanimously reversed within seventy-two hours of a hearing. You don't see that every day. The message to the Quebec court was a resounding rejection of its logic and interpretation of business law, with a slap upside the head – don't you guys understand the consequences of this?

In awarding costs of at least $10 million, all the way back to the Superior Court, to Bell, Teachers and other principals, the Supremes sent a message to the bondholders – stop bringing frivolous cases, or pay the price at the end of the day.

And in putting out its ruling, a full ten days before the deal is due to close, the Supremes were telling Bell, Teachers and the investment banks: If this deal craters it won't be because of the Supreme Court. And there is no doubt that had the decision gone the other way, it would have killed the $42.75-per-share deal for BCE's 615,000 individual and institutional shareholders of Canada's most widely held company.

Amid relief and jubilation last Friday, one Bell source acknowledged a loss in the high court "would have been hugely problematic."

While the case was argued by Bell's lead counsel, Guy DuPont of Davies Ward, the hero of the piece on the inside was Pierre Bienvenu of Ogilvy Renault, who was brought in to write Bell's forty-page factum. Arguments to the high court are mostly for show, factums are where cases are really won. And while Bienvenu held the pen, it was Bell CEO Michael Sabia who personally edited every draft.

Meanwhile, the Quebec Court of Appeal is left with its reputation as a commercial court in tatters. It is a strong court on Charter cases and the division of constitutional powers, but a very weak one on business law.

Which leaves a huge question for all us all to consider: How are we supposed to build a world-class business culture in Quebec when the highest court in the province doesn't know anything about business?

June 2008

PART TWO

People

7

BRIAN MULRONEY

WINNING ON THE COURTHOUSE STEPS

At a table by the bar of Le Mas des Oliviers, a legendary Montreal hangout of lawyers and pols, Brian Mulroney was finishing a long lunch in the company of Gérald Tremblay, lead counsel in his libel action against the federal government.

"We've had a lot of meals together in the last fourteen months," Mulroney said, "and lots of them have had funny moments, and their share of laughter, but none of them have been joyous. This is joyous."

The former prime minister took a sip of tea, and leaned back in his chair. "Life is good again," he said. "Life is good."

Tremblay is chairman of McCarthy Tetrault in Quebec. But it's in court that he's made his name not only as a leading litigator of the Montreal bar, but as one who comes to court impeccably prepared.

Over the last year, he built a case that left the government no alternative other than to settle on the courthouse steps. His case was in twenty-six boxes of paper, paper with a thousand cutting edges. Tremblay knew the RCMP had leaked the government's accusatory letter to the Swiss. So did his client.

Mulroney said so himself when he gave his deposition. On the same day, the government's lead lawyer, Claude Armand Sheppard, had assured the court Ottawa had made every effort to assure the confidentiality of its extraordinary letter to a foreign power, in which it referred to the "criminal" activity of the former prime minister. Sitting behind Sheppard in court as he made this statement, knowing it to be false, was RCMP Sgt. Fraser Fiegenwald, who in November 1995 had divulged details of the letter to a highly unauthorized source, Stevie Cameron.

"I have learned a lot about Brian's management style in this case," Tremblay said after his client had moved on to another mid-afternoon appointment. "He has been incredibly hands-on. Sometimes he drove me crazy with his requests to check this and look into that. At one point, I said to him, 'Look, Brian, I'm a pretty good lawyer. It's my work, let me do it.' But you know what? Whenever he asked for something, or wanted something checked, it usually turned out he was right."

In that sense, Mulroney was the leader of his own Dream Team, composed of Tremblay and his colleague Jacques Jeansonne, noted Montreal civil-rights attorney Harvey Yarosky and, significantly in Ottawa, former deputy justice minister Roger Tassé, later a partner in the private practice of Jean Chrétien, who had been his minister at the justice department.

It was Tassé who wrote Justice Minister Allan Rock in early November of 1995, objecting to the language of the letter, but offering his client's co-operation, and acknowledging the RCMP's right to investigate him. The letter was copied to Solicitor-General Herb Gray, responsible for the RCMP, and to RCMP Commissioner Philip Murray. According to Tremblay, there was no reply.

This was the time, fourteen months ago, when Mulroney was brought low. Before the story broke, he called his close friend and law partner, Yves Fortier, chairman of the firm of Ogilvy Renault, and asked him over to his house to discuss an important matter.

Fortier thought that, in all the years they have been friends and colleagues, Mulroney had never sounded so low.

"Brian," Fortier said, when Mulroney explained the situation to him, "I have to ask you just this once, on behalf of the firm, whether any of this is true."

Mulroney replied that it was all false.

"Yves," he said, his voice breaking, "this is about my place in history."

In nine years of office and since leaving it, he had endured the usual slings and arrows of public life, and then some. But no one had ever called him a criminal. Now the government had done so, in a letter to a foreign country. And a public that was disposed to think badly of him anyway, would now have all the more reason to do so. Why wouldn't they? Why would their government lie to them about such a serious matter? Well, of course, that must be how Mulroney paid for his house on the hill, with bribes stashed in secret Swiss bank accounts!

On a cold night in early November 1995, Mulroney went for a walk near his home in Westmount, and shared with an old friend and financial adviser the accusations that were in the wind.

"What are you going to do?" the friend asked.

"Well, I can do one of two things," Mulroney replied. "I can let it sit there, in the hope that, maybe, well, it will go away. That wouldn't cost me a nickel. But knowing these people, this will leak and I'll die the death of a thousand cuts. My life will become unbearable. The alternative is to get my lawyers together so that if and when this leaks, I'll file the most massive pre-emptive lawsuit in Canadian history."

Mulroney understood that unless he struck back swiftly and decisively that – instead of writing about the free-trade agreement, the Meech Lake accord, the acid-rain accord with the Americans, privatization and even the GST – historians would conclude that he was a crook.

Instead of noting that he was the only Conservative leader to win consecutive majority governments since Macdonald, their only historical comparison with Sir John A. would be the scandals.

And even then, Mulroney knew it would be a long and expensive battle. He knew a trial, if it came to that, would be a street fight on both sides. But then he is a streetfighter.

In two national campaigns, he had always done what it takes to win. John Turner could have told Jean Chrétien that.

Or as Mulroney said: "You can say what you want about me, I don't care about that. But attack my family or my name and you'll be in for the fight of your life."

Once committed to a trial, Mulroney was genuinely reluctant to settle. His wife wanted to go to court. His four children wanted to go to court.

"The kids have been solid on this, they have been great from the beginning," Mulroney said. There was only the youngest, Nicholas, only 10 at the time, who initially had some difficulty dealing with the usual schoolyard whispers.

In the end, in what could be called the Mila clause, the government "fully" apologized to Mulroney "and his family."

To Tremblay's knowledge, it is unprecedented in Canadian jurisprudence for a family to be included in an admission of error by the government. Harvey Strosberg, the prominent Ontario libel lawyer who was brought in by Rock to bolster the government's legal team, agrees that it was unprecedented to include Mulroney's family in the apology.

Jeansonne, who filled out Mulroney's table at lunch, suggested Mulroney did better by settling than he would have by winning in court, in that Superior Court Judge André Rochon could have ordered costs and damages in a judgment, but could not have compelled the government to apologize.

A trial would have lasted at least three months, and perhaps as many as six, and appeals could have dragged out for years in the Court of Appeal and the Supreme Court. All things considered, it was in Mulroney's interest, as well as the government's, to settle.

Getting him there proved to be an important part of Tremblay's mandate. When the government hired Bruno Pateras to seek a settlement just before Christmas, and suggested labor negotiator Alan B. Gold to mediate talks, Mulroney agreed with Tremblay that Ottawa was finally getting serious about dealing, because these were serious people for whom he had respect and, in Gold's case, genuine affection.

Gold, retired as chief justice of the Quebec Superior Court, had resumed private practice as a lawyer and ran the negotiations from his office in Place Ville Marie.

Tremblay shuffled back and forth from his office two blocks away at Le Windsor. Strosberg changed hotels on at least one occasion so journalists would be less likely to track him down. The bargaining was hard and tough, over language, and over costs.

On more than one occasion, Strosberg gathered his papers and pushed back from the table.

"Sit down," Gold told him. "You don't leave here until I tell you you can. Nobody leaves here until I say so."

At another moment, when Strosberg got up to leave, Gold repeated his message.

"I'm just going to the washroom," Strosberg said.

"That's allowed," Gold said.

The talks almost came to grief over the question of costs. Both sides have acknowledged that the government, up to and including Prime Minister Chrétien, balked until the end of last week.

Tremblay's instructions from Mulroney had been clear: "No meetings unless there is an apology on the table."

There was. But the negotiations stalled over money, and broke off on New Year's Eve.

Tremblay reached Mulroney at his rented condominium at Mont Tremblant. "OK," Mulroney said, "tell the boys you'll see them in court next Monday." It was Tremblay's turn to walk away.

But the Thursday before they were due in court, the RCMP's Fiegenwald admitted to the government what he had apparently been denying for months – that he was in fact a source of the leak of some of the contents of the justice department's letter to the Swiss.

Informed of this, Rock went ballistic. Later on Friday, the government lost its claim of privilege as to its witnesses.

It was time for the government to fold.

Last Saturday morning, the government side called Tremblay and said it was prepared to discuss Mulroney's costs, by then more than $1 million with the meters running. But as late as Sunday afternoon, the deal wasn't done, and even on Sunday night, Mulroney told a friend: "They're hot to trot, but I still haven't seen it in writing."

Strosberg confided that part of his strategy was to make substantial concessions only at the end, partly because Mulroney was himself a former labour negotiator. As Strosberg said: "The labour negotiator in him knows you always get the best deal at the last minute."

In the end, Mulroney had to agree with his partner, Yves Fortier, that the deal was "everything he wanted, everything he was entitled to."

As Fortier told him: "There comes a point where you have to say yes."

Tremblay went to see him with the draft of a settlement. When Mulroney had read it, and was assured that Ottawa had agreed to what had been negotiated in Montreal, he finally agreed.

"As long as my name is cleared," he told Tremblay, "I'll leave the rest to the lawyers."

Since the settlement, the recriminations and questions about the government's mishandling of the matter have made it clear that the case didn't really end in court.

Why did a justice official, on behalf of the minister, write to a foreign country on behalf of the RCMP and its department of the solicitor-general? Does anyone really believe that the Justice Department wrote to a foreign country, accusing a former prime minister of being a criminal, without the knowledge of someone in the central agencies of the Prime Minister's Office and the Privy Council Office?

The question remains: who at the centre knew what, and when, and how was any information acted upon? The RCMP insist the Airbus investigation is active and continuing. But what investigation can be taken seriously, when from the beginning until now, the RCMP have never interviewed or sought to interview John Crosbie, who was minister of transport at the time Air Canada purchased the A-320 from Airbus in 1988?

Time and again, senior Air Canada officials, from the former chairman, Claude Taylor, to the former president, Pierre Jeanniot, have attested to the transparency of the airline's procurement process, a file in which Mulroney was never involved.

Crosbie said this week that his own involvement was limited to calling in Jeanniot and receiving his assurances that everything was on the up and up. The American ambassador of the day, Tom Niles, had complained to Mulroney's chief of staff Derek Burney on behalf of Boeing, the loser in the deal, and passed on the suggestion of improprieties. Burney had told him: "Tom, if you have anything, bring it in."

Niles never did. But Crosbie did the snake-check anyway.

Why wouldn't someone, anyone, in the government, take seriously the representations by a jurist of the stature of Roger Tassé, who pleaded with the justice department and the Mounties to modify the letter, offering his client for interviews, only to be ignored?

And what was a serving officer of the RCMP doing talking to journalist Stevie Cameron about a sensitive police file?

Those questions, and many more, will continue to swirl around this case.

As for Mulroney, he says: "I'm going to be 58 in a couple of months. I'm going to get on with the rest of my life."

As he was putting on his coat to leave the restaurant, an acquaintance at the bar yelled congratulations over to him.

"You could be the Conservative candidate in Baie Comeau at the next election," Mulroney replied. "That's just a rumor. But tell the RCMP. They'll spread it around."

And he left, as he entered, laughing.

January 1997

∽

AUTHOR, AUTHOR

Brian Mulroney was talking about his legacy one night, so I asked what he regarded as his most important achievement. I was thinking along the lines of the Free Trade Agreement, or the acid rain accord, something like that.

He didn't hesitate: "Having a good marriage," he replied. "And being a successful parent." Well, of course.

But that's the thing with Mulroney. It is always personal. And nothing is more important than family or friendship.

He once had the PMO switchboard track down a friend who had just split up with his wife, and was staying in an Ottawa hotel with his infant daughter. "I hear you've got trouble at home," he began. "Look, if you walked down the Sparks Street Mall tomorrow, nine people out of ten will tell you they have problems in their marriage. The thing is to work through them."

The conversation went on for about half an hour, the friend later recounted. "You have more important things to do than this," the friend finally told him. "You have a country to run."

"Nothing is more important than this," Mulroney replied.

There are at least as many such stories about Mulroney as there are pages in his new book – more than a thousand. They come from personal friends and political foes alike. When Bob Rae's brother died in 1989, Mulroney was on the phone. When my daughter Grace was born in 1990, he called the hospital. "It doesn't get any better than this," he said that day.

It was because of this personal touch, *le beau geste privé*, that Mulroney was able to hold the Conservative caucus, a notoriously fractious group, together for the decade he led the party from 1983 to 1993.

There were plenty of highs, including two consecutive majorities, but also lots of lows. Mulroney was not one to hoard his political capital. Rather, he spent it down and then some. By the time he left office, the country was glad to see the back of him, but his caucus always remained solid, even as his approval rating plummeted toward single digits. "I'd follow you anywhere," Don Mazankowski told him before caucus one day as the end of his nine years in office drew near.

Equally, Mulroney invested in relationships with foreign leaders, none more so than Ronald Reagan and the first George Bush. And what did Canada get out of those excellent interpersonal relations between the Canadian prime minister and two American presidents? Well, there was the Free Trade Agreement with Reagan in 1987, and the acid rain accord with Bush in 1991. On more than one occasion, presidents Reagan and Bush rejected the advice of their advisers on U.S. positions so they could be helpful to Mulroney on his home front in Canada. "That's for Brian," Bush said of the emissions-reductions targets he agreed to on acid rain.

Many years later, Mulroney traced his relationship with Bush to his time as U.S. vice-president, when it was by no means clear that he would succeed Reagan. "I invested heavily in George Bush," Mulroney would later say of a time when many foreign leaders had difficulty looking past Reagan.

The friendship and courtesies were reciprocated in full. And they continue to this day. Brian and Mila Mulroney spent Labour Day weekend, as they have for years, as guests of George and Barbara Bush at Walker's Point in Kennebunkport, Me.

Reagan and Bush will undoubtedly figure prominently in Mulroney's book, *Memoirs*, which is what he's been calling it for years – as in "I'll deal with him in my memoirs." Lucien Bouchard and Pierre Trudeau are undoubtedly among the subjects. Clyde Wells wouldn't fare very well, either, in Mulroney's version of Meech Lake.

This was long before he finally got started to write them, around five years ago. He hired a researcher, Kingston writer Arthur Milnes. But Mulroney himself, and no one else, wrote his book. And if Mulroney is settling accounts, well, aren't all memoirs self-serving as well as revealing?

Having completed the manuscript and delivered it to his publisher in late spring, Mulroney recently said, "I now understand why you writers get the jitters before the book comes out." The writer's work is done, and now it's in the hands of others, especially the reviewers.

What he did control was the timing – he would not be pushed into finishing the book, and would not let go of it until he was done. He has always understood that this book was his one opportunity to tell his version of events as he lived them, and his version of history as he made it.

One area where the narrative may be incomplete is in his telling of the 1984 and 1988 campaigns, if only because Mulroney was always in the moment, rather like a hockey player who never sees the tape of a great playoff series.

I covered the 1984 campaign from the press section at the back of Mulroney's campaign plane, and participated in the 1988 free-trade election from the staff section at the front. The two campaigns were as different as my vantage point, but both outcomes were a result of Mulroney's unrivalled skills as a campaigner. As his friend Robert Bourassa said at a critical point of the 1988 campaign: *"Brian, c'est un maudit bon campaigner."*

He could make the case, as he did on free trade; he could force the issue, as he did by defining the negatives of his opponents; and he could close the deal. And no one since Mulroney has had the ability to carry a campaign on his back, as he did in 1988 after taking a hit from Turner – "I believe you have sold us out" – in the defining moment of the leaders' debate.

He was a highly disciplined campaigner, but he also had a gambler's instinct for living on the edge. In Victoria in the 1988 campaign, he accepted a challenge from three hecklers to debate them on the spot over Chapter 19 of the Free Trade Agreement and its associated dispute-settlement provisions. When our press secretary, Marc Lortie, came aboard the PM's bus, I asked him: "Does he know it that well?"

"We are," said Lortie, "about to find out."

It turned out that he did know it, but it was also, excuse the expression, a roll of the dice.

A week later, on a beautiful late autumn Saturday morning, we were rolling on the North Shore of Quebec, on a day that would end with him speaking in his home town of Baie Comeau. He wanted to say something about the courage of his parents' generation, who built towns out of forests. "My father dreamed of a better life for his family," he said, "I dream of a better life for my country."

"Good stuff," he said as he got off the bus that night. "Thanks."

No, sir. Thank you.

National Post, September 2007

EXPENSIVE MONEY

In the four years I wrote speeches for Brian Mulroney, I came to know the difference between his own voice and something that had been written for him.

And clearly, at the Ethics Committee of the House of Commons, Canadians heard him in his own voice. Whether you believed him or not, his half-hour opening statement was Mulroney speaking for himself, not a lawyer arguing a brief. No excuses. No qualifiers. No one to blame but himself.

The audience wasn't in the room. Not really. The members of the committee were supporting players in a fairly scripted if spirited drama. The media were just filters. The real audience was in the offices and living rooms of the country. And having heard from Karlheinz Schreiber over four days, there was a growing sense that in fairness Canadians should hear from Mulroney for at least one.

The first thing he had to do was apologize for accepting a cash retainer arrangement with Karlheinz Schreiber. So that one of the storylines of the day became "Mulroney apologizes" rather than "Mulroney refuses to apologize."

Then, after expressing regret, he needed to acknowledge it was the biggest mistake he ever made in his life. Or as he put it, "the second biggest mistake," after ever agreeing to meet a character like Schreiber in the first place.

In terms of misjudging a man's character, it ranks right up there with his misreading of Lucien Bouchard, of whom he once said, "I don't know how I could have known someone for thirty years without knowing him at all."

If Peter Lougheed knew enough to keep Schreiber away from the Alberta premier's office, if Paul Tellier knew enough to throw him out of the Langevin Building, Mulroney should never have met the man. It was Elmer MacKay and Fred Doucet who introduced him, and Mulroney's mistake, and his own alone, in meeting him.

MacKay had given up his seat for Mulroney in the 1983 Central Nova by-election. And Doucet, a senior adviser who went on to become a lobbyist, is one of the old friends of whom Mulroney was far too indulgent. Don't ask.

Mulroney said yesterday that when he met Schreiber, he knew him as a respectable businessman, as the head of Thyssen Canada, with 3,000 employees in this country. It was only later that he came to discover that he was a serial liar and sociopath, who specialized in ruining people's lives. Schreiber's certainly had a good run at ruining Mulroney's, not to mention Helmut Kohl's, with honourable mention in the last week of Jean Charest and Benoît Bouchard. The man would sell out his own mother to achieve his objective of avoiding extradition to Germany.

Beyond the apology and the admission of his error in meeting Schreiber, Mulroney had to answer a few other questions.

Why did he accept a cash arrangement with Schreiber in the first place? Because that's what he offered, when they met at an airport hotel at Mirabel in August 1993. Would he have accepted a cheque? Obviously.

What did he do to earn the money? At his own expense, he visited high level government officials of the five permanent members of the UN Security Council, to lobby them on behalf of the Bearhead light armoured vehicle project his own government had cancelled when it would have cost $100 million of taxpayers' money to build a plant in Nova Scotia.

Why the delay in paying his taxes, which he did voluntarily later on? What did he do with the cash? And by the way, how much was it?

Not $500,000, which Schreiber said had been set aside. Not even $300,000 in three payments of $100,000 each. But $225,000, Mulroney said, in three payments of $75,000 each.

Now that was the major development of the day. That it was only $225,000 doesn't diminish Mulroney's error in judgment.

But it does further destroy the credibility of Schreiber, who doesn't even know how much money he paid Mulroney. If he can't even get that straight, why should anyone believe anything he says?

For the rest, Mulroney proceeded to eviscerate Schreiber's credibility, quoting different sworn versions of the same story, and destroying Schreiber's November 7 affidavit that Mulroney dubbed his "get out of jail card," leading to this political melodrama on Parliament Hill.

Now David Johnston, the independent third party who is to make recommendations on where to go from here, is faced with a political as well as a process problem. Is there a question of the public interest, enough to justify the expense of a full public inquiry? Is there a lesser means, such as turning the whole miserable business over to the police or a public prosecutor? Or was this, in the end, a private transaction which, Mulroney having paid his taxes, isn't in the public domain?

Whether it was $300,000 or $225,000, this much is clear: it's the most expensive money Mulroney ever made.

December 2007

MULRONEY AT 70

As Brian Mulroney turns 70, he has every reason to reflect on what he calls "a good life, a full life." The former prime minister is in Florida, at his winter home in Palm Beach, surrounded by his wife, four kids and four grandchildren.

He adds: "Mila's in great shape. The kids are in great shape. The grandchildren are fantastic. My health is better than it's ever been in my life. You've got all that going for you at 70, you're beating the odds."

Before flying out to Fort Lauderdale, Mulroney took some time to chat in his law office at Ogilvy Renault, where he is a senior partner and huge rainmaker for the firm. On the window sills, book shelves and credenza, there are the photographs of a life in politics and business: with Bill Clinton and George W. Bush in the Oval Office, with the first George Bush at Kennebunkport, with Ted Kennedy, Nancy Reagan and Margaret Thatcher, all of whom have written or called to wish him a happy 70th birthday. There are other photos, with Ronald Reagan at the White House, with Mikhail Gorbachev and Boris Yeltsin in Russia, with François Mitterrand and Pope John Paul II at 24 Sussex.

Mulroney's desk, a walnut table that once belonged to Sir John A. Macdonald, was a gift from the Conservative caucus on his retirement in 1993. He points behind the desk to a large portrait of his four children, painted by the Ottawa artist Shirley Van Dusen in 1987. "That's by far the most important thing in this office, what I cherish most," he says. "It's perfect."

Looking back on his nine tumultuous years as prime minister from 1984 to 1993, he says: "I enjoyed very much being prime minister and I deeply enjoy now that my policies are being recognized as beneficial to the country. But all of that pales into insignificance beside my children. My wife, my children, my family, my friends – that's what counts. I'm thrilled with life."

He adds: "My dad would be pleased. My mom would be pleased."

Mulroney never expected to live to see 70.

"No, I did not," he says. "My dad died when he was 61, and for me that was an entirely traumatic moment. I've lived 44 years without my hero, and I feel his loss to this day."

This is what it always comes back to with Mulroney, the narrative of the electrician's son from Baie Comeau; and the father, the first Ben Mulroney, who never lived to see, or savour, his son's success.

"He used to sit in that La-Z-Boy chair that he had at 79 Champlain Street," Mulroney recalls. "He would kick back, take off his shoes and sit back with a small, cold bottle of Molson in his hand. His words are burned into my mind. He would say, 'we're almost over the hump,' and of course, with six kids, we weren't. And he would say, 'the next time we go to Montreal, I want you to see the Canadiens, I want you to see the Forum,' and of course we never got there. He never saw them play."

This was something Mulroney always thought of during his years as president of the Iron Ore Company, when he had four seats in the reds right behind the Canadiens bench; or again when he left office, when he had his own two seats in the reds beside the great Dickie Moore. More than anything he ever did as prime minister, he has said his father would have been impressed by his investiture as a Companion of the Order of Canada, when Mulroney centred a line of Rocket Richard and Jean Béliveau at Rideau Hall.

In a major new book, *Blue Thunder*, author Bob Plamondon appraises every Conservative leader from Macdonald to Stephen Harper, and ranks Mulroney second to only Macdonald himself. In an appendix rating success and failure, Plamondon ranks Mulroney in first place on the economy and prosperity, notably for "his crowning policy jewel," free trade with the United States; first on the environment for the acid-rain accord, the Green Plan and other achievements. He rates Mulroney the best campaigner of them all, for his back-to-back majorities in 1984 and 1988, particularly the turnaround of the free-trade election after losing the leadership debate to John Turner.

Plamondon sent Mulroney an advance copy of the book the other day, and the former PM says he finds it "gratifying" to be ranked "the best after Sir John A., who is obviously in a class by himself."

Their pictures being on the cover of the same book is about the only thing Mulroney shares with Harper nowadays. They've not talked since the current Prime Minister severed contact with his predecessor after Karlheinz Schreiber's affidavit in November 2007, falsely accusing Mulroney of taking up his extradition case with Harper at Harrington Lake.

But this is more Harper's loss than Mulroney's, since the PM has deprived himself of his best adviser on Quebec, and a mentor on foreign affairs, notably Canada-U.S. relations. Mulroney would have served as an early warning system on the Conservative cultural cuts and young offender proposals in Quebec.

Mulroney knew early in the last election campaign that the cultural cuts were a problem when he and his wife had Robert Charlebois and Gilles Vigneault over to dinner, and the two renowned Quebec singers spent part of the evening blasting Harper. What Mulroney didn't know was whom to call, since no one in the Harper camp was allowed to talk to him. When Harper wonders about his missed rendezvous with a majority, and the near-death experience of his government in December, it's something to consider.

The only cloud on the horizon of Mulroney's life as he turns 70 is the matter of the inquiry into his cash transaction with Schreiber, the most expensive $225,000 he ever made in his life. He's certainly paid a heavy price for it, and has already suffered great embarrassment for his bad judgment in even meeting someone like Schreiber.

It's like a pebble in his shoe that he needs to stop and shake out. Mulroney blames no one but himself for doing business with Schreiber. As he has said: "My mother used to say, when you lie down with dogs, you wake up with fleas." But as to the accusation that his retainer with Schreiber was to lobby the Canadian government, Mulroney has often said privately: "I have never lobbied the Canadian government in my life."

As for the Oliphant Inquiry, Mulroney knows he will just have to get through it. One thing is for sure: When he appears before the inquiry, it will be a quite a show.

"There is a saying that you should never be exultant in victory or craven in defeat," he says. "You've just got to keep going, that's all."

Four years ago, there was a very real question of whether Mulroney would keep going at all, when he nearly died of pancreatitis and was hospitalized for months at Montreal's Hôpital Saint-Luc. He later said it was only when his daughter Caroline showed up at his bedside, and reminded him that she was expecting twins, that he decided he was going to live.

"They say if you have a near-death experience it changes you forever," he says. "Mila says it has changed me in that I'm much less partisan than I used to be. It was really Mila who pulled me through that." In this regard, he reflects on the illness of his close friend Ted Kennedy, "a wonderful man, who is completely without malice," now on an acclaimed victory lap of life even as he lives with inoperable brain cancer.

A lifelong aficionado of American politics, Mulroney likes the lift that Barack Obama has given to American politics, and that his visit to Ottawa "has given a new appreciation of Canada in America."

Obama reminds him of Jack Kennedy, "in the sense that he has both style and substance." He has known four American presidents and ranks the first George Bush as the "finest at a human level," and Ronald Reagan, as "the best natural leader I ever met."

The interview ended and Mulroney's driver was waiting. But when he reached the sidewalk, he said to me, "it's a beautiful evening, Montreal at its best, let's walk for a bit." At the corner of McGill College and de Maisonneuve, he pointed down the street to the iconic cruciform tower of Place Ville Marie, the spot where he started at Ogilvy Renault, fresh out of Laval law school, in 1964, and to which the firm is returning this spring.

Among the firm's five floors of space, Mulroney has been assigned a large corner office, "with a view east to the Big O, south to the Port of Montreal, and north to the mountain." Imagine, he added, "me, a guy from Baie Comeau, with a corner office in PVM."

March 2009

ACCEPTING THE CALL

Jean Charest will assume the leadership of the Quebec Liberals for one compelling reason – he has no other choice.

He cannot hope to someday lead the country if he now refuses to answer the call of country.

It's inconvenient. It's unfair. It's politics.

Inconvenient, because he's at a good place in his life, rebuilding the fortunes of the Progressive Conservative Party, and moving his family into a new home in Ottawa. "I have an eight-year-old daughter," he told a friend the other day, "who is going to have her own room for the first time."

Unfair, because Charest has already given a lot to the cause of a Canadian Quebec. His role in the 1995 referendum, played with pride and passion, might have been decisive in the razor-thin victory of the federalist forces. He can honestly say he gave at the office.

It would have been better for him if Daniel Johnson had taken the hit in the coming Quebec election, allowing Charest to come in again in the event of another referendum before the next federal election.

But then, as John Lennon used to sing, "Life is what happens when you're busy making other plans."

Daniel Johnson, it turns out, had other plans. Plans for himself, and for Charest. No one who has spoken to Johnson in the last week is in any doubt that he had Charest very much in mind when he stepped to the microphone,

8

JEAN CHAREST

resigned the leadership, and stopped Bouchard's spring-election scenario in its tracks.

The problem for the Liberals wasn't the message. It was the messenger. So Johnson, in a selfless and strategic gesture, quit. But in doing so, he put the cat among the pigeons.

And so Charest is deeply conflicted, and genuinely torn, between ambition and duty, between preference and necessity.

He wants to be prime minister of Canada, not premier of Quebec.

One job is the leadership of a big country, the other of a big province. It is the difference between the major leagues and Triple-A. Except for one thing. Only in Quebec can provincial politics determine the national agenda, and the future of the country itself.

In making the switch, Charest could well be sacrificing his national ambitions, not merely setting them aside. No Quebec premier has ever gone on to lead the country. Any Quebec premier has an obligation to defend what Robert Bourassa once called "the higher interests of Quebec," which inevitably conflicts with the national interest.

If Charest were leader of the opposition, a prime minister in waiting, he could safely decline the Quebec leadership. But he's leading the fifth party in the House of Commons, not the second.

Then there's the litany of "what ifs." What if the PQ won an election it might well have lost to him? What if the Yes won a referendum that wouldn't have been held had he answered the call? And what if, in those circumstances, the country was lost?

In any of those scenarios, Charest would be finished in federal politics. And in the worst case, there is no point aspiring to lead a country that no longer exists.

On the other side of this discussion, there is the historic opportunity for Charest to confront not only the sovereignists, but Bouchard himself. It is personal between them. In his federalist phase as senior Quebec minister in Brian Mulroney's government, Bouchard asked Charest to be chairman of a parliamentary committee that rejigged the Meech Lake accord, and then ostensibly left Ottawa because of Charest's report. "I have time," Charest said then, of settling the account, and the time could finally be at hand.

Charest knows where all the bodies are buried in the Conservative Party, but he does not know the Quebec Liberals. It's up to them to persuade him that the Liberal caucus, organizers and financial levers are all there for him.

Then there are the federal Liberals from Quebec, the cousins who have made Johnson's life so unbearable. They've made very unseemly noises in recent weeks about muscling in on the Quebec campaign.

But it's important to distinguish between the Quebec and federal Liberals. The feds have been in a position to impose their leadership and strategy in two referendums, in 1980 and 1995. But in the last four Quebec Liberal leaderships, from 1970 to 1994, the wishes of the cousins have counted for little. Claude Ryan won the leadership in 1978 without Ottawa's support and Robert Bourassa regained it in 1983 over the opposition of Pierre Trudeau.

Oddly enough, it is easier for Charest to make this move as a Conservative, who worked for Meech Lake and free trade, both supported by the Bourassa Liberals, and who has opposed both the Supreme Court reference on secession and the Millennium scholarship fund, a direct invasion of provincial jurisdiction in education.

The Quebec Liberals want Charest because he moves the numbers. He has more than the gifts of a great retail politician. He has the gift of a *"rassembleur,"* bringing people together. It is the appeal of *"la main tendue,"* the outstretched hand of which he spoke in last spring's federal campaign.

Not yet 40, he is confronted with a terrible decision that will shape not only his own family and career, but his province and country. But then, this is the life he chose, and it may be what destiny has chosen for him.

March 1998

∞

MR. PREMIER

At his news conference following his victory in Election 2003, Jean Charest spoke of Quebec's leadership role in the Canadian federation, going back to Jean Lesage and the formula for opting out of the Canada Pension Plan that enabled the creation of the Caisse de dépôt et placement du Québec.

Charest also noted that even under René Lévesque, important arrangements were made to share jurisdiction of immigration in the Cullen-Couture accord. Later, Robert Bourassa negotiated and Daniel Johnson concluded agreements on manpower and training.

By way of modern Quebec history, Charest was making two important points. First, Quebec's leadership is vital in managing the federation. Second, it isn't necessary to change the constitution to make Canada more functional, for the benefit of all its partners.

And with that, Charest served notice that Quebec would be back at the table of the federation, not with the ambition of wrecking it but with the intention of making it better.

He was doing so, not as the leader of the opposition trying to get noticed at a chamber of commerce but as the premier-designate of Quebec, standing in the lobby of the legislature, announcing a sharp turn in government policy.

From the negative bias of the Parti Québécois toward Canada, Charest was affirming the positive bias of an incoming Liberal government to making Canada, as well as Quebec, a better place.

Charest was quick to add that Quebec has no monopoly on leadership in the federation, but the historical facts are just as he pointed them out. It is not only Quebec's presence that moves issues in federal-provincial relations but Quebec's pro-active leadership.

But Charest also served notice to Ottawa in his victory speech Monday that he would be coming to the table with an agenda, particularly VFI, the Vertical Fiscal Imbalance, that will see Ottawa pay off the national debt by 2020, while the provinces go deeply back into deficits, unless the feds adopt a more generous outlook on transfer payments to the provinces.

VFI is a complicated file but also as simple as the notion of burden sharing. If the provinces are expected to make new investments in health care and education, Ottawa can't be retiring the national debt while the provinces go broke.

This is the next big debate between Ottawa and the provinces and the first big discussion between the outgoing Chrétien government and the incoming Charest government. The VFI file will be Charest's first important test as a "defender of the interests of Quebec" – the basic benchmark of dealing with Ottawa and the provinces.

But Charest also comes to the premier's office uniquely prepared to conduct intergovernmental affairs with Ottawa and the provinces. First, as a former federal environment minister, a sensitive portfolio between Ottawa and the provinces, he has a broad understanding not only of federal politics but of the federal-provincial process.

And second, as a former national leader of the Conservative Party, he has a deep understanding of the entire country, where it is likely to be receptive to Quebec, and where it will be resistant. No Quebec premier in the last half-century, not even Lesage or Bourassa, has really understood the rest of Canada.

Bourassa was highly regarded by his fellow premiers and had excellent relations with Ottawa during the Mulroney years, but he made fatal assumptions about the pragmatism of English-speaking Canadians and underestimated their deep emotional attachment to the country. Thus, his disastrous "knife at the throat" strategy for forcing new negotiations after the failure of the Meech Lake Accord.

Charest will never make such a mistake. He knows the country, and its people, far too well. His network includes important premiers such as Ralph Klein (they were environment ministers together) and Ernie Eves in Ontario (who actively campaigned for Charest in the 1997 federal election).

Just before he went to vote, Charest was speaking of the end of the campaign and the large crowds he drew on the final weekend's big push. "I'm feeling pretty emotional about the whole thing," he said. He had also been talking to his predecessors, Daniel Johnson and Claude Ryan, as well as to Andrée Bourassa and Corinne Lesage. He was talking to them *en famille,* the Liberal family.

Now, he spoke for the first time as head of the larger family of Quebecers. And by invoking history as he did, he drew its mantle to himself.

April 2003

NEIGHBOURS IN THE TOWNSHIPS

Paul Martin and Jean Charest are neighbours in the Eastern Townships. Martin's farm is at Iron Hill, near Knowlton. Charest's weekend home is at North Hatley, overlooking Lake Massawippi, about half an hour away.

During the summer, they traded visits. The first, at Martin's place in July, was a bad meeting. The second, at Charest's in August, went much better.

Martin was in a sour mood at the first meeting, wondering why Charest hadn't done anything to help the federal Liberals in the election, and complaining that he wasn't moving onside with Ottawa on health care. Charest was shocked by Martin's scolding and presumptuous tone.

"Paul," he finally said, "I'm not your son. I'm the Premier of Quebec." It's difficult to overstate how underwhelmed Charest was with Martin's performance that day.

A few weeks later, Charest was at home when the phone rang around 8:30 in the morning. It was Martin, suggesting they get together.

"Sure," Charest replied, "come on over for a coffee."

Within an hour, the prime minister arrived alone on Charest's rambling front porch. Charest made it abundantly clear he had two major issues with Martin in the run-up to the health-care summit.

The first was Ottawa's insistence on accountability for any funding on health care. The second was his demand for a revised equalization formula. Both were deal breakers for Charest.

Whether Ottawa puts $9 billion of new funding on the table, or more, it isn't the amount that's important to Charest, it's the constitutional principle of provincial jurisdiction.

Martin has said that reducing waiting times is his top priority, because that's what Canadians have told his pollster, and so it is the most compelling cause of our time. Charest's view is that he'll be determining his own priorities, and by the way, check the constitution. Article 91, that's Ottawa. Peace, order and good government. Article 92, that's the provinces. Health care, day care, cities. The constitutional division of powers is the fundamental bargain of confederation.

It happens that most of Martin's program priorities are in provincial jurisdiction. For most provinces, this is merely annoying. For Charest, it's a major test of leadership. No Quebec premier, least of all a federalist one, can be seen as Ottawa's poodle. Charest cannot be perceived as anything other than a strong defender of Quebec's interests. Thus, his solidarity session with representatives of the health sector, including the trade unions, who sent him off to Ottawa with their full support. The headline in *Le Soleil* could not have been more unqualified: "Everyone behind Charest."

Charest clearly pointed the way to a deal when he invoked the opting out with compensation formula that enabled the creation of the Canada-Quebec pension plan and medicare in the 1960s. Quebec got the federal funding, but the benefits were portable. It was known as co-operative federalism and its inventor was Lester B. Pearson, who as leader of a minority government left an unmatched legislative legacy.

That's one of two courses open to Martin this week. He can follow the Pearsonian path of statesmanship. Or, like Pierre Trudeau, he can choose brinkmanship and ask who will speak for Canada. Either choice will cause heartache in the Liberal Party as between the pragmatists and the centralizers.

If Martin wants a deal, he'll follow the Pearsonian precedent. If he wants rhetoric, he can ask the premiers what they're doing to reduce waiting times. Then he shouldn't be surprised if they remind him that, as finance minister in 1995, he helped create the problem by slashing federal funding for health care. Great television, but no deal.

Priorities in health care are one contentious point. Accountability is another. Charest won't accept Ottawa dictating his choices, nor will he be told how to spend any additional money. When 75 per cent of Charest's new program spending since taking office is in health care, he understandably takes offence at the inference he would spend health money on highways.

The provinces received an additional $2 billion in health-care funding last spring, but the catch for Charest was his $500-million share of the pot was offset by a drop in equalization payments. Ontario, as one of only two have provinces, had a bad year in 2003.

The have-not provinces, including Quebec, have paid an economic price in lower equalization receipts. The news that the federal surplus will again be larger than expected comes at an inconvenient moment for Ottawa.

Here's the cutting edge of a deal. Money without strings attached for health care, and a commitment by Ottawa to negotiate a new equalization formula. Since the provinces are on solid constitutional footing, in their own jurisdiction, they have a strong hand to play.

And here's a thought for Martin's next election campaign. Run it in federal jurisdiction, for a change.

September 2004

WINNING BIG ON HEALTH CARE

Jean Charest got the power, the glory and the money. It doesn't get any better than that.

Not since Jean Lesage in the 1960s has a Quebec premier won as much as Charest did at the health-care summit in Ottawa. Forty years ago, Lesage obtained the opting out with compensation that enabled his government to set up the Quebec Pension Plan and the Caisse de dépôt et placement du Québec. Lesage's vision created the economic levers of modern Quebec society.

Make no mistake, Charest made the same kind of history last week. But just as Lesage could not have done it without the statesmanship of Prime Minister Lester B. Pearson, father of co-operative federalism, Charest would have won nothing without the generosity of Prime Minister Paul Martin.

After nine disappointing months in office, Martin defined himself as prime minister in terms of federalism. He had to choose between Pearson's and Pierre Trudeau's visions of Canada. He chose the Pearson brand of federalism, repudiating the Trudeau hard line of treating the premiers as "snivellers who should be sent packing."

Martin will pay a price for this with the Trudeau wing of the Liberal Party and the entrenched elements of the federal public service, who resist any kind of concession to the provinces. Martin will be called "a head-waiter to the provinces." The confederation-of-shopping-centres crowd will be out in force. As for who speaks for Canada, Martin's reply should be that they all do, especially when speaking about a provincial jurisdiction like health care.

Since Martin staked his election campaign, and his government, on fixing health care "for a generation," he needed a deal as badly as the provinces needed the money.

He almost blew it. The meeting was the worst organized and worst managed first-ministers conference in twenty-five years. The low point was the frat-house atmosphere, with officials spilling over all three floors of the PM's residence.

At one point, pizzas were delivered at 2 a.m. and served up over the dining-room table. Please, it's not Porky's, it's 24 Sussex.

But at the end of the day, it's the outcome that matters. And while it might not be a deal for a decade, it is certainly a big deal in terms of money – $18 billion over six years, $41 billion over ten, is not chump change.

It's an even bigger deal in conceptual terms of federalism. Martin not only recognized asymmetrical federalism, he put it in writing, noting it "allows for the existence of specific agreements for any province." Thus, the "funding provided by the federal government will be used by the government of Quebec to implement its own plan," with Quebec promising to ensure delivery "in a timely manner and at reducing waiting times."

A win-win. Charest gets the cash and recognition of his jurisdiction, as well as a separate Quebec clause. Martin gets agreement that reducing waiting times is a priority for Quebec.

Asymmetrical federalism is definitely a step away from the Trudeau model of symmetrical federalism, notably in the Charter of Rights and Freedoms. But it is not a new model, and does not represent a craven caving to the provinces. It is as old as confederation itself, and is at the heart of the Canadian bargain.

For example, in Section 93 of the British North America Act, recognizing education as a provincial jurisdiction, Quebec was able to organize its school system on denominational rather than linguistic lines. Section 133 recognizes English as well as French as a language of the courts and legislature of Quebec.

Pearson practised asymmetrical federalism when he agreed to the opting out of the Canada-Quebec Pension Plan. And that's exactly what Martin did last week. Now, as then, the winner in the short term is Quebec, but the winner in the long term is Canada.

As well as the money to deliver on his own health-care promises. Charest also got the promise of another first ministers meeting on equalization and the fiscal imbalance – whose existence Ottawa had refused even to acknowledge before last week.

But Charest's political victory is even bigger. He can say that federalism, his kind of federalism, works. He has also established himself as a strong defender of Quebec's interests.

It wasn't just his commanding performance at the table, but his role in negotiating in the back room. Charest, in deep trouble only a few months ago, might now be unbeatable in the 2007 election. That's how big a win it was for him.

September 2004

∽

IN THE MIRROR—NO ONE TO BLAME BUT HIMSELF

If Jean Charest is looking for someone to blame for nearly losing the 2007 election, he can start by looking in the mirror.

The leader is always the first one responsible for what happens in a campaign. Others shape the leader's tour, turn polling and advertising into strategy and tactics, write speeches, keep the media hounds both fed and at bay, and find a suitable role for the party's team of candidates. But it is always the leader who makes the big decisions, and carries the entire burden of the campaign on his back.

Reduced to a minority government, the real Jean Charest finally showed up on election night. He needed to appear chastened, humbled and responsive to the challenge all at once. And he did, acknowledging first that "Quebeckers have rendered a judgment, a severe judgment" on his government and himself, promising to "draw the lessons of this verdict" and "bow before this will." In other words: "Message understood." Good.

Then, at his news conference the next day, Charest took full responsibility for the outcome of the campaign. Quite right.

In the first place, it was Charest's decision to move up the election call to February from April, to take advantage of André Boisclair's meltdown in the polls. A more orderly march to an election call might have resulted in a more coherent campaign, once more focused on the future than on a record resulting in dangerously high levels of dissatisfaction.

It would also have given the Liberals more time to see Mario Dumont in the rear-view mirror, rather than his suddenly appearing in their blind spot as he did in the second week of the campaign.

Furthermore, Charest could have done a proper victory lap on the federal budget, as a sitting premier tucking the gains for Quebec into his own budget and touting them at a Liberal policy convention originally scheduled for last weekend. In the event, he was one of three candidates for his own job, all claiming or assigning credit for resolving the fiscal imbalance.

Then Charest took $700 million of "new" equalization money and announced a tax cut with the entire amount, neglecting to emphasize another $1.6 billion next year in extra federal funding under the "old" equalization formula, as well as transfer payments. The political class panned Charest's equalization cash call, and his opponents jumped on the opportunity to remind voters of his broken 2003 campaign promise to cut taxes by $1 billion a year.

While there was no constitutional issue with equalizing fiscal frameworks rather than services, there was an immediate and understandable backlash in the rest of Canada, where voters saw themselves paying for a tax cut for Quebecers, who already enjoy services such as $7-a-day child care and $1,668 university tuition fees not available in their provinces.

Apart from defending Quebec's interests in Ottawa, part of the premier's job is promoting good will toward Quebec in the rest of Canada. No sitting Quebec premier has ever had a better understanding of Ottawa and the rest of the country, or accumulated more equity with both. But last week, Charest spent it down significantly on a promise he might not even be able to deliver on in a minority House.

And then there was the general tenor of the campaign. If the Liberals wonder why they couldn't get their message out it's because, from Day 1, they lost control of the travelling media circus and never got it under control until the final week.

A fifty-minute daily media availability is an invitation to a drive-by shooting. On all three leaders' tours, the media did virtually nothing to illuminate such important issues as health care, education reform, tuition fees or fiscal federalism. The parties and leaders had positions, the media just didn't report them.

On the campaign trail, Charest performed up to his capacity only in fits and starts. But then why did the Liberals keep Charest in a premier's posture? Why wasn't the best campaigner of his generation allowed out to play? Even his best friends and closest associates were mystified, and wondered what was wrong with him.

As it used to be said of Bill Clinton – let the big dog run.

For Charest and the Liberals, that should be the biggest lesson of this campaign.

March 2007

THE ECONOMY, STUPID

In 1970, Robert Bourassa ran the Quebec Liberal election campaign on the promise of creating 100,000 jobs during a first four-year mandate. He was so closely identified with this promise, and the Liberals so synonymous with the economy, that he became known as "Bob Le Job."

In the last year alone, from May 2006 to May 2007, the Quebec economy has created more than 100,000 jobs, an unprecedented achievement in modern times.

As Statistics Canada reported: "While employment was little changed in Quebec in May, the unemployment rate held steady at its historic 33-year low of 7.2 per cent. Since the beginning of the year, employment has risen 1.3 per cent, above the 0.3 per cent growth for the same period in 2006. So far this year, increases in construction, accommodation and food services, and information, culture and recreation have more than offset losses in the manufacturing sector."

Quebec's unemployment rate of 7.2 per cent last month was only 1.1 per cent above the national rate of 6.1 per cent – significantly lower than the historical spread of two points above the national average.

Doesn't, or shouldn't, Jean Charest get some credit for presiding over the strongest Quebec economy in more than three decades? You can be sure Bourassa would have made these numbers work for him with the voters.

But Charest didn't run on the economy in the March election, which in retrospect he should not have moved up from the spring, when these remarkable numbers would have been out there.

He ran on his larger record, including health care and tax cuts, where he ran into a high degree of voter dissatisfaction with the government, which rose from 50 per cent to 57 per cent during the campaign, coming very close to the generally acknowledged tipping point of 60 per cent.

But it all played out in the way the Liberals framed the ballot question. They should have been running on the economy, and as the party of prosperity.

Instead, they had a slogan, "United for Success," which was anything but memorable, when their positioning statement should have been simply, "*Ça va bien*."

Running on the economy would have allowed Charest to slide into his achievements on managing the fiscal framework – balanced budgets, the creation of the Generations Fund to pay down debt, the two upgrades of Quebec's credit rating in New York, reducing the cost of borrowing and improving its reputation in global capital markets.

In other words, he could have played from strengths, instead of his perceived weaknesses. Even on federal-provincial fiscal frameworks, Charest took a $2.3-billion win on the fiscal imbalance, and turned it into a $700-million tax cut that reminded voters only of broken promises, and ended any further discussion of that issue with the feds.

So the party that has presided over unprecedented job creation took no credit for it, and the premier who won historic financial gains from Ottawa received no credit for them. The Liberals and Charest were on different message tracks, which very nearly cost them an election they should have won in a walk.

Which proves a very good political point: If you don't talk about your achievements, you shouldn't be surprised if the people don't vote for them.

Yet the strong economy might yet provide a political framework on which the Liberals and Charest can build a recovery. The Liberals are seen as the party of economic managers, and Charest has proposed two big ideas. One is free trade with Ontario and the other is expanding Quebec's hydroelectric exports.

A free-trade agreement with Ontario would, at long last, eliminate the ridiculous barriers to interprovincial trade. An Ottawa taxi can drop a customer at the casino in Gatineau, but if it tries to pick up a fare there, faces a huge fine.

There is a way back for Charest. It's the economy, stupid.

June 2007

∞

MAKING HISTORY

Jean Charest, who a year and a half ago seemed destined to become history, stands on the threshold of making history.

No Quebec premier since Maurice Duplessis has won three elections in a row, but Charest is only days away from doing just that. Jean Lesage and Robert Bourassa, René Lévesque and Lucien Bouchard, are all leading members of the premiers' hall of fame. None of them won three in a row.

"I feel very confident," Premier Charest was saying from his campaign bus in Quebec City. "I'm trying to avoid tempting history. But I like the sound of that."

He has every reason to feel confident. All the polls put Liberals clearly in majority territory, with the Parti Québécois in a competitive second place and Mario Dumont's ADQ on the verge of being reduced to a handful of seats in the 125-member National Assembly. The magic number is 63, and in all the seat models, Charest is poised to regain the majority he lost in March 2007, when voters returned him at the head of a shaky minority government.

What has happened since then is a two-part narrative – one part is the political redemption of Charest, the other is the utter failure of Dumont to seize the opportunity, as leader of the opposition, to present himself and his team as a government in waiting.

It wasn't just that Charest nearly lost the last election. What astonished even his closest friends was that Charest, the most gifted campaigner of his generation, failed to show up for the campaign.

That hasn't been the case this time. "This has been my best campaign in a very long time," he said. "I feel good about what we've been fighting for. I'm very happy with our campaign. We have been very steady in defining the issues, and very good at staying on message. I didn't have to say that to anyone on our team. It just showed."

Has it ever. Charest has breezed through the month-long campaign like the natural he is. In his early days in federal politics in his 20s, he was known as "the Kid." Now, at 50, concluding what might well be his last campaign, the Kid is back. His speeches have been sharp, his meetings have been well attended, and the renowned Big Red Machine has put on a near flawless tour. The fact that the campaign has been uneventful, boring as the rain, has also worked for Charest.

His ballot question is simple – the economy, and who should run it in a crisis. He began from several advantages, all of which have been reinforced by the way the campaign has played out. First, on the question of best premier, Charest leads by a wide margin over Pauline Marois and Dumont. He also enjoys a huge lead on questions like which leader is the most competent, has the best character, and the best vision for Quebec. Then there is the Liberal brand. The Liberals have unique brand equity with voters as managers of the economy, particularly in the coming storm. They are also seen as having the best team, and the best platform

Quebecers didn't want this election – three voters in four were annoyed at Charest for calling it. Unless he forced his preferred ballot question, it could very easily have got away from him. It could have become about waiting times in the health-care system. Both Marois and Dumont tried very hard to make it about the losses of the Caisse de dépôt since the stock market crashed in September. Dumont tried to revive the identity issue, which worked so well for him on reasonable accommodation last year, around the teaching of religious ethics and cultural courses rather than religion in Quebec schools. A negation of Québécois values, he said. This time, there were no buyers, only buyers' remorse from the last time.

"Imagine," Charest scoffs at the thought of making a campaign about "whether we'll allow Christmas trees in schools."

Only at the leaders' debate did Charest underperform relative to inflated expectations, while both Marois and Dumont exceeded theirs. Marois proved surprisingly engaged, while Dumont had the best manners, the only one at the table not interrupting or shouting to make himself heard. For a brief moment, he reminded voters that they had liked him well enough as a suitor for their daughter, though not as someone to run the family business in a downturn. For the only time in the campaign, Charest went off message – keep smiling, be premier. The debater and the Irish in him got the better of him. He was too hot. But there were no defining moments in the debate, and three days later, it was barely a memory.

The tumultuous events of the last week in Ottawa worked at first in Charest's favour. First of all, the crisis in Parliament knocked the provincial campaign completely off the front page, and practically out of the first section of the papers. Whatever closing arguments Marois and Dumont were making, no one was hearing them over the noise from Ottawa.

And then the chaos swirling in Ottawa's minority House – so soon after an election and in the face of the economic crisis – only reinforced Charest's message about the dangers of having "three hands on the wheel."

"What's been going on in Ottawa," says Charest, "is reason enough for Quebecers to ask themselves, if this is what they get with minority government, then they don't want it."

Charest should enjoy his moment of history. Not only is he about to make it, but he has earned it.

December 2008

9

PAUL MARTIN

LEARNING TO BE PM

One of the lessons Paul Martin has undoubtedly learned during his first days in office is that a prime minister is not supposed to think out loud.

When the prime minister speaks, he's not just making noise, he's making policy.

So when the PM suggests parliamentary review of Senate appointments, the abolition of mandatory retirement and the legalization of marijuana, as he did in a series of year-end interviews, that's news.

Opposition spokespeople speak. Commentators comment. Professors profess. Interest groups look after their interests. Bureaucrats write memos, like the one the PM would have received from the Privy Council Office, titled Separation of Powers 101.

While it might have been a nice thought in terms of redressing the democratic deficit to have MPs review appointments of senators, it was clearly unconstitutional, as Martin acknowledged when he took it back. "In terms of the Senate," he recanted, "the advice I have received is that one house should not review another house of Parliament. That is the advice I have accepted."

Since Martin has pledged to make Parliament relevant, indeed, central, to his government, he should know how it works.

This was completely off message: Senate appointments – and a slew of them are coming up – should be made on the basis of recognized merit rather than cronyism.

And on the larger issue of Senate reform, it wasn't much of a leadership statement on Martin's part to say he didn't favour an elected Senate, suggesting the premiers might come up with some ideas through the new Council of the Federation.

Actually, an elected Senate is constitutionally quite achievable, requiring only a consensus of Ottawa and seven provinces comprising 50 per cent of the population. It's when the discussion moves to a Triple-E Senate – elected, effective and equal, that it becomes a deal breaker in Ontario and Quebec. But absent the PM's leadership, it's a dead letter, leaving his ambitions for parliamentary reform curiously incomplete.

Martin was also thinking out loud when he said: "I don't believe in mandatory retirement" at age 65.

This might have been slightly Freudian on Martin's part, in that he's starting a new job at 65, but as this newspaper suggested in a subhead over the story, Martin's "remarks will reopen national debate."

No kidding. About half of the Canadian workforce is required to retire at 65, while mandatory retirement is barred in the federal civil service and several provinces, including Quebec.

Trade unions tend to be in favour of compulsory retirement, in that it opens up jobs for young people entering the workforce.

Human rights activists have another view, that compulsory retirement is discriminatory. The Supreme Court has a view, that is an acceptable limitation of freedom under the Charter of Rights. There are even implications for the administration of the Canada Pension Plan.

There's nothing wrong with the PM proposing the abolition of mandatory retirement, but the place for him to do it is in the Speech from the Throne, where it can be properly backgrounded and backstopped by the bureaucracy.

Martin has also announced he plans to revive a bill decriminalizing marijuana possession. Where the allowable quantity was to have been 15 grams or less in the bill that died on the order paper at the end of the last session, Martin is asking a parliamentary committee to review the amount permissible to avoid criminal charges. Talk about empowering MPs and erasing the democratic deficit.

Who has views on this? Well, the cops, for starters. Most Conservatives and some members of Martin's own Liberal caucus. Not to mention the Americans, even though simple marijuana possession has been similarly decriminalized in a number of states, including California and New York.

In his first week in office, Martin had an message of change. In his second week, he has been all over the place, looking unfocused, undisciplined and even uninformed.

It's all a function of his talking too much. Sometimes the best way for a prime minister to exercise power is to simply shut up.

December 2003

"MAD AS HELL"

Paul Martin will long remember the month of February 2004, which couldn't have ended a day too soon for him. And it wasn't Leap Year Day that made the Martin Liberals wonder if their month from hell would never end.

Martin must have wished he'd allowed Jean Chrétien to stick to his original departure timetable of February. If the House had not prorogued, the auditor-general's report, which must be tabled while Parliament is sitting rather than simply be released, would have come out on Chrétien's watch.

Chrétien would have stonewalled it, saying that while mistakes were made in the sponsorship program, it was born of the best intentions, to show the flag for Canada, the greatest country in the world. And that might have been the end of it.

Chrétien received the AG's report within a week of the Liberal leadership convention in November. Martin also had to be aware of its contents – if the report wasn't among the transition documents, someone missed something very important.

In their rush to take power, the Martinites forgot to beware of what they wished for. And since they got there, for all the time they had to think about it, they have looked strangely unprepared to govern.

And here's the thing – they weren't. There is simply no school for running the Prime Minister's Office, not even the Department of Finance, which Martin ran for nine years. While Finance is a power centre, it is not a crisis-management centre. The PMO has a crisis every day.

Then, Martin could have benefited from a tougher opposition over the last decade, and a more competitive leadership race. He has never really been tested until now.

So there was Martin, cruising into the corner with his head down, when he met the equivalent of Gordie Howe with his elbows up. Welcome to the NHL.

There is something else that's changed about this session of Parliament. For the first time, the opposition Conservatives can put more than one good line on the ice. A critical mass of talent has kicked in on their front bench since the merger of the Canadian Alliance and the Progressive Conservatives. Finally, they look like the gang that can shoot straight.

Martin's strategy of being "mad as hell" about the whole mess, and then getting back on his agenda message track, is extremely high risk. Most voters, while commending his courage in taking the brunt of their wrath, simply don't believe he knew nothing about it. He explains it as a machinery-of-government issue – the finance minister doesn't sign cheques, the Treasury Board does. Right. You mean, you balanced the budget but didn't know what was in it.

His appointment of an inquiry, unlimited in scope, in addition to a parliamentary committee, is a highly principled response. But it is a highly dangerous one. No one knows how the inquiry will run, including whether it will sit during an election campaign. No one knows where it will go, much less how it will come out.

Martin survived his month from hell in February but the Ides of March are still to come.

March 2004

NO WAIT TIMES

The story was just a little one-column item buried at the bottom of Page A12 of *The Gazette*. But it had a bullet. It disclosed that Prime Minister Paul Martin's family doctor, Sheldon Elman, runs a string of private health-care clinics, the Medisys Health Group.

There's no doubt that Medisys is a private health provider. Last year it was a $53-million business. The company is traded on the Toronto Stock Exchange. Its clients for executive health care are a virtual who's-who of corporate Canada. It's a very good business, built by a visionary founder, and it might be an excellent model for the private delivery of publicly-funded health care.

Which is the whole point about Martin receiving treatment there. He is prime minister. He wants to campaign on a new ten-year plan to renew public health care. He accuses Conservative leader Stephen Harper of having a hidden agenda for two-tier health care. He has rebuked his own health minister, Pierre Pettigrew, for even suggesting there might be flexibility in the delivery of health care.

Yet Martin himself receives treatment at a private clinic which, to be fair, is publicly accessible.

As noted, Page A12 with a bullet.

"I do not belong to an executive health plan," Martin declared at a news conference, insisting he uses his *carte du soleil* like everyone else. He acknowledged he receives the same benefits all MPs do from their medical coverage, and some additional benefits "as a pensioner from my previous employer." That would be Canada Steamship Lines which, uh, he actually owned.

Martin's statement was made in Chicoutimi just after all hell had broken loose in the House of Commons. Deputy Prime Minister Anne McLellan spent most of question period on her feet staunchly defending Martin from the accusation he was receiving private health care.

"The prime minister obtains his health care the same way we all do," she insisted over and over again.

Right. Medisys is just like the local CLSC. Just walk and ask for an MRI.

Harper was having none of it.

"How does the prime minister justify a clinic he claims his government doesn't support?" Harper asked.

He's definitely got a point. This is the prime minister who, just two weeks ago, denounced the nameless proponents of "chequebook health care." This prime minister poses as the defender of public health care when, as finance minister in 1995, he gutted it.

Leaving aside Martin's hypocrisy, or perhaps making generous allowances for it, the disclosure of his privately provided health care should encourage a timely debate about the reform of public health-care delivery.

If private service providers can deliver publicly-funded health care, what's wrong with that?

It's at the heart of the debate between Roy Romanow on the one hand, and Michael Kirby on the other, authors of two clashing visions of health care. Romanow, in his royal commission on health care, recommended bringing private providers into the public system. Kirby, chairman of a unanimous Senate committee report, recommended a single payer, the government, but didn't much care who provided the service.

Evaluating the two reports last year in a paper for the Institute for Research on Public Policy, economist Tom Courchene noted Romanow saw medicare "as a moral enterprise, not as a business venture."

But why can't it be both, universally accessible and publicly funded, but privately provided? Is it possible that the health-care industry, like any other, might benefit from competition and the profit motive? Or perhaps pharmaceutical companies are not in business to provide cures for customers and profits for themselves.

Health care is a $100-billion industry in Canada, but only about 30 per cent of it is provided in hospitals. The rest is spent on everything from nursing homes to clinics.

Everyone knows the system is broke, and needs fixing. Everyone has a story about waiting lists for essential treatments. Once proud of their public health-care system, Canadians know it is no longer among the best in the world.

April 2004

∽

MR. DITHERS

The Martin government is by definition the weakest since the last minority under Joe Clark in 1979. But with last week's unravelling over continental missile defence, this is now the worst government since the Diefenbaker minority in 1963.

There are striking parallels between then and now. Then, as now, the issue was missiles, whether Canada would accept Bomarcs armed with nuclear weapons on our soil under NORAD. Then, as now, the question was whether Canada would keep its word to the United States. Then, as now, the prime minister's utter absence of leadership and complete mismanagement of the issue were alone responsible for an incredible mess.

John Diefenbaker said no to John F. Kennedy, breaking Canada's commitment to accept the Bomarcs. Dief's dithering fractured his cabinet, split his caucus and resulted in the downfall of his government.

Paul Martin has now said no to North American missile defence, breaking his own word. The consequences for the Martin government are unclear, but the repercussions for Canada-U.S. relations are certain. Canada just fell off the radar screen in Washington. We have also ceded sovereignty over our own space to a foreign power. And whenever there's a discussion of missile defence at NORAD headquarters, Canadian officers will be asked to leave the room.

As in 1963, it's completely the prime minister's fault. Now, as then, a major rupture in bilateral relations was completely preventable.

On November 15, 2003, the day he assumed the leadership of the Liberal Party, Martin said: "It's pretty clear that if you're talking about the defence of North America, Canada has to be at the table."

The next step for Martin would have been to announce at his press conference of December 12, 2003, the day he took office as prime minister, that he had just got off the phone with President George W. Bush, and informed him of Canada's decision to participate in North American missile defence. Or not, had that been the case. And that would have been the end of it.

Instead, missile defence has been the making of Mr. Dithers. In Washington last April, he publicly lectured the president of the United States, saying "I told him the weaponization of space is not on." It isn't. The system will be land-based in California and Alaska. In August, Ottawa signed a memorandum of understanding with the U.S. for the system to be operationally based at NORAD headquarters in Colorado.

In the meantime, opposition to Canada's participation multiplied, not just with the Bloc Québécois and the NDP, which has promoted public hysteria by calling it Star Wars, but within the Liberal Party itself, particularly its Quebec and youth wings. The youth were bringing a resolution opposing missile defence to the floor of this weekend's national Liberal policy convention, and Martin's announcement was a pre-emptive takeout. The resolution was expected to carry easily. The youth wing of the Liberal Party is running the Prime Minister's Office.

In 1963, Lester B. Pearson unilaterally reversed a resolution of the national Liberal federation opposing the acceptance of nuclear weapons, and used his position to bring down Diefenbaker's minority government.

In 1983, Pierre Trudeau, who twenty years earlier had denounced Pearson as the defrocked prince of peace, accepted U.S. cruise-missile testing in Alberta. Demonstrations in the streets were notably absent.

In 1985, Brian Mulroney called his caucus together in the Centre Block on a Saturday morning, and informed them that Canada would not join Ronald Reagan's cherished Strategic Defence Initiative, known as Star Wars.

He then went upstairs to his office and called President Reagan at Camp David.

"Ron," Mulroney began, "I'm sorry to say we can't be with you on a big project, but Canada will not be joining in SDI. It's not in our interest, though it may well be in yours as the leader of the free world. I wanted to tell you, Ron, personally, before you read about it."

"Brian," Reagan replied, "I'm very sorry to hear that, but I appreciate you informing me yourself."

That was the end of it. There were no divisions in the governing party; the policy was determined by its leader. The caucus was informed, not consulted. There was no debate in the House. And there was no harm done to Canada-U.S. relations.

Consider, by contrast, the duplicitous and craven manner in which Martin took his decision. He was with George W. Bush at the NATO summit in

Brussels, but did not have the simple courtesy to inform the president of the United States of Canada's decision. Instead, it was conveyed by Foreign Affairs Minister Pierre Pettigrew to U.S. Secretary of State Condoleezza Rice. The Americans were informed, two days before the issue was announced in the House. The Americans were told before we were. How's that for an abdication of our political sovereignty?

And as he made the announcement, Martin had still not spoken to Bush.

There's only one word to describe this kind of leadership – spineless.

February 2005

OTTAWA DOWNGRADED

In a politically charged research note, Canaccord Capital Corporation noted the "income-trust sector lost $23 billion over the past month, largely due to fear and uncertainty caused by the federal government." It called the meltdown in market valuations "morally indefensible," and said Ottawa was accountable for "the intentional or unintentional destruction of the income trust market" which "does not need to happen."

In market terms, Ottawa got downgraded.

It isn't every day that a brokerage firm takes on Ottawa, and the minister of finance. And the normally unflappable Ralph Goodale, clearly feeling the heat on income trusts, responded with an uncharacteristic attack on the firm's integrity.

"This particular firm has chosen to take a very political, a very partisan approach," he said. Conservative MP John Reynolds had called the note to Goodale's attention and his son, Paul Reynolds, is a senior executive of Canaccord. So, Goodale suggested, "consider the source."

This is getting ugly. But it was very predictable. When Ottawa took billions of dollars out of taxpayers' pockets, to save a few hundred million for its own, it ran the risk of an investor revolt. Ottawa just didn't see it coming, because it was thinking about Bay Street, and took its eye off Main Street.

From September 19, when Ottawa suspended tax rulings on income trust conversions, market valuations for the trust sector shrank from $173.8 billion to $150.5 billion, a loss of $23.3 billion, or a correction of 13.4 per cent.

The conclusion that it's all Ottawa's fault is undoubtedly overstated. October was a bad month in the market. The price of oil retreated significantly, and the income-trust segment is heavily weighted in oil and gas trusts, which declined in value from $75.3 billion to $65.9 billion.

But the sell-off began immediately after Ottawa announced it was suspending tax rulings on corporations converting to income trusts, whose high yield monthly dividends to unit holders have increased market valuations by a factor of 10 since 2000. Ottawa's concern was that the rush to income trusts structures was depriving it of $300 million in corporate tax dollars, even though payments to unit holders are taxable as other income.

This is quite extraordinary. Ottawa is sitting on such a big surplus it could afford to bribe the NDP with $4.6 billion last spring to prop up the Martin government. But it was so concerned about a paltry $300 million that it was prepared to chill the hottest segment of the TSX.

Why have investors in general, and seniors in particular, been moving into income trusts? Because they are considered a safe investment, with a high yield.

"As income trusts offer one of the highest sources of sustainable recurring cash yield in Canadian equity and fixed income markets," writes Canaccord analyst Chris Rankin," it's no surprise that trusts are so popular and they are the preferred investment vehicle for many Canadian retirees (or soon to be retirees)."

Do you think they're talking about this down at the bingo hall, Mr. Goodale? Actually, they're putting on their running shoes, to go vote against you.

October 2005

10

STEPHEN HARPER

A BOY NAMED STEVE

For a better understanding of Stephen Harper, and his idea of the country, it helps to come to his adopted home town of Calgary as the prime minister did for five days during the Calgary Stampede. This is his town. He is their guy.

Harper flew in directly from his White House visit, where a guy named George called him Steve, and flew out nearly a week later for tea with the Queen, who would never dream of calling him anything other than Prime Minister.

At Harper's annual Stampede barbecue, nearly 1,000 people crowded into a lawn tent that had more the air of a victory party in which a favourite son had come home a prime minister. Calgary minister Jim Prentice presented Harper with a Stampede belt engraved "Stephen J. Harper, Prime Minister of Canada."

"You see that, Mother? It says Stephen, not Steve," Harper said.

Then: "If the guy wants to buy 85 per cent of our exports and call me Steve, that's OK with me."

The hometown crowd roared with approving laughter.

What a difference, as Prentice and others noted, a year makes.

Only a year ago at the Stampede, Harper's handlers dressed him in a ridiculous black cowboy outfit that made him look like the bad guy in an old Hopalong Cassidy movie. Worst of all, he had his hat on backward.

Last year, his riding association had a hard time selling 300 tickets; this year, 950 tickets were sold out weeks ago.

Last year, he was in a foul mood after narrowly failing to defeat the Liberal government because of Belinda Stronach's defection to the Liberals. In retrospect, Stronach did Harper a favour, giving him another six months to lose the angry-man image.

This year, a new prime minister made a home swing between visits to the President of the United States and the Queen, on his way to the G8 in Russia.

Harper's five-day sojourn to Calgary has probably quelled a rising chorus of complaints that he has been neglecting his base while pursuing his charm offensive in Quebec.

It has not gone unnoticed in Alberta, any more than in Quebec, that Harper reads all his opening statements entirely in French first. Fine, but three minutes at the White House?

Harper might have been born and raised in suburban Toronto, but his sense of the country, and his idea of the federation, were clearly influenced by events, mentors and friends in the West.

When he first moved to Calgary in 1984, the Alberta economy was devastated by the Trudeau government's confiscatory National Energy Program. Nearly a quarter century later, the NEP remains the hated symbol of federal intrusion into provincial jurisdiction, in this case ownership and management of natural resources.

Harper's idea of federalism, and his idea of the federation, would have been influenced by that. Thus, open federalism, and his pledge in his Quebec City campaign speech to respect the division of powers in the constitution, and his promise not to use the federal spending power for new programs in provincial jurisdiction without the support of a majority of provinces.

If he can keep these two promises, he might buy a generation of constitutional peace, simply by vowing to respect the constitution. He may also create a new Quebec-Alberta alliance such as hasn't been seen since the Mulroney years.

Harper has come to office at a time when economic as well as political power is moving West, away from Quebec and Ontario, to Alberta and British Columbia. Consider: Of the 216,000 new jobs created in the first half of the year, 69,000 were in Alberta. Stated another way, one-third of the new jobs in the country were in a province that has only one-tenth of the population.

The West is more than in; the West is where it's at.

July 2006

A MAJESTIC MOMENT

It was a majestic moment in Parliament when Stephen Harper crossed the floor to shake hands with Bill Graham after the Liberal leader's statement endorsing the prime minister's motion to recognize Quebecers as a nation within Canada. For his part, Graham had led the Liberals in a standing ovation for Harper.

Note the wording of the motion, that the House recognizes Quebecers as a nation, not Quebec as a nation. There is a very big difference between the two.

Quebecers constitute a nation in the sense that Acadians do, or the Cree among other aboriginal peoples, that is to say as a people with their own language, culture, history and territory. In other words, Quebecers are a nation in what Stéphane Dion has called the sociological sense.

Quebec as a nation is an entirely different matter and this is what Gilles Duceppe was proposing when he served notice that the Bloc Québécois would use an opposition day to bring a resolution to the House recognizing "the Quebec nation."

There being no coincidences in politics, the timing of Duceppe's gambit was obvious. He aimed to embarrass the Liberals further on an issue that has left them badly divided going into their leadership convention next week, while getting the Conservatives on the same hook.

But in a lightning play, Harper completely outmanoeuvred Duceppe, with a resolution that all federalist parties endorsed, leaving the Bloc isolated and Duceppe visibly annoyed, his eyes bulging with anger.

Quite simply, he was outsmarted by Harper. The Liberals jumped at the resolution because it solves a problem that threatened to blow up their convention. Graham had summoned all eight leadership candidates to a meeting to push for a compromise on the resolution sent to the convention by the wing of the party calling for recognition of Quebec as a nation. Problem solved.

Harper's play neatly trumped the Bloc resolution, while sidestepping the trap of the Quebec nation. What was most striking was the speed with which Harper moved. Within twelve hours of receiving word of the Bloc resolution, Harper was standing before his national caucus proposing, and explaining, one of his own. There wasn't a dissenting voice, and this in the party of John Diefenbaker's One Canada and Preston Manning's western Reform movement. The caucus gave him a standing ovation.

Over the lunch hour, Harper worked with Graham on wording that would be acceptable to the Liberals. Harper then set to work writing his two-page statement to the House himself.

While Harper was giving up short-term political advantage of enjoying the Liberals' anguished division on this issue, he was bidding to gain a greater advantage over the longer term – as a prime minister with a sense of history and a generous sense of country. Graham's statement was equally eloquent, even emotional, in his declaration that questions of country are more important than partisan divisions. He didn't mention his relief. He didn't have to. It was plain on his face.

There was such a moment in the life of the House on the Manitoba minority-language rights issue in September 1983. The Liberals set a trap for the new Conservative leader, Brian Mulroney, by proposing a motion recognizing French-language minority-language rights in Manitoba, an issue that threatened to tear the Tory caucus apart. Instead, Mulroney rallied them to support the motion, and used the occasion of his maiden address to the House to forever bury the ghosts of Conservative intolerance on the language issue. Pierre Trudeau was equally magnificent in the House that day.

Similarly, Harper seized an opportunity to offer a strong sense of history and a generous definition of Quebecers' role in Confederation, but clearly within the boundaries of a federal state.

"In landing in Quebec City," he said, "Champlain didn't say this isn't going to work, it's too far, it's too cold, it's too hard. No. Champlain and his companions worked hard because they believed in what they were doing and because they wanted to preserve their values, and they wanted a safe and longstanding country. That's precisely what happened almost 400 years later. The foundation of the Canadian state. Mr. Speaker, Quebecers know who they are. They know they've participated in the foundation, the founding of Canada in its development and in its greatness. They know that they've protected their language and unique culture, but they've also promoted their values and interests within Canada.

"The real question is straightforward. Do Quebecers form a nation within a united Canada? The answer is yes. Do Quebecers form an independent nation from Canada? The answer is no, and it will always be no."

Anytime a prime minister gets to make a vision of Canada speech, that's a good day for him. Any time the opportunity is handed to him by the leader of the Bloc, that's an even better day for the country.

November 2006

THE NIXON IN CHINA THING

It's the Nixon in China thing. It took a prime minister from Alberta to win recognition of Quebecers as a nation within Canada. A prime minister from Quebec could never have sold it in Ontario and, especially, the West.

"This," Stephen Harper was saying in Montreal, "is simply a declaration of recognition and a gesture of reconciliation."

It is "a symbolic gesture," as he said, which confers no additional powers or special status on Quebec, recognizing Quebecers as a nation within a united Canada. But while it is only symbolic, it is also deeply symbolic. Canadian unity, the very fabric of the country, is full of symbols. Symbols are the stuff of legend and icons and national mythology. And in Quebec, nothing is more symbolically important than this.

After the motion is adopted unanimously by all four parties in the House, it will be a time for healing of painful wounds from the death of Meech Lake in 1990 and, previously, the patriation of the Constitution without Quebec's assent in 1982.

In the rest of the country, Harper will have some explaining to do that this merely means recognition of Quebecers as a nation in the sociological sense as proposed by Stéphane Dion. "It's not a constitutional amendment," Harper said. "It's not a legal text. It's simply a declaration of recognition and a gesture of reconciliation. And I think it's important to recognize the reality. I know it's not easy for everyone in the rest of Canada, but I think when we talk about a nation, Quebecers are a group of people with an identity, a history, a language, a culture and the meaning of that in the vocabulary is a nation."

As he was explaining these things in French, a mostly English-speaking audience of health-care professionals broke spontaneously into applause.

Harper was at the Montreal General Hospital of the McGill University Health Centre, announcing the $260-million Canadian Partnership Against Cancer, an organization that will be run by stakeholders at arms-length from the government and the bureaucracy of Health Canada. But when it came to the Q&A, first in French and then in English, journalists went straight to the nation thing.

Harper was quite prepared to go there. Clearly he had thought about it a lot in the last few days, as he had thought about it several times since he was asked the Quebec-nation question in Quebec City on St. Jean Baptiste weekend and said he wasn't too concerned with questions of semantics.

Clearly not satisfied with his own answer, he said last month that Quebec was "an indispensable part of Canada," which means exactly the same thing in French as it does in English, saying all that needed to be said.

But then last Tuesday, when the Bloc Québécois served notice of a motion declaring Quebecers a nation – a motion calculated to sow even more disarray among Liberals at their convention in Montreal this week – Harper saw an opportunity and seized the moment. He countered with one of his own, affirming Quebecers as a nation within a united Canada.

The Liberals, at risk of being torn apart on the Quebec-nation question on the floor of a convention being held in Quebec, grabbed it like a life raft. The NDP and Jack Layton also went along with it, leaving the Bloc isolated in the House on a question they raised in the House. By Friday morning, unable to explain himself to his own voters, Gilles Duceppe announced that the Bloc would also be supporting the government motion of Quebecers comprising a nation, "within a united Canada."

"That's interesting," Harper said. "That's the third position of the Bloc in three days. First they proposed a motion. Then they made an amendment to their motion, and now they're supporting our motion, but I must say that my first responsibility as prime minister of Canada, my first responsibility is Canadian unity. If I can have the support of even the Bloc, I'm happy."

"Leadership," Brian Mulroney was saying the other day, "is the capacity to transform a challenge into an opportunity. And that's what he did."

All on his own.

November 2006

∞

CHESS, NOT CHECKERS

It's been said of Stephen Harper that he plays chess, while others play checkers.

It's very much a chess move that Harper is making, as the government introduces a binding resolution on the Afghanistan mission in the House. Nobody wants the government to fall over Afghanistan, least of all the Liberals. Which may leave them with no alternative but to bring the government down over the budget.

It's simple. The budget vote will probably come the first week of March. The Afghan motion won't come to a vote until the end of March. Because a vote on the Afghan mission would be a disaster for the Liberals no matter which way they swing (for reasons explained below), Harper is effectively making Dion force an election through other means.

How did Stéphane Dion get himself in this situation? Because he was playing checkers on Afghanistan. He's announced that he has only one possible move: Canada's "combat role" in Afghanistan must end a year from now in February, 2009.

But there's something called the Manley report, offered by a former deputy prime minister of Dion's own party, a classic Canadian compromise: Either NATO steps up and does some burden-sharing in Kandahar, or we're outta there next February. There's enough cover for Dion in that – or should be, at least.

When Dion met with Harper for about twenty-five minutes, he had a chance to buy into the Manley report. Harper handed Dion a copy of the resolution that will be tabled in the House, invited his comments and said he would entertain any improvements to the language.

Harper's understanding of the way they had left it was that Dion would get back to him the next day. Harper's office says he never heard back from Dion. After consulting his caucus Wednesday morning, Dion said he would be offering his own amendments to the government motion.

That's a different role. Harper was inviting him to be part of a welcome consensus. Dion has chosen a path that leads to an unwanted confrontation in Parliament, one that can now be avoided only by using the budget vote as a pre-emptive takeout.

And what if, in the meantime, Defence Minister Peter MacKay returns from a NATO ministers meeting with the assurance that the alliance is prepared to step up with the Kandahar reinforcements Canada is seeking? If that essential Manley-specified condition is met by our allies, how could the Liberals be out of step with that?

And what was Dion thinking when he agreed to a meeting with NDP leader Jack Layton, before meeting the prime minister on Tuesday? Did Dion think that he could persuade the NDP that Canadian troops should remain in Afghanistan in a non-combatant role? (Layton's position has long been that he will "support our troops by bringing them home.")

And what are Dion's terms for remaining in Afghanistan past next February? "You need to be prepared to fight," Dion said, "but the combat role is when you are pro-actively seeking the engagement with the enemy. It's something I have said we will interrupt in February, 2009." In essence, Dion is trying to modify his position, while sticking to it. He is describing rules of engagement that would tie the hands of commanders in the field.

What's worse, the Liberal caucus is itself divided. Many Liberal MPs are of a mind with the NDP, as if there were room for the Liberals on the left. And then there are those leading Liberals, like Michael Ignatieff and Bob Rae, who don't want to be accused of abandoning Afghanistan, to say nothing of our troops.

So rather than go to the polls on Afghanistan, it is the easier course for the Liberals to defeat the government on the budget. That's what happens when one man is playing chess, and the other one is shuffling around his checkers.

February 2008

∞

HARPER'S SELF-INFLICTED WOUND

Proroguing the House is the safer course for Stephen Harper, and the easier one for Michaëlle Jean. Which is why the first session of this Parliament will probably end as soon as today, pre-empting the non-confidence vote on the economic update scheduled for next Monday, when the minority government would be certain to fall.

By proroguing, the prime minister survives for at least another few months. He gets a cooling-off period, gets to regroup and present a new throne speech with a budget at the end of January 2009. The dangerous part for Harper is that by losing a vote next Monday, the governor-general might decline his request for an election writ and invite the Three Stooges coalition – the Liberals and NDP, propped up by the Bloc – to form a government.

Harper is already permanently damaged by this self-inflicted wound, but if he allowed the ouster of his government he would be finished as leader of the Conservative Party, which is incensed from the grassroots to the cabinet level at his reckless brinkmanship.

The easier course for the GG is that no one in her role has ever refused a prime minister's request to prorogue the House, but one has refused a request for a dissolution, Viscount Byng in 1926. One precedent weighs in favour of prorogation, the other argues against dissolution so soon after an election, especially since the three parties have answered the only question the GG must consider – the confidence of the House.

One constitutional convention points to Jean refusing Harper's request for an election, and inviting the opposition parties to form a Liberal-NDP government, propped up by the Bloc Québécois. While in any banana republic, this would be a coup, in Canada it is perfectly within the bounds of constitutional custom. But the constitutional convention around prorogation weighs heavily in Harper's favour.

Quite apart from precedent, which is in and of itself a compelling reason for the GG to sign on to proroguing the House, it is entirely clear in the

Westminster tradition that the prime minister alone determines the agenda and timetable of the government in Parliament. This is his prerogative and his alone. Period.

Then there is a further precedent of a quick end to a session after an election, and a recent one at that. In 1988, after the free trade election, Brian Mulroney recalled the House with a one-page throne speech to enact enabling legislation for the Canada-U.S. Free Trade Agreement. The session was prorogued after only ten days.

Of course, Mulroney enjoyed the confidence of the House with a majority government, as Harper clearly does not in a minority House. The opposition can also argue that Harper is avoiding a confidence vote, and that the GG should thus decline his request. He can say he is merely rescheduling, as is his right in determining the agenda. As in baseball, a tie goes to the runner.

And in the unlikely event Jean were to decline the easier course, she will be faced with the harder one on the morrow of the confidence vote. So, to switch metaphors from baseball to football, Harper will punt, and she will kick it right back to him.

Problem solved? Crisis over? Not exactly. Not for Harper, who will never again have a stranglehold over the House or his own party. The schoolyard bully has been called out, and no one will ever be afraid of him again. Well, maybe in his own entourage, but that's his problem – he is surrounded by sycophants and right wing ideologues in the Prime Minister's Office, a place desperately in need of adult supervision. If they had a shred of honour, after this unprecedented disaster, they would all resign. That starts with his chief of staff, Guy Giorno. The first rule is to protect the king. The staff's job is to take the bullet.

But before any heads roll in the PMO, Harper should have a good look in the mirror. The problem is within himself. He is usually the smartest guy in the room, but sometimes he can be all tactics, which brings out the worst in him. Giorno, a hard-core partisan from the Mike Harris era at Queen's Park, only reinforces Harper's worst instincts. There is no one around Harper to stand up to him, no one to say, "Sir, that's a very bad idea."

Ending party financing as part of the economic statement was one very bad idea in a minority House. Harper put the opposition parties up against the wall at gunpoint, and stole their money. Of course they want to take him down. Banning the right to strike in the public sector for three years, when trade unions are core constituencies for the NDP and the Bloc Québécois, was another bad idea.

Where did these really stupid ideas come from? From Harper and the PMO, which ordered them into the economic update last Wednesday, without consulting cabinet or caucus. It's a total breakdown of cabinet government and breach of party solidarity, with the disastrous consequences that have rained down on Harper since last weekend.

It is not enough for Harper to roll on this, he needs to recant. In the event he makes a TV address to the nation to explain this mess of his own creation, he should express the hope that cooler heads prevail over the holidays, and that everyone can learn from this, beginning with himself.

As for the opposition parties, they have serious problems of their own. Stéphane Dion, Jack Layton and Gilles Duceppe made a big mistake in staging a formal signing of their coalition pact on Monday. In comedic terms, they looked, as colleague Greg Weston observed, like the Three Stooges. In political terms, they looked like the coup plotters in Moscow in August 1991. The Liberals and the NDP are both taking a terrible risk in climbing into bed with the separatists.

And Dion has another problem. His reappearance on the scene as the putative prime minister after Canadians thought they had got rid of him has only reminded voters of why they were glad to see the back of him.

In the House, he was emotionally unhinged, practically spitting his questions across the floor. Clearly, the man is temperamentally unfit to be prime minister. If nothing else, proroguing will save the country such an unwanted and dangerous outcome.

December 2008

A LEADER IN TROUBLE

A good leader knows when he's in trouble. And Stephen Harper, as he turns 50, is in deep trouble. He's in trouble in the country, especially in Quebec; in trouble with the public service, which is putting down tools with his government; and increasingly in trouble with the Conservative Party, whose fault lines are cracking under the divisive and mean-spirited management style of the Prime Minister's Office.

But Harper is apparently oblivious to how much trouble he's in, because there's no one, other than Laureen Harper, who can tell him. He is a leader without confidants and without mentors. There is no one to tell him what he needs to hear, as opposed to what he wants to hear, not in the cabinet, not in the caucus, and certainly not in his own office.

There is no one to bell the cat.

In 1987, the Conservative Party sent two emissaries to see Brian Mulroney privately at Harrington Lake. Peter Lougheed and Bill Davis, who had retired undefeated as four-term premiers of Alberta and Ontario, had unique standing to carry a message to the prime minister. They told Mulroney, then polling in the low 20s, that unless he made major changes to his office, he was headed for certain defeat at the next election.

And that is precisely where Harper stands now.

Mulroney listened to the party elders, and made the changes that eventually reversed his slide in public opinion. His closest advisers were all shunted aside and eventually left. This was an extremely painful decision for Mulroney, because as he often said, "you dance with the one you came with." Loyalty was big part of Mulroney's makeup, and it cut him to the quick to let his friends leave. But at a higher level, he also understood that a prime minister has no friends, only interests to defend, beginning with a party in government.

Harper doesn't put a lot of store in loyalty. He is motivated, his close friends say, by a sense of duty, and expects the same in those who work for him. At the end of the day, he doesn't reward service, especially by his friends, and his loyalty deficit has not gone unnoticed in the party, from the rank and file to cabinet rank.

Here's the thing: Michael Ignatieff is capable of inspiring Harper to take his game to a higher level, but the prime minister can't get there with the people he's got around him now. If he doesn't shake up his office, and soon, Harper is going to lose to Ignatieff. He may lose anyway, especially in this economy, but unless he makes changes to his office, he's going to lose for sure.

It begins with his chief of staff, Guy Giorno, who in less than a year has alienated the key central agencies of Privy Council, Foreign Affairs and Finance; annoyed the entire public service; offended the Ottawa political class of lawyers, consultants and lobbyists; re-opened old cleavages between the Reform-Alliance and Progressive Conservative wings of the party; and to all appearances, written off Quebec.

Well, you can win elections without Quebec, especially in a four-party House, but you can't govern the country without Quebec. And you can't run the country if the second floor of the Langevin Block, PMO, isn't talking to the third floor, PCO, the prime minister's own department. The other key central agencies, Finance and Foreign Affairs, are often on different pages than PMO, as Finance was last November when PMO ordered the disastrous items into the economic update that nearly blew up Parliament.

Giorno arrived in Ottawa last June, known only as the last chief of staff to Mike Harris at Queen's Park. By then the Common Sense Revolution had run out of steam, Harris having left at mid-mandate in 2001. Harris was known as a big picture leader, but the people around him were known as "the little shits." Many of those same people are now running Ottawa, and they are proving that they can't play the game at this level.

"They haven't been tested yet," Harper said of his new staff during a private chat in mid-August last year.

Well, they have been since then. In the campaign, the Conservatives lost their majority by being totally tone deaf on Quebec. Then, in the parliamentary crisis last December, Harper's staff approved his polarizing address to the nation, attacking "the separatist coalition" in English. The PMO recouped with a successful budget in January and a well managed visit by Barack Obama in February, but dug another hole in March by suggesting Mulroney was no longer a member of the party. It was cheesy, cheap and utterly lacking in class, not to mention incredibly stupid.

In a larger sense, there is no real sense of public policy or public purpose coming from this government. It's all tactics and wedge politics. There are no big ideas, and no compelling agenda. That's a leadership issue, and it goes to the prime minister and his office.

Harper tends to take criticism of his staff personally, yet paradoxically he is known for learning from his mistakes. On this milestone of a birthday, he needs to give himself a shake.

April 2009

11

STÉPHANE DION

In a way, Stéphane Dion's problems began on the day and because of the manner in which he won the Liberal leadership in December 2006, coming from a distant third place to overtake frontrunners Michael Ignatieff and Bob Rae.

It meant there were two candidates ahead of him who thought they should have won. Actually, three, counting Gerard Kennedy, who would have finished third if a half-dozen of his delegates, as reported later by Joan Bryden of Canadian Press, hadn't parked with Martha Hall Findlay on the first ballot to reward her for an outstanding speech earlier on that long Friday evening at Montreal's Palais des Congrès.

It is worth reviewing the numbers of the first ballot: Ignatieff 1,412 (29.3 per cent), Rae 977 (20.3 per cent), Dion 856 (17.8 per cent), Kennedy 854 (17.7 per cent), Ken Dryden, 238 (4.9 per cent), Scott Brison 192 (4 per cent), Joe Volpe 156 (3.2 per cent) and Hall-Findlay 130 (2.7 per cent). Had those half-dozen Kennedy delegates stayed with their candidate rather than voting their symbolic approval of Findlay, Kennedy would have been four votes ahead of Dion, not two votes behind. This changed the design of the convention, creating an accidental leader.

After the first ballot, the delegates dispersed for a night of partying in Old Montreal, while the various leadership camps worked to lock in their deals for the second ballot early on Saturday morning. Already, after the first ballot, Brison and Volpe had dropped out and gone to Rae on the floor of the convention. Findlay, who had deals with both Ignatieff and Rae, showed up for Saturday morning's second ballot with Dion as a passenger on her bus. Eliminated, she was throwing her support to Dion, and that created enough separation between the third- and fourth-place candidates – two percentage points and 90 delegates – that Dion rather than Rae emerged as the stop-Iggy candidate.

As it developed, both Ignatieff and Rae stalled on the second ballot at 1,481 (31.8 per cent) and 1,132 (24.1 per cent). Ignatieff grew only two points and Rae only four points, despite two endorsements. What Rae really needed was for Dryden to drop out and go to him after the first ballot, rather than waiting until he was eliminated on the second. What Rae really didn't need was Kennedy dropping out after two ballots with 884 votes (19.8 per cent) and taking most of them over to Dion, who had 974 (20.8 per cent), creating a decisive momentum surge that allowed Dion to overtake both frontrunners on the third ballot, where Dion vaulted to first place with 37 per cent, against 34.5 per cent for Ignatieff, with Rae eliminated at 28.5 per cent. On the fourth and final ballot, Dion would win with 54.7 per cent to Ignatieff's 45.3 per cent.

The Liberals rejected the foreigner, Ignatieff, who had been out of the country for thirty years, and the stranger, Rae, who had been in another party for thirty years. Stéphane Dion became the default candidate of Liberals determined to stop one or the other, and, as it turned out, both. It was a revolt of the grassroots against the Liberal establishment.

Throughout the six months of the leadership race, Dion was never seen as a first-tier candidate, and many observers wondered why he was even in the race. He was regarded as a back-of-the-pack candidate, like Dryden and Brison, in it to make a point and a speech at the convention. And in fact, he made what was generally regarded as the worst speech of the night at the convention. Evidently, no one cared or no one was listening.

Dion was a Quebecer without much support in his own province, especially in the Liberal caucus, where his handful of supporters included MPs from anglophone and allophone-dominated ridings in the western half of Montreal. He was a former minister without a single endorsement among his former colleagues in the Chrétien and Martin cabinets, who remembered him not only for his professorial propensity for summarizing cabinet discussions, but also for his tendency to lecture them around the cabinet table on their responsibilities in their own portfolios. He was a one-issue candidate on the environment, which produced the "Dionistas," with their billowing sea of green scarves at the convention, but only set him up for a devastating Conservative attack ad within weeks of his return to the Commons.

The Tories staged a pre-emptive advertising attack on Dion's environmental credentials, quoting Ignatieff from a Liberal leadership debate, lecturing Dion: "Stéphane, we didn't get it done." The Conservatives closed the ad with the tag line: "Stéphane Dion, not a leader."

Said pollster Nik Nanos of Nanos Research: "The Conservative strategy of proactively defining Stéphane Dion from day one is one of the most effective communications strategies I've ever seen. Usually, there's a honeymoon period for a new leader. But the decision of the Conservatives to roll out the ad strategy stole the honeymoon, wrote the narrative and defined his image."

In the House, the new environment minister, John Baird, known as both a thoughtful and a highly effective partisan, taunted the Liberals and Dion for their collective and personal failure to meet the Kyoto emissions reductions targets they were advocating. Baird even made a Power-Point presentation to the House environment committee with a trend line pointing out that during the Liberals' 13 years in office, Canada's greenhouse gas emissions rose by 27 per cent above 1990 levels – a 33 per cent miss in terms of Kyoto targets of reducing them by 6 per cent below 1990 levels.

Dion obviously had a plan for breaking out of the back of the pack of the leadership race, but none for moving the party forward in the unlikely event that he won. In Montreal, the Liberal convention managers, led by national director Steve MacKinnon, did an outstanding job of staging an exciting three-day delegated convention – with tremendous excitement and suspense on the two days of speeches and balloting. But beyond that, there was no plan for organizing a policy convention for the party's intellectual renewal. There was no venue for planning and shaping policy frameworks. And, significantly, Dion overlooked the need for humility – something Liberals don't do very well – when in his acceptance speech he said the party had to get back in power as soon as possible to save the country from the Conservatives. With the Liberals barely turfed out after four consecutive terms in office, Dion was suggesting a dynastic renewal based on nothing more than the resilience of the Liberal brand, which had nothing to do with the renewal of ideas or the party's grassroots, from one generation to the next.

Furthermore, as all the defeated candidates sitting around a luncheon table with Dion on the morrow of the convention knew well, the party was broke and facing huge financial challenges arising from the leadership campaign. The candidates were limited to spending $3.4 million by party rules, a far cry from the $12 million raised and spent by Paul Martin to secure the Liberal leadership in 2003. But that was in another era, before Jean Chrétien's legacy campaign finance reform included leadership campaigns under an umbrella that prohibited corporate and union donations, and set a $5,000-a-year limit on personal donations. It was also before the Harper government's 2006 Acountability Act, which initially further reduced individual donations to $1,000 per person. The effect of these strictures was such that more than a year later, both Ignatieff and Rae were still holding fundraisers to liquidate debt from their relatively modest $2-million leadership campaigns, and Dion himself was still facing a leadership debt of $850,000, with no prospect of paying it off in the event he were to lose a general election. In 2008, not only were the leadership campaigns still paying off debts from 2006, they were competing against the party in its attempts to raise money for the next election. And the Liberals were not doing very well on that front. In 2007, the Conservatives raised four times as much money as the Liberals, from a much broader donor base.

In sum, the Liberals were broke; the candidates were in debt; the party was essentially bereft of new ideas or a process for renewal; a party of government was stranded in opposition, in an unseemly hurry to cross the floor to power again. And their new leader, whom the Tories mercilessly taunted as "not a leader," allowed the Conservatives to define him in his first weeks on the job.

Then, when he turned up in the House as Liberal leader in 2007, Canadians discovered that Dion's English was heavily accented and his syntax painfully awkward. Eventually, the country also discovered that he was a leader without standing in his home province of Quebec. So that voters in Ontario, who like to elect national parties with good prospects in Quebec, saw a leader without a base, like a prophet without honour in his own land. Or, as Dion himself put it in a memorable line at the National Press Gallery dinner in October 2007, his problem was that English-speaking Canadians "can't understand me," while French Canadians "just can't stand me." It brought the house down with howls of appreciative laughter, mainly because there was as much truth as humour to it.

The huge problem looming for the Liberals is what's known in the political class as the "echo effect" or the "mirror effect," between Quebec and Ontario, which together send about 60 per cent of all members to the House of Commons. Quebecers like to elect winners. Ontarians like to elect national governments. The voters of Quebec and Ontario look and listen to each other across the Ottawa River, creating a mirror or echo effect. Pollsters can't quantify this, but politicians and their managers not only believe in it, but take it as an article of electoral faith.

And the echo effect kicked in, big time, on the night of September 17, 2007, when Dion's Liberals took a pounding in three Quebec by-elections. In Montreal, a hand-picked Dion candidate lost the Liberal fortress of

Outremont to the NDP's Tom Mulcair by nearly twenty points, marking the first time Jack Layton's party had ever won a seat on the island of Montreal. Even worse, the Liberals finished a bad third to the Conservatives or the Bloc Québécois in two by-elections outside Montreal, in the so-called ROQ – Rest of Quebec. The party of Laurier, St. Laurent, Trudeau and Chrétien, now led by another Québécois named Dion, was a bad third among francophone voters. And the Conservatives had replaced the Liberals as the competitive federalist party against the Bloc outside Montreal. To borrow or steal a Liberal campaign slogan from the 1990s, one that now turned to the advantage of *les bleus*, the Conservatives were now the "Block the Bloc" party for federalists outside Montreal.

The importance of this cannot be overstated, in terms of both the echo effect and of the prospects for Harper to grow from minority to majority status from one Parliament to the next. For Harper, the road to a majority clearly lies through Quebec, with its 50 seats outside Montreal.

Pollsters say there comes a point where the numbers are talking. In this regard, the point where the numbers talked was a CROP poll for *La Presse* at the end of March 2008. The top line was troubling enough for the Liberals, showing the Bloc and the Conservatives virtually tied at 30 and 29 per cent respectively, with the Liberals at 20 per cent and the NDP at 15 per cent.

And in the critically important 418 region – Quebec City and east – the CROP poll was even worse for the Liberals, showing them in fourth place at 14 per cent, behind even the NDP at 17 per cent, while the Conservatives were poised for a regional sweep at 41 per cent, with the Bloc at 25 per cent.

Quebec is Dion's home province, and Quebec City is his hometown, where he was born, was raised and attended university at Laval. Pollster Nik Nanos looks at such numbers and says: "Quebecers, who know the leader best, don't like him."

The echo effect is what worries Liberals the most. "The worst part," says one leading Liberal senator from Quebec, "is the word of it getting out." It's out, all right. The CROP poll had significant resonance in Ontario, where Liberals were reminded of the extent of Dion's problems in his home province. The CROP poll followed an extraordinary meeting of the Liberal Party's executive in Quebec after several senior Liberals openly criticized the leader's performance, and offered a gloomy assessment of the party's prospects in Quebec. None of Dion's outspoken critics even bothered to couch their comments anonymously or on background.

All of them went on the record, essentially a declaration that no one was afraid of him. "I'm the leader," Dion declared, "and I don't want people to be undisciplined." It is impossible to imagine Pierre Trudeau or Jean Chrétien ever reduced to making such a plaintive statement to his party members in his home province of Quebec. After the meeting, many members came away shaking their heads that the leader was completely disconnected from the reality of the party's prospects in Quebec.

But the gloom was unmistakable. One Quebec senator told a top member of the national campaign committee from Ontario: "If we're going into an election, you can't count on us in Quebec for more than 12 seats." Jean Lapierre, the party's Quebec lieutenant under Paul Martin and now a radio and television commentator, said, "I never thought things could be worse than they were during the sponsorship scandal, but this is the worst I've ever seen."

Dismissing reports the party was having difficulty recruiting Quebec candidates for the next election, Dion and his Quebec lieutenant, Céline Hervieux-Payette, declared at the end of the meeting that they had 50 out of 75 candidates confirmed. They wouldn't give names, but *La Presse* columnist Vincent Marissal later obtained a list of only thirty-two names from party sources. When he called the Liberal Party for comment, it went to court to obtain a late-night injunction against publishing the list. When it turned out in court the next day that the list wasn't Hervieux-Payette's own top secret list of candidates, the Liberals hastily withdrew their request for an injunction. At this point, the entire political class was doubled over in laughter, and furious Liberals from across the country, as well as Quebec, were demanding Hervieux-Payette's head on the gates of Parliament Hill.

But even if Dion were to dump Hervieux-Payette as Quebec lieutenant, senior party insiders say that wouldn't change the fundamentals. "He's got to mobilize the party around something," said one Liberal senator from Quebec. "He needs a mobilizing event."

A major part of Dion's dilemma is the lack of a coherent policy agenda, and the obvious inconsistency of denouncing the Conservatives in the House, and then not showing up to vote against them.

In the absence of a plan endorsed by a policy convention, Dion has made a series of one-off announcements. One day it could be corporate tax cuts. The next, green mortgages for the environment, before musing about a national carbon tax in April, an idea first put forward by Ignatieff in the leadership race. Then, he endorsed a Liberal private member's bill on registered education savings plans, which passed the House, only to fold when the Conservatives put in a poison pill tying it to the budget implementation bill. Beginning with the Throne Speech last fall, Dion has time and again threatened to defeat the government, only to fold his hand. He has been continuously outmanoeuvred by Stephen Harper on both tactics and strategy.

The House of Commons is a theatre best appreciated from the galleries, for the off-camera body language as well as the repartee and derisory comments never recorded in Hansard.

Before Question Period every day at 2:15, the House sets aside 15 minutes for statements by members, normally to note the achievements in their ridings, such as Roberval as Hockeyville, or to mark events such as National Wildlife Week or the 90th anniversary of Vimy Ridge. Occasionally, members from all sides use their allotted 60 seconds for a purely partisan purpose, as Conservative MP Jeff Watson did on April 9 in suggesting Dion's closest adviser was his dog, Kyoto.

"Kyoto says, 'down boy,' and the Liberal leader responds by driving his poll numbers in Quebec way down," Watson said. "Kyoto says 'sit' and the Liberal leader responds by having his caucus sit vote after vote. When Kyoto says 'roll over,' the Liberal leader obliges on every significant matter of policy and confidence in our government. However, the Liberal so-called leader is saving Kyoto's best advice for last. In the next election, which Liberals now pretend they will call in the dog days of summer, their so-called leader will finally play dead."

Waiting to ask his lead question, Dion sat virtually expressionless throughout these cruel comments. But the Liberal benches, instead of erupting in outrage, sat mostly in silence throughout the indignity of it. It was a telling moment.

In Question Period that day, the newly arrived Bob Rae rose in his place to ask a question, arising from the Olympic torch relay, on China and human rights in Tibet. "We have all sorts of different factions in the Conservative government," he began. He got no further, as he was interrupted by howls of laughter from the government benches, led by the prime minister pointing to the Liberal front bench. Even Rae had to smile. The next day, when Rae asked another question in his capacity as foreign affairs critic, it was taken by Deepak Obhrai, the parliamentary secretary to the absent foreign affairs minister. "I appreciate the response from the Prime Minister's stand-in," Rae resumed.

To which Obhrai replied: "I appreciate the question from the Liberal stand-in leader." Once again, the House erupted in laughter.

As the House broke for a recess, the Liberals were once again faced with a decision about whether to defeat the government, this time over the immigration reform legislation, which the Conservatives cast as a matter of confidence by tying it to the budget implementation bill.

And Dion, for his part, kept saying he wouldn't vote for the bill as it stood, though he wouldn't say for sure he would vote against it.

But Dion was still clinging to strategic ambivalence. Maybe he would force an election, and maybe not.

Policy Options, May 2008

12

MICHAEL IGNATIEFF

Welcome home, stranger

When it comes to Quebec, Michael Ignatieff is either completely tone deaf, or he just doesn't get it.

He continuously bandies around loaded words and terms without any apparent consideration for their context or consequences.

First, there his was musing that "we want to avoid civil war" as an outcome of a third referendum, though he was quick to add he had every confidence we would avoid it.

Why, you'd think he was talking about the former Yugoslavia or some place torn by ethnic cleansing.

Now in his vision statement for the Liberal leadership campaign, Ignatieff recognizes Quebec as "a nation" but then adds "it has all the powers necessary to make its society flourish and grow."

Well, either it means something or it doesn't.

For Ignatieff, it clearly means rhetorical ruffles and flourishes, signifying nothing.

As in this declaration at the unveiling of his campaign manifesto: "I speak for all those who say that Quebec is my nation but Canada is my country."

This is a variation of a time-honoured Quebec quotation: "*Le Québec, c'est ma patrie; le Canada, c'est mon pays.*"

Ignatieff has adapted that to: "*Le Québec est ma nation, le Canada est mon pays.*"

A homeland is one thing – it's where you live. A nation is different, it's a place with its own language, distinctive culture and geographical territory. A nation has all the attributes of a country, except, in this case, political and territorial sovereignty.

In Quebec, we have been going in circles on this since the 1960s when the first Premier Daniel Johnson declared a doctrine of two nations, with the slogan, *Égalité ou indépendance.*

In the 1968 federal election, Progressive Conservative leader Robert Stanfield campaigned on a platform of two nations, only to be flattened by Pierre Trudeau, who declared that Quebec should be put it in its place, and that its place was in Canada.

Ignatieff explains his choice of words with an academic lecture, noting there are 5,000 recognized nations in the world, but less than 200 countries at the UN.

"The Scottish people consider themselves a nation, but they regard Britain as their country," he writes. "The Basques and Catalans regard their people as nations, but accept Spain as their country. So it is with Quebec. Quebecers, by considerable majorities, consider Quebec their nation, but Canada as their country."

Having opened one Pandora's Box, Ignatieff promptly opens another, noting Quebec has never signed the 1982 Constitution Act, and until it does, "our federation's architecture remains unfinished."

When the time is right, he suggests, "Canadians should be prepared to ratify the facts of our life as a country, composed of distinct nations in a new constitutional document."

Part of this new constitutional framework would include "the acknowledgement of the national status of Quebec and the indigenous nations of Canada."

Furthermore, he is suggesting "a constitutional division of powers among aboriginal, territorial, provincial and federal orders of government, with clear procedures to sharing jurisdictions that overlap."

A guy named Joe, as in Joe Clark, once talked about "a third order of government" recognizing aboriginal peoples. This was in the summer of 1992, during constitutional talks that resulted in the Charlottetown Accord, decisively defeated in a referendum. The whole package of aboriginal rights, an elected Senate and recognition of Quebec's distinctive character, sank under its own weight.

Ignatieff is proposing something much bigger: a reapportionment of the division of powers between Ottawa and the provinces under Sections 91 and 92 of the British North America Act, consolidated with the Charter of Rights in the 1982 Constitution Act.

You're kidding, right, Michael?

Apparently not.

He's talking about a constitutional amendment, which requires agreement by Ottawa and seven provinces representing 50 per cent of the population, the 7/50 amending formula.

In BNA federalism, the division of powers is at the heart of the constitutional bargain, along with the asymmetrical nature of the federation in Article 93 entrenching the denominational, now linguistic character of Quebec schools and the status of French and English as recognized languages of the Quebec courts and legislature. In Charter federalism, the emphasis is on rights, not powers, and by its nature it is symmetrical, with all provinces created equal.

"All provinces should be equal," Ignatieff affirms, "but all provinces are not the same."

We tried that in Meech Lake, with Quebec as a distinct society within Canada.

Ignatieff is proposing much more, but even less, for Quebec, recognition of nationhood without transfer of power or tax points.

We've had two Quebec referendums and two failed constitutional amendments over the last thirty years. For most of that time, Ignatieff was living outside the country.

It shows.

September 2006

∞

WORDS ARE IMPORTANT

Michael Ignatieff is a very smart guy. But there is a difference between school smart and street smart. Ignatieff isn't at Harvard anymore, he's in a leadership campaign. And he is rapidly using up his allotment of unforced errors, to the point where his judgment, or lack of it, is becoming a serious issue among Liberals.

First, Ignatieff said he wasn't losing any sleep over civilian casualties in southern Lebanon during the summer war between Hezbollah and the Israelis. Then he laid down a hard line on conditions for Quebec's access to independence. Clear rules were needed, he said, "because we want to avoid civil war." He quickly added we would avoid one.

Then, in his campaign manifesto, titled *Agenda for Nation Building*, he opened a huge Pandora's box by proposing a constitutional amendment that would recognize Quebec as a nation within Canada, even though this would be essentially meaningless.

Then, after opening this issue, Ignatieff writes "constitutional review is for the future." In other words, words aren't important.

Well, there's nothing more important than the fundamental law of the land. And in this party, there's nothing with more potential to divide Liberals than the question of Quebec's role in the federation. And it represents a strategic opportunity for Bob Rae to make the point that reopening the constitution is a really bad idea.

Then Ignatieff appeared on Radio-Canada's *Tout le monde en parle*, which everyone watches on Sunday night for its cheeky irreverence. For any politician, it's a very high-risk outing, as Ignatieff discovered.

He was trying to make amends for his indifference to civilian casualties when, once again, he went a sentence too far.

"I was a professor of human rights, and I am also a professor of the laws of war," he said, "and what happened in Qana was a war crime and I should have said that. That's clear."

The comment went unnoticed and unremarked by the French-language media, but once it got translated, all hell broke loose in English Canada.

Accusing Israel of war crimes is a fairly serious matter. But to make it stick the Israelis would have had to deliberately launch a missile attack on a building in Qana where twenty-eight civilians were killed, rather than targeting a Hezbollah rocket launcher nearby. And the Israelis say it was an accident, so there was no war crime under the Geneva Convention.

In the fallout from his comment, Ignatieff lost his Toronto campaign co-chair, Susan Kadis, who abruptly resigned and wrote him a sharp note saying he should have known better. Kadis is the MP from Thornhill which, in terms of Jewish voters, is to Toronto as Mount Royal is to Montreal. Everyone from the Israeli ambassador to the Canadian Jewish Congress quickly jumped all over Iggy.

But he was not for the turning. At a Toronto news conference, he said: "I believe war crimes were committed in the war in Lebanon. They were committed on both sides."

There's an intellectual stubborn streak about Ignatieff, bordering on obstinacy, that is quite like another Canadian politician – Stephen Harper.

Rather than leaving Ignatieff alone in the hole he dug for himself, Harper dug one of his own, saying Ignatieff's comments were "consistent with the anti-Israeli position taken by virtually all of the candidates for the Liberal leadership. I don't think it's helpful or useful."

Neither were Harper's comments, except to Bob Rae, who was well within his rights to be shocked and appalled, inasmuch as his wife and three daughters are Jewish, and his staunch support of Israel was one of the reasons he left the NDP.

But the larger question is about Ignatieff's judgment. He is achieving a critical mass of gaffes that is prompting Liberals to ask how he would respond under the pressure of an election.

There is such a thing as a tipping point in all campaigns. Ignatieff is getting there.

October 2006

THE QUÉBÉCOIS NATION

For Stéphane Dion, Quebecers are "a national group in the sociological sense." For Michael Ignatieff, Quebec is "a nation in the civic sense."

This is hair-splitting, right? Nope. It's an issue that Ignatieff has forced onto the Liberal leadership race in a manner that could blow up the convention at the end of November in Montreal.

This is because the Quebec wing of the Liberal Party has adopted a resolution recognizing Quebec as a nation. It will now go to the convention where it will be debated and voted on in a plenary session. And if it's defeated, what then? Another humiliation for Quebec. It would certainly be a humiliation for Ignatieff.

The question of Quebec's status – special, distinct, unique, or whether it constitutes a nation within Canada, is the one issue, in this party, that could tear it apart.

This is, after all, the party of Pierre Trudeau, who in the 1968 campaign rejected Robert Stanfield's vision of two nations, and famously said he would put Quebec in its place, "and its place is in Canada." It's the party of Jean Chrétien and the Charter of Rights, which entrenched equality of the provinces in part of the amending formula. Ottawa and nine provinces could vote to abolish the crown, but a 10th, say, Prince Edward Island, could veto such a constitutional amendment.

If you think the Liberals were sorely divided over Meech Lake – and their 1990 convention was a donnybrook on the weekend Meech died – that was a tea party compared to how Liberals could split over this.

Like, right down the middle between French- and English-speaking Canada, between East and West, between the Trudeau-Chrétien and Martin-Turner wings of the party.

And between Dion and Ignatieff. Dion, father of the Clarity Act, is being pushed between a constitutional rock and a hard place, a very uncomfortable spot for him to be put in as a favourite-son candidate in Quebec, and particularly at a convention being held in his hometown.

It's not clear what the Ignatieff camp hoped to gain by forcing this issue. After all, he's already got just about everything he's going to get in Quebec in terms of delegates. He did very well in the September "superweekend" sweepstakes, winning 39 per cent of the elected delegates (14 of them from each of the 75 Quebec ridings). As for the ex-officio or automatic delegates, they are the establishment of the party, and the establishment of this party cares only about one thing – winnability.

Ignatieff had already made his case for Quebec as a nation in his campaign manifesto – that he saw Quebec as a nation in the civic sense, one of 5,000 in the world, not to be confused with the 195 nations at the United Nations, all of them sovereign countries. The recognition of Quebec as a nation would not confer any additional powers on Quebec, since it already has sufficient powers under the current constitution, although Ignatieff proposes a new division of powers between Ottawa and the provinces and territories that would include aboriginal peoples.

The Ignatieff forces played a second card, recognizing the vertical fiscal imbalance between Ottawa and the provinces. This, again, put Dion in the difficult position of denying its existence, as he did when he was minister of Intergovernmental Affairs in the Chrétien government. In Quebec, this is the equivalent of opposing glasnost during the Gorbachev years – it is considered revealed wisdom, the doctrine of the day.

Just to make sure Dion's embarrassment was complete, the Iggyites roundly booed him.

Now, how, after all that, is there any way for Dion to move to Ignatieff as the kingmaker after the second or third ballot?

And how is Ignatieff to measure his own embarrassment if he cannot carry this issue on the floor of the convention? The Ignatieff campaign doesn't have the muscle to force this issue through. Not at 30 per cent of the elected delegates, they don't. Not even with his share of ex-officios, which would normally bring him about three points higher. Not even with two-thirds of the Quebec delegates voting in favour, as they did last weekend.

So Ignatieff has little to gain, and much to lose, by forcing this issue onto the floor of the convention. And the question is, once again, what was he thinking?

Here's a theory: There's a fundamental disconnect in the Ignatieff campaign between the anglophone and francophones. Much as in Paul Martin's PMO, the English-speakers don't know Quebec and defer to the French-speakers, without considering the consequences in the rest of Canada.

October 2006

∞

THE PALACE COUP, NO FINGERPRINTS

Being descended from Russian nobility, Michael Ignatieff evidently knows how to run a palace coup.

With lightning speed, Ignatieff deposed Stéphane Dion, and forced Dominic Leblanc and Bob Rae out of the succession for the Liberal crown. And Iggy's fingerprints aren't to be found anywhere on the gun.

And here he is, duly installed as the overwhelming choice of the Liberal caucus, national executive, and various elements of the party establishment to lead them against Stephen Harper's minority Conservative government in the House of Commons.

Think about it – only a week ago, Dion was still barricaded in the opposition leader's fourth floor office in the Centre Block. Today, Dion is out, and Iggy is in, having been officially confirmed as leader, after Dion was forced out, while Leblanc and Rae dropped out.

The party had no choice but to dump Dion after the failed parliamentary coup and the bungled delivery of his blurry videotaped address to the nation. In every coup, the first thing they do is take over the TV station. These clowns couldn't even find it. Instead, as in every failed coup, the leader was stood up against a wall and shot.

On reflection, the coup was doomed the moment the coalition leaders – Dion, Jack Layton and Gilles Duceppe – appeared together at a solemn signing ceremony. That's when the penny dropped that the opposition leaders were mounting a coup that, while perfectly constitutional in terms of the confidence of the House, was politically illegitimate in the eyes of voters. Hadn't there just been an election? Didn't they just get rid of Dion? Hadn't he just been dumped as Liberal leader? So how come he was back, flanked by the socialist and separatist leaders?

Dion's very public flameout in the House the next day was proof positive that he was unfit to be prime minister, even for a day. The tape was the final straw – my daughter has better videos on her cell phone, and she knows how to find the TV station.

It is the failed coup, and only the failed coup, that forced Dion out, and has saved the Liberals the time and expense of running a divisive six-month leadership race.

The Liberals can thank Stephen Harper for saving them all that trouble. It was the government's economic statement – killing public financing of political parties and banning strikes in the public service – that brought the coup plotters together in the first place. Why they thought they could engineer the defeat of the government, when Harper was perfectly within his constitutional right to ask the governor-general to prorogue the House instead, is a tribute to their delusional fantasies. It's hard to determine which side was more reckless – the government in provoking the crisis or the coalition for taking the country to the brink.

And Dion, who was forgotten but not gone, is now gone but not forgotten. He had a respectable run as a cabinet minister in the Chrétien and Martin governments, and as an accidental leader he had an extraordinary opportunity to grow into the role, which he never did. Even his defeat in October was a fairly honourable thing – at least he stood for something, the Green Shift. But the coalition coup was a naked power grab, and an ignominious end to Dion's career. Rather than spending one Christmas at 24 Sussex, as he briefly thought he might, he is packing his bags at Stornoway. He is lucky the Liberal Party doesn't throw him out on the sidewalk.

Harper, who could have had Dion to kick around again for another six months, will never again face such a witless or incoherent opponent in the House.

Ignatieff, as he has just proven, is not only smart, he's also tough. He's also just proven that he knows how to move the pieces around the leadership chess board.

December 2008

A WORK IN PROGRESS

Michael Ignatieff is still learning his trade as Liberal leader, and his speech to the party's Quebec wing was a reminder that his leadership is a work in progress.

Ignatieff still doesn't understand the difference between a lecture hall full of undergraduates and a convention centre full of political activists. It's one thing to dazzle an adoring group of students with your brilliance, and another to bring a crowd to its feet.

Ignatieff has what it takes; he just isn't there yet. Political science is one thing; political theatre quite another. His respect for the importance of speeches is obvious in the care with which he crafts them. What he hasn't mastered yet is the discipline of delivering the message. At the podium, his eyes are on the page, when they should be on the crowd. This just in, Michael, they have these wonderful things called teleprompters. Get one. The Liberals aren't that broke.

Ignatieff's entourage also oversold expectations for his speech, billing it as a major address, a vision speech of Quebec's role in the federation, when it was long on generalities and short on specifics. That was just bad staff work, falling into the expectations trap, and then allowing the media to say the speech was relatively disappointing.

First, he told the Liberals of his intent to bring the party back to the centre, where elections are won in this country, and where enduring Liberal coalitions have been built. "We need a practical idealism," he said. This was an interesting echo of John F. Kennedy's motto: "To be an idealist without illusions."

Under the unlamented leadership of Stéphane Dion, the Liberals tilted too far to the left, for example, with a Green Shift that couldn't be sold, and a leader who couldn't sell it.

"We are a great party of the centre," Ignatieff said, quoting Sir Wilfrid Laurier to the effect that a party of the centre can equally be a party of reform, it being necessary to hold office to achieve anything.

And that was Ignatieff's second point, his core message, the promise to bring Quebec and the Liberal Party back to power in Ottawa. The Liberals, he said, are "a party in which Quebecers have always played a preponderant role." Ah, the party of Laurier, St. Laurent, Trudeau and Chrétien. The party built on Ontario and Quebec.

"Quebecers don't deserve to be in permanent opposition in Ottawa," he declared. "Their place is in power."

This was the only line in the speech interrupted by a standing ovation. If there is one message Liberals appreciate, it is the promise of power.

And here was Ignatieff's third message, as he deftly played the identity card, saying he saw no contradiction between being a Quebecer and a Canadian, adding he didn't care which identity Quebecers chose first, as long as they chose both. This is not a message that would play well in Ontario, where they see themselves as Canadians first, but it plays well here, where there is dual *"appartenance,"* a sense of belonging to both Quebec and Canada. Ignatieff spoke of "the liberty of belonging" to both. A very elegant turn of phrase.

Ignatieff has legitimate credentials in this regard, since he had been intending to bring a Québécois-nation resolution to the floor of the last Liberal leadership convention in Montreal in December 2006. It would have been very divisive inside the Liberal tent, pitting the Trudeau wing of the party against more moderate elements. As it happened, Stephen Harper saved the Liberals the trouble when he proposed his own Québécois nation resolution in the House the previous week, taking the Liberals off the hook.

And this led to Ignatieff's fourth point, a pitch to soft nationalist Bloc voters "to give us a chance to prove what we can do for your family and for you." Rather than calling voting for the Bloc a waste of time and money, as the Conservatives did to disastrous effect last fall, Ignatieff said he understood why voters supported the Bloc as a question of identity, but they also had to understand it wasn't getting them anywhere. This is a direct echo of Harper's campaign theme that the place of Quebecers isn't in the stands, but on the ice.

No speech before a partisan crowd would be complete without a bit of partisanship, and Ignatieff obliged with a riff that "my deepest instinct about the prime minister is that he's a divider." But there was a sense that was largely playing to the crowd, a bit of red meat.

Indeed, there was a clear sense from Ignatieff's subsequent news conference that his message is one of building a larger tent, of proposing a post-partisan framework. In explaining his approach to Quebec, he even quoted Sir John A. Macdonald's famous line about treating French Canadians as a nation and they will act like one, treat them as a faction and they will behave as one. So, a Liberal leader got to wrap himself in the mantle of the great Conservative founding father.

Ignatieff even had a kind word for Brian Mulroney, whom he had called to wish a happy 70th birthday, speaking of him as someone he disagreed with, but "who did good things for Canada." Not only was this a graceful note, it was in contrast, as Ignatieff well knew, with Harper, who is a prisoner of his own policy against having any contact with his Conservative predecessor until the Karlheinz Schreiber matter is cleared up by the present inquiry, and thus could not even call to wish Mulroney well on a milestone birthday.

March 2009

THANK YOU, STEPHEN

At the annual Liberal leader's fundraiser in Toronto, Michael Ignatieff was introduced by his friend and rival of a lifetime, Bob Rae.

At this point in the Liberal leadership race, Iggy and Bob should have been tearing one another to pieces, rather than holding a public meeting of their mutual admiration society. Not only would the Liberals have presented the image of a house divided, they would have been broke. In the usual course of events, the speaker would have been Stéphane Dion, in his last weeks as lame-duck leader, and hardly anyone would have paid to come.

Instead of a divided party in dire financial straits, the Liberals presented an impressive united front, as more than 1,000 people paid $500 a head to pack the big old ballroom of the Royal York, while hundreds more paid a premium for a cocktail with Iggy.

The Liberals have only one person to thank for their good fortune – Stephen Harper.

If Harper hadn't tried to put the Liberals out of business, by ending public subsidies to political parties in last fall's economic update, the Liberals might have done it to themselves.

Instead, Ignatieff leads a united party to Vancouver to a convention that's been transformed into a coronation. And a party that would have been drained financially by the fundraising demands of several leadership camps is instead raising millions toward the next election. The Liberals are also going to Vancouver resurgent in the polls, particularly in Ontario and Quebec, the two keystone provinces of Liberal dynasties since Laurier's time.

Instead of having had Dion to kick around again for another six months, while Iggy and Bob pounded each other on the leadership trail, Harper faces a united party that is once again in the hands of political professionals.

Life for the Liberals under Dion was a continuous comedy of errors, culminating in December's Three Stooges coalition and the grainy televised video that finally resulted in Dion's sudden ouster.

The truly admirable thing about the palace revolt against Dion was that it was a bloodless coup, organized and staged by Ignatieff loyalists, without his fingerprints on the gun. In accepting his appointment, rather than his election, as Liberal leader, Ignatieff was positioned as simply answering his party's call to public service. In noting that Ignatieff was the overwhelming choice of both the caucus and the party's grandees, Rae acknowledged that "I can count."

Looking back on the seven-day parliamentary crisis, the question is why Harper risked so much when the Liberals were already broke and in disarray. Quite apart from rescuing the Liberals from the incompetent Dion, and sparing them a divisive leadership campaign, Harper's actions renewed suspicions in the country of a certain meanness of spirit, to say nothing of a hidden agenda.

Then there's the economy, stupid. While events like the London G20 summit have played to Harper's strengths, (other than his getting lost in the washroom on the way to the class photo), the recession is taking an inevitable toll in Conservative voting intentions. The Liberals quite rightly regard every lost job as one less vote for the Tories, or one less for the NDP.

As he did in Montreal, Ignatieff told his Toronto audience that the Liberals are the party of the dynamic centre. He is on a mission to build a big tent party, bidding to take votes back from the NDP and the Greens on the left, and the Bloc on the soft nationalist flank in Quebec.

The Liberals have always been a party of management, and the country's Toronto-based management class didn't recognize itself in the party of Dion, starting with his non-aggression pact with Green Party leader Elizabeth May, and culminating in the December coalition with Jack Layton, propped up by Gilles Duceppe. The December coalition was a perfectly constitutional play, since the only question is the confidence of the House, and the coup plotters had the numbers. But it was politically illegitimate in terms of the confidence of the country, and the Liberals' own base, and would have led to disastrous consequences for the party in English-speaking Canada.

So Harper's play last November saved the Liberals from a leadership campaign, and Dion's failed coup saved the party, in that he was immediately forced out.

A funny thing happened on the way to the convention. The only reason for going through with it is the coronation, the laying on of hands, which will give Ignatieff the legitimacy he needs to take to the voters.

April 2009

∞

A CORONATION WITH NO CROWN

"There is no crown, you know." Michael Ignatieff was saying over lunch in a sun room at Stornoway, the opposition leader's gracious residence in Rockcliffe.

"It's your house," he said, "the public's house, have a look around." A portrait of Sir Wilfrid Laurier, founder of the first enduring Liberal dynasty, hangs behind the desk in Ignatieff's study. And a detailed map of the coast of Newfoundland by Captain James Cook, better known for exploring the West Coast of Canada.

George Drew – whom Iggy's father, George Ignatieff, later knew at the Canadian high commission in London – lived here. John Diefenbaker and Mike Pearson, Joe Clark and Pierre Trudeau, Brian Mulroney and John Turner, Jean Chrétien and Stephen Harper have all lived here on their way to or from 24 Sussex. The difference between the two is that Sussex is a house, while Stornoway is a home.

It's Pearson, among his predecessors as Liberal leader, for whom Ignatieff feels the most affinity. Pearson spent a good part of his career outside Canada, in places like Britain and America, much as Ignatieff has done.

The lure of politics, and the prospect of leadership, brought Pearson home after a lifetime in the foreign service, much as it brought Ignatieff home after nearly thirty years as a public intellectual, author and commentator in Britain and the United States. Pearson was 65 when he became prime minister, after five years and two elections in opposition. Ignatieff, 62 next month, is looking at an election this fall or next spring, after two terms in opposition.

As Pearson did, Ignatieff is having to learn his new trade as he goes, and learn about the country in the lonely travels of an opposition leader – a life of flying economy, room service at midnight, and way too much coffee on the road to riding associations, campus clubs, legion halls, seniors' groups, chambers of commerce, and the summer barbecues. Welcome home, Michael.

"A lot of Mike Pearson's work rebuilding the party was done in this house," Ignatieff said. And when you consider Pearson's achievements, as foreign minister and winner of the Nobel Peace Prize, Ignatieff observes it's remarkable he agreed to stay on for five years in the wilderness following the Diefenbaker landslide of 1958, rebuilding the Liberal Party from the ground up.

Ignatieff realizes that notwithstanding the recent Liberal surge in the polls, there is much work to be done to restore the fabled Liberal brand and rebuild the party's ground game across the country. Or, in the words of Sir Wilfrid, whom Ignatieff is fond of quoting: "It is not enough to have principles, we must also have organization."

Brian Mulroney used to put it another way, when as he often said, the leader of either the Liberals or Tories, the two parties of government in

Canada, had only three jobs: "Unite the party, fill the campaign coffers, and win the election."

Ignatieff nods approvingly of both quotes. "I think both Mr. Laurier and Mr. Mulroney are speaking well. It sounds right to me," he says.

But thanks to Stephen Harper and his disastrous November economic update, as well to Stéphane Dion and the Three Stooges coalition, both of which took Parliament and the country to the brink, a competitive Liberal convention, which would have diverted millions of dollars from the next campaign has been transformed instead into a love-in for Iggy. After a quarter century of bruising leadership battles, the Liberal party is united and beginning to fill its coffers for the election ahead.

When it's considered that Harper could have had Dion to kick around for another six months, while Ignatieff and Bob Rae spent millions on a rocky road to Vancouver, the Liberals have every reason to be grateful. Ignatieff has another reason to send Harper flowers on his 50th birthday this week. Had Harper not blown a majority in Quebec in last fall's campaign, the Liberals would have been looking at another four or five years in opposition, and could well have looked past Ignatieff to the next generation of leadership. Fate and destiny have dealt another hand.

And so instead of telling the Liberal Party why he should become its leader, Ignatieff has an opportunity to tell the country why he should become its 23rd prime minister.

His acceptance speech in Vancouver is an opportunity on twin message tracks. The first is Iggy's chance to introduce himself to the country, to tell Canadians who he is, and where he comes from. The second is his chance to tell Canadians his idea of the country, and where he wants to take it, as well as its role in the world. The vision thing.

Ignatieff has written a lot about both sides of his family, the Ignatieffs and the Grants, without telling very much about himself. The Ignatieffs were Russian blue-bloods. The Grants were WASPs from central casting, from somewhere between Queen's University and External Affairs.

Ignatieff writes about his mother's side of the house in *True Patriot Love*, a slender new volume that was timed for the leadership campaign. His uncle, George Grant, was a high Red Tory who famously wrote *Lament for a Nation* in 1965, and regarded Pearson as a traitor to his class, a sell-out to the Americans.

Yet Ignatieff's own children, Theo and Sophie, are absent from the story, living their own lives in Toronto and at the University of Edinburgh. Ignatieff says they are very cool with what their dad is doing, and that he couldn't more grateful for their support.

And here is the divide between public and private life. In a way, it is none of our business, but they are part of his narrative, and in that sense the public is entitled to know something about them. Ignatieff, in his acceptance address, needs to find a way to bring them into his story. He can look it up under Barack Obama. There is still too much about him that Canadians don't know.

They know he's smart enough to be prime minister. And after the bloodless coup he staged for the Liberal leadership, they know he's tough enough. What they still don't know is who he is, and his idea of our country.

April 2009

13

PROFILES

BERNARD DEROME

Here's the thing about Bernard Derome: nobody ever knew how he voted. Especially on the Quebec question.

It never stopped people from guessing. He occasionally wore his Order of Canada pin, and that presumably made him a federalist. But on the night of the last referendum, he spoke sympathetically of the painful loss evident on the faces of Yes supporters, and that supposedly made him a sovereignist, or at least a soft nationalist.

But nobody ever knew whether he even voted, and over the more than a quarter century that he anchored Radio-Canada's *Telejournal*, that was a good thing. More than the town crier, he was a *rassembleur*, someone who brought viewers together.

So viewers rewarded him with their trust. And trust is not something they give to airheads. Trust, as Derome himself once defined it in a speech honouring his friend Lloyd Robertson: "is a question of judgment, integrity, openness and profound honesty."

Just so. Which is why, for many years, Derome has been the most-trusted public figure in Quebec with, in one survey, a higher approval rating than Céline Dion.

There's accumulated recognition and respect in that. Just as Walter Cronkite became "Uncle Walter," Derome eventually grew into the role of "Mon Oncle Bernard." Derome has sat in the Radio-Canada anchor chair for half of his entire life. He's been doing it longer than anyone else, but also better than anyone else.

"As an anchor," said Peter Mansbridge, who knows something about it, "he's been one to watch with so much awe and respect."

What has always struck colleagues, in English as well as French, is Derome's work ethic. Mansbridge, who has worked a few feet away on any number of CBC specials, said "the thing that has always impressed me is that he is so ready. He always comes with all this paper, and he has always read it all."

The other thing Mansbridge always noticed was Derome in talkback mode, off-air with the people talking in his ear.

"You've got to be an anchor," said Mansbridge, "to know that on the big, live show, you're on-air almost all the time, so that during the few opportunities you have to talk to your producers, they are listening to you, not out of fear, but with respect. I always got that sense with Bernard."

At the 1984 Liberal leadership convention, I happened to get a close-up view of this during four days while working as a guest commentator in Derome's anchor booth.

The first thing about Derome was the voice, crackling with urgency even in rehearsals. The second thing, as a television journalist, was that his words always filled out the visuals. The story of that convention was John Turner vs. Jean Chrétien, or in Derome's memorable turn of phrase, "man of ice vs. man of fire."

Then, Derome was at once a control freak and the calm centre of the storm. He was not a guy for small talk on the set, and if you wanted to speak to him during the broadcast, you'd better be giving him something to tell the audience.

But away from work, he was someone who loved to stop and share the latest political gossip, and in his job he knew it all. And sometimes, because he cared for the story so much, he got it first. When first ministers reached a surprise agreement on the constitution at Meech Lake in 1987, prime ministerial press aide Marc Lortie said "I've got to call Bernard Derome," which is how Radio-Canada had it on the air first.

June 1998

∞

MARK WAINBERG

Mark Wainberg, newly elected president of the World AIDS Society in Geneva, was describing the dimensions of the epidemic.

"During the seven days we were in Geneva," he was saying, "100,000 people around the world became infected with HIV."

Pretty scary stuff. But Wainberg, a microbiologist who heads the McGill AIDS Centre at the Jewish General Hospital, has been in the field of AIDS research since HIV was first identified nearly fifteen years ago.

"I'm committed to the fight against AIDS, both in Canada and around the world," he said. His team has already developed, with BioChem Pharma of Montreal, an anti-viral cocktail ingredient known as 3TC.

For the next two years, Wainberg will be the world's most prominent advocate of education, research and treatment of a disease he warns might be "potentially the leading cause of morbidity and mortality in the world."

The HIV-positive numbers for Canada and the United States are forbidding enough – 50,000 in this country and two million in North America. But worldwide, the number is a frightening 35 million, and growing exponentially in the Third World.

AIDS is not an equal-opportunity disease. It discriminates. It picks on poor people who don't know about it, can't read about it and can't get treatment for it.

In sub-Saharan Africa, and on the Indian subcontinent, Wainberg says, the epidemic is full blown. Countries such as Zimbabwe and Botswana, he says, have been hit particularly hard, with a reported HIV incidence of 25 per cent among adults.

"In parts of Zimbabwe," Wainberg says, "the rate of HIV infection is 35 per cent among girls between the ages of 13 and 18."

There is good news, he says, in that when those "girls become pregnant, we can treat them so as to virtually eliminate HIV among their babies." The bad news is that the mothers can still pass it on by breast-feeding. Or the mothers often die, leaving their children "to become orphans at a very young age."

For his two-year mandate, Wainberg hopes for a global effort at education. "Prevention," he says, "is always better than the cure." Abstinence equals prevention, and the message is the same for teenagers whether in South Africa or the South Shore.

"We have to stop horizontal transmission, sexual transmission," Wainberg says. He adds: "We have to promote safer sex wherever we can."

For Wainberg, that means promoting the use of condoms, and recommending monogamous relationships. "Two monogamous gays who are not infected," he says, "are not going to be."

Getting the message out is the priority. Not to the 3,000 journalists covering the biennial conference in Geneva, but to the countries of the devel-

PROFILES 199

oping world. "Too many countries don't even have billboard campaigns," Wainberg says, "something that we take for granted."

Wainberg takes very little for granted in the fight against AIDS, which he knows is a long, twilight struggle. He has been an activist from the beginning, and has worked with Robert Gallo, the co-discoverer of the virus, at the National Institutes of Health in Washington, D.C.

Wainberg's personal journey is a fairly familiar story of achievement in Montreal's Jewish community. Outremont High, McGill University, a house in Côte St. Luc, a wife named Susan and two grown sons. It is the work, and the commitment, that sets Wainberg apart.

"Were you the school nerd?" he was asked.

"Many people still think of me as a nerd," Wainberg said as he sat in an office decorated with brilliant African masks and a desk piled high with transparencies from his lab down the hall at the Jewish.

It is his work as a microbiologist that set his course when AIDS emerged in the early 1980s. Microbiology, he explains, "is the study of germs and their behaviour."

The HIV germ, he says, behaves irregularly. It is a smart germ, constantly changing its identity.

"It mutates," Wainberg explains. "It refuses to wait for us to finish it off with either a vaccine or drugs."

But they're working on it at the McGill AIDS Centre, which Wainberg says has Canada's "largest critical mass of scientific funding by the Medical Research Council to work on the problem."

One area where he would like to see Ottawa move more quickly is the drug-approval process at Health Canada. Wainberg cites the example of one drug, Nevirapine, approved two years ago by the Food and Drug Administration in the U.S., but not yet approved by Ottawa. Ironically, Wainberg says, most of the research for the drug was conducted in Canada. Drugs are expensive, and no more than a palliative. But as Wainberg says, they can maintain patients in reasonably good health as productive members of society. Basketball star Magic Johnson, seven years since he was diagnosed HIV-positive, and still the picture of apparent health, is a famous case in point.

The quest for a vaccine continues, but Wainberg explains that it's not like polio, where the invading germ had a single identity. A gripping piece on "exposed uninfecteds" in *The New Yorker* magazine suggests that a study of gay men who have developed immunity may provide important clues in developing a vaccine.

"The analogy many of us use is diabetes," Wainberg said. "We want to help keep these people going, until they die of old age."

Wainberg was finishing up a plate of pasta and a diet Pepsi in a downstairs cafeteria when a woman stopped by to congratulate him. "*Mazeltov*," she said. "We're all very proud of you."

The fight is hard. The hope endures.

July 1998

∞

JOHN CIACCIA

There are gentlemen and there are players in politics, and John Ciaccia has proven to be both.

His twenty-five years in the National Assembly have been evenly divided between government and opposition, from the James Bay treaty he negotiated to the Oka crisis he survived, from one language crisis and one referendum to the next.

It is not every politician who gets to leave by the front door, as Ciaccia has in announcing he won't be running again for the Liberals in Mount Royal. Nor it is every one who reminds us, as Ciaccia has by his exemplary service, that politics is an honourable calling.

Along the way, he's traveled Highway 20 to and from Quebec at least 1,000 times, picking up his share of speeding tickets, especially in the days he owned a British racing green Jaguar. "I have paid my share," Ciaccia said. "I have made my contribution."

To share a meal with Ciaccia in any Italian restaurant in Montreal, as at Porto Fino on Mountain Street the other night, is to realize his standing in that community.

He was born in a town called Ielsi, between Rome and Naples, and his family moved here when he was four years old. He went to law school at McGill, worked on the real-estate side of the Steinberg grocery empire, made a lot of money and bought a big waterfront house in Beaconsfield before moving into politics and government.

"I feel at peace with this decision" to step down, Ciaccia said. "It's twenty-five years. The party is in excellent shape to win the next election. It's time."

The achievements, and the anecdotes, of a quarter century in public life are enough to fill a book, the one Ciaccia is writing now.

Robert Bourassa recruited him as a star candidate in 1973, when Ciaccia was working for Jean Chrétien in Ottawa as an assistant deputy minister of Indian affairs.

Though he was clearly *"ministrable,"* the numbers of non-francophone cabinet members worked against him. But he ended up doing a more significant piece of work as the government's negotiator with the Indians affected by the James Bay project.

The 1975 treaty not only allowed Bourassa's cherished hydro-electric "project of the century" to go ahead, but is recognized to this day as a landmark agreement in relations with aboriginal peoples.

If the James Bay agreement was Ciaccia's best moment in aboriginal affairs, the Oka crisis of 1990 was clearly the worst. And the worst moment of that terrible summer came when Ciaccia, as minister for native affairs, was photographed with the chief justice of Quebec Superior Court, as a couple of armed Mohawk warriors looked over their shoulders. At that moment, the government and the judiciary both appeared to be held hostage by gun-toting dissidents.

"The low moment was my not being able to resolve it," Ciaccia said. Yet after the shooting of one police officer, as he also noted, "there were no further deaths" over the more than two months of Oka, before the cold autumn nights and the army closed in.

As minister responsible for international trade in the early '90s, Ciaccia saw Quebec move "from a $3 billion deficit when I got in to a $6 billion surplus when I left."

All of these events occurred during the twenty years that Bourassa was the dominant figure of Quebec politics and public policy. When he died in 1996, Ciaccia spoke as the dean of the legislature, and paid a moving tribute to the former premier, whom he describes as "the finest person, on a human level" he met in politics.

Best debater? Claude Charron of the Parti Québécois. "Without question he was the best," Ciaccia said. "He could get you going, but that's the game."

Best Quebec City restaurant? "The Café d'Europe. Because it's Italian."

Regrets? "Not being there more, when my son, Mark, was growing up."

But now there are two grandsons, whom Ciaccia clearly dotes on. While he is a first-generation Canadian, they can claim a connection, through Ciaccia's daughter-in-law, Kim Routhier, to Basil Routhier, who wrote the original French lyrics to O Canada.

Ciaccia told a story of going with the family to a park in Town of Mount Royal, as he has on July 1 every year, and singing the national anthem.

"It's O Canada, not Eh Canada," his 3-year-old grandson told a bystander.

Not one for Ciaccia's book, but clearly one for his album of memories.

September 1998

☯

PAUL TELLIER

Only in Canada would there be whinging and hand-wringing over the kind of deal Paul Tellier has pulled off, merging Canadian National Railway with Burlington Northern Santa Fe to create the largest freight railway in North America.

Assuming regulatory approval in both Canada and the United States, the new North American Railways will be headquartered in Montreal, with a Canadian CEO, 67,000 employees, 80,000 metres of track from Montreal to Mexico, and revenues approaching $20 billion.

"CN conquers the continent," went the headline in *La Presse,* getting it exactly right. But in certain English-Canadian precincts of punditry, the news was greeted as a requiem for the Canadian dream. As one railway tied the country together at the beginning of the century, another railway was being absorbed by continentalization at the end of the century.

You'd think Burlington Northern had swallowed CN, and moved it to Chicago, instead of the other way round.

With characteristic bluntness, Tellier dismissed such concerns. "I have no time," he said at a Montreal news conference, "for nationalists who think they can draw a gate around this country." Far from representing the Americanization of CN, he said, the merger would transform CN into a North American player, "while retaining a strong Canadian identity."

That's pure Tellier, cutting right to the chase. Anyone who has ever dealt with him, either as the country's senior public servant when he was clerk of the Privy Council, or as head of CN for the last seven years, knows that Tellier gets straight to the point.

Once, working on a major prime ministerial speech, he looked up from his conference room table and asked: "What's the headline, and what are the main points, in English and French?"

At a Rideau Hall ceremony for a minor cabinet shuffle, Tellier was approached by a minister who had been moved from one junior portfolio to another. "What do I now?" he asked.

"Minister," Tellier replied, in a scene straight out of *Yes, Minister,* "you get in your car and your driver will take you to your new office."

When he left the public service, Tellier had already refused the presidency of the CBC. Instead, he opted to become head of CN, knowing it would get him out of Ottawa, and into the business world.

He also knew that he would be the executive who privatized CN, as part of its cultural transformation to a competitive railway. CN's initial public offering, and the road show that Tellier put on with it, became the Canadian IPO of the decade.

Tellier has already pulled off one major American acquisition, but the Burlington deal raises a host of regulatory and political issues in both countries. In an echo of the old Crowsnest Pass Rate, U.S. legislators from the Midwest have already put down markers about moving grain to markets.

Canadian political concerns will be more complex, with Canadian ownership and identity mixed in with the issue of competitiveness. Ottawa's stance on mergers has been driven by electoralism rather than allowing business to create the critical mass it needs to be internationally competitive.

Among the preposterous reasons it gave for refusing the bank mergers last year, Ottawa noted that banks sponsored pee-wee hockey teams. Fortunately for the Department of Finance officials who wrote this paper, none of their names appeared on it. More recently, in the takeover battle between Air Canada and Onex Corp. for dominance of Canada's skies, Ottawa wrung a long list of promises from both sides.

The CN merger is different. It's not about pee-wee hockey. It's not about frequent-flyer points. It's about freight.

It's also about getting Canadian products to markets. Quebec, for example, now trades more with the United States than it does with the rest of Canada. More trade crosses the Detroit River from Ontario to the United States than crosses the Pacific Ocean from Japan to the U.S. Most of it moves by rail, including containerized cargo transshipments from Europe to Chicago through the Port of Montreal.

That's a lot of freight. And Tellier wants to carry it.

December 1999

LUCIEN BOUCHARD

Family, career, party. That would have been the order of priorities for Lucien Bouchard. While he never put his party before himself, he always put his family before everything.

Though often ruled by his volatile emotions, Bouchard is also a rigorously logical man whose career has been devoted to processing information and presenting arguments.

Given the order of his priorities, that led to the logical conclusion – he announced his resignation as premier of Quebec and leader of the Parti Québécois. It's an outcome with which he is quite serene, after what amounted to a closed retreat, a period of reflection over the Christmas holidays.

As he used to say, when he made up his mind about something important: *"Je suis sûr de mon affaire."*

Bouchard wouldn't have consulted anyone, other than his wife, Audrey Best. As for the Parti Québécois caucus, it was the last to be informed, before his statement in the Salon Rouge of the National Assembly.

Family, career, party. In those terms, it was not a difficult decision. In those terms, it is a very good decision.

As he said: "My years are counted, and I have a young family." As he added, with a breaking voice, of his sons, 11 and 9 years old: "Alexandre and Simon need me, and I need them."

Family first. Bouchard's first marriage was childless, which left a certain sadness to his life. And then he met this California girl, and together they had two sons, who became the great joy of his life.

To those who knew Bouchard when he met her, there was never any doubt that Audrey was the one, rather than just another of the women seduced by his many charms. To those who knew of his longing for children, there was never any doubt family would ultimately prevail among the priorities of his life.

Like many men who come to fatherhood later in life, Bouchard was astonished to discover that being a successful parent was by far the most important achievement of his life.

As an older man with a young family, he's always had a clear sense of the importance of their time together and has increasingly resented their time apart.

He worked in Quebec, at least three days a week. They lived in Montreal, seven days a week. Even as he thrived on the work, and the premiership was the great ambition of his life, he hated the arrangement.

He has long since learned to live with the disabling effects of the flesh-eating disease that cost him a leg, and very nearly his life, in 1994. He dealt with it with great courage and great dignity, and moved on.

Bouchard has been continuously in politics and public service for the last fifteen years, the prime earning years of his life. As Canadian ambassador in Paris, as a federal minister, as leader of the opposition in Ottawa, and finally as premier of Quebec, he made a reputation but never made any money.

Any Montreal law firm would be lucky to have a counsel of Bouchard's abilities, and his network of government and business contacts.

The PQ, an ungovernable party, is no longer his problem. He never has to attend another party council meeting and give one more speech about sovereignty being just around the corner. He doesn't have to explain the absence of winning conditions for another referendum. He doesn't have to be in the same room as those who belittle the Jewish Holocaust experience or question the people's right to vote as they please in a democracy.

Not Lucien Bouchard. He's outta there. In his own time, on his own terms, by the front door.

January 2001

THE QUEEN

Pierre Trudeau, John Turner, Brian Mulroney and Jean Chrétien would all agree on two points about Queen Elizabeth – she's a very nice woman, and she knows her Canadian files.

If she's been more successful as a monarch than a mother, that's probably because she's spent more time at it, including 20 visits to Canada during her half century as queen. Today marks her 50th anniversary.

She's been through ten British prime ministers, including Winston Churchill, and nine Canadian prime ministers, from Louis St. Laurent to Chrétien. (Paul Martin and Stephen Harper would make eleven.) All of her Canadian prime ministers have enjoyed working with her; all of them have been struck by how seriously she took her job, or rather, her role.

I can personally attest to how hard she works, having worked for her on several speeches during the Mulroney era. The Prime Minister's Office provides "advice" to the queen, including words for royal occasions.

There are two kinds of speeches by the queen, the kind where she says "I now declare this bridge open," and the kind where she has something significant to say. In my experience, when you gave her a meaningful text, she worked on it, edited it, added her own touches and invariably improved the final product.

It was always very clear that she knew her own mind and had a highly nuanced understanding of Canadian issues.

At Quebec City in October 1987, she decided entirely on her own that she wanted to go further in approving the Meech Lake Accord than the pro-forma endorsement we had written into her speech. She told Mulroney she wanted to be helpful. She was. The subsequent headlines across the country sent opponents of the constitutional deal into a rage.

"Even the Queen herself is forced to say the accord is a good thing," Trudeau grumbled as he began his famous anti-Meech testimony to the Senate in 1988. Trudeau should have known better. Nobody puts words in her mouth.

In 1990, the Queen's visit to Ottawa on Canada Day had been set up for her to proclaim the Meech Lake constitutional amendment. When it cratered instead a week earlier, she decided she couldn't let the occasion pass without comment.

"I am not just a fair-weather friend," she told the Parliament Hill crowd, "I am glad to be here at this sensitive time."

She added: "Knowing Canadians as I do, I cannot believe that they will not be able – after a period of calm reflection – to find a way through present difficulties."

These and other rhetorical ruffles and flourishes were entirely her own handiwork. Seasoned royal-watchers from Fleet Street said they had seldom, if ever, heard her give such a pointedly political speech. What they didn't know was that she wrote, or rewrote, most of it herself.

Two years later, the Queen was back for another Canada Day address to the nation, this time on the 125th anniversary of Confederation, and her speech was overtly political, intended to give a boost to the federal-provincial talks that, later that summer, led to the Charlottetown Accord.

The queen had no problem with her text but wanted to add something, which she brought up during a morning meeting with Mulroney at 24 Sussex. "Prime Minister," she said, "we really should say something about your peacekeepers in Yugoslavia."

Why hadn't we thought of that?

She wrote it in as a marginal note at the end of her text, and it became the spontaneous applause line of her speech: "They serve both Canada and the cause of peace with courage and conviction."

Whatever we think of the institution of the Canadian constitutional monarchy, or of the dysfunctional royal family, it's impossible not to admire this woman for the irreproachable way she's done her job.

She is famous for saying "my husband and I," so I once tried to fit it into one of her Canada Day speeches. She took it out. Evidently, the Queen was not amused.

February 2002

ANTONINE MAILLET AND ALISTAIR MACLEOD

My Cape Breton grandmother, Martha Anderson MacDonald, used to say that Nova Scotia's biggest export was brains. There was statistical evidence of that in the census, indicating a decline in the population of Nova Scotia.

And there was literary proof on the stage of Moyse Hall at McGill University, where Alistair MacLeod and Antonine Maillet joined forces in a reading called "Across the Divide," as part of a two-day symposium organized by graduate students around the theme Canada: Rupture or Continuity.

This is pretty fast company for students to be keeping. Maillet is the author of *La Sagouine*, and winner of the Prix Goncourt, France's equivalent to the Booker Prize. She writes of a country, l'Acadie, that as she said, "no longer exists," and of a people, the Acadians, who are still here "simply because we decided not to die, but to live."

MacLeod is the author of *No Great Mischief*, a novel of a migrant family's struggle over generations in Cape Breton, and winner of the Dublin Award. It is a stunning achievement. The power of MacLeod's writing is in its spareness. He writes, as he said, of "unity, belief and loyalty, because these themes have always intrigued me."

MacLeod's Scots and Maillet's Acadians, she suggested, "are two people who went through a great ordeal," so that they could express the same literary language, "though in two different languages."

As Maritimers, MacLeod replied with evident pleasure, "the same ocean touched us both."

Their common themes are dislocation and a return to roots. In a way, they have done their own Canadian census, except that the numbers talk. The census reminds us that Canadians, a nation of immigrants, are always on the move for new opportunity. Writers such as Maillet and MacLeod remind us where we come from.

Maillet is so short that she needed to stand on a box to peer over the podium, "so that you can see me." But her height has nothing to do with her stature. And she works a crowd better than any politician.

"The Acadians exaggerate a lot," she said, "because if we didn't, there wouldn't be enough of us."

MacLeod was an English professor at the University of Windsor and a writer of admired short stories, before *No Great Mischief* came out three years ago. He wrote it in longhand. It took him thirteen years to complete. It certainly puts the lie to the old saying that those who can, do, and those who can't, teach.

His narrator, Alexander MacDonald, and his sister were raised by grandparents after their parents drowned in a winter ice crossing. He is driving his older brother home from Ontario to Cape Breton, to die. Along the way, he narrates the family history, two centuries of sorrow and hope.

Reading it at the cottage last summer, I could hear the voices of my own grandparents. My Nana Donald, as she was called, used to spend her mornings baking cookies on a wood-burning stove in her country kitchen in Hillside, Mira. Then she would sit down for a cup of tea and gossip. It seemed to me then that she knew the family history of everyone in Cape Breton. "Now, she was a MacAskill from Marion Bridge," she would say, "and she married a MacPherson from Gabarous."

My grandfather, a Glace Bay insurance broker named Angus J. MacDonald, did not like leaving Cape Breton, and didn't particularly like Nova Scotia, which he called the Mainland. The narrator's brother, in his determination to get home, drives across the flooded Canso Causeway in a terrible storm. My grandfather would have understood that.

March 2002

FRANÇOIS BEAUDOIN

The worst moment in what François Beaudoin calls "the ordeal" was the second time they came to his front door with a search warrant.

It was 6:45 a.m. on December 13, 2001, when the doorbell rang. Beaudoin was in the basement study of his Town of Mount Royal home. "I could hear the doorbell, and my wife went to the door, and I could hear her scream, 'Not you again, not you again.'"

Beaudoin was president of the Business Development Bank of Canada until he was fired in 1999 after he recommended recalling a $615,000 loan to the Auberge Grand-Mère. As head of the federal bank, serving at the pleasure of the prime minister, Beaudoin had been personally lobbied by Jean Chrétien on three occasions to grant the loan. The PM once had an interest in the hotel.

Following his dismissal by Chrétien-appointed BDC chairman Michel Vennat, Beaudoin's severance and pension package were rescinded by the bank. Beaudoin sued, and the bank countersued, alleging he had abused his office. Search warrants were issued on several occasions for Beaudoin's home, cottage, office, even his golf club.

Finally, in a scathing judgment entirely in Beaudoin's favour, Judge André Denis of Quebec Superior Court wrote last month that the bank had waged a "vendetta" against Beaudoin.

Beaudoin, spoke of his life during the fifty-one months from firing to vindication. That December morning, he said, three officers of the RCMP presented a search warrant demanding he turn over a personal computer, hard drives and diskettes containing information belonging to the bank.

With his wife, Manon, in tears, Beaudoin read the search warrant and told the police it was "a false statement" – there was no such information on his laptop.

"It was a Mac, a PowerBook," Beaudoin recalled, "used by my daughters and my wife. It had all my daughters' university projects. I can remember my daughters begging the police to allow them to keep the diskettes that were clearly their own." The police were deaf to the tearful pleas of Marie-Caroline and Chantal.

A few days earlier, the RCMP had raided Beaudoin's locker at the Royal Montreal Golf Club, and the club's office as well. They were looking for his wife's golf chits – one of his perks had been a family membership for green fees at the club, to which he had already belonged for twenty years.

"Can you imagine," he asked, "the members of Royal Montreal reading about their club being raided?" Founded in 1873, Royal Montreal is the oldest golf club in North America, and one of the most prestigious.

"It is to the credit of the members of Royal Montreal," he said, "that through the years of this, they were fully supportive. They never looked the other way. They supported me warmly."

In one of the ironies of this case, Jean Carle, Chrétien's former director of operations, was sponsored by Beaudoin when he applied to join the Royal Montreal. The BDC paid his $32,000 initiation fee.

According to Beaudoin, Pelletier mentioned that Carle was looking to return to the private sector. Beaudoin had an opening. Though Carle had no experience in the public-relations field, he was hired at a salary of $133,000 after being identified as the only serious candidate in a search conducted by Vennat's former wife, Manon Vennat, a highly regarded head hunter.

So what were the RCMP looking for at Beaudoin's house, and who sent them knocking at sunrise? Denis answered both questions in his devastating judgment.

"On April 11, 2001," he wrote, "Mr. Michel Vennat filed a complaint against Mr. Beaudoin for making and using forgery with Mr. Giuliani Zaccardelli, Chief Commissioner of the RCMP. On May 2, 2001, Mr. Vennat asked the RCMP to conduct an investigation on Mr. Beaudoin for misappropriation of the BDC's property and services."

Previously, the bank had obtained a bench warrant on a Saturday afternoon to raid Beaudoin's home, his cottage in the Laurentians and his office at PriceWaterhouseCoopers, the accounting and management consulting firm.

Whatever they were looking for wasn't there. Beaudoin, on leaving the bank on October 1, 1999, had left all his personal and business papers at the office. Within weeks, a forensic team from KPMG conducted what Judge Denis denounced as a "huge blind search" and, as one searcher admitted, "took everything."

"They learned the most intimate details of the Beaudoins' family life," Denis wrote. "Mr. Beaudoin's charitable donations. Mrs. Beaudoin's orthodontic fees, the schools attended by the couple's two daughters ... tax accounts ... hundreds of details."

Beaudoin is savouring his vindication in a case in which the entire machinery of the state was brought down on him for adhering to the rules of good governance and good banking. A bank that was barely breaking even when he took it over was making $100 million a year when he left. Its profits have since plummeted to less than $40 million a year.

With his lawyer, Doug Mitchell, he is considering suing the bank for damages to his reputation, loss of income, and anguish to himself and his family. When Beaudoin got the judgment, on the morning of February 6, he called home from his car. On hearing the news, his younger daughter burst into tears and told him: "Dad, you're a champ."

March 2004

∞

JOE CLARK

A quarter century ago, Joe Clark was giving an interview in a Montreal hotel suite when his young daughter Catherine skipped into the room. "I remember, you called her Muffin," Clark was told.

"I still do," replied Clark, who is leaving the Conservative leadership for the second time. In the blood sport of politics, it is useful to recall that the players are also people whose important achievements include raising accomplished children, as Clark and Maureen McTeer have done with their daughter.

Nothing else comes even close in measuring life's accomplishments, not even being prime minister at 39. Nothing else so mitigates the disappointments, even being former prime minister at 40.

Now, just a week short of his 64th birthday, Clark prepares his second exit from the political stage. Twenty years ago, when Brian Mulroney wrested the Conservative leadership from him, Clark left by the back door. Nor was there any tribute to Clark at the 1993 Conservative convention, the one that chose Kim Campbell over Jean Charest, to the party's everlasting regret.

Honour is due. When Clark receives the tribute of the Tory faithful at the opening of their leadership convention in Toronto, he will be recognized for rescuing the Conservative Party from assumed oblivion in the 2000 election, and making it competitive again as the clear, though still very distant, second choice of Canadians.

Clark had left politics in 1993, but thought he was answering a call when the Conservative leadership opened up again in 1998 with Charest's departure for Quebec. But then it took Clark nearly two years to get back to the House of Commons, the one place where he has consistently outperformed expectations. Along the way, there were the mishaps and misjudgments of the kind that have always seemed to dog Clark, notably his opposition to the Clarity Act in the face of a caucus that supported the bill setting out rules of the road to Quebec's separation from Canada.

Still and all, he says it has been "very much worth coming back."

And he speaks of "an unexpected bonus – it forced me to take a look at my modern country, a country that has changed immensely."

Once bitter rivals at the 1976 and 1983 conventions, Clark and Mulroney will share the spotlight in preliminary tribute events tomorrow night and Friday morning. Any review of Clark's resumé should also include his seven years as foreign minister in Mulroney's government.

"I really came to appreciate his skill as minister of Foreign Affairs," Mulroney said. "He was easy to work with, and respected around the world. With the exception of Lester Pearson, he was the finest foreign minister we've ever had in Canada."

Also of note, suggests Mulroney, "was his decision to seek a seat in Alberta in the last election. It was very courageous, and became an important turning point. It proved we could win in the West again."

The man from High River went home to win an unlikely seat in Calgary. At the time, it seemed like an odds-against proposition. Then again, that's the story of his life, and in his own way, the compelling grace note of his career.

May 2003

PETER LOUGHEED

When Peter Lougheed took office as premier of Alberta in 1971, the price of oil was $3 a barrel, before the OPEC oil cartel tripled it to $9 a barrel in 1973, and before it tripled again to $27 a barrel after the Iranian revolution in 1979.

But did he ever, during his fourteen years in office and more than twenty years since leaving it, foresee oil at $75 a barrel?

"No, I didn't," Lougheed said the other day. "I knew it would go up steadily, but I never expected that. It wasn't in my forecast."

From his corner office on the top floor of the 47-storey Bankers' Hall tower, the entire booming city of Calgary, building out to the foothills of the Rockies, lies before him. The foundations of today's energy boom were laid in the 1970s. The bust precipitated by the disastrous National Energy Program in the 1980s is a bitter reminder that no one in Alberta takes prosperity for granted.

Both the boom of one decade, and the bust of the next, occurred on Lougheed's watch between 1971 and 1985, by any measure one of the most significant and successful provincial premierships of the 20th century. He founded the Progressive Conservative political dynasty that still reigns after thirty-five years in office, with no sign of it ending any time soon.

In the 1970s, he was the face of Alberta's prosperity, carefully husbanding its new-found wealth with the creation of the multi-billion-dollar Heritage Fund. In the 1980s, he was the staunch defender of Alberta's interests against Ottawa's incursions onto its energy turf.

When he walked away from it all in 1985, he left by the front door. His career since is proof there can be a fulfilling life after politics. He joined the boardroom Calgary law firm of Bennett Jones, accepted a bunch of corporate directorships, signed up for volunteer roles such as the chancellorship of Queen's University, and kept up his interest in the public-policy process.

"It's been a good balance," says Lougheed, still a commanding figure, and still with that famous steely voice. "I didn't want to be a CEO. I didn't want to run anything, I'd been running the government of Alberta."

Lougheed knows the influence of the elder statesman is measured in inverse proportion to the frequency of his declarations. His interventions on public policy are highly infrequent, thus, duly noted. And lately he has had something on his mind, the overheated Alberta economy and the runaway development of the province's oil sands.

For one thing, he's opposed to using natural gas to extract the oil from the oil sands. For another, he's concerned that the royalty regime short-changes the people of Alberta. He also worries about the inflationary effects of an overheated economy.

"The Alberta government has let the development get ahead of the infrastructure," Lougheed says. "And when that happens, you start to pay a price for it."

And by infrastructure, he means, "the highways, the utilities, the schools, the hospitals and all the services that are required at Fort McMurray." Not to mention a chronic housing shortage.

Lougheed, who recently toured the Fort McMurray area by helicopter calls it "a mess" and "a moonscape" and is suggesting a pause in further development until the infrastructure catches up.

Moreover, he says serious cost overruns in building oil-sands plants will delay royalty returns to the government that will kick in at the conventional rate of about 20 per cent only when the net costs of development are met. Meantime, royalty payments are a measly one per cent. One plant forecast at $5.5 billion came in more than 100 per cent over budget, and Albertans are paying for the cost overrun in foregone royalties.

"What about the people of Alberta?" Lougheed asks. "How do we get our return?" Again, he refers to "the people of Alberta, who own the resource. A lot of people in this town have a problem with the word ownership, but the ownership is with the people."

As for using natural gas for extracting the oil, Lougheed sees that "as an environmental issue, but it's also an economic issue."

And finally he worries about Alberta's 7 per cent wage inflation in an overheated economy that is creating one-third of all the new jobs in Canada and still faces a serious labour shortage.

"Who are the beneficiaries of all this?" Lougheed asks. "First of all, you create an inflationary environment in the country, that's one thing. And we see right here in the city of Calgary, the cost of housing is far higher than it should be (up 35 per cent in the last year alone). You are going to pay in a bunch of ways. People on lower incomes are going to suffer in a city and province of this nature. There's a lot of negatives in an overheated economy, and we truly have an overheated economy in Alberta today. The question is its sustainability."

Clearly, Lougheed is at ease in the role of elder statesman, still motivated by public policy and the public interest, but with no trace of nostalgia for being at the centre of the action. "We're fine," he said with a smile.

He certainly is.

July 2006

CONRAD BLACK

The Conrad Black you've been reading about – living the high life and cutting corporate corners at shareholder expense – isn't the person I know.

When he owned newspapers, including this one, he was a very good proprietor (as he would put it), who invested in the product, seldom interfered in the newsroom, and would never dream of telling you what to write.

And when he started a newspaper, the *National Post*, he changed the economic and editorial rules of the game in this country. He broke the *Globe and Mail*'s monopoly as a national newspaper, created a platform for conservative ideas and, not least, paid good writers top dollar. For that alone, journalists in this country are permanently in his debt.

He also created shareholder value, buying the Southam papers for a song, then selling them at the top of the market. It wasn't Conrad Black who turned Hollinger Inc. into a penny stock, but the guys running it now.

None of these facts is particularly pertinent to his recent trial in Chicago, where he has been convicted on four counts of mail fraud and obstruction of justice, while winning acquittal on nine other charges, including two counts of tax fraud.

So while he still faces jail time if he loses his appeal, he has also won a significant, if partial, victory. The dismissal of the tax charges means he won't be hounded by revenuers in the U.S. and Canada. As for the so-called lifestyle charges, and Black was very much on trial for his lifestyle, a jury of ordinary men and women threw them out.

And while he must endure the humbling proceeding of a bail hearing tomorrow, he has already been deeply humbled, as in how the mighty have fallen. The trial has cost him millions, and he's already lost his power, which he valued much more than money. What matters most to him is his reputation, which should be the best guarantee to the judge that he won't skip bail.

Is Black the author of his own misfortune? Well, a public company can't be run like a private one, not where the rules of corporate governance are concerned, particularly in the United States and especially in the post-Enron era. In hindsight, Black might have saved himself a lot of trouble by not listing on the New York Stock Exchange in the first place.

Does he have only his own arrogance to blame for his plight? While it's true he doesn't do humility very well, his personality has nothing to do with the formidable powers of the state that have been arrayed against him. In seeking to portray Black as a villain, the prosecution transformed him into an unlikely underdog.

Here's what I know about him, as a friendly acquaintance of many years: His humanity and humour, neither of which has been much in evidence in the Chicago media circus, shine through.

Two anecdotes of a mutual friend will illustrate, and if Nick Auf der Maur were here, he would tell the first one himself.

When Nick was struck with cancer in 1996, he had to suspend his column during his treatments, and since he was a freelancer here with no benefits, he would be losing his only source of income at a time when he needed it most. Conrad very quietly sent word he should be paid for the duration of his illness.

Then when Nick died in 1998 and we were putting together what became the bestselling book of his columns and tributes from friends, Conrad was delighted that we asked him to contribute. He made the deadline, stayed within the word limit, and in one of the best pieces in the book, told stories of Nick at his own expense.

Since then, I've dealt with Black on magazine excerpts from his massive biographies of Franklin Roosevelt and Richard Nixon. No author in my experience has ever been more helpful or courteous. In the Roosevelt excerpt on Pearl Harbor Day, he even pointed out, for the purposes of the photo cutline, why FDR was wearing a black arm patch (his mother had recently died). For the Nixon excerpt on the Kennedy-Nixon debates, in *Policy Options*, he took time from the trial to read and approve the edit.

As for the sense of humour, it's dry, and admittedly an acquired taste. When he was in Washington in 1988 for a White House dinner for Brian Mulroney, I ran into him in the lobby of the Madison hotel. He explained why he had decided not to invest with Pierre Peladeau in a new Montreal tabloid, the *Daily News*.

"I figured if I'm going to be a press baron," he said, "I should have controlling interest."

July 2007

LEO KOLBER

Leo Kolber has led the life of a man of influence, seldom at the centre of the spotlight, but never far from it, in business, politics and philanthropy.

As the *consiglière* to the Bronfman family, he managed their investments for decades and built Cadillac Fairview into Canada's premier real estate developer. As the bagman for the Liberal Party of Canada, he raised untold millions for Pierre Trudeau and Jean Chrétien, and later became chairman of the powerful Senate Banking Committee. In Montreal, he raised millions more for McGill University and the Montreal Symphony, and he is a legendary fundraiser in Montreal's Jewish community, notably for the Jewish General Hospital and Israel.

Along the way, he's known every Liberal prime minister from Lester Pearson to Paul Martin, and been on very friendly terms with Brian Mulroney. He's known every Quebec premier from Robert Bourassa to Jean Charest. In Israel, his close friend of half a century is Shimon Peres. He's had nights out with stars like Cary Grant and Frank Sinatra. In business, he was a surrogate son to Sam Bronfman, and close friend and advisor to his sons, Charles and Edgar.

It has, as Kolber says, been "quite a ride." Now he has reached his 80th birthday, the latest milestone in his remarkable life. On his 40th birthday, Danny Kaye delivered smoked meat to his house. On his 50th, he sang a duet with Harry Belafonte. Kolber isn't saying, or doesn't know, what surprises are in store for tonight's black tie gala at Le Windsor.

Upstairs in the splendidly restored former Windsor hotel, Kolber still puts in full days in an eighth floor corner office at Claridge, the Bronfman holding company and associated foundations.

In a room where family photos outnumber shots of the rich and famous, there's one memento that stands out: a designer's sketch of the Toronto Dominion Centre framed in a brass teller's cage from the bank branch that was demolished to make way for the largest office complex in Canada.

Building the TD Centre in the 1960s, Kolber says, was the outstanding achievement of his business career at Fairview, later Cadillac Fairview, where he had started out building suburban shopping centres.

"It put us on the map, it put me on the map," Kolber said the other day. "It transformed Fairview from a small shopping centre company and put us in a position where real estate developers were bringing major deals to us."

The TD Centre transformed the Toronto skyline, announcing its arrival as a world class city and financial centre. The other big five Canadian banks all followed suit and built their own signature skyscrapers that form the centre of the Toronto skyline.

And it was all done on a handshake between Kolber and Allen Lambert, the CEO of the TD Bank who later said the TD Centre transformed the bank from a regional to a national player.

Decades later, Kolber says, people would say to him, "Hey, you're the guys who built the TD Centre." That was Kolber, and his architect, the

PROFILES 217

renowned Mies van der Rohe, whom Kolber brought in at the suggestion of Sam Bronfman's daughter, Phyllis Lambert, famously a student of Mies who had hired him to build the Seagram Building in New York.

To this day, when he flies into Toronto and looks down at the TD Centre, Kolber recalls not only the pride in the achievement, but the anxiety about building and renting it. As he says: "I know as much about building a skyscraper as I know about nuclear fission." He was putting 1.25 million square feet of prime office space on the market, and the bank was taking only 10 per cent of it. "I had many sleepless nights over that," he says.

Fairview and the TD Bank, equal partners in the massive project, each put only $6-million into it and financed the rest. When Cadillac Fairview sold its 50 per cent of the TD Centre at the top of the market in 1987, it walked away with $500-million.

After putting the company on the map, the TD Centre led to the Eaton Centre a few blocks north, the first of the great downtown shopping malls in Canada. It also led to Pacific Place in Vancouver, and other massive projects across Canada. And when Cadillac Fairview more or less ran out of things to build in this country, Kolber and his associates turned their eyes south, building skyscrapers and regional malls in Atlanta, Dallas, Houston, Los Angeles and Washington, D.C.

The culture of the world-competitive Canadian company, says Kolber, is something he learned from Sam Bronfman and the Seagram experience. "Mr. Bronfman used to say you can hone your skills in Canada," Kolber recalls, "but if you want to be really successful you've got to look south to the U.S. and then to the rest of the world. Canada is a fabulous country, but there is not enough room to grow here."

As the Liberal Party's bagman for two decades, he raised millions at a time when there were no limits on donations, and corporate contributions were allowed for parties and leadership campaigns. As the founder of the Liberals' Laurier Club, Kolber chaired numerous events at $10,000 per couple, and once even organized a series of small dinners at 24 Sussex. But Kolber was an equal opportunity donor – he and Charles Bronfman donated $100,000 to Brian Mulroney's leadership campaign in 1983. They couldn't do that today – it wouldn't be legal.

Kolber supported Chrétien's 2003 campaign finance reform that banned corporate and union donations, and isn't troubled by Stephen Harper's 2006 bill limiting personal donations to $1,100 a year. He has always played within the rules. "The unfortunate part is that the Liberals haven't adjusted to it," he says. "The Conservatives are loaded with money. And when you look at Barack Obama, he raised $700-million, most of it in small donations online."

As the former chairman of Senate Banking, Kolber takes the most satisfaction from its recommendation to reduce the capital gains tax from 50 to 25 per cent as well as its landmark 2002 report supporting large bank mergers. Of the current turmoil in financial markets, he says only that "they created a bubble," and this is the reckoning.

For Kolber, there is no reckoning tonight, only a celebration of a life well lived.

National Post, January 2009

∞

JEAN BÉLIVEAU

With the weekend's all-star festivities in Montreal, hockey celebrates the centennial of the Canadiens, 24-time Stanley Cup champions, the most storied franchise in the game.

The greatest Canadien of them all, Jean Béliveau, has his name on the Stanley Cup 17 times – 10 as a player (including five as captain of *les glorieux*), and seven more as an executive. No one else in the history of the game even comes close to matching his achievements, on the ice and off.

If Rocket Richard was fire on ice, Béliveau was the majestic prince of the game. For the 18 years he wore the uniform, and in all the years since his retirement in 1971, he has personified the best attributes of hockey. No one has ever played our game, or represented it, with such class.

In our games of street hockey in Montreal, there were only two kinds of kids, those who wanted to be the Rocket and wore No. 9, and those who wanted to Big Jean, and wore No. 4. I feel quite privileged that Béliveau, the idol of my youth, became a friend as an adult.

As it happened, we were members of the same golf club, Laval-sur-le-Lac, in the 1980s, and occasionally he would invite me to join his regular Saturday morning game. Walking down a fairway with Jean Béliveau, it was easy to imagine what it must have been like skating down the ice with him – he did everything, and he made it look so easy.

And he was always so considerate, not just of his playing partners, but of the caddies carrying his bag. He would spend at least as much time talking to them ("Are you having a good season?" he would ask), and he would always buy them lunch after nine holes. Between shots, he was happy enough to talk hockey, but he always wanted to talk about politics. For if he was a master of one game, he was a student of the other. Prime ministers, from Pierre Trudeau to Stephen Harper, may not have taken his advice, but they have certainly enjoyed his company.

Brian Mulroney offered to put him in the Senate. Jean Chrétien offered to make him governor-general. He declined the first offer because he didn't want a partisan line on his resumé; and the second because of a family tragedy, when his son-in-law committed suicide and Béliveau decided his granddaughters needed him full time.

When I asked Béliveau once where he had learned to stick-handle, he said it was on the outdoor rinks and ponds of his youth in Victoriaville, halfway between Quebec City and Montreal. "We skated 'till our mothers called us home," he said. "It's how we learned the game." It's impossible to imagine that anyone took the puck away from him. That was his special grace on the ice – he controlled the tempo of the game, even while being one of the most selfless players in its history.

When the Forum closed in 1996, he was kind enough to do a radio interview with me, and stayed for half an hour on a morning show I was hosting. We talked about his last Stanley Cup victory, a quarter century earlier in 1971, after the Canadiens had ousted the Big Bad Bruins of Bobby Orr and Phil Esposito, and gone on to clinch the Cup against the Black Hawks of Bobby Hull and Stan Mikita. It was in Chicago that Béliveau began the tradition of the winning captain skating around the ice with the Cup. "I wanted," he said, "to bring the Cup closer to the fans."

"Anything to declare?" the customs man asked Béliveau when the team returned home to Dorval Airport that night.

"Just the Stanley Cup," he said.

"We will just mark 'Canadian Goods Returned'" said the customs agent.

But here's my favourite Béliveau story. Eleven years ago, during the Winter Olympics in Nagano, Japan, the two of us were having lunch. Somehow, the question of hockey rules came up, and how the NHL had changed its rule on short-handed play to align with international hockey and allow an opposing team's player out of the penalty box after a power-play goal.

"I was responsible for having that changed," Béliveau explained.

"How was that?"

"One night, on a power play against Boston, I scored three goals in 44 seconds."

"Really?" I replied. "Who was in nets for them?"

"Terry Sawchuk," he said. Not just any goalie, but perhaps the greatest of all time.

National Post, January 2009

MICHAEL SABIA

The first time I met Michael Sabia was twenty years ago in the third floor corridor of the Langevin Block, which the Prime Minister's Office shares with the Privy Council Office. He was then working for Paul Tellier, clerk of the PCO and head of the public service, as his top financial adviser.

"This is Michael Sabia," said the person making introductions. "He's the guy who invented the GST."

"You're the one," I said. "Do you know how much trouble you've made?"

He had, indeed, made a lot of political trouble for the Conservative government of the day. But the GST proved to be a highly efficient consumer tax, and a highly successful replacement tax for the hidden 13.5 per cent manufacturers' sales tax. Since the 7 per cent GST didn't apply to exports, it came off at the border, giving Canadian exports a huge competitive advantage in selling to the United States at the very moment the Canada-U.S. Free Trade Agreement was coming into force.

The GST, which came to be worth about $6 billion a year of revenues per percentage point to Ottawa, also drove exports, creating jobs and profits, creating even more personal and corporate tax receipts. Paul Martin, finance minister in the Chrétien years, would be the first to acknowledge the role of the GST in balancing books and launching our decade-long virtuous cycle in 1997.

By then, Sabia was long gone from Ottawa, gone to Montreal with Tellier, to help him engineer the turnaround of CN, from worst to first among North American railways. The privatization of CN, and its initial public offering in 1995, was one of the most successful IPOs in Canadian history. Anyone who bought CN stock then, and held it, has done very well by Tellier and Sabia.

Then at BCE, as president and CEO from 2002 to 2008, Sabia re-focused on its core competencies in telecom, selling off non-strategic investments in Telesat, CGI and CTVglobemedia, all of which previous management had overpaid for, creating a cash kitty of $3 billion. The Bell operating companies, in wireless, wireline, satellite and Internet, struggled to retain and gain market share, and the share price flatlined for years. But in 2007, Sabia negotiated the biggest leveraged buyout in history, in which the Ontario Teachers' Pension Fund would have taken it private at $42.75 a share, creating a 50 per cent premium for shareholders over its previous price languishing in the mid-20s. The deal cratered only weeks before it was to close in December last year, under pressure from the stock market crash and a bizarre KPMG accounting report that there was too much debt in the deal. By then, Sabia had left the company in the hands of new management last July, at the request of Teachers.

That's his story so far, but now Sabia, 55, has been named the new president and CEO of the Caisse de dépôt et placement du Québec.

It's not immediately clear why Sabia, at this point on his life, would want to take on such a challenge, and it certainly is a steep one. "Michael likes public service, it's as simple as that," says one close friend and colleague.

He isn't doing it for the money, and in relative terms, it doesn't pay a lot of money. At half a million dollars a year, there isn't the head of a single financial institution in the country who would even consider it. And then there's the grief of running an institution that is a public trust. Not only is the Caisse Quebecers' pension fund, it has, along with Hydro-Québec, become an important source of *la fierté Québécoise*. There's a lot of scrutiny, and a lot of heat, that come with the territory.

Especially now, with the Caisse having lost $40 billion, or 26 per cent of its value, last year. Until this week's rally in equity markets, the stock market was off another 20 per cent already this year, a bear market within a bear market. So the Caisse's $120 billion portfolio, depending on its weight in blue chip equities, is certainly worth even less today.

At his news conference, Sabia laid out a three-point turnaround plan, starting with enhanced risk management, and a better balance of risk and return, while emphasizing the importance of the team at the Caisse.

There will be complaints that Sabia is not only an outsider, but not even a Quebecer, as there were yesterday from one surprising source, the normally erudite André Pratte of *La Presse*, who wrote on his blog: "For several reasons, the name of Michael Sabia shouldn't even be on the list of candidates. In the first place, as is obvious, the CEO of the most important Quebec economic institution should be a Quebecer. To name someone from another province or another country is to send a signal to the world that there are no Quebecers competent enough to run a financial organization of this size."

Sad to say, I don't recognize my friend André Pratte in these words. Sabia has lived here for nearly twenty years. What does it take to make a Quebecer? For that matter, Paul Desmarais, the owner of *La Presse*, is also from Ontario, from Sudbury. That should be an interesting conversation.

When Toe Blake and Scotty Bowman were behind the Canadiens bench, all anyone cared about was how many Stanley Cups they won – thirteen.

That's all anyone should care about now – whether Sabia can make the Caisse a world champion again.

March 2009

MONIQUE JÉRÔME-FORGET

She was known as the handbag lady, *la dame à la sacoche*. As the keeper of Quebec's public purse, Monique Jérôme-Forget was fond of saying she treated it as she would her own – with great care.

And when she stepped down as Jean Charest's finance minister, she didn't leave shoes to be filled so much as the legacy of the purse. Her successor, Raymond Bachand, popped out one of her trademark designer handbags in a cartoon by Serge Chapleau in *La Presse*.

Everyone on the Grande Allée knew the budget was her last one, and it was entirely in character for her to leave now, rather than putting in another three months until the end of the session in June. That's Monique: I'm done, I'm outta here. She's got a husband, Claude Forget, himself one of the outstanding public policy advocates of his generation. They've got grandchildren. They've got a place in Mexico.

She will be missed. She had style, and substance, and you don't see that every day in politics. The style was evident not just in her purses and power outfits – all white or all red. She had a way of arriving in a room. And she had a manner at the podium that said, listen up. She was a woman who could stand in there with the boys, absolutely on her own terms, and deliver a message.

The message invariably came back to *la sacoche*. For most of the last six years she was responsible for raising money as finance minister, and spending it as president of the Treasury Board. Every nickel, on the way in, and the way out, went through her. Each job is enough for any minister. Monique was very comfortable doing both. Charest called her "the boss".

In last fall's election, which restored the Liberals to a majority, she was the key figure in the Liberal campaign, other than Charest himself. If Charest promised a steady hand on the wheel, she was in the passenger seat, giving directions.

The metaphor of the campaign was the coming economic storm, and her role was to provide a certain amount of reassurance, especially to women voters worried about their families' incomes and jobs.

It was also her role to skate the opposition into the boards – fending off concerns about a deficit in a recession, as well as the vociferous warnings of Pauline Marois that the Caisse de dépôt, the province's pension plan, was heading into big trouble.

On that file, Marois has serious I-told-you-so money, although she overplayed her hand in demanding both Charest and Jérôme-Forget be called on the carpet before a committee of the legislature. When Jérôme-Forget finally appeared there last month, she made it very clear she was on to the opposition's game, and made no effort at all to conceal her annoyance. At that, she only appeared at the insistence of the premier's office, and made no effort to conceal her annoyance over that, either.

This led to stories of a falling out between the premier and the finance minister, when the two are always supposed to be on the same page. Moreover, she was initially reported to be miffed that she wasn't properly consulted, as the minister with nominal oversight on the Caisse, on the appointment of Michael Sabia as its new CEO. In fact, while she may have had some reservations initially, she became an enthusiastic supporter of the appointment, which while it was made by the Caisse's board, came from Charest's office.

The Caisse's 26 per cent decline last year – honey I shrunk the pension plan – is not something that can be laid at her door. She wasn't the one buying asset backed commercial paper, and the stock market did lose a third of its value in last fall's crash.

As for going into a deficit in her last budget, it is obviously not the handbag lady's preferred outcome. But every province with the exception of Saskatchewan is in deficit territory. Even oil rich Alberta. It's no mystery, government revenues are down – Quebec's alone went off a cliff, down 19 per cent in January alone, as Jérôme-Forget said worriedly at the time. Welfare claims and other entitlements are up. And there is the stimulus spending, as in, we are all Keynesians now. But Monique's deficit amounts to about 1 per cent of GDP, compared to 2 per cent for Jim Flaherty in Ottawa, and a staggering 12 per cent in Barack Obama's U.S. budget. Relatively speaking, Quebec is in good shape.

It will be years before the handbag lady's legacy can be fully appreciated. But in the pantheon of Quebec finance ministers, she already casts a long shadow.

April 2009

14

TRIBUTES

ROBERT BOURASSA

Robert Bourassa would have liked his funeral. He would have liked the seriousness and spareness of the occasion. He would have liked the way it showcased the dignity and inner strength of his wife, Andrée. He would have liked the role of his son, the jazz pianist François Bourassa, of whom he was terribly proud, in selecting the music.

He would have liked the way the occasion brought people together, all factions of the Quebec Liberal Party, and all elements of Quebec and Canada's political class – Ontario's Mike Harris arrived with every former living premier of Ontario, from Bill Davis to Bob Rae, an extraordinary reminder not only of Bourassa's political longevity, but of the high regard in which he was held.

He would have liked the way his wife opened the balconies of Notre Dame to the public. Most of all, he would have liked the applause, streaming down from the galleries, as Daniel Johnson, Jean Chrétien and Lucien Bouchard entered the cathedral. He would have been surprised by the ovation from the crowd on Place d'Armes when his casket was carried into the golden autumn afternoon.

He might have done a couple of things differently. Had he been consulted on Cardinal Jean-Claude Turcotte's eulogy, Bourassa might have suggested a few statistics, like how many jobs had been created in his time as premier of Quebec.

All that was missing was a sense of Bourassa's humour and his irony. But the guests in Notre Dame's pews had their own memories of that.

For the essence of the private Robert Bourassa was that he was at once a very humane and good-humoured man.

During the period of his life known as "the exile," he went to a dinner party at a friend's house. At the end of the meal, the host raised a glass to Robert Bourassa and his wife "in thanks for their service to the people of Quebec."

Bourassa, his eyes bright with mischief and humour, never missed a beat. "We are," he said, "still available."

That was Bourassa, at once amusing and disarming, moving off the emotion of the moment even as he was touched by it.

But there was equally a serious side to his comment. He was still available, and intent on making himself inevitable, against all odds. He once asked a former campaign aide to assess the odds of his regaining the leadership of the Liberal Party and the premiership of Quebec. Not wishing to encourage him, the one-time assistant replied: "Robert, I would put your chances at one in 100."

Bourassa, who had the ability to stand aside from himself, wasn't in the least offended. But he had another view. "I'd put it at about one in twenty," he said, "but as long as it's even one in 100, I'll never give up."

Because his public pronouncements were marked by what he himself called "zig-zaggage," Bourassa was thought to be ambivalent and ambiguous about everything. But as with everything else, his ambivalence served a higher tactical purpose of keeping the media and the opposition in a state of confusion.

By the time he returned to the Liberal leadership in 1983, Bourassa had learned the hard lessons of his earlier premiership, when he was too young, too impressionable, and too accessible. "You know, at 50," he said then, "you have maybe ten good years left. I want to make the most of them."

When he completed his astonishing political comeback by winning the 1985 election, he was ready to govern as he had not been in his earlier two terms of office. By now, he knew more about the job than his advisers and officials.

This was apparent at Meech Lake, late in the afternoon of April 30, 1987. The first ministers were meeting alone in the second-floor conference room when Bourassa had to leave the room to take an urgent call.

"I have a budget leak," he informed his colleagues as he excused himself. If ever there was a legitimate pretext for Bourassa to leave the meeting on the constitution, this was it. No one would have blamed him for leaving, and more than one may have suspected Bourassa as the source of the leak.

Bourassa went to a phone in the next room and instructed his finance minister, Gérard D. Lévesque, to release his budget that evening instead of the next day. With markets closed, there was no breach of budget secrecy. "You look after it," he told Lévesque. "I've got things to do here."

And with that, Bourassa returned to the constitutional talks. From that moment, his colleagues knew he was there to make a deal.

A few weeks later, the first ministers met again at the Langevin Block in Ottawa. This time it wasn't so easy. First, this was a legal text rather than an agreement in principle, and then the prime minister and premiers had lost the element of surprise that had worked in their favor at Meech. By the time of the Langevin meeting, more than one premier was feeling the heat.

As the long day turned into an even longer night, Bourassa walked back into the conference room following a break, opened his briefcase and pulled out a sweater. It was his way of saying he was there for the night.

The next day, when he signed the agreement under the television lights in the old Ottawa railway station, he finished his signature with a flourish and two words: "It's done." At that moment, the room exploded in thunderous applause, and Bourassa later admitted that he was almost overcome by the ovation.

For all his apparent ambivalence, Bourassa knew what he wanted on the big issues. And he wanted Meech Lake.

For Bourassa, it held out the prospect of redemption for the Victoria Conference of 1971, when he left money on the table. He had walked away from a constitutional veto for Quebec because the province's political class told him he needed more control over social programs.

He was fond of quoting Fouché, Napoleon's minister of police: "Worse than a crime, it was a mistake."

Bourassa knew that Victoria was one historical error, and he also knew that the death of Meech was another.

When Meech failed, Bourassa felt he had to get out in front of the sovereignist parade to slow it down. He then let three little genies out of the bottle – Bill 150, requiring a referendum within two years, the Belanger-Campeau Commission on Quebec's constitutional future, and his own party's Allaire report, which he soon recognized was out of control. But by then, the fall of 1990, he was away from his post, fighting his first bout of cancer. When he finally got to a party convention in 1991, it took him all of two days to put Allaire where it belonged, on the shelf.

In the 1995 referendum, he played a minor supporting role, until panic swept the tents of the No forces in the final days, and they put him on the road again to prop up their "B" team. He was only too happy to answer the call. In truth, he had been waiting for it.

Last October 30, late in the afternoon of referendum day, he returned a call, and ventured a prediction that the No should win with about 51 per cent. "We should be OK," he said. His only concern was the high turnout. "Over 88 per cent," he said, "and anything can happen." Anything almost did.

In his final illness, Bourassa would call around to his friends, as always, doing his own damage control. "We'll see," he would say. "We'll tough this out." As he had in another life, as long as there was even a 1 per-cent chance, he would never give up.

And he never did.

October 1996

∞

NICK AUF DER MAUR

My favourite Nick story involves Melissa. Naturally. Nick was in his office at the bar of Winnie's when I walked in on a Friday afternoon in March 1985.

"Melissa's turning thirteen on Sunday," Nick announced.

"That's great. What are you getting her?"

"All she wants is a birthday card."

"So?"

"A personal birthday card from the prime minister."

"Uh-huh."

"And the president," he added.

"You mean, the president of the United States."

"So what do you think?" he asked.

"I think you'd better call Fox."

Bill Fox, a mutual friend, was press secretary to Prime Minister Brian Mulroney. Fox was quite busy with the advance for the Shamrock Summit of the prime minister and president in Quebec City on St. Patrick's Day, Melissa's 13th birthday.

Melissa had told her Dad in no uncertain terms: the prime minister is your friend, the president is his friend. I'm Irish and Canadian on my father's side, and American on my mother's.

Fox understood. He was Irish, and he had a daughter, too. So did the prime minister, when Fox briefed him on the request.

"Great idea," Mulroney said with a laugh. "Nick will love it."

When Ronald Reagan got off Air Force One in Quebec that windy Sunday afternoon, he inspected an honour guard in a hangar, exchanged words with Mulroney about their common Irish ancestry, and climbed into the back of a bulletproof Cadillac for the drive into town.

Mulroney, just back from the funeral of Soviet leader Yuri Andropov, was the first Western leader to brief Reagan on the new Russian leader, Mikhail Gorbachev, who sent a message that he wanted to meet the American president at an early moment. There were other things on the agenda. Acid rain. Free trade.

But first, Mulroney explained the Melissa situation to the president.

"I have an unusual request from a friend of mine, who was a candidate for me, who is particularly close to his daughter."

"Sure, I'd be delighted," Reagan said. "What an interesting name. Auf der Maur. It doesn't sound Irish."

When they got to the Château Frontenac and up to the suite, Mulroney hauled out this huge custom-made card. Here's what he wrote.

"Dear Melissa: Given your unique Canadian-American heritage (to say nothing of the Swiss!) the president and I wanted to send warm greetings and good wishes on your birthday." And they both signed it.

As Nick later wrote in his column, it was "the first document of the Shamrock Summit."

Nick, who had been invited to the gala where Mulroney and Reagan sang *When Irish Eyes Are Smiling*, was stopped by colleagues and informed that Canadian officials had briefed the international media on the Melissa Accord, as Mulroney later said, "the first agreement of the summit." The briefing official somehow thought Auf der Maur was Swedish rather than Swiss, but that just made the story better in the telling, and Nick told the best stories.

After the gala, Mulroney spotted Nick in the crowd and dragged Reagan over to meet him, introducing him to the president of the United States as his good friend and as Melissa's father.

Nick had Melissa's birthday card framed, and it hung in the hall of his house on Tupper Street.

The story of Melissa's birthday card says a great deal about Nick.

About his love for his daughter, who was the great joy of his life.

About his attachment and loyalty to his friends. About his wonderful capacity for making the ridiculous into reality.

His sense of fun also translated into something of his way with women. Strong feminists would be offended if Nick didn't try to pick them up.

There were many women in Nick's life, but really only three whom he deeply loved. His Swiss mother, who brought him his Bible and his Canadiens jersey in the Parthenais Street jail when he was locked up in the October Crisis of 1970. Melissa's mother, the brilliant and beautiful Linda Gaboriau.

And their Canadian-American-Swiss-Irish-French daughter, the child of their particular and peculiar destiny.

Melissa was the flower girl at her parents' wedding in 1976. Later on, Nick never really forgave himself for the failure of his marriage and he never stopped making up for it to Melissa. All week long, he would look forward to their weekends together. He would drop out of sight after lunch on Friday, and we wouldn't see him again until Monday, when he would be full of stories of his weekend with Melissa.

Many years later, when my own daughter came along, he would always ask about Gracie. And when I worried about her being the child of a failed marriage, he always had a gentle word of advice. "Wait till she gets old enough for you to travel together," he said once. "Those will be the best holidays for both of you."

When Melissa bloomed into a musician and, later, a rock star, he took his greatest pride as a parent in the fact that she was so grounded, and had such values.

And Nick's friends. Well, they were everyone he ever ran with, in every party he ever ran for. And there were a lot of both. People he ran against, John Lynch-Staunton and Warren Allmand, were among his best friends. One of Allmand's circulars, in the 1984 federal election, included a positive piece Nick had done on him. Jean Drapeau appreciated Nick's wicked sense of humour, as well as his sense of occasion, as when he proposed a motion of congratulations at city council on the mayor's birthday.

And Mulroney, who recruited Nick to run for him against Allmand, came within a couple of thousand votes of having him in his cabinet. Nick figured the Tories were the only party he had never belonged to and, besides, what did he have to lose? Nick had to settle for being a friend of a prime minister, and he probably preferred it that way. He wouldn't have passed security clearance, anyway.

"Comrade Prime Minister," Nick always called Mulroney, in deference to his own Marxist origins. This was a guy who was once escorted out of Moscow by the comrades when, at a Kremlin reception, Nick proposed a toast to a free Czechoslovakia after the Soviet occupation of 1968.

Ottawa would have taken him out of Montreal, and he hated leaving Montreal. In his entire life, he never got a driver's license. Why would he when he could walk or take a cab to wherever he was going? He hated weekends in the country. He hated leaving the city.

Nick lived his life as if he were immortal, and so we always assumed he was. When it turned out he wasn't, he confronted his illness with courage and humour and, as always, brought an amazing number of people together.

Including the people who worked so hard to save his life, whom he wrote about with gratitude and with pride in his city, which was his world.

And Melissa, who was the centre of it.

April 1998

THE ROCKET

In the last years of his life, Maurice Richard thought a lot about his death, as if he sensed the magnitude of the event.

Not that he was preoccupied with his passing in a morbid sense, but the Rocket wouldn't have wanted anything inappropriate to be done in his name, such as a red or blue flag being draped on his coffin.

He needn't have worried. The Rocket was in good hands. His family. His church. His team. His community. All of them understood his sense of occasion.

We've never seen anything quite like the events of this week, and it's unlikely that we ever will again. The Rocket dies only once.

There's never been such an outpouring of affection and respect as we've witnessed this week. The largest funeral in the history of the city, and perhaps the country, wasn't for a prime minister or premier, a titan of industry or a prince of the church. It was for a man who was, as he said, just a hockey player.

But it was the way he played, and the team he played for, that fired the imagination of the public. It is forty years since the Rocket retired, now beginning the third generation of people who never saw him play.

Yet rather than fading, the Rocket's reputation only grew. His records were long since eclipsed, but somehow never surpassed.

In any event, the Rocket's enduring fame wasn't based on statistics – even his most impressive ones. First to score 50 goals in 50 games. First to score 500 goals. Or his 82 playoff goals, or his six playoff goals in overtime. Or his eight Stanley Cups, of which he was Canadiens' captain for four.

Rather, it was that he owned one third of the ice, from the blue line in. It was his intensity, his heart and his will to win that brought people to their feet. There was nothing quite like the sound of the Rocket being cheered to the echo in the Forum on a Saturday night.

And those who never saw him play heard about him in oral history classes, at their father's knee. They heard how he carried the team, how he carried opponents on his back, how he carried the hopes of an entire people.

It was not a burden he could lay down at his retirement. Somehow he was expected to go on being a hero. It wasn't a career, but a lifetime role. At some level, the Rocket understood that, accepted it, and got on with it.

In his own uncomplicated way, the Rocket was a very shrewd and sophisticated man, able to distinguish between his public obligations and his private life. He wasn't interested in making a lot of money – the Rocket wasn't the sort of man who charged for an autograph.

He had his family, a close circle of trusted friends, his fishing. He looked after the legend, too, but not in a self-serving sense. The Rocket played or refereed old-timers hockey in every tank town in the country. It was a way of staying in the game, and of giving back to it.

And he knew his public, because he never got out of touch with them.

There was a moment early in the week when his son, Maurice Jr., said the family knew what their father meant to the people, and were prepared to share their grief.

But they came to the Molson Centre not in grief so much as in gratitude for the Rocket's life, which enlarged the life of Quebec and all of French Canada. They came also with pride in his unique achievements. They came wearing sweaters he had signed, clutching pictures with him at pee-wee banquets, holding the hands of sons named after him.

By nightfall on Tuesday, it was clear the Molson Centre would not be closed until the middle of the night. It was another standing-room-only crowd for the Rocket. The only quiet crowd of his career. The most respectful crowd ever seen.

Thus the Rocket, who closed the Forum with the ovation of the century in 1996, opened the Molson Centre this week in the sense that it is now a meaningful place. Something historically significant has now occurred there.

As there was the laying in state of Howie Morenz at the Forum in 1937, so there was now the laying in state of the Rocket in 2000. Three generations from now, they will still be talking about the day more than 100,000 people lined up to pay their respects.

And then there was the Rocket's funeral at Notre Dame, a basilica of overpowering beauty. There was an eloquent simplicity in the eulogies, notably in Maurice Jr.'s observation: "We are now in the temple of love. Yesterday, I had the impression we were in the kingdom of love." Or in the farewell of Cardinal Jean-Claude Turcotte: "*Bon repos, Maurice, bonne pêche.*"

There have been many standing ovations at Notre Dame, for *The Messiah* and other performances. But never before has there been a prolonged standing ovation for a man who was just a hockey player, as his teammates from two decades took a final shift with him and guided him on his way.

Dickie Moore has said the Rocket was the Babe Ruth of hockey. Yes, and Jean Béliveau was hockey's Joe DiMaggio. One was an incomparable hero, the other a majestic figure of the game.

Béliveau was supposed to be the last pallbearer on the right. But he gravitated to his natural position at centre, behind the Rocket, setting him up in the slot.

Wherever he is now, don't get between the Rocket and the net.

June 2000

JEAN DRAPEAU

In public, Jean Drapeau had a solemn sense of occasion. In private, he had a wicked sense of humour.

He once returned a reporter's call and left a message from "the mayor."

"Sorry I missed your call, Mr. Mayor," I explained. "I was over at the bank paying a parking ticket."

"By all means," Drapeau replied, "buy them by the dozen."

He had a weakness for puns and bad jokes, in both official languages, and whenever he heard one he liked, he would write it down and put it in his pocket.

With his passing, in the last months of the twentieth century, he ranks as Montreal's mayor of the century and, without any doubt, its man of the century.

He had a slogan, "one island, one city" that he never saw realized. But in his time, there could have been another motto for Montreal: "one city, one man."

He set out to put Montreal on the international map and ended up on it himself. No other Canadian mayor could claim to have been introduced from the audience by Ed Sullivan, who called him "Gene Drapoo."

This was in the run-up to Expo '67, the most successful world's fair of the century, which Drapeau had the harebrained idea of putting on two islands which didn't exist in the middle of the St. Lawrence River, but which were created in part with landfill from metro excavations.

The fair was his centennial gift to Canada, and to this day remains celebrated as a high water mark of confederation, a historic moment when Canada shed its inferiority complex and recognized itself as one of the leading countries of the world.

The subway is his enduring legacy to Montreal. It became the city's new central nervous system. The mid-town core of the city shifted north to de Maisonneuve Boulevard, and dozens of office and apartment buildings sprang up "on the metro."

And then there were the Olympics, Drapeau's billion-dollar baby. The costs spun out of control, largely because Drapeau wanted a stadium of monumental proportions, one with a tower and a retractable roof. To the end of his days, the Olympic fiasco remained a sore spot with Drapeau. He was always writing his version of what happened, but never got around to publishing it.

He needn't have bothered, because the people of his city had long since forgiven him for it. At least he was thinking big, and they liked that about him. They also knew that his ambitions were always for the city, never for himself.

Neither did he see any contradiction in being a reformer and ruling city hall with an iron fist. He called it disciplined democracy, and said the entrance to his Civic Party was narrow, while the exit was wide. The party headquarters was a phone and filing cabinet in his private office on Sherbrooke Street East. Membership was by invitation and consisted of his caucus at city hall.

The media railed, the opposition flailed, and the voters agreed with Drapeau. In 1978, though tarred by the Olympic mess, he was swept back into office with all but two seats on city council. For Drapeau, it was a sweet moment of vindication. "*Vox populi, vox dei,*" he said on election night, looking pointedly at press row.

But after his final election in 1982, Drapeau began to slow down after his first incapacitating illness. Walking with a cane, he was no longer the civic whirlwind. "The head is willing," he said at a 1983 ground-breaking ceremony, "but the body is not."

Drapeau always said he didn't want to hang around the city after he left office, like the ghost at the banquet, and Brian Mulroney obligingly named him ambassador to UNESCO, which took him to Paris for a few years.

As for his legacy, if you would see it, look around you, all around you.

August 1999

∞

PIERRE TRUDEAU

On a Monday morning in May of 1980, Prime Minister Pierre Trudeau met with several advisers from his referendum war room to discuss strategy for his fourth and final speech of the campaign, a monster rally at the Paul Sauvé Arena in Montreal.

One of the communications advisers, Claude Morin, pointed to a small story in the day's newspaper clippings. No more than a few paragraphs under a one-column heading, the clipping told of how René Lévesque had said Trudeau wasn't really a French Canadian because his mother's name was Elliott.

Some people didn't think much of it, but Trudeau was very interested in the story, and thought he could somehow use it in his speech.

He turned to André Burelle, his chief speechwriter, and asked him for a list of Parti Québécois luminaries with English names. Everyone around the table knew them: Pierre Marc Johnson, Robert Burns, Robert Mackay, Gratia O'Leary, Louis O'Neill. They began to see where Trudeau was going with it.

Burelle didn't write a text for the speech – just some baseline notes that Trudeau would commit to memory. But Burelle did compile the names, and passed them on to the prime minister.

Two days later, the day of the Paul Sauvé speech, Trudeau had Jean Chrétien around to lunch at 24 Sussex, and asked his justice minister what he should say.

Chrétien's advice was characteristically simple. "Give it to them, Pierre," he said.

Eight hours later, on an arena stage that had always belonged to the PQ, Chrétien introduced Trudeau as "the pride of Quebec and the pride of Canada."

Trudeau knew the speech had to be meaningful and so it was, with his solemn promise to put the seats of his Quebec members on the line for constitutional change.

Trudeau switched to English and delivered a memorable sound bite about the separatist agenda for fracturing Canada. "They want to tear it down? They want to take it away? No, that's our answer."

By now, Trudeau was in full gunslinger mode and the crowd was in full cry, cheering him to the echo. Then he turned to Lévesque's comments about his name.

"*Bien sûr que mon nom est Pierre Elliott Trudeau. Elliott était le nom de ma mère, voyez-vous?*"

The crowd sensed what he was onto, and their cries of "Trudeau, Trudeau," turned to "Elliott, Elliott."

Most journalists covering the event later agreed it was the best speech they ever heard. Afterward, a bunch of us adjourned to the Auberge St. Tropez on Crescent Street, where the usual argument ensued about the headline.

Patrick Gossage, Trudeau's press secretary, said the headline had to be the promise of constitutional reform.

"That might be the headline," I replied from across the table. "But it's not the history. He made history with Elliott tonight." And so he did, in what remains the defining rhetorical moment of Trudeau's career, and surely one of the great Canadian speeches of the 20th century, one that began with a one-column clipping.

For those of us who followed Trudeau around for a living, he was never anything less than interesting. He always challenged us, and he usually rose to any challenge that lay in his path.

On foreign trips with Trudeau, even the separatist scribes wanted him to do well, since they were also proud of him as a favourite son of Quebec.

Every now and then there would be a moment of truce, usually late at night, aboard his plane.

One night in the spring campaign of 1979, Trudeau was flying somewhere over Quebec when columnist Charles Lynch broke out his harmonica and began to play *Un Canadien Errant*. It was a heartstopping moment, with Trudeau joining the most hardbitten reporters and cameramen in singing and humming along.

The 1979 election was Trudeau's most difficult campaign in every sense. It was also his bravest.

His marriage had crumbled, and his prospects for re-election were dim. It was a measure of his dignity that while everyone on the press bus felt for him, no one felt sorry for him. No one even felt the need to cut him any slack.

Such as the long day, the very long day, the bus rolled out of Quebec at 6:30 in the morning, bound for the South Shore and the Lower St. Lawrence. By the time he got to La Pocatière in mid-afternoon, it was already his fourth event of the day, and the town-hall format worked to his disadvantage. All the questions were on agriculture, and finally Trudeau snapped: "Everyone knows farmers are grumblers."

Which happens to be the dead truth, but not the sort of sound bite that makes a prime minister's day. "Farmers grumblers, Trudeau says." Gotcha. It was the journalistic equivalent of a drive-by shooting.

Trudeau got killed on the news that night, and the rest of his day never happened. But being Trudeau, he never complained and never explained. He simply pulled himself together for the next event.

And that night in Rimouski, far too late for anyone to file on it, he stood in gunslinger pose and delivered one of the great speeches of his career. It was about Quebec's future in Canada, the one issue that never failed to stir the passions of his heart.

This country, this continent, he said, had been discovered and explored and settled by French Canadians. All of it belonged to them, and they should never give up such a precious birthright.

Though it was still early in the campaign, Trudeau had clearly determined in his own mind that if he was going to lose, it was going be about things that mattered to him.

The circumstances were very different in the winter campaign of 1980, when time and chance combined to deal him a winning hand. It was the greatest performance of Trudeau's career. For two months he successfully impersonated a sleepwalker, hiding his intellectual and rhetorical gifts behind a hefty podium that his staff derisively called the coffin.

But in St. John's he broke free of the handlers and engaged a crowd of boisterous Memorial University students who demanded that he turn over ownership of the offshore oil resource to their have-not province.

"I'd like to tell you you could have it all, it would be all yours, and wouldn't it be wonderful," he said, "but that wouldn't be Canada, which is about fairness and sharing."

The students responded with a standing ovation. And in the front row, we were reminded that he still had it.

Clearly, as he told colleagues, if he was going back as prime minister, it was going to mean something. The 1980–84 Trudeau government was the most activist of his four terms of office.

There was the 1980 referendum and the subsequent two-year struggle to patriate the constitution with the Charter of Rights and Freedoms. There was the North-South Initiative and the Peace Initiative. There was the National Energy Program and record deficits and debt.

Not all these policies were successful or right for the times, and some of them, such as the NEP and the fiscal framework, were outright disasters.

But to the end, Trudeau was always able to summon the energy to defend them.

As he said, somewhat grandiloquently, in his farewell address to the 1984 Liberal leadership convention, whenever he felt thwarted, he would "go over the heads of the multinationals, over the heads of the provinces, over the heads of the superpowers, to the people of this land."

Not that the superpowers cared much about the people of this land, but Trudeau always gave the impression that he did, simply by never talking down to them.

And so he defined not only the political texture of his times, but the touchstones of two generations of Canadians – baby-boomers who grew to early middle age with him, and Gen-Xers who grew up with him as the only prime minister they ever knew.

In the next federal election, there will be millions of Canadians voting who have no memory of Trudeau as prime minister.

In that sense, he was like Rocket Richard. Millions of Canadians never saw him. But they heard about him. And they knew he could play the game.

Better than anyone.

October 2000

TED BLACKMAN

Ted Blackman was a complete Montrealer in journalism and broadcasting. Real Montrealers, Ted once wrote, walk on the north side of Ste. Catherine Street.

Well, of course. The sunny side of the street. And this real Montrealer once famously painted a green line down the middle of it before the St. Patrick's Day parade. City Hall got the message.

In the news business, many people move on to other markets, but Ted was made for this one. In both print and radio, he hired a lot of people who later achieved national prominence. One of the reasons he needed satellite television with hundreds of channels was to watch all the talented people who got their first break from him in local radio.

His column wouldn't have read quite the same in any paper other than this one. It is equally difficult to imagine him doing radio commentaries in Toronto on the Leafs, Blue Jays and Argonauts. His teams were the Canadiens, the Expos and Alouettes; he gave them his lifelong allegiance, and knew everything that was going on with them.

A couple of years ago, he called to say that Maurice Richard had only hours to live.

"How do you know that?" I asked.

"Because I just talked to Jean Béliveau at the hospital," he said.

Ted had great news judgment, and an unerring sense of the city. He knew the Rocket died only once, that it was a uniquely important Montreal occasion, and correctly predicted that 100,000 people would come to pay their respects at the Molson Centre. How do you cover a funeral on radio? Ted did it brilliantly, by getting everybody on the air.

He knew everyone. Only Ted could have given Scotty Bowman's cell phone number to Brian Mulroney so that the former prime minister could call and congratulate him on winning his ninth Stanley Cup.

All the people Ted knew had one thing in common – he had met them along the way in Montreal. He was a tireless ambassador for Montreal, and never gave up on the city, even in its most troubled times, notably the exodus after the first election of the Parti Québécois in 1976 and the anguish following the 1995 referendum.

He knew the city from first light to closing time. There was no doubt that Ted should have taken better care of himself, and as it was once said of the Rolling Stones, if he'd known he was going to live this long, he would have. His hard living was not conducive to longevity. But like his friend Nick Auf der Maur, he lived the life he chose, and lived it fully.

And the way he looked at life after his liver transplant, he had another seven years. But rather than ease back with the comfortable hours of doing sports in the afternoon-drive show, he returned to the punishing schedule of doing a morning show.

Three things made Ted, in his prime, a superlative journalist. One, his huge network of contacts. Two, his ability to get the story behind the story. Three, his instinctive sense of the big picture, whether it was sports or politics.

And because he started out as a wire-service reporter, he got the story out fast. His *Gazette* coverage of the 1972 Team Canada series from Moscow was breathtaking. He was writing to deadline, from eight time zones ahead, from the user-unfriendly Soviet system. But he got it all, including the post-game quotes.

Two other points about Ted. One was his loyalty to his friends, at all times and in all circumstances. The other was his love of women. He was married three times, to three very accomplished women, and had the gift of being on very good terms with all of them. In his own way, he was a strong feminist.

And underneath the gruff exterior, he was not called Teddy Bear for nothing. His close friend George Balcan remembers the end of his own farewell broadcast from Mount Royal and looking over at Ted and seeing him in tears.

There might be some tears for Ted at his memorial service. There will certainly be a crowd at Erskine and American United Church. On the north side of Sherbrooke Street. The side real Montrealers walk on. Ted would have liked that.

October 2002

∞

PIERRE BOURGAULT

It was Pierre Bourgault whom Pierre Trudeau had in mind during the 1980 referendum campaign, when he asked scornfully what had become of "the knights of independence," eclipsed as they were by the ambiguous advocates of sovereignty-association.

Bourgault never put the water of association in the wine of sovereignty. His kind of sovereignty never came with a hyphen in it. He was for independence, period, full stop. Thus, in Trudeau's terms, Bourgault was a true *"chevalier de l'indépendance."* At least Bourgault was honest, you had to give him that.

Firebrand and radical that he was, he was also an extraordinarily nice man. I first met him in 1979, when he was a guest on a CBC television show I was hosting on the referendum. He had just torn into me in his *Gazette* column for one I had written, taking down the Parti Québécois white paper on sovereignty-association as a bad deal that English-speaking Canada would never go for.

Bourgault walked onto the set and came over to introduce himself with a handshake and an apology.

"If I can't take a little heat myself," I replied, "I should get out of the kitchen."

"Yes," he said, "but we are both in the same kitchen."

That was Bourgault – he had a great sense of humour, and he was very quick with it. He was famously an angry man – it went with the territory. But I knew him more for his laughter. He had a wonderful sense of the absurd and used it to great advantage in his writing and broadcasting.

Then in the 1980s, someone got the idea of putting the two of us together on a radio talk show, perhaps in the hope we would yell at one another. Instead, we got on famously, and no one listened. He treated colleagues with courtesy and opponents with respect, as a result of which many of them became his friends.

There was, for example, no better road show in that first referendum than Bourgault and Robert Bourassa on campus, one an outcast of the separatist movement, the other regarded as a leper by federalists. So they went where no one else would go, when no one else would have them. Bourgault would set the room on fire with his brilliant oratory, and then Bourassa would extinguish it with a remorseless flood of statistics.

On that first referendum night, they appeared together on a Radio-Canada panel. "This is your victory," Bourgault quite generously told Bourassa on the air.

Typically, Bourgault was friends with an adversary and couldn't stand René Lévesque, who had brought the sovereignty movement from the margins to the mainstream.

Bourgault had every reason to despise Lévesque. After dissolving his Rassemblement pour l'indépendance Nationale and joining the new Parti Québécois in 1968, Bourgault was never again given a prominent role in the independence movement. From Lévesque's standpoint, the dislike was equally visceral.

"Lévesque didn't like it that Bourgault was gay and felt uncomfortable in his presence," says Graham Fraser, author of the definitive *René Lévesque and the Parti Québécois in Power*. "And fundamentally, he thought Bourgault was disruptive, destabilizing and threatening, representing all the things he didn't want the PQ to be."

The party Bourgault wanted the PQ to be would never have been elected in 1976, and Lévesque understood he couldn't win an election on a *pur et dur* platform. Lévesque also understood that while Bourgault and the hard-liners had nowhere else to go, his job was to broaden the sovereignty movement's base.

Which, on an intellectual level, left Bourgault back where he began, storming the barricades of respectability. And that, more or less, is how he spent the remainder of his life. If there was an occasional tone of bitterness in his newspaper column after the second referendum in 1995, perhaps it was because the dream died hard.

When one of his books came out during our radio period, he brought a copy to the studio already inscribed to me. "If we're not careful," he had written, "we will end up as friends."

June 2003

CLAUDE RYAN

Claude Ryan used to say he was "a three-career man" – social activist, journalist and politician. In all three, he made a lasting impression and left an enduring mark as a man of ideas who was also committed to action.

In all three careers, he personified the motto of Thomas Aquinas, "Observe, judge, act," that motivated his postwar generation of Quebecers in the lay Catholic Action movement later described as "the beachhead of the Quiet Revolution."

First as general-secretary of Catholic Action from 1945, then as editor and later publisher of *Le Devoir* from 1962, and finally as leader of the Quebec Liberal Party from 1978, he was known for his forceful intellect and authoritarian personality.

Ryan made no apology for a style variously described as abrasive, arrogant and ascetic. As he once put it: "I do not impose myself on others, but if I am appointed to lead, I expect to lead."

In this, he had both the qualities of his faults and the faults of his qualities. He set such standards of intellectual rigour, it was easy to forget he was all too human, capable of blood feuds, vendettas and settling scores. But that was Ryan – you took him as he was, or not at all.

His complex character, and the contradictions between his essential generosity and meanness of spirit, were what made him so interesting. A profoundly and devotedly religious man, he would be the first to acknowledge he was a sinner, not a saint.

But in all that he did, in all of his careers, no one ever suggested he was in it for anything other than the highest of motives – building a stronger Quebec within an enduring Canadian framework. Many disagreed with his ideas, but no one ever questioned his intellectual capacity, or the lucidity with which those ideas were presented.

The generation of Quebec public figures to which he belonged was undoubtedly the most activist, and the most accomplished, of the 20th century. The Catholic Action movement produced politicians such as Jeanne Sauvé and Gérard Pelletier, public servants such as Pierre Juneau and Fernand Cadieux, writers such as Guy Rocher and Fernand Dumont, sociologists such as Maurice Pinard and Soucy Gagné, economists such as André Raynauld and Albert Breton. Empowered by the force of ideas, this generation threw off the intellectual constraints of Duplessisism.

From his travels across Canada, first in Catholic Action and then as president of the Canadian Institute for Adult Education in the 1950s, Ryan developed an understanding of the entire country that was unusual for a Quebecer in those days.

Rooted in Quebec, he was also interested in Canada, an outlook that made him an ideal choice as editor and then publisher of *Le Devoir*. Later, his nationalist Quebec perspective within a Canadian context also made him the obvious choice to become Liberal leader at a time when the party was desperate to counter the sovereignist thrust of a Parti Québécois government on the road to the first referendum on sovereignty in 1980.

At *Le Devoir*, Ryan's editorials were must reading for the political class. Noted for their clarity and coherence, they were usually written with the speed of a wire-service reporter on deadline. It was nothing for Ryan to knock out 1,500 words in an hour. But he also put the paper on a sounder footing by insisting it be run as a business rather than a charity. He was notoriously tight. His idea of a power lunch was St. Hubert BBQ. When a decorator once asked him how he wanted the office painted, he replied, "in white."

By most conventional assessments, his leadership of the Liberals would be considered a failure because he was unable to win an election against René Lévesque in 1981. But that doesn't take account of what he did to restore the credibility of the Liberals as a party of ideas, the indispensable role he played as an advocate of renewed federalism, or the huge machine he built to fight the 1980 referendum.

As a politician, he was highly unconventional, an anti-charisma candidate who didn't care if his meetings got on television. In the 1980 referendum and 1981 election campaigns, he refused to spend money on polling, forcing his advisers to get figures from the feds or the media.

But he gave the Liberals the intellectual content and credibility they needed to fight the first referendum. And his stature was somehow undiminished by his election defeat. Like Robert Stanfield, whom he greatly admired, Ryan thought it was more important to have principles than to be in power. It was a measure of Ryan's standing that when he was succeeded by his predecessor, Robert Bourassa asked him to stay on, and gave him prominent portfolios such as education.

When he completed his third career in 1994, each one had lasted about sixteen years. In the last decade, he enjoyed a fourth career as elder statesman and conscience of the Liberal Party, a role cut short by the illness that ended his life. Typically, he acknowledged the finality of his cancer, refusing remedial treatment, and even putting it out that he was dying.

He was a great Quebecer, and a remarkable Canadian. As he often said: "*Très bien, très bien. Formidable, formidable.*"

February 2004

PETER JENNINGS

On the day before the 1995 Quebec referendum, a small group of journalists was standing outside the Ritz when Peter Jennings came through the front door of the hotel.

We introduced ourselves, and he had a word with everyone.

"You've beaten the *Times* badly on this story," he told a beaming Charlie Trueheart of the *Washington Post*.

Jennings was on his way to shoot some stand-ups for the opening of his show the next night. He had brought ABC *World News Tonight* to Montreal because he thought it was an important international story. It wasn't just that, as a Canadian, he cared about the potential breakup of his country. He thought U.S. viewers should know about it.

"What do you think?" he asked me.

"It's very close."

The next day, I sent him an analysis I'd done, suggesting a narrow No victory as the most likely outcome. The morning after, the phone rang in my hotel room.

"Hi, it's Peter Jennings," he said. "Thanks for sending me that piece. It was quite an evening, wasn't it?"

We chatted about mutual acquaintances, including my father-in-law's brother, Jack Van Dusen, who had given him his first job at CJOH television in Ottawa.

"Here's my private home number," he said as he rang off. "Please call the next time you're in New York."

And here's the point – although he was very aware of the fame that went with being a major U.S. network news anchor, he also remembered where he came from. And that informed his work. He looked at America from the outside in.

When Ronald Reagan died and Brian Mulroney was asked to deliver one of the eulogies, Jennings understood it was unprecedented for a foreign leader to speak at the state funeral of a U.S. president. He led his broadcast that night with a clip of the former Canadian prime minister rather than the other two speakers, both named George Bush.

He kept hiring Canadians as correspondents, producers and writers, to the point where there were mutterings about it at ABC News, particularly in its Washington bureau. Even when he became a U.S. citizen in 2003, he was criticized for taking so long to do it, as well as for retaining his Canadian citizenship. He also retained a cottage in the Gatineau, where he usually spent most of August.

In some right wing circles in the United States, his Canadian origins were cited as proof of liberal bias. Jennings never dignified such nonsense by acknowledging it. He simply got on with his job, and did it better than anyone else, for longer than anyone else. He was worldly, urbane, elegant and dashing. No one ever fit a trench coat better.

But no one lasts a quarter century in an anchor chair on presentational skills alone. The core attribute in connecting with viewers is trust. And, with his unfailing sense of occasion, Jennings inspired trust.

There are two standards of excellence in television news – Walter Cronkite in one generation and Peter Jennings in the next. Cronkite was a born reporter who became a great anchor. And Jennings was a born anchor who became a great reporter.

Cronkite worked his way up from war correspondent to the anchor chair. Jennings worked his way down from the anchor chair to war correspondent. When he was made ABC anchor the first time in the mid-1960s, he was only 27, clearly too young.

But at least he knew it. Most U.S. networks use the White House beat as a grooming ground for stardom. It is life in a bubble. Jennings went out and saw the world, from Vietnam, to the Middle East, to London where he became ABC's international co-anchor. The next time he sat in the anchor chair in New York in 1983, he was ready.

Cronkite's signature event occurred on November 22, 1963, the assassination of John F. Kennedy. Jennings narrated the events of September 11, 2001. Each not only informed the audience of something awful, but shared his own humanity and helped their viewers get through it.

With Tom Brokaw of NBC and Dan Rather of CBS, Jennings formed a generational triumvirate whose appointment newscasts were increasingly challenged by all-news cable channels. This resulted in a certain dumbing down of the news, in a parochial American sense, that Jennings must have found discomfiting. He undoubtedly preferred to leave the Michael Jackson trial where it belonged – on Court TV. It wasn't for nothing that his program was called *World News Tonight*.

He refused to bow to the lowest common denominator and perhaps as a result, his ratings suffered. Still, it was reassuring to know a story had to meet his standards to get on the air.

As Canadians, we were immensely proud of him. He not only was our best. He was *the* best.

August 2005

SIMON REISMAN

The first thing anyone noticed about Simon Reisman's office was the black rotary phone. At the dawn of the digital age, he insisted on this relic of an earlier era, almost as a condition of accepting his ambassador-rank appointment as Canada's negotiator in the free-trade talks with the United States in 1986.

No beige touchtone phone for Simon. Not even a hold button. Just an old black phone they had installed especially for him.

It was the only thing about Simon Reisman that was out of date. For the rest, he was forward-looking, a visionary, bold and energetic until his death, at 88, of complications from heart surgery.

Consider: He was present as Canada's negotiator at the creation of the General Agreement on Tariffs and Trade, in 1947. He negotiated the Canada-U.S. Auto Pact, signed by Prime Minister Lester Pearson and U.S. President Lyndon Johnson in 1965. And he was the principal negotiator of the Canada-U.S. Free-Trade Agreement in 1987, under which our exports to the U.S. have tripled.

Three generations of Canadians have benefitted from his vision. Millions of Canadians, in our export reliant-economy, owe their jobs to this remarkable man. Yet most Canadians have never heard of him.

But in Canadian-government circles and among trade-policy experts worldwide, he was a legend.

He was also, as Brian Mulroney said in a speech last fall, "tough as nails." It was one of the two reasons why, as prime minister in 1986, he asked Reisman to lead the free-trade talks with the United States. The other was his institutional memory. He knew everything there was to know about bilateral and multilateral trade.

"When I sat down to think about who could do this, there was only person on my list," Mulroney said from his winter home in Florida. "He did a brilliant job. And he was a delight to work with."

He was also known for eating people alive. The first time I went to see him, at the trade negotiations office in June of 1986, I was terrified at the prospect of meeting him. I was writing a TV address to the nation for the prime minister, announcing the trade talks with the U.S. Reisman knew everything about it. I knew nothing.

"Come on in," he said with a big smile and a friendly wave. "What can I do for you, young man?" He couldn't have been nicer. And he couldn't have been more helpful.

I had unwittingly discovered his secret. There were two Reismans, the public figure who intimidated everyone, and the private gentleman of the old school. "Are you motoring back to Ottawa?" he once asked me after a conference in Montreal.

The public figure, on instructions of his government, walked out on the free-trade talks just two weeks before the negotiating deadline of October 3, 1987. "If it weren't for you, we could have had a deal a year earlier," U.S. Trade Representative Clayton Yeutter, later told him.

"Yeah," Reisman retorted, "if we settled on your terms."

The last time I saw Reisman, he and Connie, his beloved wife of sixty years, were attending a tribute dinner for Mulroney last October on the 20th anniversary of the Free Trade Agreement. The organizers of the event, Tasha Kheiriddin and the Montreal office of the Fraser Institute, had thoughtfully invited the Reismans to the head table and graciously seated them in a place of honour.

When Mulroney paid tribute to Reisman's role in negotiating the FTA, the room erupted in such an ovation that Reisman got to his feet, and in his clear, resonant voice, said, "thank you, Prime Minister."

He addressed all his prime ministers that way, even after they left office. He served them, and our country, with exceptional distinction. Canada is deeply indebted to him for a full life that has enriched us all.

April 2008

MARIAN AGNES ROACH MACDONALD

Marian Agnes Roach MacDonald belonged to what Tom Brokaw famously called "The Greatest Generation" – my father in uniform for the duration of the Second World War in the Army Corps of Engineers, my mother on the home front as a nurse.

The Greatest Generation fought the war, won the peace, and created the prosperity we have inherited today. They built an industrial democracy and a social model that is the envy of the entire world. Along the way, they raised families, the baby boomers, the largest cohort in world history.

They never sought or received any thanks for it. They were just playing their parental role and doing their job. And in all circumstances, they carried on.

They didn't do empathy very well. It wasn't in fashion. It wasn't even in their vocabulary. They just got on with it, and expected you to do the same. They measured performance by results, in reports in school, in dishes washed at home, in attendance at church. All these things were expected – no explanations, and no excuses.

We all have difficulty sometimes in understanding the environment that shaped our parents and our own family life. That was the world our mother came from, of her family's sacrifices to send her to a convent school, of her own struggle for acceptance as a Catholic girl marrying into a high Presbyterian family – my grandfather boycotted her for years before coming to his senses; of the lonely war years in Ottawa while her husband was away in uniform, a young major in charge of electrical installations on the entire East Coast of Canada.

And of the even lonelier years after our father's death half a century ago at the age of only 43 – she did what she always did. She carried on.

She went back to work as a nurse, as a casual float at first, then as a night nurse, later becoming the matron of the Queen Mary Veterans' Hospital. She paid down a mortgage, saved for her retirement, and found the means to send me to private school, while my sister finished college. She kept a box with my father's medals in it, but had none of her own. She was just an unsung Canadian hero, doing her job.

And if she didn't tell us she loved us very often, perhaps she assumed we knew it, for all she did for us.

She was as parsimonious with her praise as she was with her pennies. She didn't say she was proud of us very often, either. She just thought we knew that.

She never talked to me about my work – but after my sister closed her apartment when my mother went into a residence ten years ago, she gave me a box full of clippings of my newspaper columns from *The Gazette*, and positive reviews of my books. The first one was a bestselling biography of Prime Minister Mulroney, in which I had saved writing the dedication page to the last – "to the memory of my father, Arthur Lamond MacDonald." It was my closure with him. I signed the dedication page to her on her birthday that year – "to Mother, who also shares this page in my life."

Somehow I think my mother, a staunch Liberal, disapproved of the entire project. For she believed in God, Queen, country, and the Liberal Party. This did not, however, prevent her from accepting the prime minister's invitation to meet the Queen on Canada's 125th birthday in 1992, nor from attending a tea graciously offered by Mila Mulroney at 24 Sussex when Lisa and I were married in 1989. There were limits to her partisanship, even within the family.

If we suffered from an affection deficit, she made up for it in other ways. My mother wasn't a great cook – she made cardboard roast beef. But she was a great baker. Her chocolate chip cookies were famous, and she would allow me to eat them fresh out of the oven, right off the cookie sheet.

And twice a year, on my birthday and at Christmas, she made her famous pound cake. Her secret – butter and sugar. After she'd put on the vanilla icing, an inch thick, she'd give me a spoon and allow me to scrape the bowl. That was her way of saying I love you. By the way, she was competitive – she always refused to share her recipe with her sister, my Aunt Marg, the best cook in the family.

It is hard for me to imagine my parents' life, and impossible to pass judgment on it. Like all parents, they were all too human, when as children we only wanted them to be perfect.

Years ago, when Gracie was only five, and I was driving her to her kindergarten in Washington, she asked me a question from the back seat.

"Daddy," she said, "tell me about Grandpa Arthur."

"Well," I said, "he's up in heaven looking down on you, and he loves you very much because you're his granddaughter."

And I thought, whew, good save.

"Daddy," she said, and I looked again in the rear view mirror. "He's looking down on you, too, and he loves you very much because you're his son."

I nearly drove the car off the road.

And now there is another one, looking down on the next three generations of this family.

There is a saying, for every death, a baby is sent.

When our father died, my sister and I never got to say goodbye. This time we did. I told my mother: "I love you. There's a baby coming."

Two, actually. Christina is expecting her second child, my mother's seventh great-grandchild, in July. And Tasha is expecting her first child, my second, and my mother's last grandchild, in June. As Tasha says: "It's a miracle." We are truly blessed.

I had secretly hoped she would stay with us for awhile yet, so we could present the baby to her. But though she was present with us in body until Sunday, a larger part of her mind and spirit had left us some time ago.

Perhaps this is better – she can be looking down on this baby from heaven where we hope and believe she has been reunited at last with our father.

At her own wish, her ashes will be buried with my father and his parents at Hillside, beside the Mira River in Cape Breton. For those of you who know the famous Cape Breton song, *Song for the Mira*, that's where she will be.

As delivered, Ascension of Lord Church, December 2008

PART THREE

Potpourri

15

MONTREAL LANDMARKS

ST. PATRICK'S OF MONTREAL

If the walls of St. Patrick's could talk. For a century and a half, it has been a sentinel on the city, keeping watch from the top of Beaver Hall Hill.

Gray and forbidding on the outside, miraculously warm and majestic within, St. Patrick's is seven generations of touchstones of the Irish and English-speaking Catholics in this city.

This is a community that has defined the essential minority experience in Canada, divided by language but united in faith with Quebec's francophone majority. The story is all there, in 150 years of church records, and in the larger history of Montreal over the last two centuries.

A father of confederation, two prime ministers and six mayors of Montreal have come from this community. The leaders of the federalist forces in two referendums have been called Ryan and Johnson. The Irish have struggled up from Griffintown and Point St. Charles below St. Patrick's to the summit of Montreal above it.

This is big-picture stuff, and it doesn't even get into the rough and tumble of ecclesiastical politics. Alan Hustak has packed all of this into a fine little book, *St. Patrick's of Montreal*.

"I called a publisher and told him I was writing St. Patrick's biography," Hustak says. "He said they already had a book on Patrick Roy."

Even Simon Dardick, whose Véhicule Press specializes in the obscure and arcane, had his doubts about it.

"I hesitated," says Dardick, "but then I read the manuscript." The walls are a rich tapestry of anecdotes. The church bell, *"la vieille Charlotte,"* named for the consort of His Madness, King George III. The fights over the number of Irish and French-speaking tradesmen hired for the five-year job of building St. Patrick's, a foretaste of all the wars since waged in the Montreal building trades. The turf battles between the Sulpicians and the Jesuits, and between church and state.

As premier, Maurice Duplessis went to St. Patrick's rather than the French Cathedral, then as now seat of the Archdiocese of Montreal, because of his blood feud with Archbishop Joseph Charbonneau. During the October Crisis of 1970, the War Measures Act was denounced from the pulpit, as one of St. Patrick's parishioners, Nick Auf der Maur, admittedly the black sheep of the flock, was locked up by the Trudeau government.

In a way, Hustak's little book is the end page on the year-long observation of St. Patrick's 150th anniversary. It was the fate of St. Patrick's to open in June of 1847, the Summer of Sorrow, when 5,000 immigrants died of the plague at Grosse Île, the quarantine station downriver from Quebec, and thousands more died in sheds in Point St. Charles, buried, as Hustak writes, "anonymously in a mass grave which is today marked by a lugubrious black stone in the middle of Bridge Street leading to the embankment of Victoria Bridge."

When St. Patrick's reopened, after $5 million of restoration, the result was justly hailed as a stunning achievement, every bit as beautiful as Notre Dame on Place d'Armes.

In a way, it was the first election of the Parti Québécois in 1976 that rescued the St. Patrick's parade from folkloric status and restored the event to the standing of a community-wide celebration.

"I think there's something to that," acknowledges Brian O'Neill, the last ranking Montreal-based executive of the National Hockey League, which has long since moved to New York.

O'Neill is also president of the St. Patrick's Society, which as he notes, "is the oldest organization in the city, founded on St. Patrick's Day in 1834, a few months before the St. Jean Baptiste Society."

The challenging aspect of St. Patrick's Day falling on a Tuesday is that it becomes a five-day event. Sportscaster Dick Irvin, Irish for the day, speaks to 1,000 people tomorrow at a breakfast organized by the Erin Sports Society.

Then, at a Tuesday lunch, they're giving the St. Patrick's Society Community Award to Brian Gallery, patron saint of many lost causes. With lawyer Peter O'Brien of Stikeman Elliott, he has raised $1.3 million for the Canadian Irish Studies Program at Concordia University.

St. Patrick's remains very much the focal point of all this, rather as in a small town than a big city. Jean-Claude Turcotte, the Cardinal Archbishop of Montreal, will be presiding there on Sunday.

Turcotte stumbled into the constitutional issue last Christmas, when he told *Le Devoir* that the federal government's Supreme Court reference on Quebec's unilateral right to independence would make no difference to an issue that would be decided by the people. This is exactly where 88 per cent of Quebecers came out on this question in a subsequent poll.

In the ensuing imbroglio, Turcotte was reminded of his vows of humility, before providence, in the form of the ice storm, intervened to rescue him. Still, some hard-liners from English-speaking precincts were unsatisfied with his explanation that his comments were imprudent. It is rumoured that they may walk out on Sunday.

"Let them," says O'Neill. "We need the seats. He's been a very good friend of the Irish community and of the English-speaking community. I have the highest respect for the man."

One thing for sure. Nothing dull ever happens at St. Patrick's.

March 1998

∽

ST. MONICA'S

The cardinal is coming, and that's always a big thing in a place like St. Monica's in Notre-Dame-de-Grâce, where they're celebrating the 50th anniversary of the parish.

Except that Cardinal Jean-Claude Turcotte, a man of touching humility, will probably come in a cab, wearing nothing fancier than a Roman collar.

Which wasn't how Cardinal Paul-Émile Léger used to arrive at parishes like St. Monica's, where he would sweep up in a chauffeur-driven Chrysler Imperial, complete with police escort, and alight in garments all red, truly a prince of the church. This was in Léger's triumphalist phase, around 1960, before a personal crisis led to his resignation as archbishop and his work among lepers in Africa.

Not for nothing did news photographers of the day call Léger "Kid Kodak."

To a group of altar boys waiting on the sidewalk, including me, he was a pretty impressive figure. In later life, I could claim to have served mass for two cardinals, Léger and Emmett Carter, who would go on to become archbishop of Toronto, but was then living at St. Monica's while he ran St. Joseph's Teachers' College. Carter had to be out early for work, which meant he said an early mass, and he was known to us as the fastest gun in the West. He could get through a low mass in about 12 minutes, which worked for us as well as him.

For those of us who hung around the sacristy in those days, St. Monica's was more than a church, it had very much to do with our sense of belonging, and in a larger way with our sense of community.

"It's still like that," Father John Walsh was saying.

It was a little world unto itself, the simple red-brick church at the corner of Benny and Terrebonne, St. Monica's elementary school across the street, Monkland High across from Benny Park, and Benny Farm itself, a housing project for war veterans.

"Benny defined the neighbourhood," Walsh said. "All those young men, back from the service, all starting families."

Including my dad, and such memories as I have of him, for he died when I was very young, are largely of things like punting a football on the front lawn of Benny Farm.

The great Sam Etcheverry lived up the street and we would gather in front of his apartment just to watch him arrive home from practice, hoping he would throw a few with us which, being the nicest man in the world, then as now, he usually did.

For those of us who hung around backstage at St. Monica's, it was kind of like a clubhouse. As teenagers we played bridge in the church hall and a couple of young seminarians named Ernie Schibli and Joe Cameron took us under their wings.

To the extent that I've had a career in broadcasting, it began at the lectern of St. Monica's, where Don Ferguson – of *Air Farce* fame – and I were among a stable of Sunday-morning readers of epistles and gospels. St. Monica's got us over the shyness of standing at a microphone in front of nearly 1,000 people. "Are you coming to be a commentator?" Father Adelchi Bertoli asked when I called about their anniversary.

He has been there more than thirty years and, in partnership with Walsh, runs a parish which, confounding the expectations of non-observance, carries 1,500 families on its books. The wailing room that was built in the back of the church – mass under glass, we used to call it – still gets a surprising amount of use. "We have twelve baptisms next month," Walsh was saying.

The demographics have changed. "We have about 20 per cent Italian families, and a growing group from the Caribbean."

The work has changed, too. Walsh spends a lot of time on community work, with shelters and hot kitchens and so forth. "We have to be out there," he said.

Tomorrow, Walsh has the cardinal, with whom he's still on a Jean-Claude basis after seventeen years as colleagues in the archdiocese office. "We know that he'll come and be very touching and very appreciated by everyone," Walsh said.

Turcotte was called in last winter when Expos chairman Jacques Ménard needed to close a deal to keep Felipe Alou on board as manager of the baseball club. Ménard knows Turcotte from fundraising for the cardinal's endeavours.

Alou had said God was his agent, and so Ménard brought in Turcotte as his closer. "Jean-Claude, I need your help with this," Ménard explained when he reached Turcotte at his cottage.

The phone later rang at Alou's place in Florida.

"I am," the cardinal said, "calling on behalf of your agent."

May 1999

∽

THE ROYAL MONTREAL CURLING CLUB: HOME OF MY DAD'S TROPHY

My father was a curler. On Saturday mornings, he would take me along to sit behind the glass while he skipped his rink at the St. George Curling Club.

When he died of a heart attack at the Quebec Bonspiel in 1958, his club donated a trophy in his name for competitions with the Beauchâteau Curling Club in Châteauguay.

He would have liked that. Curling was the passion of his life. As an engineer, he was drawn to the precision of the game and fascinated by its tactics. He kept newspaper clippings documenting the feats of a friend named Ken Weldon, who once missed winning the Brier for Quebec by a single shot. Above all, he loved the fellowship of the game.

As a boy, I heard about the Art MacDonald Memorial Trophy, but never saw it, and never thought anything more about it. And I never took up curling – it was my father's game, not mine.

Two years ago, Jim Robb called to ask a favour. The guest speaker had canceled at a dinner of the Royal Montreal Curling Club, and he wondered if I could fill in.

In the politics of this town, Robb is one of those people you meet along the way, a backroom adviser to John Turner and Robert Bourassa, a man of influence in Liberal councils and a senior partner in one of the city's largest law firms, Stikeman Elliott.

"Just come and have a drink, meet people before dinner," said Robb, assuring me there was no problem with a speech on politics at a curling club.

The Royal Montreal is one of those buildings people walk by without even wondering what's inside. Leaning up against the south side of de Maisonneuve Boulevard, near the Guy metro, it looks like a think-tank in need of funding. Only the initials, RMCC, carved in stone over the front entrance, give even a hint of what goes on there.

And what goes on there, since 1807, makes it the oldest curling club in North America. Pictures of monarchs and governors-general adorn the walls, and there are three sheets of ice, with viewing areas in the main-floor bar and upstairs dining room.

"So, do you curl?" one of the members asked.

"No, but my father did."

"Really. Where?"

"At the St. George Club. On The Boulevard. It's a school now."

"We have quite a few members from the St. George Club. Wilf Marchant, do you know him?"

"Wilf Marchant was my father's best friend."

Then I explained about the trophy.

"What was your father's name?"

"Art MacDonald."

"We have an Art MacDonald trophy."

"Where?"

"There, in the corner."

Sure enough, among a collection of other club trophies, there was a silver claret jug under glass, with the crests of the St. George and Beauchâteau clubs, and my father's name engraved on the front.

Up to that point, I had been doing Jim Robb a favour. As it turned out, he was doing me one. Forty years on, I was seeing my father's trophy for the first time. No one had any idea of how it came into the possession of the Royal Montreal.

"We have to do something about this," Robb said. "Leave it with me."

A few weeks ago, Robb called again to invite me to a Royal Montreal lunch. "We would," he said, "like you to present your father's trophy to the club. We're going to put it in competition for young curlers."

It was one of those invitations where you don't check your schedule. You just accept.

They do these things by the book. The lunch followed a morning of curling with guests from Nashua, New Hampshire. Robb proposed a toast to the President of the United States and the Queen of Canada and Scotland. Later, the Royal's membership chairman, Jim Mathewson, played keyboard-perfect versions of *The Star Spangled Banner* and *O Canada*.

The guest speaker was the journalist and author Graham Fraser – as it happens, one of my closest friends. And the man sitting on my other side was Wilf Marchant, my father's closest friend, whom I hadn't seen in all those years. As a moment, it was only perfect.

At 84, Wilf is working as a stockbroker at Scotia McLeod, and still curling.

"Ken Weldon," he recalled, "needed one shot to win the Brier, and missed it." In more than half a century of curling, Wilf has amassed thousands of club pins, which he is thinking of selling on the Internet.

"How old was your dad when he died?" he asked.

"Forty-three."

Though my father left the party too early, it occurred to me then that he did leave me with two things, a love of sports and of this city.

We would drive to Victoria Pier and stand under the Sailors' Clock, and looking uptown, he would point to the Sun Life building, calling it the tallest in the Commonwealth.

He had season tickets for the Alouettes, in Section K, on the north side of Molson Stadium, in the years when Sam Etcheverry ruled. Occasionally, he got the company tickets to the Forum, in the blues before they were painted red, and one night we saw Maurice Richard break in from the blue line and score a trademark goal against Boston.

And my dad loved baseball, especially double-headers between the Montreal Royals and the Havana Sugar Kings. He had a blue Spalding scorebook that looked like a set of architectural plans.

One of my regrets is that he never got to go a ball game with his granddaughter. On summer nights at the cottage, we sit on the deck and watch the stars come out over the lake. The first one, the wishing star, Gracie calls "Grandpa Arthur's star," and she talks to him.

Now she can tell him about his trophy.

April 2000

QUEBEC'S OLDEST LIBRARY? WESTMOUNT, OF COURSE

A Scottish architect named Robert Findlay was passing through Montreal on his way to a job in Mexico when he received word that his prospective employer had died.

This was in 1885, and Findlay decided to stay on in Montreal, with results that can be seen around you to this day. He designed the original Sun Life headquarters on Notre Dame Street, Victoria Hall and city hall on Sherbrooke Street in Westmount, as well as dozens of homes on the mountain and along the Golden Mile.

He built the Sir Mortimer Davis house on Peel Street that became Purvis Hall at McGill University, the Hubert Molson house on Avenue du Musée that became the Russian consulate and the eagle's nest on Belvedere Road that became Sam and Saidye Bronfman's house on the hill.

But Findlay's most celebrated and ultimately his most enduring work is Quebec's first municipal library, the library in the park in Westmount, which opened 100 years ago.

"The opening of the library on June 20, 1899," wrote Laureen Sweeney in *Polishing the Jewel*, her book on the restoration and renewal of the library in the present decade, "was an occasion of flags, flowers, caterers and an orchestra."

There may not be an orchestra at the 100th-anniversary celebration, but there will be strawberries and champagne, and readings by authors, including Bill Weintraub, author of the best-selling *City Unique*, which chronicles the lives of many of the robber barons whose homes on the hill were built by Findlay.

The library has grown well beyond the original Findlay wings that were completed a century ago at a cost of $11,500, with stacks and space for 3,000 volumes, and segregated reading spaces for men and women. After all, it was the Victorian era, and the library had been conceived three years earlier as a project for the Queen's diamond jubilee.

Findlay added a children's pavilion in 1911, now the reading room, and another wing in 1924 and continued his practice in Montreal into the late 1930s, when he received the first order of merit from the Quebec Association of Architects, of which he had been a founding member in 1890.

The Findlay trademark is the Victorian look, red brick, turrets and leaded-glass windows, much of which had fallen into disrepair or been painted over by the early 1990s, when the gifted Montreal architect Peter Rose was hired to do a $7.5-million restoration and expansion at the library.

Now teaching architecture at Harvard, Rose had a reputation for designing new spaces that were respectful of old surroundings, as in the Canadian Centre of Architecture he built for Phyllis Lambert around the beautifully restored Shaughnessy House.

But the library restoration was dogged by controversy from the beginning, partly because every librarian and architect who lived in Westmount felt they owned a piece of it. The mayor, Peter Trent, went so far as to conduct a focus group of two dozen librarians. For a time, Rose must have felt like the president of a synagogue, a job which comes with a lot of annoying free advice.

But there was real heat over the original plan to close Findlay's door on the park. As Trent asked at the time, and as quoted in Sweeney's book: "Can you imagine closing off the park entrance to a library in the park?" Rose's plan also called for the demolition of a 1959 annex and replacing it with the present Rose building, which is joined to the older wings by a central spine that has a contiguous, unifying effect.

The result is a brilliantly restored and enhanced library with 130,000 volumes, including a growing French collection, as well as thousands of videos and CDs, and all the computerized bells and whistles of a new age in which librarians are known as information specialists.

The best investment is the children's library, downstairs in the Rose building, where my daughter spends a good part of her summer.

"I like the cage of gerbils where you can walk around and look at them freely," Gracie was saying. "And I like all the National Geo videos they have.

"I like how they have the computers you can play on if you want," she continued. "And I like how they have a kids' theme every summer. Last summer it was medieval times. I'm really into myths.

"This summer, it's detectives."

Maybe Kathy Reichs, or her Tempe Brennan, will show up.

June 1999

∽

EATONS'S DOWNTOWN

There is a saying that retail is detail, something they evidently forgot at Eaton's, to the point where they can't even run a bankruptcy sale.

Knowing what day of the week a sale begins is a pretty important detail, as in Wednesday, not Monday, and prices should be going down, not up.

But this confusion is only symptomatic of decades of mismanagement and neglect of Eaton's biggest asset – its brand name. There isn't a Christmas tree in Canada that an Eaton's box hasn't been under, and that's called trademark value.

But if you had to trace the decline of the Eaton's brand, you would begin with its growth, namely its expansion to the suburbs in the 1960s, in Montreal and across Canada. From the moment Eaton's became an anchor tenant in malls like Fairview, its downtown flagship stores became dinosaurs.

While "going shopping" had been a downtown experience – checking out Eaton's, Simpson's and The Bay – there was no longer any reason to hit Ste. Catherine Street on a Saturday afternoon. An entire generation of kids never went downtown, but grew up instead as mall rats, and became mall moms.

The downtown stores, far too big to begin with, were never redeveloped to reflect the times. It took the closing of Simpson's and years of the building standing empty, before its current renaissance as Simons in a significantly smaller space, sharing the larger space with the Paramount movieplex and a mix of shops and restaurants. And where Simpson's was staid, Simons is sizzling, with one of the hottest retail launches of the decade.

Simons is hot because it has figured out what Eaton's forgot – what the brand stood for and where the market niche was. Long before Simons moved into Montreal, there was a network of career women who shopped at the Quebec City store. Simons built the brand on items like quality handbags and sweaters at affordable prices, and went from there.

Eaton's downtown Montreal flagship, nine storeys of an entire city block, is one of the largest department stores in the world, about a million square feet. Even Macy's in New York isn't much bigger, in the heart of a retail market several times the size of Montreal.

It's a rule of retailing that every floor you go up, your revenues are cut in half. So that if you do $1,200 a square foot on the ground floor, it's $600 on the second floor and $300 on the third. By the time you get to the ninth floor, the margins are pretty thin.

Taking the escalator at Eaton's, and walking its aisles, is to marvel at wasted space, in everything from furniture to appliances. In the lyric of the Dire Straits song: "We got to move these refrigerators/We got to move these colour TVs." But nobody was. This high-end segment had long since moved to specialty retailers like Brault & Martineau.

Eaton's renowned ninth-floor restaurant might be a marvel of art deco, and a wonderful place to take your grandmother for lunch, but it's pretty hard to justify in a business where results are measured in dollars per square foot. The first-class dining room of the *Titanic* was a nice place, too.

Eaton's had years to reconfigure its space and redefine its market niche, and did neither, either under family management or in the two years of its new lease on life since the company went public with a stock offering that was sold on the brand name rather than anything Eaton's was doing.

Eaton's could have made the downtown space pay for itself by downsizing the retail and outsourcing space to boutiques as, for example, Ogilvy's did in its successful and widely copied re-fit of its downtown store a decade ago.

Some day, someone will build it, and people will come. Already, people in the real-estate industry are speculating on the future of the downtown Eaton's building. "It could become residential on the University Street side, offices on the de Maisonneuve side and stay retail on the Ste. Catherine side," suggested one industry source. "But it's just too much square footage for a department store."

Timothy Eaton, the founding father, might have been the first to acknowledge that. With the Internet as the equivalent of the Eaton's catalogue, electronic commerce is rendering the old retail models, including the mall model, obsolete. But if IBM had stayed only in the mainframe business, it would be out of business. Somehow, Eaton's let the decade of the '90s go by as it ran the retail version of mainframe.

Eaton's being Eaton's, its demise has attracted significant comment from politicians, notably in Quebec. Lucien Bouchard thought he detected sinister motives in the Montreal stores closing their doors for a day last week, while remaining open in the rest of Canada.

This is a chip off the old shoulder. Or, sorry, I don't speak French, as it used to be said of Eaton's sales clerks, more in the telling of the tale around the table of the Quebec family than in the real world of retailing. This has been a bad rap against Eaton's. Long before it became a requirement of the linguistic regime, Eaton's required bilingualism of its employees in Montreal.

And while notably inhospitable toward efforts to unionize those employees, Eaton's has always been known as a good employer, especially to the many thousands of students who got their first jobs there.

My first summer job was at Eaton's downtown, selling sporting goods on the fifth floor. There was a feeling of taking a step out into the real world, and earning that first paycheque.

"Sixty-five dollars a week," I was telling my daughter on the way up the escalator. We were going to the ninth-floor restaurant, where she dropped a couple of pennies into the gorgeous wall fountain under the fresco with the hunting theme.

She ordered dessert, a huge piece of chocolate fudge cake and a glass of milk, brought by a kindly waitress named Yolande, who thought there might be hope for the restaurant, inasmuch as the government had already moved to protect it as an art-deco treasure. But a look around the room showed the demographics were decidedly in the wrong direction.

"Going down, ladies," an elevator operator called on the way out. She carefully closed the cage, and described the departments on a stop on the sixth floor.

In a way, that elevator symbolized what was wrong with Eaton's – run by the nicest people, but hopelessly out of date.

August 1999

PVM: THE BEST ADDRESS IN TOWN

William Zeckendorf desperately needed an anchor tenant for his new office complex known as Place Ville Marie. The Royal Bank of Canada was the perfect prospect, except for one thing – it already owned its own head office in the financial district at 360 Rue St. Jacques.

So Zeckendorf bought the old Royal Bank building for one dollar, and the cruciform building became the Royal Bank Building at 1 Place Ville Marie. The Royal later regretted not holding out for having the entire complex named for the bank, a deal it could easily have swung, and the place was never known as anything other than PVM.

Zeckendorf was a New Yorker, a visionary developer with a big-picture view of things. Where there was a hole in the ground with trains running into Central Station, he saw an underground shopping mall and a rooftop restaurant, Altitude 737.

He hired a brilliant young architect named I.M. Pei, who would go on to win such important commissions as the East Building of the National Gallery of Art in Washington, the John F. Kennedy Library in Boston, and the Pyramid at the Louvre in Paris. But PVM, finished in 1962, was Pei's first major commission. PVM became the signature of the new Montreal skyline. It also gave birth to Montreal's underground city.

With the country's premier bank as his anchor tenant, Zeckendorf was able to sell PVM as the city's new prestige address, and the cruciform building quickly filled up as the headquarters of Alcan, Air Canada, Montreal Trust and major law firms like Ogilvy Renault.

A good thing, too, since it was a lot of space – 1.6 million square feet. Like many developers, Zeckendorf's visionary reach was beyond his financial grasp and his company, Trizec, ended up in other hands. There is a saying in the real-estate business, that the pioneers get the arrows and the settlers get the land.

Now Trizec is in the process of selling both PVM and the old Royal building to SITQ, the real-estate arm of the Caisse de dépôt, which owns a number of other properties around town, including Westmount Square – a Mies van der Rohe knockoff of his own Seagram building in New York.

PVM remains the city's best corporate address, about 97 per cent leased, though most of the earlier tenants have long since moved on. Air Canada moved down the street to its own tower at 500 René Lévesque Blvd. W., before selling it off in the 1991 recession and relocating to the airport at Dorval. Its current headquarters is a dump, and nothing compared with the splendour of both its former downtown offices, where most vice-presidents – and there were dozens of them in those days – had private washrooms.

Among other charter occupants of PVM, Alcan moved uptown in the mid-1980s to its heritage headquarters on Sherbrooke Street, a pet project of its former CEO, David Culver. The Royal eventually gave up the pretense of being a Montreal bank and moved the last of its national operations to Toronto. Even Ogilvy Renault, which had moved into 1 PVM because they were the Royal Bank's outside counsel, eventually moved up the street to 1981 McGill College, a crummy building compared with PVM, and a move that longtime Ogilvy secretaries complain about to this day.

Among former PVM tenants, it's a common complaint that in their new building, there's nothing down below. The shopping mall at PVM had an ambience that was unique in a Montreal way. Where there is a food court today, there was once of a bunch of bars and restaurants called *Le Carrefour des Canadiens*, and for years it lived up to its title as the gathering place of Montreal. It also lived up to its nickname, the Swamp. And when snowstorms occasionally shut down the city, rather than calling in the army as they do in Toronto, Montrealers would repair to the Swamp.

During the heady days of Expo '67, a young Montreal lawyer named Brian Mulroney introduced a shy cabinet minister named Pierre Trudeau to the crowd at the Swamp. In those days, nobody thought of either one of them as a future prime minister. When Trudeau came back only a year later, in the Trudeaumania campaign of 1968, there were 50,000 people waiting to see him on the plaza at PVM.

Mulroney was an up-and-coming lawyer at Ogilvy, even then known as the Factory, the largest firm in town, and the only one with two different postal codes in the same building.

February 2000

(Postscript: Still known as the Factory, Ogilvy Renault moved back to PVM as one of its main tenants, with five floors of space, in May 2009.)

∞

WINDSOR STATION—GATEWAY TO A NATION

They were arguably the most famous and glamorous couple of the 20th century and, ultimately, among the most tragic.

But all of that lay ahead of John F. Kennedy and his bride, Jacqueline Bouvier Kennedy, as they stepped off a train at Montreal's Windsor Station. It was December 1953, just three months after their wedding, and a decade before Dallas.

The platform was virtually deserted except for an official from the American consulate, on hand to greet the 36-year-old junior senator from Massachusetts and his 24-year-old wife. And there was Arnold Harrington, a young staff photographer for the Canadian Pacific Railway, who was there to get an arrival shot.

"What do you want us to do?" Kennedy said, when Harrington asked for a picture.

"Can we get one of you stepping off the train?" Harrington asked.

"Sure," Kennedy said.

That was one shot. And there was another with Jack Kennedy holding his briefcase, and Jackie Kennedy looking right through the camera. Two pictures, and Harrington's job was done.

"I never thought about the importance of those pictures when I took them," says Harrington, retired as manager of Canadian Pacific's photography department. "I never thought of him as the future president of the United States."

But nearly half a century later, Harrington acknowledges that he captured something about them.

"They were," he says, "a very striking couple. And there was an aura about her."

The Kennedy photos went into the Canadian Pacific archives at Windsor Station. They are among 800,000 photos in the archives, filed away on the ground floor of Windsor Station – from which millions set out for a new life in the West, millions more set out for two world wars, where the Montreal Canadiens of the 1950s dynasty set out for other conquests, and where the Dionne quints and Cardinal Paul-Émile Léger were greeted as conquering heroes.

"It is a treasure trove," says Judith Nefsky, the Canadian Pacific archivist. "And endless. It takes several lifetimes to catalogue it."

It's not a research archive in the usual sense. Students can't walk in off the street. As Nefsky notes, it serves a corporate purpose; it is available to the media and is developing a vocation as an image bank.

"We consider ourselves a stock agency in Canada," says Bob Kennell, co-ordinator of the Canadian Pacific photographic collection.

What stock. And what a collection. Because Canadian Pacific is uniquely connected to the history of this country, its photography collection is, among corporate archives, uniquely historic.

There was, first, a railway to be built across Canada, then land to be sold to settlers, ships to be filled with passengers and hotels to be filled with tourists. All of it was photographed, over more than a century, by dozens of CPR staff shooters.

At its peak, the CPR photo department employed eighteen photographers and technicians. When the Queen visited Canada in the summer of 1959, Harrington was one of half a dozen CPR photographers and technicians who followed her across Canada.

What was John F. Kennedy doing in Montreal? "He was here for a speech," Harrington says. "That's all I can tell you."

The photo caption says only December 1953. There is no mention of the visit in *Gazette* files for that month. But an e-mail to the Kennedy Library in Boston brought a same-day response that Senator Kennedy was here to speak "to students at the University of Montreal on Dec. 4, 1953."

The text of his Montreal address is available from his presidential library.

And there is the Page 4 headline in the *Montreal Star* the next day: "Canada, U.S. urged to set amity example for World."

"I know I speak for the majority of the American people," Kennedy told the U. de M. Literary Society, "when I tell you that the United States values highly its friendship and association with Canada.

"If you and I, the citizens and officials of our two great countries, can all emphasize those positive values and traditions which insure the continued amity of the U.S. and Canada, then there will be less danger of a deterioration of our relationship arising from temporary, insignificant or politically inspired controversies."

Kennedy's Montreal visit is not mentioned in any of the JFK biographies, and his Montreal speech is fairly unremarkable, except when measured against the temper of the times, the Red Scare and McCarthy witchhunts in the U.S., and other issues that spilled across the border.

There was another reason for the Kennedys' Montreal visit, as the newspaper reported:

"Senator Kennedy was the guest of honour later at the annual St. Mary's Ball in the Windsor Hotel. He was accompanied by Mrs. Kennedy."

And there, on the social page of the same day's paper, is a four-column photo of Jack and Jackie Kennedy, he in white tie and tails and she, stunning in an off-the-shoulder creation, standing in a receiving line with the hosts of the St. Mary's Ball, Mr. and Mrs. Thomas V. Burke, who, among other distinctions, were the parents of Montreal sports columnist Tim Burke.

Among the young Catholic ladies of Montreal presented that night, quite a few had a turn on the dance floor with Kennedy and one of them, Catherine O'Brien, recalls all these years later, that "he had very good rhythm."

Catherine's brother, David P. O'Brien, is now chairman and chief executive officer of Canadian Pacific Ltd., the latest in a line that goes back to Lord Strathcona, Lord Mount Stephen, Sir William Van Horne and Lord Shaughnessy, the legendary railway barons whose 20th-century successors included Sir Edward Beatty, Buck Crump and Ian Sinclair.

All of them were strong personalities, with well-developed egos and an equally strong sense of corporate destiny. From the beginning, they hired people to photograph every aspect of a company whose operations had a reach and scale like no other.

O'Brien himself tells the story of a tourist who arrived in Quebec on a CP ship, checked into the Château Frontenac, bought CP travelers' cheques, and sent a CP cable to Vancouver, asking what time it was there. "Eleven o'clock, Canadian Pacific Time," replied the desk clerk. "Don't tell me," the tourist said, "you own the time, too."

CP's operations might have moved West, but its history, and so much Canadian history, is in its Montreal archives, not forgotten and gathering dust, but organized and catalogued and very much alive.

"There is," Nefsky said, "a real thirst for this kind of material."

Among the most fascinating and significant pictures in the Canadian Pacific archives are rare photos of the two wartime summits at Quebec and the Château Frontenac, where Prime Minister William Lyon Mackenzie King played host to Winston Churchill and Franklin Roosevelt.

The first Quebec summit, in August 1943, approved Operation Overlord and the liberation of Europe. The second, in September 1944, saw talks on the shape of the postwar world.

There is Churchill, riding in an open car with Mackenzie King at the 1943 Quebec summit, an event meticulously recorded by the Canadian prime minister in his diary.

King's adviser and biographer J.W. Pickersgill quoted the diary in *The Mackenzie King Record*: "On Monday, August 23, at noon, Churchill and Mackenzie King 'drove through the streets of Quebec. It was a triumphal procession from the time we reached the Garrison Club at the foot of the Citadel until the time of our return. There was a great demonstration in front of the City Hall. Churchill was visibly pleased. He remarked on the happy expression of the people. Indeed as we looked at the people from the car, it was like a vast throng hailing a deliverer.'"

Churchill had arrived in Halifax after a secret crossing of the Atlantic on the *Queen Mary*, and taken a special train up to Quebec. Before the Quebec conference, he traveled on by train to Hyde Park, for a visit with the Roosevelts at their estate on the Hudson River, before returning to Quebec for the summit. Churchill landed in Canada on August 9 and didn't leave until August 31, and then only for Washington.

After the conference, Churchill was even able to get in a few days trout fishing with his wife, Clementine, at Lac des Neiges, north of Quebec City. Churchill, wrote his biographer Martin Gilbert, "worked on the broadcast he had agreed to give to the Canadian people," which he made when he eventually returned to Quebec after his five-day fishing excursion in the middle of World War II.

"Here at the gateway of Canada," Churchill proclaimed from the Citadel on August 31, "in mighty lands which have never known the totalitarian tyrannies of Hitler and Mussolini, the spirit of freedom has found a safe and abiding home."

The success of the first Quebec conference was such that Mackenzie King was able to persuade Churchill and Roosevelt to return a year later, though it meant another ocean crossing for Churchill, and a tiring Roosevelt was in the middle of the 1944 re-election campaign.

Even then, the essence of Canadian foreign policy was about having a seat at the table, and Mackenzie King proudly noted that he had arranged for the Canadian Red Ensign to fly in the centre of three flagpoles between the Union Jack and the Stars and Stripes.

Again, the pace was leisurely enough that Churchill and Roosevelt found time after the conference to receive honourary degrees from McGill University. But as Clementine Churchill wrote: "Instead of having to go to Montreal for the ceremony, the dignitaries of the university kindly came here."

In fact, as Pickersgill notes in his biography, Mackenzie King had hastily arranged the honourary degree ceremony after receiving the request in a phone call from *Montreal Star* publisher J.W. McConnell. "The president said he had no clothes," King wrote in his diary. "I told him I would have hoods and gowns brought along."

Afterward, there was a session with reporters and photographers, as Martin Gilbert writes: "to whom Churchill also spoke, noting that as a result of the earlier Quebec conference, 'decisions had been taken that are now engraved upon the monuments of history.' Out of that first Quebec conference, he said, had come 'arrangements by which the vast armies were hurled across the sea, forced their way on shore in the teeth of the enemies' fire and fortification, broke up his armed strength and liberated, almost as if by enchantment, the dear and beautiful land of France, so long held under the corroding heel of the Hun.'"

Churchill was accompanied at both Quebec summits by his "darling Clementine," while Eleanor Roosevelt accompanied her husband to the second one.

The energetic Mrs. Roosevelt wrote that "the ladies have no duties, so I'm being lazy and luxurious." Her idea of laziness? "Did two columns this a.m." Her column, *My Day*, ran in hundreds of American newspapers.

Eleanor Roosevelt, at 5-foot-11, towered over Mackenzie King as he escorted her to a reception at the Château Frontenac. Mrs. Roosevelt and Mrs. Churchill also did a broadcast to Canadians, in French, from the hotel's radio studio.

But there is also a remarkable photo in the Canadian Pacific archive, of Eleanor Roosevelt at Quebec doing a stupid pet trick with the president's faithful dog, Fala, before an appreciative Mackenzie King, who had his own dog, named Pat.

Fala went virtually everywhere with Roosevelt in the last five years of his life. There is even a display case of Fala memorabilia at the FDR Library at Hyde Park. Franklin Roosevelt once famously observed: "The Republicans have not been content with attacks on me, or my wife, they now include my little dog, Fala."

March 2000

∽

THE MAA'S STORIED TRADITION

No sporting club in North America can match the storied history of the Montreal Amateur Athletic Association, home to three Stanley Cup champions including the first one in 1893, and a century of Canadian Olympic medalists.

Founded in 1881, the old MAAA also came to symbolize much that was wrong with the city – living off its former glories, with an aging and shrinking English-speaking clientele and an old building on Peel Street that was falling apart.

Like Montreal itself in the 1990s, the MAAA desperately needed a rebirth of confidence and a renewal of its infrastructure. The city's proudest athletic facility was down to 450 members and was several million dollars in debt.

The place was on the verge of bankruptcy when its members bailed it out in partnership with a Toronto club-management company, the Cambridge Group. With a $4-million capital infusion, they paid down the debt and, in only six months, renovated the landmark building from the ground up.

Relaunched and repositioned as the Montreal Amateur Athletic Club, losing the last A along the way, le Club Sportif MAA has even ditched its trademark Winged Wheel logo, stolen decades ago by the Detroit Red Wings.

"The old logo," suggests general manager Jocelyn Robert, "was old, English, dated and bankrupt."

The transformation, in both look and feel, is stunning. The musty old MAAA had somehow missed the Nautilus revolution and the culture of the personal fitness trainer.

The new MAA opens onto the street, literally, with a ground-floor workout area in a huge window that is a salesman for sweat. The workout machines are all from the digital age, as are the high-resolution TVs tuned to Canadian and U.S. cable news channels.

Some things couldn't be changed. The old swimming pool was six inches short of twenty yards, which was why none of Dick Pound's swimming records there ever counted. It's still short, only now it's measured in metres. But his Commonwealth records in the 1960s were enough to gain Pound admission to the MAAA Hall of Fame.

And there's still a bowling alley in the basement, with four lanes of duckpins. How many jock clubs have that?

The old MAAA had never resonated with the francophone community or the French-language media, and Robert did a very smart thing when he hired Nathalie Lambert, the Olympic double gold medalist in short-track speedskating, as his marketing director.

Lambert leads a representational outreach that has resulted in dozens of corporate memberships, and an infusion of young francophones from new-economy companies. But with her television tapings, right in the workout room, she's also created a buzz in the French-language media.

With her medals and skates in a display case in the lobby, Lambert is also a link to the MAA's Olympic heritage, reaching all the way back to Étienne Desmarteau, who won Canada's first gold medal for the hammer throw in 1904. Lambert's trophy case is also a reminder that the MAAA hosted the world speed-skating championships in 1897.

Anne Montminy, the silver medalist in tower diving at Sydney, is the latest in a line of champions in water that includes Carolyn Waldo, the gold medalist in synchronized swimming in 1988.

The first two Stanley Cups were won by the MAAA Winged Wheelers in 1893 and 1894, and a third one was added in 1903. Even before Lord Stanley donated the cup, the MAAA had won six consecutive Canadian amateur championships. There's also a historic sense of community and continuity with events like the MAA's snowshoe race on Mount Royal for the Friends of the Mountain, and its triathlon, which has raised hundreds of thousands of dollars for cancer research.

It would have been very sad, if all that history had been lost in a bankruptcy. Sometimes, a proud tradition can be among the best reasons for creating a new one.

March 2001

TORONTO—MEGACITY CENTRAL

Trust Toronto to call itself a megacity. They closed a civic merger there with the election of Mel Lastman as mayor of six communities, population 2.4 million, that have been joined at the municipal hip.

This was meganews, in and of itself, the triumph of suburban kitsch over the downtown smart set. Lastman, a man with such a bad hair weave he once carried business cards showing his before-and-after look, has been mayor for a quarter century of the sprawling suburb of North York.

The hilarious highlight of Lastman's campaign was his statement that he had never met a homeless person in North York. The one homeless person in his borough was, unfortunately, found dead, later that same day, in a subway station.

This helped the Toronto news media, aided and abetted by the pollsters, turn a runaway race into one supposedly too close to call, as Lastman was reported to have squandered a thirty-point lead in five weeks.

This turned out, on election day, to be so much wishful media thinking as the suburbs proved that the only people in Canada who hate Toronto more than the rest of the country are those in its own back yard.

The organization of the election itself, in the suburbs compared with the city, offered conclusive proof of why Lastman won. In his own borough of North York, the polls functioned efficiently and closed on time. In the city,

16

CITIES

they ran out of ballots at some polls nearly two hours before closing, and had to send downtown for more.

This, combined with many names being left off lists, created long lines of disgruntled voters standing outside after the polls closed.

Toronto's merger is a shotgun wedding arranged by the government of Mike Harris at Queen's Park, a place where, when you ask directions to the premier's office, they tell you to turn left off the elevator and follow the demonstrators.

Harris has been using up his political capital at an enormous clip. Ontario, not used to the social cleavages that have long marked public-policy debates in Quebec, is badly bruised from a province-wide teachers' strike. Under the Harris government, going to the barricades has become a commonplace occurrence.

The municipal merger should have been a slam dunk, but Harris was perceived as imposing it from on high, and in non-binding plebiscites at the borough level last spring it was roundly rejected. Undeterred, Harris went ahead anyway.

There were two political subtexts that meant trouble for Harris. First, Toronto is a city that takes its municipal politics seriously. In the era of Jean Drapeau's thirty-year reign in Montreal, Toronto mayors Nathan Phillips, David Crombie and John Sewell not only tolerated opposition at city hall, they thrived on it.

Where Drapeau practised what he called "disciplined democracy," inviting voters to stay home between elections, Toronto would have televised public hearings on everything from street names to smoking bylaws. It has taken Montreal decades to catch up with Toronto on public engagement on municipal issues. Only in Toronto would Jane Jacobs, who writes books on cities, be a celebrity.

Toronto is like Montreal in one sense: it is very much a city of neighbourhoods. And residents, in the city and suburbs alike, were concerned about preserving the character of those neighbourhoods. In the city, Rosedale is to Westmount as Forest Hill is to Hampstead, while the Beaches has the real neighbourhood qualities of NDG. The suburban boroughs – Scarborough, Etobicoke and the three Yorks – sprawl 60 kilometres on either side of the 401.

Until now, Toronto's metropolitan government has existed, pretty much like the Montreal Urban Community, as a dysfunctional body politic that oversees police and public transit. For the rest, the six communities have been left to provide their own services and levy their own taxes.

Until now, Metro Toronto has existed mostly in the minds of headline writers at the *Toronto Star*. For example, when Mikhail Gorbachev became general-secretary of the Soviet Union in 1985, the *Star* recalled in a front-page story that, on an earlier visit to Canada as agriculture minister, he had visited the CN Tower. The famous headline: "New Soviet leader loved Metro."

The megacity moniker is also the creation of headline writers, and it adds to Toronto's world-class reputation for self-absorption.

But a unified Toronto raises competitive issues that will give Montreal real things to think about.

For starters, the integration of municipal services will allow the new city to cut about 5,000 employees from its cumulative payroll of 55,000.

The real competitive issue is the critical mass of municipal services that will give Toronto a significant advantage over Montreal. This may well hasten the day when Montreal goes beyond the "one island, one city" notion of metropolitan government first enunciated years ago by Drapeau, and moves to a vision of a greater Montreal that includes Laval and the South Shore.

For the moment, Toronto has moved ahead, and is already growing quickly. As I was leaving Toronto on election night, a taxi-driver said it would become the fifth-largest city in North America. By the time my plane landed in Dorval, a local cabbie said he'd heard it was the fourth-largest, which, if you exclude Mexico City, it is, after New York, Los Angeles and Chicago.

November 1997

∞

THE BIG COMMUTE MONTREAL–TO

It was one of those out-of-Montreal experiences. A couple of us were sitting in a client's conference room when we noticed that the corporate paintings all depicted Montreal and Quebec scenes.

Nothing unusual about that except for one thing – the art collection, one of corporate Canada's best, was in Toronto. The artists were all big Quebec names, including John Little, Lorne Bouchard, René Richard and Marc-Aurèle Fortin.

It was a weird feeling to be looking out the window at Bay Street, while looking at the walls and Sherbrooke Street.

The explanation is really quite simple. The company headquarters is now in Toronto, but it used to be in Montreal. When they left, they took their paintings with them.

They moved for a perfectly good reason – they're in the consumer-products business, and they've gone to where the customers are. Nearly half the Canadian retail market is in Ontario, and one-fifth of it in a region known as the GTA, the Greater Toronto Area.

Some of their employees have moved with them, and some continue to commute between their work in Toronto and their homes in Montreal. When they talk about "catching the 6," they're not talking about the train to Dorval, but the plane.

There are commuters in the management ranks of nearly every company that has relocated from Montreal to Toronto. The reasons are always the same. The work is in Toronto. The family is in Montreal. With a daughter in high school, it doesn't even get to a family vote. A husband or wife can't move, or won't, for professional or lifestyle reasons.

It's not like commuting to Calgary. When Canadian Pacific moved its corporate head office as well as railway operating headquarters from Montreal to Calgary, employees either went or were left behind.

What's left, in the splendidly renovated Windsor Station, is a facade as empty as any set in Hollywood. But then CP, too, was going where its business was, with most of the rail traffic, and most of its other operating companies, in the West.

Montreal to Toronto is a sufficiently short commute that a surprising number of people stretch their lives to accommodate both their careers and their families.

They can go home for dinner on Friday night and be back at their desk on Monday morning. Three nights at home, four on the road. They talk of working late and eating takeout.

Once in a while, it works the other way, with a company like Molson Inc., refocusing on its beer origins, moving to Montreal from Toronto. Somehow, you don't hear as many stories of families who refuse to forsake the pleasures of Mississauga for Montreal.

With all these Montrealers in Toronto, it's not surprising that a niche market has developed there. The current *Toronto Life* magazine has a cover piece by Jacob Richler on where to find Montreal in Toronto.

There was supposed to be a piece of it, or a taste of it, when Moishe's opened a steak house in First Canadian Place, in the heart of the Bay Street financial district.

I'd never really thought of Moishe's as a movable feast. Much of its ambience is uniquely Montreal, with prosperous patrons complaining about how bad things are in the rag trade.

How do you take a steak house from the Main and put it down on Bay Street? The answer, evidently, is with great difficulty.

"It doesn't look like the one in Montreal at all," confided a member of Montreal's diaspora. "It's all chrome inside."

The day we walked around at lunchtime, there was nothing inside but stacked chairs and a notice posted on the doors saying that the landlord had reclaimed the premises in an apparent disagreement with the tenant.

Mind you, there are some things about Toronto that will never change. Determined to put down jaywalking, they have posted large signs that exclaim: "Pedestrians obey your signals."

Somehow, that wouldn't work in Montreal, in either language.

November 1999

∞

SNOW STORMS

With November's election safely behind him, the mayor of Montreal needn't concern himself with snow clearance. But it's very much on the mind of Mel Lastman, mayor of Toronto, where snow has been falling in Montreal-like quantities – which is to say, enough to close down Canada's self-styled megacity.

With Toronto "in chaos" according to the *Globe and Mail* headline, Mayor Mel said he was "petrified" by the prospect of more snow on the way. With 65 centimetres of snow accumulated in the last week, and without the infrastructure to move it, Lastman called in the army. The Toronto subway was closed, because part of it runs above ground.

As for Pearson Airport, don't go there expecting to get out. Since it is the hub of Canadian civil aviation, even if you're going somewhere else from Dorval, chances are your plane is on the ground in Toronto.

Being Canada's world-class city, Toronto had the bright idea to buy machinery that melts snow rather than move it. This high-speed marvel of high technology moves at less than two kilometres an hour, fills sewers to overflowing and turns streets into skating rinks.

This Rube Goldberg–like contraption actually made the ABC News the other night, with anchor Peter Jennings furrowing his brow in apparent surprise over the inability of his fellow Canadians to cope with the onset of winter. When he was growing up in Ottawa, they might not have had snow-melters, but they had shovels, eh?

Message to Toronto: welcome to Canada.

Yet here's an opportunity, unique in this century, for Canadians in the rest of the country to express their solidarity with Toronto's plight.

CITIES 277

Don't everybody run for that Toronto Helpline at once. Why aren't broadcasters, which organized Marathons for Manitoba in the 1997 floods, organizing Telethons for Toronto?

Seriously, if Toronto were a city in China rather than Canada, Bourque would be sending in snowblowers, as Jean Drapeau once did for New York Mayor John Lindsay when a blizzard closed Gotham in the late 1960s.

It would be a great story for television to follow down the 401 – unilingual francophone Montreal road crews coming to the rescue of unilingual anglophone Torontonians.

Lastman, being the mayor of super-rich Toronto, would insist on paying for it, and the windfall would wipe out Montreal's deficit. Outsourcing is one of the world's fastest-growing service industries, so why shouldn't Montreal be part of it? After all, the mayor of Moscow sent a task force early in the 1990s to see how it's done.

In point of fact, Montreal has the equipment to deal with snow and the mindset to live with it. The first wave of plows is generally followed by the Armies of the Night, the phalanxes of snowblowers and trucks. If the snow isn't removed within three days in your neighbourhood, you simply voted the wrong way. In Detroit, it doesn't matter which way you voted. The city doesn't remove snow on residential streets.

There aren't many North American cities with a winter culture. Washington, for example, of which Franklin Roosevelt once quipped that its founders had in mind a city of northern efficiency and southern charm, and ended up instead with a city of northern charm and southern efficiency.

Never more so than during winter-weather emergencies, both real and apprehended. It's a city where schools close on the forecast of snow, sleet or freezing rain. My daughter's elementary school has snow makeup days built into the calendar.

On the first prediction of a major snow event, invariably dubbed The Big One, panic buying hits supermarkets, which run out of water, milk, toilet tissue, salt and shovels. Among downtown street vendors, sunglasses are replaced by rubbers, gloves and ear muffs.

On the Capital Beltway around the city, trucks spread abrasives even before a freezeup. It's a wasted precaution in a city where people drive their 4x4s with the brakes on.

The other day, one Washington TV station issued a dire warning of freezing conditions overnight. Freezing what? And then when the Big One actually does hit, as it did in January 1996, the capital of the most powerful country on Earth shuts down. Bill Clinton was a prisoner in the White House for a week, with nothing to do but grope Monica Lewinsky. He couldn't even get out for a Big Mac with fries and a large Coke.

Americans may not have as much experience at this, but our own standards of doing business as usual in winter might be slipping. An operator called from Ottawa to say a snowstorm was on the way, and wondered whether everyone would still be available for a conference call this morning.

Peter Jennings would definitely disapprove.

January 1999

CAPITAL CITY—OF POTHOLES

While driving along a quiet Washington street the other day, I was making a mental note of things this city had in common with Montreal when my car hit a huge pothole.

That, too.

Washington potholes are, if possible, even deeper than the ones in Montreal. They are caused by the tropical rains, rather than spring heaves. And they are the main reason the DC police lead the world in disabled patrol cars. The problem is so serious that the city wants to put welfare recipients to work patching 2,000 potholes this summer. Meanwhile, its streets look more like a third-world capital than the New Rome.

Some of the cabs would be right at home in Havana, where they specialize in spare parts for 1958 Chryslers, the last model year before Castro arrived in town. And for reasons known only to the immigration authorities, and possibly not even them, most of the cabbies here are not only from out of town, but out of country.

This makes it very difficult for them to get around a city designed as a quadrant with avenues named for states cutting diagonally across parallel numbered streets running into dozens of traffic circles, designed by Pierre l'Enfant so people would get lost. The worst of them, Chevy Chase Circle, feeds in traffic from seven directions. It is not much different than driving around the Champs Elysée in Paris, another capital designed by l'Enfant.

Because no one who lives here is from here, Washington offers the bad driving habits of 50 states. Put it all together in a city of workaholics, and you have the worst traffic in America, after Los Angeles, according to *USA Today*.

The political expression "Inside the Beltway," as in Inside Baseball, derives from a ring road around the U.S. capital where many lawyers and lobbyists now put in long billable hours on their cell phones.

The Washington metro is in some ways patterned after Montreal's and in others an improvement on it, beginning with air-conditioning. The Washington metro is the city's pride, with five lines converging on downtown DC from the city and suburbs in the neighbouring states of Virginia and Maryland.

If you thought the politics of metropolitan transit was intricate between Montreal, Laval and the South Shore, try bringing in the county executives of two sovereign states and get them all on the same page as to where the metro should grow next.

Surface-transportation jurisdictions still change at the DC line. So do a lot of other things. On one side of a street named Western Avenue is the District of Columbia, on the other the state of Maryland.

If you move across the street, you must change your driving license, registration, license tags and insurance. You also change your area code, get a new phone number and new voice-mail pickup. You even get a different cable guy. On the DC side of the street, garbage day is Thursday, on the Maryland side, it's Wednesday.

So the metro is a model of regional co-operation. Though Washington has its share of drive-by shootings, schoolyard stabbings and crack-house murders, its metro is remarkably crime-free. In about thirty years of operations, there has only been one murder on the metro.

The metro is only ten minutes from downtown to National Airport, renamed for Ronald Reagan, in honour of a president who once fired the air-traffic controllers.

Montreal is also like Washington in the sense that it has two airports, one just minutes from the centre of the city, and the other more than 50 kilometres from downtown. Except that Mirabel is a white elephant and Dulles has become one of the busiest airports in the world, and is getting busier all the time, with a high-tech corridor on either side of the Dulles toll road.

Something else Montreal and Washington have in common is Frederick Law Olmsted, the American landscape architect who designed Mount Royal Park. New York's Central Park is probably Olmsted's most famous creation, but he also designed the National Zoo, 163 acres backing on to Rock Creek Park in the middle of Washington. It's truly a national treasure, and as part of the Smithsonian complex of museums, there's no admission charge.

Then, both Montreal and Washington, with Boston, are the leading university cities on the east coast of North America. A McGill University survey last winter indicated Montreal had the highest per-capita university enrolment on the continent, edging out Boston by a fraction of a percentage point. Washington is not far behind, with Georgetown, George Washington, American University, Johns Hopkins, Catholic University, Howard and UDC.

Montreal and Washington each have fine symphony orchestras that perform in arts centres, Place des Arts and the Kennedy Center, which serve multiple purposes but not the particular purpose of classical music. Charles Dutoit of the Montreal Symphony Orchestra and Leonard Slatkin of Washington's National Symphony are reputable leaders of orchestras condemned to perform in Salle Wilfrid Pelletier and the Kennedy Concert Hall, which are to music what the Olympic Stadium was to football.

Still, Montreal has one thing Washington doesn't – Major League Baseball. For the moment, anyway. Which could be one more thing the two cities finally have in common – the Expos.

June 2000

LIGHTS OUT

In the middle of a summer heat wave, there was no electricity in the largest city in the country. There was no air-conditioning, and the people suffered great discomfort. There was no refrigeration and food was wasted. In a country rich in oil, there was no way to pump gas. Hospitals cancelled all surgeries. There was only a 24-hour supply of water. With no way to transact commerce, the local economy quickly came to a halt. With banking machines shut down, there was no money. When night fell on the city, there was widespread fear of looting.

Baghdad in the summer of 2003? Nope. New York. And Toronto. The most important cities in the United States and Canada, as well as most of the state of New York and the province of Ontario were struck by a rolling blackout that within minutes, left twenty million people without power. From New Jersey in the south to Michigan in the west, from Ottawa to Windsor and Detroit, the east coast of North America came unplugged.

Terrorist attacks on power plants? Thankfully not, though somewhere in a cave near the Afghan-Pakistani border, Osama bin Laden undoubtedly noted the vulnerability of the power grid of eastern North America, a vast network of aging utilities, interconnected for sharing electricity, but equally interconnected when power fails. It's the industrial version of an Internet virus.

Interrupting a Los Angeles fundraiser to assure Americans it wasn't an act of terrorism, President George W. Bush allowed it was time to look at modernizing the North American power grid. A complete no-brainer. Electricity is a mature industry, built as geographic monopolies by public utilities that financed and built power stations, generated and transmitted electricity and sold it to customers at fixed or bundled rates.

Then along came deregulation, and utilities were privatized and broken up into power generators and transmitters, selling at market prices, including the spot market. If public utilities were lazy and inefficient, the market forces haven't done a better job. It's not the market's job to keep supply and demand in perfect balance, that's what moves markets. The electricity industry is now about 85 per cent privatized in the U.S., but private utilities don't really have the public-policy vision or the financial leverage to build new capacity. The James Bay energy projects would never have been built without the vision of Robert Bourassa, or the good reputation of Hydro-Québec in borrowing markets.

Electricity is a $200-billion industry in the U.S., worth about $60 billion in the northeast alone. Hydro-Québec is one of the niche players in this market, reaping windfall profits from selling to the U.S. at "needlepeak" prices, especially when demand spikes in summer heat waves.

One of the ironies of the Ontario-wide blackout was that while Parliament Hill was in the dark, the lights were blazing across the river at the casino in Gatineau. Of course, it being Ottawa in August, nobody panicked because no one was in town. The first thing Ottawa Mayor Bob Chiarelli declared was that he wasn't declaring an emergency. The Americans know how to do these things. By the same time, New York Mayor Michael Bloomberg had agreed to go on *Larry King Live*.

So, whose fault was it?

The first of many confused reports on CNN was a power station went out "near Ottawa," triggering a chain reaction. Blame Canada, eh? Having none of it, the Prime Minister's Office at first said lightning struck a power station at Niagara Falls, N.Y. – an odd assertion given the PGA golf championship was playing down the road in Rochester without so much as a cloud in the sky. Then Jean Chrétien's office changed its version to, as CNN's headline put it: "Canadian PM: Cause of Power Outage Fire at Con-Ed Plant." The Americans went ballistic, maintaining the Niagara Falls plant in question never went down. Later, Defence Minister John

McCallum blamed a failure at an American nuclear plant. So, three different official Canadian versions of the event, with Chrétien himself nowhere to be seen. In Ottawa, they didn't need to be without power to have the lights turned out.

August 2003

17

LIVING

SELLING THE MIATA

"I sold the Miata."

"What do you mean you sold the Miata?"

This has been my conversation-stopper recently, about trading in my 1991 Miata Limited for a much more sensible Subaru Forester.

My friends, men and women alike, have been uniformly shocked and appalled. The Miata was a beautiful car, all right, in British racing green with tan interior and walnut-knobbed stick shift, the sort of car that got a lot more looks than the person driving it.

The Miata became the car of the 1990s for one very good reason – it was the baby-boomer generation's mid-life crisis present to itself. Everyone who didn't own one wanted one. It was the MGB they'd always wanted when they were growing up.

It was partly the sleek design, partly the superb handling, and partly the feel of the road eighteen inches under the clutch. There was room in the boot for a golf bag, and perhaps two overnight pieces. When the 1990 Miata first rolled out, it came in only three colours: red, white, or blue. British racing green came along a bit later, and all the shades of black, blue, and silver since then.

It instantly became the hottest thing on the road and sparked the renaissance of the two-seater. *Esquire* magazine did a piece suggesting the sports car was like your mistress while the family vehicle was like your wife.

Not only was this sexist, it was wrong. Among the people who kept asking if I wanted to sell my Miata was a former girlfriend in Washington, a broadcasting executive who used to love driving it out into the Virginia countryside during weekends. My ex-wife used to look forward to child and car swaps so she could drive around with the top down after getting her roots done. She used to joke that she wanted the Miata in the divorce, but had to settle for the Mazda 626 instead.

I happened to take delivery of mine on my daughter's first birthday, in July 1991. When I asked the sales agent for a British green one, he just laughed, explaining they only shipped 300 copies of the Limited to all of Canada. But he found one on a dealer's lot, the last one in Montreal. "It's a five-speed," he said, "a standard."

"What do you mean, a standard? Can't I get an automatic?"

"Nope, only comes in standard. It's supposed to be a sports car."

I couldn't drive a standard. Hadn't ever. Lessons were in order. I called my pal Bill Fox, who happened to own a red Miata.

"Do you think we could go around this parking lot for about half an hour?" I asked.

"I'm not sure you can get it in half an hour," he said.

In an hour, I must have stalled fifty times.

"You pop the clutch," Fox explained. "You hit the sweet spot."

"What's this down at the bottom of the gear shift?" I asked.

"That's reverse."

Somehow, I later managed to drive my car off the lot, down the Decarie Expressway, and out to my cottage in the Gatineau, generally avoiding traffic, steep hills and stop signs.

When I went to Washington to work at our embassy in the fall of 1992, I drove the Miata down through the mountains of New York, Pennsylvania and Maryland, and at the end of a perfect top-down day, across Memorial Bridge, around the flood-lit Lincoln Memorial and into a new life.

During the years I lived in Washington, the Miata usually stayed in the driveway, except during weekends. But once in a while, on a fine morning, I would take it to work, on a route that swung around the South Portico of the White House and up Pennsylvania Avenue to our chancery in the shadow of the U.S. Capitol. It was quite a kick.

Moving back to Montreal in 1996, I rediscovered something the Miata wasn't made for: winter. There wasn't enough snow clearance and it tended to fishtail on icy roads. That's not to mention the body damage caused by road salt.

But in spring, it was a fine way of declaring the end of winter. And until I changed the plates, it might have been the only Miata in Montreal with Maryland tags. No matter where I pulled in to gas up in Quebec, attendants always spoke to me in English, asking how I liked it here.

Then I began seeing someone who liked it well enough for short spins around the city, but not weekend trips out of town. "You can't even invite anyone to the cottage," she pointed out, correctly.

Since she does not travel with just carry-on luggage, even going to the airport became a problem. "Stupid damn car," she said as we were heading off one time, suggesting I take the spare tire out of the trunk to make room for one of her bags. "Wouldn't fit anyway," I replied lamely. It went on her lap.

That was the beginning of the end for the Miata, though she suffered guilt pangs when I decided to trade it in. "I whined and nagged until you got rid of it," she said, full of remorse.

Nope. It's just that a Miata doesn't go to the beach or cottage with an eight-year-old, or anyone else. It also has to do with turning 50, and getting on with the rest of life.

When I drove it into the dealer's lot, I gave it one last lingering look. "Thanks, babe," I whispered, "you've been great."

July 1998

CHURCHILL'S FISHING CAMP

Here's a fishing story, the true story of how Winston Churchill went trout fishing in Quebec for three days in the middle of the Second World War.

It happened after the Quebec Conference in August 1943, when William Lyon Mackenzie King hosted Churchill and Franklin Roosevelt, an event the Quebec government memorialized this year when it dedicated busts of the British and American wartime leaders, but not Canada's prime minister.

Churchill, and his wife, Clementine, joined a group of anglers at Lac des Neiges in Parc des Laurentides, or "Lake of the Snows," as he wrote of the fishing trip in *Closing The Ring*, Part 5 of his epic six-volume history, *The Second World War*.

At the Quebec Conference, the allies approved Operation Overlord, the Normandy landings of 1944. When the conference concluded on August 24, Churchill remained behind at the Citadel to prepare a radio broadcast to Canadians scheduled for August 31. But after a few days, he wrote, his mind turned to the possibilities of fishing.

"There was so much to say and not say in the broadcast," he wrote in *Closing The Ring*, "that I could not think of anything, so my mind turned constantly to the Lake of the Snows, of which glittering reports had already come in from those who were there."

He had been invited by his Canadian military aide, a Colonel Clarke, "who owned a ranch amid the mountains and pine forests from which the newspapers get their pulp to guide us on life's journey."

Churchill thought he "might combine fishing by day with preparing the broadcast after dark," and so "set out with my wife by car."

What made the visit all the more remarkable, apart from such light security in the middle of the war, was that the area was then quite inaccessible, and would have taken a good day to reach by car from Quebec. Indeed, Churchill wrote of a "wonderful all-day drive up the river valley."

To this day, the last 80 kilometres into Lac des Neiges is a terrible dirt road that climbs spectacularly to a 20-km-long finger of a lake, some 700 metres above sea level.

The first I heard of Churchill's angling adventure in Quebec was on a fishing trip at nearby Lac Brulé. The host was Claude Bruneau, one of seven authors of the 1964 pro-federalist manifesto titled For a Functional Federation, which brought an obscure academic named Pierre Trudeau to the public's attention. While Trudeau became prime minister, Bruneau became chairman of an insurance company and later an adviser to Paul Desmarais at Power Corp.

Rummaging around in a cabinet drawer after dinner one evening, I came upon an old guest book. Out tumbled these old black and white Kodaks of Churchill holding up a line of huge speckled trout. In one picture, he was standing in a boat, without a life jacket, looking very pleased with himself. There wasn't a security man anywhere in the picture.

On his page of the guest book, one of the greatest figures of the 20th century wrote a lavish inscription with a fountain pen, and signed it, unmistakably, Winston S. Churchill. Clementine and others in his party signed below.

"Have you seen this?" I asked my host.

"Sure," said Bruneau, "It's been in that drawer for years."

"Churchill was here during the war?"

"Lac des Neiges. It's a few miles from here."

Both lakes were in the middle of a timber concession run by the Price company, which may be how the guest book and photos came to be in the possession of the forestry company at Manoir Lac Brulé, one of those corporate fishing camps that dot Quebec.

As it happened, the next summer, I was invited to Lac des Neiges with another fishing group.

Lac des Neiges is now a fishing camp maintained by the Quebec government for members of the National Assembly and their guests, who pay an equivalent commercial fee for two or three days of fishing.

There are actually two camps on Lac des Neiges, a spare and modern one complete with hot showers, guides and three square meals a day, and a rustic one with log cabins along the lake, where Churchill supposedly stayed.

There is in fact some uncertainty about where Churchill slept. He wrote that he arrived "at a spacious log cabin by the lake," which fits the description of Manoir Lac Brule, and raises the distinct possibility that his party slept there and fished over at Lac des Neiges.

But there is no doubt that he fished there. "My wife and I sallied forth in separate boats for several hours, and though we are neither of us experts, we certainly caught a lot of fine fish."

He added: "We were sometimes given rods with three separate hooks, and once I caught three fish at the same time. I do not know whether this was fair."

Certainly not. And, by today's rules, certainly not legal. But the Kodaks were the proof of his catch, and the guest book the proof of his presence. The trip almost assumed larger significance in that Roosevelt, as Churchill wrote, "had wanted to come himself, but other duties claimed him."

Getting Roosevelt, in his wheelchair, into Lac des Neiges, would have been quite a feat even today. As it was, Churchill wrote: "I sent the biggest fish I caught to him at Hyde Park."

As for his address to the Canadian people: "The broadcast made progress, but original composition is more exhausting than either arguing or fishing." And at the end of the third day, he returned to Quebec.

Nowhere at Lac des Neiges is there any acknowledgement that Churchill took time for a Quebec fishing holiday in the midst of the war.

A modest memorial plaque, quoting Churchill's description of the visit, perhaps even in English as well as French, might be appropriate.

August 1998

"WORKING OFFLINE"

My laptop computer is in the shop, being fixed. And my cell phone, which died, is in my car. In Washington.

It's only when these tools of the new economy are unavailable to us that we are reminded of how much we've come to rely on them.

The problem with my laptop is that the plug won't plug in, and the battery won't recharge. Conclusion: the new economy runs on electricity, a commodity distributed by regulated monopolies from the old economy, like Hydro-Québec.

No computer, no dial-up access to the Internet. No way to read e-mail, much less download it. No way to do online trading or check on the latest tech meltdown on the stock market. No way to send a fax, since that's part of the computer-software package. No way to do the column, which is being written in the office at a borrowed workstation.

When I bought my Compaq Presario three years ago, it was cutting-edge technology, with an Intel Pentium sticker and everything. This means that, according to Moore's Law, it has been obsolete for the last year and a half.

Gordon Moore, the co-founder of Intel, Mr. Intel Inside himself, once posited that computer capacity would double every eighteen months. Which means there is more power in your laptop than in the onboard systems that took Apollo astronauts to the moon.

Moore made this pronouncement back in the late 1970s, when Ken Olson, the president of Digital Corp., said he saw no need for people to have computers in the home. In those days, about 99 per cent of the world's computer power was still in mainframe, and today 99 per cent is in personal computers, in desktops and, increasingly, in laptops.

Which is why, if IBM hadn't invented the PC in 1980, it would have gone out of business. Today, computer manufacturers such as Compaq and Dell ship about seventy million PCs a year worldwide. And the business is still growing, especially given convergence and connectivity.

Buying a laptop computer is a very personal choice, and since it goes everywhere with you, a very personal statement. People check you out on airplanes, in coffee shops, in bookstores, and other places that make office space increasingly redundant.

My Presario came recommended by Bernard Hudon, the proprietor of the friendly neighbourhood computer store. A helpful young woman named Marise asked what kind of software I wanted loaded into the thing.

"WordPerfect."

"WordPerfect 8, right?

"Nope, WordPerfect 5.1."

"You're kidding," she said, with a pitying look that tech heads reserve for real people.

"I just want WordPerfect 5.1 It gives you white type against a blue screen. Shift F10 to save. It's all I need. I just need word-processing."

"You need Word," she insisted. "You'll get over it."

Bernard himself intervened.

"Michel Tremblay is one of our clients," he said. "He also refuses to use anything but WordPerfect 5.1. Writers definitely like it."

There are WordPerfect people in the way there are Apple people, cult-like in their devotion. We don't like Word, and we don't like Microsoft.

WordPerfect people have been following the Microsoft anti-trust case with interest. In the current penalty or remedy phase, the U.S. Justice Department is asking the judge to break up the company into "ops" and "apps," the Windows operating system that most of the world's computers run on, and the software applications as well as new media brands that Bill Gates has been foisting on people.

Actually, my Presario came with a present from Bill Gates – a free Encyclopedia Encarta on compact disc. All the knowledge that used to be in 26 volumes in your basement is now on one thin CD. Gates said in a speech not long ago that he was discussing this with Warren Buffet, who owns World Book Encyclopedia and sells about 300,000 copies a year the old door-to-door way, while Encarta does about 3 million copies a year on CD.

Bernard also threw in a free Virus Scan from McAfee, which came in handy during ILOVEYOU week. It's becoming pretty clear that the new economy is vulnerable to the kind of dirty tricks perpetrated by Mafia Boy, who police say is a West Island teenager, and who may well be negotiating the movie rights to his story.

Like Matthew Broderick, who nearly started a nuclear war in *War Games*, Mafia Boy crashed major Web sites and sent share prices tumbling. He took billions of dollars out of equity markets, but the media can't name him because he's just a teenager, whose punishment is to stay offline.

I know the feeling.

April 2000

DIARY OF A CRAZY WEEK

Monday: Foolishly predict on the radio the Liberals will win the Mercier by-election by five points. Mercier is to the Parti Québécois as Outremont is to the Liberals. But it's a by-election, and PQ candidate Claudel Toussaint has been clobbered by negative coverage of his personal life. Plus, the separatists are running a candidate, Paul Cliche, making a strong bid for the Ralph Nader vote. Plus, the Liberals have a quality local candidate in Nathalie Rochefort, and they're not running her in red. The earth tones of her posters look very Péquiste. Plus, there's enough people in the Plateau angry about their rent to vote against the government, any government.

Jump in the car and race to Ottawa for a business lunch. Note the Île aux Tourtes Bridge is actually open, all six lanes of it. Decades after it was finished, the bridge is finally open, at least until summer. Crossing the Ontario border, also note the sudden absence of potholes.

Ottawa never changes. Still a village. Talk of the town is the escalation of the Grand-Mère affair with the weekend raid on the homes and offices of former Business Development Bank president François Beaudoin, suspected of leaking bank documents to the *National Post,* which had faxed them to the Prime Minister's Office and the bank for comment. What a coincidence, and how fortunate for the bank to find a judge working on a Saturday. Luckily for Jean Chrétien, Parliament isn't sitting.

Drive back to Montreal. Liberals win Mercier by five points. Quit while you're ahead.

Tuesday: Fly to Toronto for an afternoon meeting. Get to the airport only ten minutes before scheduled flight departure. No time to park, so leave the car with valet parking. It's right outside the terminal, and while it's $24 for the day, it's still less than half the cost of taking a cab out to Dorval and back.

At the check-in counter, told flight is closed and oversold, but given a boarding pass anyway. Name called at the gate. Given a seat, and in business class. Nothing like flying for free in the wide seats. Who says Air Canada service is lousy?

Leaving downtown Toronto at 4:30, note again the Air Canada Centre is a much better building than the Molson Centre. And they're still playing hockey there.

"Take your time," cab-driver is told, "my flight's only at 6."

"You'll make the 5:30," he says. We get to the Rapidair door at five minutes to five. "You might even make the 5," he says.

"If you run," says the gate agent.

Airbus 330 pushes back from the gate on time, an unheard occurrence in Toronto. On the ground in Montreal at 6:05, home at 6:30. Downtown to downtown in two hours, a personal record.

Wednesday: Drive to New York to pick up daughter for Easter vacation. Stay in Manhattan exactly one hour. Load car with kid, cat, and guinea pig and turn around to drive home.

Daughter's taste in traveling music runs to Britney Spears. But not in clothes. "She dresses like a tart," 10-year-old daughter says.

Last of countless trips to New York and Washington, as daughter and her mother are moving to Montreal. What a concept, living in the same city as your kid.

No papers for guinea pig. Fear she will be seized in a foot-and-mouth sweep. Cat has more papers than daughter has for English school in Quebec. Waved through by smiling Canadian customs agent.

Montreal at its magical best on crossing of Champlain Bridge, lights twinkling on the still waters of the St. Lawrence. "Awesome," daughter says. "But I won't get to see this as much because I won't be driving into Montreal any more, I'll be living here."

Montreal – New York – Montreal in an elapsed driving time of 14 hours. Also a personal record. Completely wasted.

Thursday: Daughter wants to check out new school. After seeing library and science lab, wants to start right away. "Can I skip Easter vacation?" she asks.

Friday: Sleep in.

April 2001

∽

SALMON FISHING, KING OF SPORTS

The great thing about fishing is that you never run out of excuses. The water is always too high or too low. There's always too much rain or, as is the case this summer, not enough. It's either too windy or there's a dead calm. Too early in the day or too late. And, of course, too sunny, fishing being the only sport where people complain about the weather being too good.

The abundance of excuses is very important in the quest for the elusive Atlantic salmon, perhaps the noblest and certainly the most sought after species in angling.

The Sainte-Marguerite River, a tributary of the Saguenay, is one of the fifty great salmon rivers of Quebec. By the time the Atlantic salmon enter it, they're on the final leg of an epic return voyage across the Atlantic Ocean.

They're going home to spawn – the females to leave their thousands of eggs in the riverbed and the males to fertilize them. The last obstacle, on a journey of perhaps 15,000 kilometres, are the anglers in the pools of the Sainte-Marguerite.

The entire length of the river is a ZEC, a Zone d'Exploitation Contrôlée, with the number of anglers and their catch severely limited. Any grilses under 62 centimetres or 2.5 kilograms may be kept and consumed. Anything larger is strictly catch and release.

The Sainte-Marguerite Salmon Fishing Club, on the banks of the river near Sacré-Coeur, was founded by American interests in the 19th century, passed into the hands of the Price forestry family in the early 20th century and was assumed by Alcan around mid-century.

Under successive leaders of the aluminum company, notably David Culver, the fishing camp has been painstakingly restored to its original state. Culver is as renowned along the river as he is in Montreal for having built the company's award-winning world headquarters on Sherbrooke Street.

There is more to conservation than catch and release. Above the camp, a major research effort is under way at the Inter-University Research Centre for Atlantic Salmon. Students from Laval, McGill and other Canadian universities spend the summer doing fieldwork on the river, and professors analyze the results on the migratory patterns of the Atlantic salmon.

They know how many fish leave the river, and how many come back. And the numbers are dwindling. It's much the same worrisome story along many of Quebec's salmon rivers.

The problem with the Sainte-Marguerite isn't the river. The problem for Atlantic salmon in Quebec is beyond the rivers. On their two-way journey, the salmon must contend with native fishing, commercial overfishing and, not least, the predatory seals that have multiplied since the end of the seal hunt.

"In the very good years at the beginning of the '90s," camp manager Claude Poirier says, "it wasn't unusual to catch about 900 salmon in a season." With only a month to go in the current season, he has written only about 50 salmon into his log book, half of them released.

It certainly isn't because of the guides. From lifetimes spent on the river, they have developed a kind of night vision, seeing things the rest of us don't. Paulo Dufour has been on the Sainte-Marguerite for thirty-three years, and his father for thirty-five years before that. His grandfather was on the river his entire life. Talk about local knowledge.

We were at a bend of the river one morning, and the salmon were jumping at a pool named Powell, for an angler once guided by Paulo's grandfather. It was cloudy and cool, following an overnight rain, with just enough wind to stir the pools.

Paulo tried a dry fly called a Bomber, and suddenly there was no mistaking the bend of the line. The salmon hit the water with more a thud than a splash.

"*Baptême!*" Paulo exclaimed, "I haven't seen one like that in years."

"I forgot the net," I said lamely.

"We don't need a net for this," he replied, as we brought the salmon into the rocky shore. "I'll pick it up by the fins. You just bring it in."

"You can do that?"

"Been doing it all my life."

And so he did. After only twenty-seven minutes, a thirty-pound female was photographed in his hands and sent on her way.

Back at the camp, I came across an article written forty years ago in the *Atlantic Salmon Journal*. The writer, Alexandre Marcotte, was director of the marine-biology station at Grande-Rivière.

"If you have ever done battle with the fighting Atlantic silver salmon," he wrote, "think of this muscular juggernaut whom you first met in the clear, fresh water of a stream. It mattered not really whether you won or lost. If you can think like this, there need be no conflict of interests, and this greatest of all fish, the salmon, will with your help and mine, survive the age of industrialization."

July 2002

SEEING EYE HEALTH CARE

Nearly everyone has a story about the health-care system, and now I have one, too.

A few weeks ago, I suddenly started seeing black dots moving around in my left eye. A few days later, when my vision clouded over completely, a friend referred me to his ophthalmologist at the Montreal General Hospital.

"He isn't here today," his receptionist said on the phone. "What's your problem?"

"I can't see out of my left eye."

"You have to come into the emergency at the General," she said. "There's an ophthalmologist on call 24 hours."

So began my four-week journey through the public and semi-private health-care system in Quebec. Along the way, I learned there is no neat dividing line between public and private medicine anymore, as I found myself having to make choices outside the system that saved time inside it. Luckily, I was able to afford those options, which cost about $750 for everything from blood samples to an ocular axial lens for my eye.

Health care is a $130-billion industry in this country, of which about $30 billion is privately delivered, much of it within the public system. But I am getting ahead of the story.

I went to emergency at the Pine Avenue entrance of the General. "I need to see an ophthalmologist," I said.

"It doesn't work that way," said the woman at the registration desk. "First, you see the triage nurse, then you come back here, then you wait to see a doctor who will decide whether you need to see an ophthalmologist."

It was 3 o'clock on a Thursday afternoon. "Now for the hard part," she said.

"The waiting?"

"The waiting."

Everyone waits. Fifteen patients were lying on gurneys in the corridor of the ER, stacked up like cordwood. In some instances, consultations were held in the corridor. It looked like the Third World.

Three and a half hours later, a young doctor called me into an examination room and looked at my eye.

"I recognized your picture from the newspaper," he said. "You have floaters. You need to go up to the ophthalmology clinic on the fourth floor."

Two and a half hours later, they called my name to go upstairs.

David Lederer, a fourth-year resident in ophthalmology, would be the first of seven ophthalmologists I would meet over the next four weeks.

"It seems like it's just a broken blood vessel," Lederer explained. "But there could be a torn retina. It needs to be looked at again. The problem is, you can't see out, and we can't see in.

"You have a choice," he continued, "you can stay in the public system and go to the clinic at the Jewish General tomorrow, or you can see Dr. Chen at his semi-private clinic in the morning."

Six hours in a waiting room has a way of clarifying choices. John Chen's office, the Montreal Retina Institute, had a room full of patients waiting to see him and his three partners. The visits are covered by the *carte du soleil*, but the drops for dilating the eye cost $30, credit card or bank card only, no cheques or cash.

"You're lucky it wasn't twelve hours," said Saad Al-Khalifa, a fifth-year post-doctoral fellow from Bahrain who did his medical studies at the University of Dublin. It takes nine years of study from first-year med school to full accreditation in ophthalmology, and as long as twelve years, including sub-specialty training, to do what Chen does.

"Why did you choose ophthalmology?" I ask Chen as he peers into my eye for the first time.

"Because it allows me a mix of diagnostic work and surgery," he replies. Most of the time, the operation is a success and the patient doesn't die.

A McGill University graduate, Chen works out of his clinic two-and-a-half days a week, and does surgeries on Wednesdays at the Royal Victoria Hospital of the McGill University Health Centre, as well as half a day at the RVH's free clinic.

On any given Wednesday, says Terry Mercer, the orderly on Chen's surgery team, "we do between seven and twelve operations."

"Surgery," says Chen, "is by far the most relaxing thing I do. I'm sitting down the whole time. The clinic, that's the most stressful thing I do. People are waiting, sometimes for as long as three hours, and we're always trying to clear the backlog. You feel their frustration. It's very understandable."

It's also a thriving business. Chen and his partners recently moved from rented space on Union Street downtown to owned space in an office condominium on Ste. Catherine Street, across from Westmount Square. By 9 o'clock any morning, his waiting room is already full. The demographic is mostly 60 and up. And as the first wave of the baby-boomer generation turns 60 in 2007, the demand for ophthalmologists is only going to grow.

According to the Canadian Institute for Health Information, there were 1,066 ophthalmologists in Canada in 2004. Chen was one of 285 in Quebec.

The question is, why isn't Chen at Harvard or Johns Hopkins, research-rich institutions where public health care and waiting times are not an issue?

"We get solicited like that all the time," says Chen. "I like it here. I make a very good living. I do all the research I want to do with my patients. Plus, my parents are reaching the age where one of their children needs to be close by." He and his wife, Angela, have three school-age daughters. She runs the business side of his clinic. They are active in the community – he just stepped down as board chair of the Centaur Theatre, she volunteers with the women's auxiliary of the RVH.

It's McGill itself – world-renowned in medicine – and a critical mass of excellence in the practice of ophthalmology, that attract doctors and students from every corner of the globe. Chen is also an associate professor in the McGill medical faculty and has twice been voted best teaching professor by student residents.

"McGill is absolutely one of the reasons I'm here," says Al-Khalifa, a member of Bahrain's royal family who will return home to open his own practice after one more year. "But it's also the opportunity of working with people like Dr. Chen. He is the best."

How Chen came to Canada and Montreal from Taiwan at the age of 15 is a story in itself. His father, Peter, is a Paris-trained lawyer and politician who abruptly decided to leave Taiwan after Richard Nixon's visit to mainland China in February 1972. He thought that once the United States abandoned Taiwan, the "commies" would soon be coming across the Strait of Formosa. Because he was French-speaking, he chose Montreal over Vancouver.

Chen lays out the options at our first meeting – waiting until the eye clears, which could take weeks, or surgery to clear the blood and repair any damage to the retina. "There may be a slight tear," he says. "If that's the case, we can laser it. At this point, it's an elective, but the risk in waiting is that it could detach in the meantime."

Having a pathological fear of doctors and hospitals, I choose to wait. After four weeks, the eye finally clears enough for Chen to see into it, but he doesn't like what he sees.

"The retina is detached," he says at his clinic on the last Tuesday in October. "You have to have surgery tomorrow. I'm also going to remove a cataract. You have to come back here in the morning to have your eye measured for a lens to replace it. Then you need to go across the street to the Westmount Medical Centre and get an EKG and some blood work done before the surgery. Bring the results to the hospital with you."

This is where the semi-private part of the journey becomes expensive. The ultrasound to measure for an ocular axial lens costs $150. But it's done in half an hour the next morning. A walk-in visit to the private clinic in Westmount Square costs $129 for the EKG and blood samples. But the waiting time is one minute, the tests take twenty minutes and the results of the blood work will be faxed to Chen's office within an hour by the laboratory. It's only 9 in the morning, and Chen has scheduled emergency surgery at 1:30 in the afternoon.

There's enough time to reflect that I can afford to opt out of the system, and opt back in, significantly reducing diagnostic waiting times. But what happens to people who can't?

They wait. In its 15th annual report, *Waiting Your Turn: Hospital Waiting Lists in Canada*, the Fraser Institute finds actual waiting time for a scheduled ophthalmology procedure in Quebec is 11.8 weeks, three months, as opposed to a reasonable median waiting time of 7.9 weeks, or two months. The waiting time between diagnostic services – the work-up and prep for scheduled surgery – is usually two to three weeks. Because my case turned out to be an emergency, the EKG and blood work were done within half an hour of walking into a clinic.

"You go to day surgery about an hour before," Chen says. "Go to floor 6-S. They will prep you and bring you down to the surgery."

The outpatient surgery is down one of the Royal Vic's famous labyrinth of corridors, where people have been wandering around lost for generations. The back office of the hospital is a disaster, with paint peeling from the ceilings and broken windows repaired with cardboard. The information technology systems are hopelessly antiquated. Though the General and the Vic are MUHC hospitals, patients need separate client cards for each. In the day surgery, patients are prepped in front of other patients and privacy is nonexistent.

That being said, the quality of the care and compassion of the staff are truly outstanding.

Two nurses, Linda Geronimo and Dina Fernandez, prep up to four patients at a time. They ask questions, they probe and prod, and tell you to change into a hospital smock.

Then Terry Mercer, friendly and reassuring, arrives to wheel patients down to the OR.

"Hi, I'm the head nurse," Josée Cloutier says outside OR No. 6, on floor 5-S, one of two surgeries dedicated to ophthalmology. "Are we operating on your right eye or your left eye today?"

"Ha-ha-ha."

"Well, it's the first time I'm seeing your chart," she replies. "You weren't on the schedule. We're doing you as an emergency."

"Tell you what, make sure it is my chart."

"Are you allergic to anything?" she asks.

"Yes, hospitals."

"Me, too," she says.

A young woman named Joanna Ng-Mangun arrives. "I'm a fourth-year student, and I'm here to help with the IV," she says, sizing up the veins in my left wrist. "Don't worry, we're going to take very good care of you. Dr. Chen is famous."

Al-Khalifa looms overhead, hardly recognizable in his hygiene shower cap.

"Remember me?" he asks.

"Sure, oil-rich Bahrain."

"Not so rich," he says. "You are in the very best hands."

Josée Cloutier is back to explain another choice.

"The lens Dr. Chen is going to put in your eye," she says, "there's one that comes free with the operation, or there's the deluxe model that costs $300. We have to know now."

"I don't exactly have my credit cards with me," I reply. "What does Dr. Chen recommend?"

Chen comes around to explain. "The standard one that comes with the operation is very good, but the deluxe one is better."

"I'm going to write about this," I tell him.

"Then," says Chen, "please point out that the $300 goes to the hospital, not me."

My credit cards are upstairs, with my former wife, Lisa, who has accompanied me to the hospital. "You can tell them upstairs to have Lisa put it on my bank card," I tell Cloutier.

"How are you feeling?" Chen asks.

"Terrified." One week short of my 58th birthday, I'm about to have the first operation of my life.

"Everything will be fine."

In their green hospital scrubs, Chen and his team look like masters of the universe.

"Here's a nice warm blanket," says Cloutier, as I slide onto the operating table. "Is there anything else you need?"

"A double scotch."

"What we're going to give you," says Chen, "will make you feel a lot better than that, without the hangover. You have a choice of music, classical or rock."

Classical, this is definitely not a rock 'n' roll moment.

The local anaesthetic allows him to operate while the patient remains fully conscious. I can't see what he's doing, but I can hear him: cleaning, clipping and finishing with a laser-like flourish. There is no pain and no discomfort.

"Some people have out-of-body experiences," Chen had warned me.

In my case, I decide to interview him during the operation.

"How much would this cost if I were paying for it myself?" I ask him.

Snip-snip.

"In the States?" he replies. "About $7,000."

Snip-snip.

In less than two hours, he is done.

I went into the prep at 1 o'clock in the afternoon and walked out of the hospital at 4 o'clock. There was never any question of staying overnight. "I don't want you to get an infection," Chen had said wickedly.

I started the day of the operation with a semi-private visit, followed by a private consultation, followed by a publicly-funded surgery. It was all done within the space of one working day. The semi-private and private procedures significantly reduced my diagnostic waiting times, and allowed for one less person making intermediary demands on the public system.

"In the best of worlds," Chen says in a reflective moment, "the public health system would be able to provide the best of everything, and there would be no waiting times for anything. All doctors are social democrats at heart and we'd all like it to work that way. But it doesn't. The service I provide at my clinic should be regulated, I should not be able to charge what I want. But I should be able to provide the best care. For me, it's a question of pride."

I'm very aware how fortunate I am to be able to afford these choices. The waiting times in emergencies and for scheduled procedures are clearly a source of intense frustration with the public, whose insurance premiums pay for care they are not receiving in a timely and dignified manner.

Yet the fault lies with an overburdened system and obsolete infrastructure, not with the health-care providers. From orderlies and nurses to students and surgeons, they deliver a remarkable quality of care that compensates for the inadequacies of their workplace.

The most striking element of all is the world renown of McGill. Not one of the seven ophthalmologists I met was from Canada. Without exception, they were attracted to Montreal by the fame of McGill in medicine, and the reputation of local practitioners.

"The institution of McGill is very important," Chen says. "But the network is also important. Because it's so international here, people come to study from all over the world. And when they go home, they advertise. Saad Al-Khalifa will be the first retinal surgeon in Bahrain. Others will follow him here."

I'm exceedingly grateful to Chen and his team. I felt I was in the hands of a highly motivated and thoroughly professional team, with an outstanding leader. They represent a culture of excellence and take exceptional pride in what they do. They are the best.

November 2005

ROOTING FOR THE RED SOX

It was time for closure on the Expos, so in Maine the other day, I bought a Red Sox cap at the drug store in Ogunquit. This was an intensely personal and exceedingly painful decision.

In the years since the Expos left Montreal for Washington, I haven't been able to wear my favourite baseball hat, an authentic red Expos warmup cap given to me by my friend Jacques Ménard, when he was chairman of the consortium that bought the team from its founder Charles Bronfman in 1990, for the express purpose of keeping it in Montreal.

From the Expos we learned that baseball is a game to break your heart, as in 1981 when we lost the pennant to the Dodgers in the ninth inning of the deciding playoff game. Or 1994, when Montreal had the best team in baseball, but was deprived of post-season play by a season-ending players strike.

My daughter loved going to see the Expos, from childhood to her early teenage years. She once stood in line for a pre-game autograph from Vladimir Guerrero, who was blessed with wondrous gifts and a sweet disposition. He signed his colour photo on an Expos calendar, and gave her a dazzling smile. She still remembers the moment and still has the calendar hanging in her room.

"Daddy," she asked, when it was announced the Expos were really, really leaving Montreal, "why are we losing our baseball team?" I blamed it on a man named Jeffrey Loria, who gave carpetbaggers a bad name.

In the unkindest of all fates, Loria traded in the Expos for the Florida Marlins, and won a World Series. The Expos became the Washington Nationals, but even though they now played in a city where I had lived for five years, I couldn't even bear to read the National League standings.

Wearing another team cap was out of the question. Certainly not the Yankees, the most expensive team money could buy. And decidedly not the Toronto Blue Jays, Canada's other team. And if you don't know the why of that, then you're not from Montreal.

Even when the Blue Jays won the World Series, in 1992, I couldn't wear their hat at a Canadian Embassy reception in their honour in Washington.

They were invited to the White House, as is customary, by the first President Bush. As head of the public affairs department I suggested that we invite the Jays to the embassy's sixth floor, with its unexceeded views of the U.S. capitol, the night before. "Great idea," enthused our ambassador, Derek Burney, who set it up with the Blue Jays.

We even arranged for them to ship the actual World Series pennant, which we unfurled down the side of the embassy, right on Pennsylvania Avenue, a very in-their-face gesture which was widely noted in Washington.

But wear their hat? Never.

With the passage of time, the Red Sox seemed an obvious candidate as a newly adopted team. Since winning the World Series in 2004 and again in 2007, they are no longer beautiful losers, but still have an enduring legacy of heartbreak with which any Expos fan can identify.

Their eighty-six years of World Series frustration is exceeded only by the Chicago Cubs, who in 2008 mark a century of futility since their last victory. If you want to start a conversation in Boston, just mention 1946, 1967, 1975 or 1986, defining moments in the history of heartbreak. Besides, the Red Sox are a regional franchise, right on our doorstep, which claims the allegiance of all New Englanders. Moreover, they are endearingly struggling anew, currently trailing the Tampa Bay Devil Rays, whom I generally think of as the team in the Dennis Quaid movie, *The Rookie*.

So, finally, a Red Sox cap. Made in China, of course. In regulation blue, with the trademark red "B". Other hues of the hat are available, including red, a legitimate heritage colour, since Boston wore red caps a couple of decades ago. But pea green? Ugh. Light blue? That's the University of North Carolina's colour.

And there's pink, a big seller judging by the women at the beach, and a matter of some controversy among purists and Fenway fanatics.

"Why is this pink hat so hated?" asked the *Boston Globe* in a screaming headline on its Style section page. One fan, himself the father of two girls, suggested pink hats should be banned from Fenway Park.

This is a serious business. In a bar in Nashua, New Hampshire, the other night, a lively debate developed between two Red Sox fans and a woman in a Yankee cap. They took it outside into the parking lot where the Yankee fan rammed the Sox fans as they were driving off in their car. The Sox fans were injured and criminal charges have been preferred. The Yankee fan has no chance of getting a fair trial anywhere in New England, also known as Red Sox nation.

Meanwhile, back at the beach, the parking-lot attendant at Ogunquit beach expressed strong approval of my new cap.

"I like your hat," he said in that distinctive New England accent. "Couple of Yankee fans in that car just ahead of you."

Thanks for the heads up.

July 2008

MAINESTAYS

For decades, Quebecers have been coming to the beaches of Maine in summer.

In a seasonal sense, they are following in the footprint of those French Canadians who, a century ago, migrated by the thousands to the mill towns of Saco and Biddeford, just south of Portland on the Maine coast. Long since assimilated, they are still called Canadians – not French Canadians, much less Québécois.

While their forebears came here to make a living, Quebecers now come here to play, from St. Jean Baptiste Day in June to Labour Day in September.

They populate the beaches of southern Maine, from York and Cape Neddick, to Moody and Wells, from Kennebunkport and Cape Porpoise to Goose Rocks, Fortunes Rocks and Biddeford Pool. From Ocean Park and Old Orchard to Prout's Neck and Higgins Beach.

And they come to Ogunquit. According to local lore, this is an Algonquin term for "beautiful place by the sea" – which it most assuredly is.

At low tide, the beach is a quarter-mile wide and four miles long. Ogunquit is one of the great walking and jogging beaches in America.

My daughter, now 17, learned to boogie-board in Ogunquit's surf. Since she was six, Gracie has also floated down the Ogunquit River to the sea with the amazingly fast currents at low tide. She has decided that, after a one-year hiatus for being a camp counselor-in-training, she'd rather come back to the beach.

There has seldom been as much French spoken, on the beach or in the retail outlet malls of Kittery, as in the summer of 2008, a season of exchange-rate parity.

Seldom has there been as much French overheard on the Marginal Way, the renowned walk along the cliffs under hotels and gracious summer homes, joining Ogunquit to Perkins Cove – which, with its pedestrian footbridge, fishing boats and shops, is a scene right out of *Murder, She Wrote*.

Only instead of Angela Lansbury, there is Billy Tower, a former lobster fisherman who scraped together the money to start his own lobster and seafood restaurant, Barnacle Billy's, in the cove forty-six years ago.

All these years later, Billy still rides to work on his moped, dressed in the same immaculate white uniform with name tag as the students who wait on tables in his two restaurants. He acquired the second one, famous as the Whistling Oyster but now called Billy's etc., in a bankruptcy proceeding in the 1980s, when the onetime fisherman wrote a cheque for over $1-million.

For nearly half a century, students have worked their way through college waiting tables at Billy's. His alumni association surely numbers in the thousands.

It is also a good place to measure the mood of Quebecers on a summer evening.

Thirty years ago, in the nationalist heyday of the Parti Québécois, you could occasionally hear a chorus of *Gens du pays* drifting across the cove. René Lévesque called it "our national anthem by anticipation."

Nobody from Quebec talks politics anymore. All the conversation is about family, lifestyle and how far their dollars go.

It's true. Only six years ago, the loonie was mired at 62¢. Today, it's at par with the greenback. Canadian exporters may not like it, but Canadian tourists sure do. Stated another way, where it once took more than $1.50 to buy a U.S. dollar, a dollar is now a dollar.

And Canadians who used to come here for a week can in many cases now extend their visit to two, as we have.

My landlord of many years, Dick Drisko, is very happy to have us stay on in our cottage just off the Marginal Way above Perkins Cove.

"Welcome home," he said as we arrived.

That's just how it feels.

National Post, July 2008

18

COTTAGE LIFE

CONNECTIVITY

Going to the cottage isn't quite the rustic experience it used to be.

Take the television, for instance. We used to have an old RCA TV. It was connected to one of those huge rooftop antennas of the kind that crumpled during the great ice storm in 1960, after which everyone in Montreal got cable. That antenna brought in two channels, CBC English and French, both of them snowy.

We finally got a new television with digital colour and a little dish that connects us to the 500-channel universe. We've got CNN, BBC World News, Newsworld, and RDI, to say nothing of all the sports and learning channels.

And so, doing some lakeside channel surfing, we learned with everyone else that John Kennedy's plane was missing. It was one of those breaking news stories in the category of oh-no-not-again, in which you automatically feared the worst even while hoping for a miraculous rescue. Maybe, like his father in the Second World War, he could swim three miles to a nearby island, pulling his unconscious wife along with him. Maybe they had a rubber raft onboard, and would wave at a rescue plane.

We watched with another kind of dread fascination when an unknown French qualifier stood on the 18th tee at Carnoustie, leading by three shots, needing only a double-bogey six to win the British Open, and played a triple-bogey seven, setting up his playoff loss.

Even after an errant drive, all Jean Van de Velde had to do was to lay up, land a pitching wedge and take three putts, and he would have had his name on the Claret Jug with the likes of Walter Hagen, Bobby Jones, Jack Nicklaus and Arnold Palmer. But like the Kevin Costner character in *Tin Cup*, he had to go for it, bounced a drive off the greenside grandstand into knee-high grass, chipped into a water hazard, and from there into a bunker beneath the hole before finally sinking a pressure putt for his triple. Just a walk in the park.

The cottage connection to the outside world used to be a rotary phone, but now it's a modem that links to the Internet and lets me pick up my e-mail back in town. We now get the Internet editions of the *New York Times* and *Washington Post*, as well as *The Gazette*, at the lake.

And I can sit out on the dock and write this on the battery-powered laptop, then go to the phone and file it. No need to go into town, especially in this heat. It's a new world, all right.

When I bought the place in the Gatineau in 1988, the idea was to get away from Ottawa in the summer. It was forty-five minutes from the Peace Tower to St. Pierre-de-Wakefield and the lake.

It was one of those smart things you do by accident. I was then working for the prime minister and figured, if we're going to be stuck in Ottawa waiting for an election to be called, I'll come in from the cottage. A colleague spotted an ad for a cottage in one of those departmental newsletters and I went and looked at it. Being one of those Montrealers with an aversion to Ottawa, I was just looking to rent, but it was only for sale, so I bought it.

It came with a reminder that if there was a lot of bad rock'n'roll in the 1970s, and a lot of polyester, there was also a lot of bad carpeting, in this case wall-to-wag shag, in burnt orange the approximate colour of Youppi. When the roof fell in over the fireplace one year, we finally replaced the carpeting with a more restrained shade of gray.

But the cottage also came with a fieldstone fireplace, a stone barbecue, a beach, a boat and a sprawling deck where you could watch sunsets over the rolling Gatineau Hills.

Two summers later, Gracie came along, and every summer since, we've had her birthday party there, with all her cousins from the Ottawa area, where her mother is from. Throughout the '90s, through marriage, separation and divorce, the lake has always been my daughter's grounding place. After her mother and I finally split up for good a few years ago, Gracie and I were out in the boat fishing early one evening when she turned to me and said: "Daddy, whatever else happens, we're not selling the lake."

So we kept it, though I live in Montreal again and she lives in Washington with her mother. For a few weeks every summer, we go to the lake.

She plays on the beach and can now swim out to the raft. At night we do what she calls the-head-under-the-chin thing, where she sits on my lap and we watch the sun go down and the stars come out and she undertakes my continuing education on nature.

The other evening, she was counting the kinds of birds we have at the lake. There's Mr. and Mrs. Loon, who showed up for her birthday party last weekend. A family of ducks that turn up around dinner time. A blue heron perched on a rock. Blue jays and hummingbirds in the morning.

All these birds mean our lake is full of fish, notably rainbow trout and brown trout, catfish and smallmouth bass, none of which I have seen lately on the end of my line.

"Daddy, can I ask you something?"

"Not now, honey, I'm doing the column."

"Daddy, when can we go fishing?"

As a matter of fact, right now.

July 1999

∞

BEAVER FEVER

We are at the lake where, until recently, we've had uninvited guests, namely a pair of very busy beavers.

They caused some commotion, and considerable consternation, when the male chopped down a huge tree at the cottage next to ours. It made quite a splash as it fell into the water, narrowly missing our dock.

It was the second tree taken down in our bay by the male, a huge 50-pounder I immediately nicknamed Bucky.

"Excuse me," Gracie interrupted, "I believe I'm in charge of naming the animals at the lake."

"Well, have you got a better idea?"

"Actually, Bucky is a good name. We'll call him Bucky."

At first, Bucky and Betty seemed harmless enough, turning up every evening just before sunset to chew on their trophy tree. Before long, the water was littered with chewed-up pieces of the tree, stripped of the bark.

That, apparently, wasn't the only problem with the water.

"Beaver fever," said my niece, Christina, an avid outdoorswoman who once did a six-week wilderness canoe trip in Ontario's Algonquin Park.

"Beaver fever?"

"Yes, they pollute the water, causing a kind of dysentery. Bad for the swimming, too."

"What can we do about it?"

"Call the game warden."

There's never a game warden around, except when you're fishing without a license. Betty wasn't really a problem, but Bucky was becoming something of a nuisance, especially when he started chewing on the end of our dock. There must be something about untreated cedar that beavers find tasty.

"What else can we do to get rid of it?"

"Shoot it."

"Shoot it?"

"Shoot it."

"I can't shoot our national symbol."

"The beaver is basically a rodent," Christina reminded me.

Shooting it was an option, but it presented certain problems. For one thing, I don't own a shotgun. For another, I don't know how to use one. Furthermore, shooting it would leave a bloody mess in the water. It might also require damage control – I had visions of fending off Greenpeace demonstrators swooping in on our dock.

Finally, Gracie was dead set against it. "We are not," she announced, "shooting the beaver."

After a couple of weeks, our next-door neighbour, Buck Schwarz, went to the town hall of Val-des-Monts to report the beaver.

"What did they say?"

"They said shoot it."

Sure. We were going to observe the 25th anniversary of the beaver being named Canada's national symbol by shooting one off the end of our dock.

Come to think of it, what does it say about Canada that our national symbol is a rodent? Well, beavers are admittedly industrious. And Canada's origins as a trading country can be traced to the fur trade.

But beavers have recently given Canada quite a bit of bad international publicity. In Washington last year, Canadian beavers invaded the Tidal Basin around the Jefferson Memorial and chopped down a couple of the U.S. capital's renowned cherry trees. The beavers were eventually caught and peacefully relocated. It remained a mystery how they got from Canada to the Potomac River.

Beavers are certainly not an endangered species, at least in the Gatineau, where they have become an even bigger annoyance than personal watercraft. Peter Mansbridge, the CBC news anchor, has a cottage not far from us on Lac St. Germain, and he mentioned on the Canada Day broadcast that anyone who wanted Canada's national symbol would be more than welcome to come by his lake.

I thought of calling the Biodome and asking if they wanted two more beavers for their Laurentian ecosystem exhibit. With Gracie's birthday party coming up, and the prospect of twenty kids contacting beaver fever, the beavers clearly had to go.

In the event, our other neighbour, on whose property the beaver had felled the tree in the first place, called a tree surgeon who cut away the trunk and hauled the tree out of the water.

That evening, when the beavers came by at their usual time, they swam around for about half an hour, obviously confused and disoriented by the absence of the tree.

Having been told that beavers don't like human contact, I thought of encouraging them to be on their way.

"And another thing, don't come back!" I yelled after Bucky and Betty as they swam off.

Just then, Bucky raised his huge tail and slapped it down on the water.

They haven't been seen since. And Gracie's tenth birthday went off last weekend, with lots of kids in the lake, and no reports of beaver fever.

July 2000

ONE BARBECUE, NO ASSEMBLY

The dread moment finally arrived when the other handle broke on the lid of the barbecue. This meant the inevitable could no longer be avoided – we would have to buy a new one.

Barbecues usually come unassembled, and unassembled barbecues are a leading cause of divorce.

The old one came in 129 pieces, and since it had to be assembled upside down, could only be done indoors. It took eight hours, on a very rainy day at the cottage. A friend once received a barbecue as a gift, from someone who obviously didn't like him very much. After he had spent a day putting it together, he couldn't fit it through the back door of his apartment.

There's a very strong possibility that barbecues were the inspiration for IKEA torturing its customers.

For a decade at the lake, we made do with a barbecue that was never fully functional, with an ever-increasing number of broken and missing parts.

For starters, the starter never started. This is apparently an industry standard. For years, I've been turning on the gas and dropping matches in, narrowly averting singed-eyebrow syndrome. Lighting a barbecue with a match is an especially daunting challenge when a prevailing wind is blowing in off the lake.

The side burner never worked, either. The efficiency rate of side burners is only slightly higher than starters. Nice chrome, though. Then the top shelf of the grill collapsed in mid-cookout, bringing a dozen hamburger buns crashing down on the meat patties.

Then the clip tying the propane tank to the barbecue broke, forcing us to put the tank directly under the coals, resulting in a hot drip that eventually melted down the plastic handle which connected the hose to the tank.

Then one handle on the lid broke, and finally the other.

I went to McClelland's in nearby Poltimore, where they have everything. J.B. McClelland and Sons have been in business in the Gatineau for more than half a century. It's a grocery in the front, a dry-goods store in the middle, and a hardware store in the back.

Darrell McClelland was sitting on his usual stool by the cash in the hardware section, wearing his customary expression, somewhere between faintly concerned and definitely harried. While he's talking to suppliers on three lines, there are usually three live customers lined up to see him.

"Do you sell assembled barbecues?" I asked, in an imploring tone.

"That's the only way we sell them," he replied pleasantly.

For the rest, as he said, it depends what you're looking for, and how much you want to pay. He had one barbecue on his floor for $795 and another, a knock-off built by the same company, for $550. He even had something in a catalogue for under $200.

"This is what I've got at home," he said, showing me one for $449.95. Plus $25 for assembly. Plus $50 for a new propane tank. Plus GST, plus QST.

"Of course," he was quick to add, "the starter will only work for about the first six months." It must be something about the corrosive effects of the Canadian climate.

Never mind. It was assembled.

"I'll take it."

Perhaps it is because of our climate that Canadians are such avid barbecuers. In all these summers at the lake, I've never cooked indoors, even on rainy days.

Montrealers even barbecue on their balconies, violating both their leases and fire ordinances. This may be the only city in the world where hibachis, those little Japanese barbecues, sell out in April.

You can imagine my anticipation, when I moved to Washington, where the barbecue season is about eleven months long.

"I'd like a couple of steaks, about this thick, for the barbecue," I said to a man behind the meat counter.

"You mean, the grill," he replied.

"No, I mean the barbecue."

He looked at me as if I was from another country.

"Where you from, man?"

"Canada."

He patiently explained that steaks might be great on the grill, but that "barbecue" was actually a combination food and cultural experience favoured by African Americans.

Montreal's Mark Phillips, London correspondent for CBS News, had a similar experience when posted to Washington in the early 1990s. "I had a cameraman from the deep south," Phillips recalled the other day, "who explained it like this: 'where ah'am from, if it ain't pork, it ain't barbecue.'"

Pork ribs, steak, salmon, trout. Whatever. It is, as the Americans say, great on the grill.

It is also very much a League of Guys thing. The feminist movement has not yet got around to liberating the barbecue, where men stand around doing nothing more than admiring the fire or making comments on burger-flipping techniques.

At my daughter's recent birthday barbecue, her aunt snuck in and flipped a line of burgers, while her brothers had their backs turned.

"Don't ever try that again," one of them warned her.

The other day, we unloaded the new barbecue and rolled it out on to the patio. To my great surprise, when I pushed the red starter button, it actually worked. And on the very first try. Liftoff, we have liftoff.

July 2000

THE FLAG ON THE DOCK

We needed a new flag for the dock, the old one being faded and frayed after a decade of summers flying at the end of a makeshift flagpole at our cottage.

People who would never dream of flying a flag in the city have no hesitation in doing so in the country. Somehow, it's just the Canadian thing to do, and dozens of cottagers do it along the five bays and 50 kilometres of coastline on Lac St. Pierre.

I called my niece, Christina Smith, who works for Stéphane Dion, the unity minister. Flags, they've got. She personally delivered one, the very next day, "courtesy," as she said with a wicked smile, "of the Liberal government."

Last weekend, we took down the old one, folded it in a proper triangle and put it away in one of those old chests of drawers you find only in the country. And we put the new one up at the end of the dock, where it's been billowing nicely ever since.

Coincidentally, the next day, the *Ottawa Citizen* ran a full-page article recalling how we got the single red maple leaf with red borders on a white field, when the prime minister of the day, Lester B. Pearson, wanted a trio of red maple leafs with blue borders representing the motto, "From sea to sea."

The issue was sorely divisive, not only in Parliament, where the Liberals were a few seats short of a majority and where Conservative leader John Diefenbaker led a bitter fight to retain the Red Ensign, but in the country as a whole. Early in 1964, Pearson had courageously gone before the Canadian Legion to argue for a distinctive Canadian flag, and while he was booed in the hall, he carried the case to the country.

Needing the New Democrats for a majority, the Liberals supported an NDP motion in committee to recommend the design that was later adopted, and the Tories, certain the PM would veto it, were effectively tricked into supporting it, making a unanimous vote out of committee.

But Pearson went along with it. Appropriately, the choice of the Canadian flag was a Canadian compromise, and the red maple leaf was unfurled on Parliament Hill on February 15, 1965.

In a memorable tableau, Pearson grinned from ear to ear, while Diefenbaker wiped away a tear. At his death in 1979, Dief had issued orders for the Red Ensign to be displayed along with the maple leaf on his coffin at his lying-in-state.

As it happened, a quarter century later, in January 1990, I was called in by Lucien Bouchard to help him with a speech to the Empire Club of Toronto, where he wanted to argue for the Meech Lake accord in front of a prominent English-language audience.

"When is it?" I asked, looking out the window of his fifth-floor corner suite in the Centre Block.

"February 15th," he replied.

The 25th anniversary of the flag. Why not, I suggested, draw a parallel between the two debates, how they seemed so divisive at the time.

He liked that, and it was the only paragraph in the draft that survived the cut. Even then, Bouchard was not interested in making a case to English-speaking Canada; he wanted resonance in Quebec.

To Canadians of my daughter's generation, the red maple leaf has always been there. It's unimaginable to them that there could have been such a sound and fury over something they wear on their backpacks, as a matter of course as well as of pride.

During the years when she lived in the United States, summers at the lake and the flag on the dock became a part of her Canadian identity. In her Grade 3 class in Washington, she caused an incident by refusing to recite the Pledge of Allegiance because, as she said, "I'm Canadian."

Every summer, on her birthday, we would take a picture of her beside the flag on the dock. In the earlier ones, she's sitting on my knee, and though she now stands behind me, the flag is in every shot.

And now we have a new one, snapping smartly in the prevailing westerly breezes of summer in the Gatineau.

August 2001

MUSKRATS UNDER THE DOCK

First we had beavers eating our dock. Now we have muskrats living under it. Welcome to our annual nature crisis at the cottage.

A few summers ago, Bucky and Betty Beaver, as Gracie named them, chopped down a big tree in our bay. Now it's Molly the Muskrat, and her family of young ones. They're living in a mud hut under the dock, built on top of the flotation foam. Every evening, Molly swims out from under the dock, returning several times with tree branches as food for the family. Catching up with her on her return the other evening, I jumped up and down on the dock, yelling as loud as I could, hoping to scare her away. No such luck.

Next, I Googled "muskrats," only to be informed by Encyclopedia.com that they are "aquatic rodents." Charming. They live in "marshes, quiet streams and ponds throughout most of North America." And in lakes. Under our dock. Another entry noted the importance of muskrats to the "wetland ecosystem," adding their lodges "can be entered by swimming under water." Yes, by swimming under our dock.

Female muskrats have anywhere from two to six young ones each season, so depending on the head count, there are as few as three and as many seven muskrats living under our dock.

I'm assured by my neighbour, Buck Schwarz, that Molly and her family will eventually move on to another neighbourhood. I'm not so sure, when she's living rent free in ours, with no shortage of frogs to eat along the shore line, including King, the bull frog who likes to sound off after dark, just as we're going to bed.

We were discussing the muskrat problem the other day when a garden snake turned up in the living room, scattering women and children to all corners of the cottage.

We've recently made some additions at the lake, including a 16-foot Bluewater fibreglass canoe that Gracie has christened Big Red. Because she recently went on a five-day canoe trip at Camp Kanawana in the Laurentians, she is the family expert on proper canoeing technique and has concluded I'm quite hopeless.

Big Red weighs only fifty pounds and is incredibly light on the water, especially in early evening, when the wind goes down, and the lake is a glassy calm. When Big Red glides, and the loudest sound is the paddle rippling the water, that's pretty close to perfection.

This summer's major project is the new deck, built of western red cedar. Quite a lot of cedar, since the sun deck is 38-feet long by 13-feet wide, complete with railings, two staircases, four flower boxes and six inches of trim all around. Since it has been raining much of the summer, it has taken much of the summer to complete.

The rebuilding of the deck has given me a whole new take on softwood lumber. For years, I've been reading about it as a dispute between Canada and the United States. More recently, I found myself in Darrell McClelland's lumberyard in nearby Poltimore, buying cedar wood from British Columbia. What a great country! Softwood that started out in the coastal forest of B.C. ended up by a lake in Quebec. Along the way it went to a B.C. mill, was sawed into pieces 16-feet long, moved 4,800 kilometres across the country by train, and trucked to a lumber yard in the Gatineau, where all we have is trees.

Because of the construction boom, the price of red cedar has recently gone through the roof, or at least the deck. But nothing beats western red cedar, either for beauty or durability. The Weyerhaeuser Web site, CedarOne.com, claims it has "one of the longest life spans of any North American softwood." Neighbour Schwarz, who served as foreman on the job, was admiring his handiwork the other day and suggested the new deck was "good for thirty years – Gracie's children can worry about the next deck."

It sure is nice to look at. People from all over the lake have been coming by to admire it. We even have new rules – no food or drink on the deck. We'll see how long that lasts – not the summer, I suspect. Perhaps not even today, which marks Gracie's 14th birthday, every one of them spent at the lake.

We have something else new at the lake – a Muskoka chair, sitting out beside the flag at the end of the dock. It's the perfect place to watch the sun setting over the Gatineau Hills. And to keep an eye on that darn muskrat.

July 2004

∞

HEWERS OF WOOD, DRAWERS OF WATER

You never know how many trees you have until one falls on the roof of the cottage.

Until the tornado, I never looked, counted or cared. The lake was out front. The trees were out back.

Then, in seven minutes, the tail end of a tornado, or cyclone, or something, suddenly tore down Lac St. Pierre, ripped through the narrows of the bay, and snapped the tallest pine tree at our place in two.

We were the lucky ones. On its way down, the top half of the towering pine got caught up in the branches of a giant maple tree. Otherwise, falling from that height, it would have crashed through the cottage roof with the force of a guided missile. Luckily, no one was home at the time.

The neighbours weren't so lucky. Four places over, the summer storm blew through every window in the house, and snapped majestic old-growth pines like matchsticks.

When the cleanup began, I started counting the kinds of trees. We've got pines, cedars, firs, birches, maples, elms and poplars, many of them living and some of them quite dead.

And now we have firewood, which in the Gatineau is about as scarce as coals in Newcastle. Enough firewood for three years in the cottage and several summers of bonfires on the beach.

If all work can be divided into policy and operations, then in cottage country the division of labour is simple: The policy guy is the one with the chainsaw, and the operations guy is the one stacking the wood.

So, my neighbour is the one with the chainsaw, while I'm the one building the woodpile. It's hard to say which will burn best, the top half of the pine tree or the dead birch with its lovely strips of bark.

It being the cottage, there is always something. The polite word for it is upkeep.

For example, the plumber was here for ten hours a week ago Saturday, fixing the kitchen sink, the bathroom sink, the shower, and the hot water tank, which wasn't giving us any hot water. In fact, the system, which pumps water in from the lake, wasn't producing any water at all. It is very difficult to explain to the girls that there is no hot water for their showers and, in fact, no showers.

The plumber was exceedingly well paid for his time and his trouble, but he came on a Saturday morning. Try getting that kind of service in the city.

The trees were cleared, and the water was finally running, but that was before the flood.

Then it rained overnight, and rained and rained. It washed out the dirt road, felled more trees, knocked out the power (again), and forced the closing of Highway 307 when part of it disappeared at St. Pierre-de-Wakefield.

It also flooded our beach, with the runoff from the famous Gatineau Hills completely washing away the neighbour's beach. At our place, there was so much water in the little fishing boat it nearly sank. At McClelland's, I bought an eight-litre pail to bail it out. There were at least 600 litres of water in the boat.

The lake now comes up to the retaining wall, which is normal in the spring runoff, but unheard of in July. It rose so high, our dock slipped from the poles to which it was attached, and started floating away. It was quite a sight, complete with Muskoka chair, pole with Canadian flag, and fishing boat with motor, all floating off into the sunset. We finally pulled it in, and while we all understand that floodwaters must rise before they can recede, our lake has this curiously dead look of standing water to it.

This summer, the cottage is a reminder of Canada's economic origins. Once again, we are hewers of wood and drawers of water.

July 2007

THE INVASION OF THE MUSKOKA CHAIR

This appears to be the summer when Ontario has successfully invaded Quebec cottage country. The Muskoka chair has arrived on docks in *la belle province*.

For several years, the Muskoka chair at the end of our dock was the only one to be seen along our bay. No longer. Their numbers have multiplied, like Ontario trilliums by the side of the road, to the point where they have taken over the neighbourhood.

In a chair count on a canoe ride around the bay the other morning, it turned out that fourteen out of twenty-two docks had Muskoka chairs on them.

It must be said that not all of them were authentic. Some were plastic. Some were painted. But all of them had the Muskoka look – the seven ribs on the rounded back, the contoured seat and the large armrests. The perfect outdoor chair for reading, watching a flag snap in the breeze or contemplating the possibility of a glass of white wine to accompany the sun setting off the end of the dock.

Not all Muskoka chairs are made in Muskoka. Indeed, there is a spirited discussion about whether the Muskoka chair is itself authentic, or a Canadian knockoff of an American original, the Adirondack chair.

According to Wikipedia, the Adirondack chair (or, in some parts of Canada, a Muskoka chair) "is a type of chair used primarily in an outdoor setting." (Another Wikipedia entry hilariously describes Muskoka as "approximately two hours north of Toronto." The writer clearly never made the drive on a Friday night.)

It seems that the original Adirondack chair was designed by a man named Thomas Lee for his summer home in Westport, New York, in 1903. It was patented as the Westport chair in 1905 by a local carpenter, Harry Bunnell, who made thousands over the next two decades.

How the Adirondack chair got to Muskoka might be a matter of some dispute among the permanent residents of Huntsville and Bracebridge, not to be confused with the 100,000 cottage owners and two million visitors who enjoy the region's 1,500 lakes every summer. In their mind, the question might be how the Muskoka chair got to the Adirondacks.

What's in a name? A thriving cottage industry, quite literally. A quick Google search brings up any number of local manufacturers, including the Muskoka Chair Company, which advertises matching footrests on its Web site, and Muskoka Chairs, whose cedar chairs can be outfitted with headrests.

For Muskoka chair purists, footrests and headrests may seem a heretical notion. But not as heretical as the plastic Muskoka wannabes, stacked up in the outdoor aisles of hardware stores. And whether in wood or plastic, the classic wood stain colour is clearly giving way. One of my neighbours has three Muskoka chairs on his dock, in three different colours – red, yellow and green.

As far as that goes, we are acknowledged Muskoka chair traditionalists. While our chair was built in an Ottawa garage by a neighbour's son, it was proportioned and stained to Muskoka specifications. And a splendid chair it is, in all kinds of weather. The aerodynamics of the Muskoka chair are perfect – built low to the ground, with wind space between the back ribs. It would take a tornado to blow it off the dock.

A Muskoka chair is also a statement: that the owner is serious about residing in cottage country. Its display at the end of a dock is equally a statement that someone is home. And this is usually enough to discourage breaking and entering. (This summer, the smart thieves on our lake are confining themselves to stealing gas from boats.)

But what is to explain the sudden proliferation and presence of an Ontario trademark chair in Quebec? Perhaps it's the proximity to Ottawa, where most of the 500 cottagers on our large lake come from.

This could be something for the cultural mavens of the Parti Québécois to keep a vigilant eye on. They mustn't allow any diminution of Quebec's precious *patrimoine*.

National Post, August 2008

19

GRACIE

THE BIG ONE

Snowstorms aren't what they used to be before there were weather channels. They had us set up for the Big One the other day, but in the end it turned out to be nothing more than a lame excuse to stay home from work in a week when the boss is away anyway.

Gracie was not impressed.

"I was in the Storm of the Century," she announced.

Washington is a city where they close the schools on the forecast of snow, and where they have snow make-up days written into the school calendar. Just a prediction of an inch of snow is enough to cause panic buying in supermarkets.

America being a demand-driven society, they sell out snow shovels along with milk.

Usually it turns out to be no more than an inch or two, and the biggest menace on the roads is yuppies trying out their four-wheel drives, usually without snow tires.

The other problem is that the mayor of Washington, Marion Barry, has more of a reputation for putting white stuff up his nose than for getting it off the street.

But two years ago, it was the real thing – at least three feet of snow, driven by howling winds, in a city with neither the capacity nor the culture to deal with the event. The storm blew in on a Sunday, and it was the following Monday before a semblance of normalcy was restored.

The government of the United States, the world's only superpower, was shut down for an entire week, not by a budgetary crisis, an annual event there, but by the weather. The president was trapped in the White House. Maybe it was then that Bill Clinton got the idea to charge campaign contributors $1 million a night to sleep over in the Lincoln bedroom.

Seeing the world's most important capital, and its government, completely immobilized, it was a good thing the Cold War was over. The Americans finally understood what Nikita Khruschev meant when he said, "We will bury you."

It would have been the week for the comrades to take over. Or the Canadians, swooping in from the north on their snowmobiles, which was actually the only means of transportation for days.

This discussion actually occurs at the highest levels of the Canadian embassy every time it snows in Washington. Should we bow to local sensibilities and close? Or should we be hardy Canadians and make it into work? And if we close, what about the Canadian television correspondents sending stories home about the wimps at the Canadian embassy, slacking off at public expense?

Here in Montreal, the politics of snow clearance isn't what it used to be. This used to be a matter of civic pride, to the point that Jean Drapeau once offered to lend a caravan of trucks to John Lindsay, then mayor of New York, when the Big Apple was crippled by a major storm.

We still have armies of the night to clear our streets, so the problem isn't snow clearance – it's the dire forecasts of the weather networks.

These people have taken the fun out of snowstorms. They used to be festive occasions in Montreal. When offices closed early, people would go to bars instead of going home.

Whatever the amount of snow on the ground, it's definitely good weather for skating. Gracie, who is 7, wanted to try out her new skates, and so the other afternoon we headed off to the Bell Amphitheatre at 1000 de la Gauchetière.

We were having a quiet family dinner in our favourite neighbourhood restaurant, when Gracie had an idea.

"Let's drive up to the mountain and the lookout," she suggested. "That would be a neat thing to do on New Year's Eve." So we did, and the city, with its blanket of snow and its great twinkling of lights under a clear night sky, looked simply wonderful.

"There are two Montreals," Gracie said. "The one on that side of the river and the one on this side. Is it all Montreal?"

"Sort of."

"It's like the view from the Empire State Building."
"How's that, sweetie?"
"You can see forever."

January 1998

―

A TALE OF TWO CITIES

Most of my summer has been spent discovering two cities, Montreal and Washington, through the eyes of my 8-year-old daughter.

It's a quite different view. We've been going places and doing things that I'd otherwise never see.

The Biodome, for instance. It's Gracie's favourite place in Montreal. Together with the Insectarium and Botanical Garden, it attracts several million visitors a year. Without my daughter, I would never have set foot in the place.

The Biodome turns out to be someone's brilliant idea, for which Jean Doré, who was mayor when it opened six years ago, and Pierre Bourque, who was then director of the Botanical Garden, can both legitimately take credit.

One thing is for sure – as the world's largest disused indoor velodrome, part of the debt-laden Olympic legacy, the building that became the Biodome had no functional future. As a $58-million municipal reclamation project, it now pays its way in admissions and in the looks of the sheer joy of discovery on children's faces.

The learning experience of the Biodome is simply in walking through it, from the tropical rain forest, to the Laurentian forest to its polar ice cap – three ecosystems under one big roof.

"My favourite is the Laurentian forest," Gracie explains, "because it has otters and beavers and is very Canadian."

Two of my daughter's favourite places in Montreal and Washington, Mount Royal Park and the National Zoo, happen to have been designed by the same man, the renowned Frederick Law Olmsted.

Each is a tribute not only to Olmsted's brilliance, but to the vision of the politicians of the day who set aside the land, as they did in New York, where Central Park is another jewel in the Olmsted crown.

What are the prospects that any of these three parks, each in the very centre of the city, would have been approved by today's civic authorities?

Washington's National Zoo, established more than a century ago, is truly an American treasure. It's practically right downtown on Connecticut Avenue, a ten-minute cab ride from the White House.

Because it's part of the Smithsonian Institution of national museums, admission is free.

And within its 163 acres, there's a lot more to do than look at animals, though there are plenty of those. Gracie is particularly fond of a group of African crown cranes she calls "the bad hair dudes."

It's also a working science centre. For example, the cheetah conservation station not only houses several of these sleek cats, but has seen one 5-year-old bred by artificial insemination. You learn that this endangered species has always known a 90-per-cent infant-mortality rate, while their numbers have declined a further 90 per cent in the last half-century. In this conservation effort, Washington is part of an international network that includes the Metro Toronto Zoo.

The National Zoo allows kids to think as well as look. They emerge from a tropical rain forest called Amazonia, much like the one at the Biodome, into a state-of-the-art information centre full of click-on computer screens.

You could easily spend a week there, and in fact my daughter has spent the last two weeks there, in a zoo camp during the mornings and hanging out with me in the afternoons. By now, as she says, we're both pretty well "zooed out."

No matter, there's plenty of other free things to do in Washington, where Gracie lives with her mom. The Air and Space Museum, directly across from the Canadian embassy on the Mall, is a regular stop for us. There are two things hanging from the ceiling inside the main entrance. One is Charles Lindbergh's *Spirit of St. Louis*. The other is the Apollo 11 space capsule. And that's just the beginning. Our own aviation museum in suburban Ottawa splendidly details Canadian achievements in flight, but it can't compete with being first across the Atlantic or first on the moon.

Our other frequent Washington stop is the Museum of Natural History, which Gracie simply calls the dinosaur museum. All of these free attractions are right on Washington's blissfully air-conditioned metro.

But a good part of this summer has been spent in Montreal. The best thing about Montreal? "That's easy," Gracie says. "No school."

One of the advantages of being a telecommuter – someone who essentially works out of home – is that it's allowed me to sit in on my daughter's swimming lessons at the municipal pool in Westmount.

There was a moment when she went from the shallow to the deep end of the pool that I'll simply never forget. "Daddy," she said, as she came off the diving board, "this means I can swim out to the raft at the lake without my life-jacket."

One more thing: having spent most of the summer with my daughter, I've been reminded again of the incredible respect we owe single parents, especially working mothers, the rest of the year. They drop the kids at school, pick them up after work, cook their meals, help with the homework, tuck them in for the night, and manage in most cases to get on with their lives.

Finally, I had been wondering if, living in Washington, my daughter's sensitive antennae had picked up on the Bill and Monica matter. It turns out she has.

"The president should have known better," Gracie said the other day.

"He shouldn't have kissed that lady. She wasn't his wife."

August 1998

FLYING SOLO

Gracie took her first plane ride alone the other day. It was a nerve-racking experience – for her parents.

My daughter has been flying since infancy, to Barbados, to Britain and Ireland, to Florida, but mostly back and forth between Montreal and Washington, where she lives with her mother. But always, she has been accompanied on her travels by one parent or the other.

After much discussion, it was agreed that Gracie might be ready to fly up by herself for the Easter holidays. But not without novenas by her grandmother and a scapular medal pinned on her dress by her mother.

"Mummy couldn't find a St. Christopher medal," Gracie explained later, "so she lent me her Blessed Virgin."

Allowing a child to travel alone is a big step for any mother. Women seem to develop a fear of flying when they become mothers. They think, if they get on the plane, they'll never see their kids again. They also think that if their kids get on the plane without them, it's sure to crash.

This just in from the League of Guys: Men are also afraid the plane will crash, especially if they insist the kids get on it alone. Which is why hardly anyone ever insists.

We've all seen children walking through airports, wearing tags around their necks and holding on for dear life to airline employees. I called a friend at Air Canada to check it out.

"Well," said Nicole Couture-Simard. "She would be a UM."

"A UM?"

"An unaccompanied minor."

I explained to Gracie's mother that Air Canada takes every precaution with children, and that its regional jet is one of the safest planes in the world, and one of the most fun to fly. (The pilots love it, because it's like driving a sports car; the flight attendants hate it because they have to work a fifty-seat jet alone.)

"Let me try and get my mind around it," she said doubtfully. "I'll get back to you." Finally, on the morning of the flight she called back to say that our daughter would be on the afternoon non-stop from DC to Dorval.

According to usually reliable sources, Gracie's mother walked her right to the gate – they let you do that in the States – and watched the RJ push back, taxi, take off and disappear into the clouds somewhere over Washington's famous 14th Street bridge, into which an Air Florida plane once crashed because it hadn't been sufficiently de-iced in a snowstorm.

At the Montreal end, Gracie's father fretted through an afternoon of endless meetings, forgetting everything the clients said, thinking only, she's on her way to the airport, she's taking off, oh-mi-god, she's in the air, I better get to Dorval.

And there, on the arrivals board beside her flight number, was the dreaded word: delayed. At least there wasn't the most dreaded word: canceled.

Since the retro-fit of the terminal at Dorval, you can again watch the planes taking off and landing through the big windows of the departure level. I figured it wouldn't be hard to see an RJ with the Air Canada colours touching down safely.

When the arrival was finally posted, there was still the long walk in from Gate 23 – basically walking in from Pierrefonds to Dorval – as well as customs to be cleared.

But there she finally was, walking through the swinging glass doors at international arrivals, looking quite grown up in a new dress, and a carry-on trailing behind her. Quite properly, the Air Canada man asked for a photo ID and made me sign for her. A message was left on her mother's voice mail, that she was safely on the ground.

"So, how was the flight?"

"It was nice. I got to go up to the cockpit."

They also gave her a kids' meal, a kids' puzzle book, and a really neat UM tag that designated her as an "official skyrider."

"Were you nervous?"

"A little bit, at the beginning. But I had my Harry Potter book."

She also had her binder full of Pokemon trading cards. Fortunately for the other passengers, none of them asked her to explain Pokemon, which she is always happy to do. We are talking about a girl who went out last Halloween dressed as Pikachu.

When I told her about the stabbing at a Montreal school over Pokemon cards, and suggested that they should be banned from schoolyards, she had an interesting reply.

"Maybe," she said, "they should ban knives from schoolyards instead."

It's been a hectic week, skating with her friend Natacha, buying Pokemon stuff, and going to see the Expos.

The definite highlight was sitting behind the Expos dugout the other night and getting Vladimir Guerrero's autograph.

"Can you go and ask for me?" she asked.

"No."

"Why not?"

"Because," I said lamely, "I sometimes have to write about these people. I can't go around asking for their autographs."

She gave me that "yeah, right" look and went to stand in line with the other kids. A nice usher made sure she didn't get squeezed out by a bunch of pushy boys, and the very nice Guerrero signed his picture on her Expos calendar and gave her that beautiful Guerrero smile.

The calendar is hanging on her bedroom door, open to Guerrero's month of July. On the doorhandle hangs her UM tag, a souvenir of a rite of passage.

"I can't wait," she says, "until I can fly alone again."

April 2000

A BRIDGE TO AVONLEA

My daughter wanted to see *Anne of Green Gables*. And I wanted to see the Confederation Bridge. So we got in the car and drove to Prince Edward Island.

"It's one of those places I feel like I know, even though I've never been there," said Gracie, who is 10, "because I've read about it so much."

Anne of Green Gables was on her summer reading list for her Grade 5 class. "I wasn't too thrilled about having to read it," she said, "but then I started it and couldn't put it down." That led to *Anne of Avonlea* and *Emily of New Moon*, other classics by Lucy Maud Montgomery set in Cavendish on the North Shore of P.E.I.

The road to Avonlea now leads over the Confederation Bridge, at 13 kilometres the world's longest bridge over troubled waters, the icy Northumberland Strait. It was more than a century, and more than $1 billion in the making, and it is truly a wonder of the world, which in only three years has changed the Island Way of Life.

In the Prime Minister's Office back in 1985, we called it Charley's Bridge. Charley McMillan was the senior policy adviser to the prime minister, and he covered an entire wall of the PM's boardroom with a mural of a private-sector bridge proposal linking P.E.I. to the mainland.

His brother, Tom, was then tourism minister and later environment minister in the Mulroney government, but economist Charles McMillan was the real power from P.E.I. in the government, and quite determined to build a fixed link that had been the talk of his native province since Confederation.

There was only one problem – Brian Mulroney had ordered that it be built by the private sector, at no cost to the government. One of the largest public works projects in Canadian history was privatized even before it was built.

Stanley Hartt, the Montreal lawyer who was then deputy minister of finance, did some creative accounting that solved the financing problem. He simply amortized the replacement cost of the Northumberland ferry over thirty-five years and came up with the money.

After P.E.I.'s late and beloved Premier Joe Ghiz had taken Islanders where they really wanted to go in a 1992 referendum on the issue, the Confederation Bridge was finally built by the Strait Crossing consortium, with Ottawa kicking in $42 million a year of ferry money over 35 years, after which it will become the owner of Charley's Bridge.

It's built to last a century, and it had better be, given the iceberg-like dimensions of the ice floes that pound it beneath the windswept waters of the Northumberland Strait. The debate may continue that long, as to the impact of Confederation Bridge on the fishery, and the Island Way of Life.

There's no doubt about the economic impact. P.E.I.'s exports to the U.S. have doubled since 1997 to a projected $500 million in only three years, and that's not in potatoes, but in value-added sectors such as aerospace.

"The bridge has brought nothing but good," says Laurie Gauthier, who operates the Green Gables Bungalow Court in Cavendish, next door to the Green Gables House, down the street from Avonlea, and across the road from the famous dune beaches of P.E.I. National Park, where the surf is the warmest north of the Carolinas.

Avonlea is a theme village with authentic touches, including a restored one-room school house where Maud Montgomery actually taught. It's been done in remarkably good taste, in striking contrast to the *Ripley's Believe It Or Not* museum down the road, complete with a mini-putt and a Tim Horton's.

Avonlea is a fictional place, of course, existing only in the mind of L.M. Montgomery, and in five generations of girls from around the world. My daughter spent a delightful afternoon hanging with Anne at the village store and being hectored by Maud in her class.

In truth, Anne is more than a legend on this island, she's an industry, who attracts tourists from as far away as Japan, where Anne of Green Gables is dear to the heart of every school girl.

I never knew this until it was explained to me by Charley McMillan, who met his wife, Kazayo, when she was visiting P.E.I. as a student. For the Japanese, coming to P.E.I. isn't tourism, it's a pilgrimage.

It's very easy to do all-Anne, all-the-time. *Anne of Green Gables*, the musical, is completing its 35th season at the Confederation Centre of the Arts and the Charlottetown Festival.

With apologies to MasterCard: theatre tickets – $76. The look of sheer enchantment on a child's face – priceless.

August 2000

A CHRISTMAS TREE IN NEW YORK

For weeks, a young Quebec woman named Sylvette has slept on the sidewalks of New York.

Far from being desperate about her circumstances or despondent about her prospects, she's working full time, selling Quebec Christmas trees by day, and watching over them by night.

Sylvette is one of hundreds of seasonal workers from Quebec who tell American customs they're going to New York for the weekend, and who a month later tell Canadian customs they've just been to New York for the weekend.

They certainly have nothing to declare, least of all the hard-earned tax-free cash in their pockets, in U.S. dollars, from a month of working without a green card.

"It's hard, but it's fun, and the people in this neighbourhood are nice," Sylvette was saying at her Christmas-tree stand on the Upper East Side of Manhattan, around the corner from my daughter's school.

Gracie and I were walking by on our way to a movie when we heard the unmistakably Québécois accents of Sylvette and her partner, talking about the weather.

It's especially cold at night, when they huddle up in a makeshift lean-to, with only their trees to cut the wind that howls all the way up from midtown Manhattan. "We have a heater," Sylvette explained. "It's not so bad."

The money is very good, especially when compared with seasonal work in the Gaspé, where she is from. On Christmas Day, when she heads home to be with family, she'll probably have several thousand U.S. dollars in her jeans. By then, all her trees will be gone. "If there's any left on Christmas Eve," she said, "we send them over to another stand over in the Bronx. They'll all be sold."

The scene is typical of dozens of New York neighbourhoods, where Christmas-tree vendors from Quebec sleep in their cars or little sidewalk shacks, or in Sylvette's case, right on the sidewalk. It's New York, and if the sellers didn't keep an eye on their trees, chances are they wouldn't be there in the morning.

Christmas trees don't grow in Brooklyn, they grow in Quebec. The bulk of our production is for export to markets as far south as Florida. But New York is the biggest single market, and the best.

A full Quebec balsam will easily go for $80 in most New York neighbourhoods, which – allowing for the exchange rate – is anywhere from two to three times the price on the street in Montreal.

But in Montreal as in New York, Christmas-tree selling is also about location, location, location.

In our neighbourhood, Bob MacLeod and his family have had the best location for years, at the corner of Greene Avenue and de Maisonneuve Boulevard, outside the Cinq Saisons market.

They have a tree farm near Weedon in the Eastern Townships, where they annually export thousands of trees to the U.S. market. They sell many hundreds more at their familiar stand in the city. But the MacLeods don't have to sleep with their trees.

"We just tarp them," Bob MacLeod said. They sleep at their place in town.

"Depending on what you're looking for," as MacLeod said, his prices run between $10 and $50, but no higher. He donates a portion of his profit on every tree to the Missing Children's Network. So MacLeod's Christmas-tree stand works in a lot of ways.

"Do you deliver?" a woman asked him last Saturday, perhaps the busiest day of the season.

"No problem," he replied. "But it would be better if you came back tomorrow."

MacLeod charged us only $40 for a balsam that would reach the high ceiling of our living room and open up beyond the corner to the edge of the fireplace.

The object of all this is Gracie's annual tree-trimming. The deal is that each guest brings an ornament for the tree and a new toy for Sun Youth. The kids put the decorations on the tree and wrap the toys for Sid Stephens' kids. When Gracie went there last year and helped distribute the toys she was donating, she had another view of Christmas.

"Daddy," Gracie interrupted last night. "Can we put the angel on the tree now?"

Excuse me. Merry Christmas!

December 2000